English Questions

PERRY ANDERSON

London · New York

First published by Verso 1992

Verso
UK: 6 Meard Street, London W1V 3HR
USA: 29 West 35th Street, New York, NY 10001-2291

Verso is the imprint of New Left Books

ISBN 0 86091 375 9
ISBN 0 86091 591 3 (pbk)

British Library Cataloguing in Publication Data
A catalogue record for this book is available from the British Library

Library of Congress Cataloging-in-Publication Data
A catalogue record for this book is available from the Library of Congress

Typeset in Sabon by York House Typographic Ltd, London
Printed in Great Britain by Biddles Ltd

Contents

Acknowledgements

'Origins of the Present Crisis' was first published in *New Left Review* 23, January–February 1964, and 'Components of the National Culture' in *New Left Review* 50, July–August 1968. They appear here shorn of some of the bombast and excess of the period to render them more readable, if not defensible. 'The Notion of Bourgeois Revolution' was first given as a talk at Cambridge in March 1976. 'The Figures of Descent' appeared in *New Left Review* 161, January–February 1987, and 'A Culture in Contraflow' in *New Left Review* 180 and 182, March–April and July–August 1990. I am indebted to all my colleagues on NLR for work together, without which they would not have been written.

Felici le nazione in cui uno stesso aggetivo significa 'nazionale' e 'popolare'

Sebastiano Timpanaro

Foreword

This book looks at some of the shapes of modern English politics and culture. In form it divides into two parts. The first of these consists of a pair of essays, one on politics and the other on culture, written on the eve of and during the Labour regimes of the sixties – followed by a short coda dating from the seventies. The second contains texts on the same set of subjects, written under the Conservative regimes of the eighties, and is completed by a conclusion from the current period. It may be helpful to say something about the background to this sequence. The initial pieces were published in *New Left Review* simultaneously or alternately with a series of essays by Tom Nairn on closely related themes.[1] In subsequent discussion on the left, the ideas developed in these pieces were often referred to as the 'Nairn–Anderson theses', and identified with the journal of that time. A modest secondary literature grew up about them, which provides one reason for republication today. To understand them, however, it is necessary to recall the intellectual context in which they were produced.

At the time when we embarked on this early writing, there was little sustained literature on the general development of the United Kingdom as a distinct state and society in the twentieth century. In the early sixties, Marxist scholarship had not yet fully flowered, although its promise was evident: significant ground had been opened up in the seventeenth, late eighteenth and early nineteenth centuries, but contemporary history remained a weakness. More conventional approaches, of a liberal or conservative tenor, rarely touched on

1. For reference to these, see note 1, p. 121 below, which includes texts down to the mid seventies. The conceptions of British society developed in *New Left Review* were the work of more than just these two signatures. Anthony Barnett's *Iron Britannia* (London 1982), analysing the politics of the Falklands War, was a central intervention of the early eighties.

structural topics at all. Sociology, as a positive influence on the writing of history, indeed as a source of ideas or findings in its own right, was still a rather marginal discipline in England – confined, in effect, to little more than dining rights at the two oldest universities. Nor, on the other hand, was there much tradition within the political Left of conjunctural analysis of contending social forces, against the background of the longer *durées* of modern British history. In all these respects, the situation in the eighties is very different. There will be occasion to reflect on that difference in a moment. For the present, it suffices to note the rather sparse character of public debate then on issues which have since – over two decades later – accumulated a formidable weight of research. It was that situation which prompted us to block out in crude lines what we took to be the major contours of the economy and society, politics and culture confronting the British Left. We were at once unaided and unawed by the presence of a consolidated scholarly literature on many of these issues: hence a resort to intuition, and also a lack of inhibition, that would have been impossible later. In retrospect, the costs of such an operation are obvious. But, however amateur, they formed a starting point which it is difficult altogether to regret.

What was the intention of these essays? In the first instance, they sought to draw a general map of English class society, derived from its trajectory since the Civil War, and of the balance of power between its principal forces. It was this dimension of the enterprise that attracted most debate. At the same time, they also tried to sketch a framework for understanding the national crisis of British capitalism – the economic decline and social deadlock whose symptoms were then just starting to come into public focus. Our argument was that the roots of this crisis lay in the particular constellation of social forces given by the long-run prior evolution of English society. From this diagnosis, we deduced various conceptions of possible advance for the Left. The enterprise as a whole owed its main intellectual inspiration to one source, then still unfamiliar in Britain.

In the early sixties, Gramsci was a little-known name for most of the Left. Few of his texts had been translated, and no secondary discussion surrounded them. The *Prison Notebooks* did not form part of the mental universe of even that (still small) sector of socialist culture that defined itself as Marxist. This situation was not peculiar to the UK. Internationally, they had not yet made much mark. *New Left Review* seems, in fact, to have given the first systematic reception to Gramsci's thought outside Italy. (Curiously enough, the only comparable episode occurred in Argentina, a country whose history was to interlock with Britain's twenty years later, where there was a near-simultaneous assimilation in the journal *Pasado y Presente*.[2]) What were the motivations in our case? Essentially, we found in Gramsci two central themes which spoke to our situation. He was the first Marxist to trace the national features of his own capitalist society back to the particular forms, as he saw it, of the bourgeois revolution which had ushered it in; and the first revolutionary to acknowledge the need for a specific strategy for socialism in the industrialized West, after the advent of universal suffrage. With these concerns as our cue, the 'Nairn–Anderson theses' represented an attempt to apply Gramsci's categories consistently across the English social and political landscape. Amongst the earliest Gramscians outside Italy, we were also amongst the most thoroughgoing.

The 'we' here is in some ways misleading. Tom Nairn was the first source of the ideas developed in *New Left Review* in the sixties. A season at the Scuola Normale in Pisa had given him a knowledge of Gramsci's work which, I think, had no equal in Britain at the time. My own awareness of it dates from my encounter with him. The seminal text for our enterprise, from which all the others grew, was an essay he published in the cultural journal of the PCI, *Il Contemporaneo*, in 1963, 'La Nemesi Borghese'. This contains the nucleus of the account of the British social formation that we later developed in *New Left Review*. The Gramscian direction of our theses was thus originally his. My own intellectual formation had been rather different – a major element in it Sartre; a minor one Lukács. Such influences, however, did not appear discrepant at the time. Rather they seemed to prepare the ground for a common kind of enquiry. Sartre had argued that the decipherment of particular social totalities – what he called, after Hegel, 'concrete universals' – was the highest test of any creative Marxism; he was also responsible for one striking, if also strained and flawed, analysis of French society as a nationally specific field of class forces. Lukács's concern with the ideological forms and functions of class consciousness in history looked not dissimilar to Gramsci's preoccupation with the cultural patterns of domination and submis-

2. Founded in 1963 by a group of young intellectuals in revolt against Communist orthodoxy, that included José Aricó, Juan Carlos Portantiero and Sempat Assadurian, *Pasado y Presente* was denounced by the PCA as the expression of an 'Argentine New Left'. The parallels between the two journals were in many ways uncannily close, in ideological reference and national iconoclasm: see, in particular, the keynote essay by Aricó, 'Examen de Conciencia', *Pasado y Presente* no. 4, January–March 1964. The journal ceased publication after the Cordobazo of 1968. Twenty years later, Aricó was to write the retrospect of this experience and its sequels in *La Cola del Diablo*, Buenos Aires 1988.

sion; he too had written a significant essay on the particularities of German national development.[3] In my texts, then, the Gramscian palette had some Sartrean and Lukácsian subtones.

The critical point, at all events, is that the theoretical background of our essays was external to most of the familiar landmarks of the British Left at the time. Not only was a serious edition of the *Prison Notebooks* yet to be published in England; the *Critique of Dialectical Reason* and *History and Class Consciousness* were also to wait several more years for translation; even a great deal of Marx, including the *Critique of Hegel's Philosophy of Right* and the *Grundrisse*, was still unavailable in English. By taking optics such as these for viewing British society, we inevitably found ourselves looking at it in ways that differed from traditional approaches on the native Left. An alien idiom suggested an oppositional stance; and so it was generally held to be. This circumstance coloured much of the debate that our early essays aroused. The most notable and sustained reply to them was written by Edward Thompson. His powerful rejoinder 'The Peculiarities of the English' is a classical statement of his historical vision in its own right.[4] The gravamen of his critique of our account of British history and society was that it had consistently underestimated the political ascendancy of the industrial bourgeoisie in the nineteenth century; the social achievements of the working class in the twentieth century; and the cumulative national culture produced by both. The detailed historical issues at stake here were not an artifice of transient intra-mural dispute on the Left. They represented problems with a considerable intellectual past preceding our engagement, and capable of vigorous survival beyond it. Some of their echoes recur later in this volume.

However effective particular replies to Thompson's claims may – or may not – have been,[5] there were two general objections he made to our account which unquestionably struck the mark. The first of these was essentially political. He was right to sense, and to criticize, what appeared to be an indiscriminate rejection of English cultural traditions in much, at any rate, of my own writing. Some part of this youthful

3. 'On Some Characteristics of Germany's Development', *The Destruction of Reason*, London 1980, pp. 37–92.

4. Originally published in *The Socialist Register 1965*, and republished in *The Poverty of Theory*, London 1978.

5. Written to parry what seemed the cutlass of an attempt at summary execution, my response at the time – 'Socialism and Pseudo-Empiricism', *New Left Review* 35, January–February 1966 – exceeded Thompson's attack in the vehemence of its defence. For some later amends, see the discussion in *Arguments within English Marxism*, London 1980, pp. 139 ff.

tirading had healthy precedents, which he overlooked. The scorn of Marx and Engels for German provinciality and philistinism, of Lenin and Trotsky for Russian religiosity and oblomovism, of Gramsci for Italian operatics and sentimentalism, were among them. No classical Marxist ever showed much complaisance towards his or her own national culture: they certainly despised every form of spiritual patriotism. This was a temper far removed from the exaltation of the nation and its values that came to characterize official Communism from the time of the Popular Front. On the other hand, it was also an attitude free from the rhetoric of deprecation to which Thompson took exception. It was Isaac Deutscher who brought this distinction home to me. Commenting on our essays, which met with his qualified approval (he dissented from our judgement of English capital, but agreed with our view of English labour), he remarked that they were nonetheless culpable of 'national nihilism'. The term was new to me. Its background was appropriately Polish – coined in the twenties to describe Rosa Luxemburg's error in opposing independence for her homeland before the First World War. The authority of Deutscher's criticism was the greater in that his own conversation was notable for its cool detachment towards Polish political traditions, which he would often contrast unfavourably with the greater depth of Russian counterparts. This was a reproof not easily ignored.

The second general objection brought by Thompson was more historical in character. Built into our analytical programme, he suggested, was the assumption of a 'normal' standard of bourgeois revolution, and a consequent 'normal' pattern of working-class development after the establishment of a capitalist state. English society was seen in this light as an exception or deviation from a modal rule. These were the terms in which – for example – the English Civil War, as a starting-point of modern political development in Britain, was deemed an anomalous experience; or in which the political paramountcy of a landowning class in the mid-Victorian age was described. The justice of this criticism is evident. The source of the error was close at hand. Here we were in fact moving in parallel with Gramsci's own procedures. For the extended meditations on the origins of modern Italian politics and society in the *Prison Notebooks* always tend to take the form of a contrast between a – fallen – national reality and a standard historical norm. The standard is provided by France. Gramsci's whole theory of the limits and deficiencies of the Italian Risorgimento, as a bourgeois revolution, is constructed through the controlling paradigm of the French Revolution, which in its heroic Jacobin phase generated precisely that unitary national-popular force, capable of rallying peasantry to bourgeoisie on the basis of agrarian reform, which the broken dualism of Moderates and Mazzinians – each equally divorced from the rural masses – fatally missed in Italy. The consequences of this shortfall are pursued throughout the *Notebooks*: from the gap of a true Romanticism in Italy in the nineteenth century to the lack of a real popular literature in the twentieth, from the fragility of Italian national identity to the chicanery of the Italian parliamentary state, it is the French model that provides the gauge of the verdict.

In our writing, there was no such overt and insistent reference. But tacitly the structure of argument was much the same. British history and society were analysed as exceptional against an unspoken background of what was taken as typical, derived from French experience. The primary plane of contrast here, as in Gramsci, concerned the shapes of what were taken as the bourgeois revolution in the two countries – in this case French 'maturity' acting as foil to an English 'prematurity', rather than Italian 'postponement'. But there was also a silent secondary opposition between the labour movements that emerged within the capitalist states thereafter – British moderation versus continental radicalism – not to be found in Gramsci, for obvious reasons. Indeed, it was at least as much the Italian party and class he had led, as anything this side of the Alps, which provided the coded contrast for us. Edward Thompson rightly sensed this bias in our method, and rebuked us memorably for it. That, of course, was the ironic force of his title 'The Peculiarities of the English'.

On the other hand, Thompson's own intervention here did not go much beyond denial of any classical standard or typical model in the emergence of modern capitalism. The result appeared to leave only a medley of historical differences, mutually unrelated, each equally significant in its own right. Such a pluralism could be worn easily enough by most liberal or conservative historians. It was they, after all – Alfred Cobban in the van – who had initiated the critique of the 'myth' of the French Revolution itself, as the archetype of a bourgeois political overturn of the Ancien Régime. It was less satisfactory for Marxists, committed in principle not only to an empirical knowledge – shared alike with non-Marxists – but also a theoretical understanding of the variant national paths of capital into the world. The hunt for 'peculiarities', logically pursued, led into the sands of an indeterminable nominalism. Confronted with this impasse, each of the authors of the original NLR theses changed course, in differing directions. From the late sixties onwards, the focus of Tom Nairn's work increasingly became that historical reality which had been most neglected by Marxism – the nation. The result was an international theory of nationalism, as a response to the uneven development of capitalism on a world scale, that gave a powerful resolution to some of the dilemmas of our earlier work. For here historical contrasts – in their most clamant subjective form – were generated by an intelligible principle of differentiation, paradoxically and remorselessly general in its sweep. This conceptual transformation – the institution of a genuine dialectic of the singular and the universal – allowed Tom Nairn to return to the fate of contemporary British society from a quite new angle, as multiple national conflicts broke out within the United Kingdom at the turn of the seventies. The fruits were the series of remarkable essays – on Scotland, Northern Ireland, Wales, England, and the all-British Union clamped over them – published in *The Break-up of Britain.*

In my case, it was not the nation but the state which formed the principal object of subsequent reflection. The result was a work of the same period centred on absolutism, rather than nationalism. There were a number of reasons for this difference of interest. One was no doubt personal background. Active Scottish origins were more likely than residual Anglo–Irish ones to produce a sharply critical but sympathetic understanding of the ambiguities of popular nationalism; although the example of my brother's work shows that post-colonial aftershocks could yield their own insights here.[6] Another was, so to speak, historical horizon. By this time the critical date in the narrative of modern socialism, for Tom Nairn, was 1914: when the major labour movements of Western Europe embraced the First World War. For myself it was more conventionally 1917: when Russian crowds overthrew Tsarism. Such starting-points suggested differing lines of enquiry. The Reichstag war credits logically led to the study of nationalism, which had inspired the vote for them; the Russian Revolution to the study of Absolutism, whose last bulwark it had destroyed. The analytic tack, however, was quite similar in either case. Methodologically, I too had to look outwards to the European matrix of Absolutism as a whole, in order to trace its overall structures as a form of rule embedded – the first in history – within an articulated inter-state system. A comparative survey of the main Absolute monarchies of the Continent, East and West, was then possible within this framework.

Absolutism was the classical state form lying across the transition from feudalism to capitalism. For that transition to be completed, the complex of political upheavals which the Marxist tradition described

6. See Benedict Anderson, *Imagined Communities* (enlarged edition), London 1991. For our family background, see his vivid introduction to *Language and Power*, Ithaca 1990.

as bourgeois revolutions was everywhere necessary in the epicentres of advancing capitalism. It was at this nodal point, of course, that our original theses on Britain had been most vulnerable. What the detour through its prehistory, the ramified record of Absolutism, had shown was that only a general theory – international in scope – could enable the specificity of any given national case to be accurately captured. Nowhere was this precept more applicable than to 'bourgeois revolutions', a group of historical events for the most part treated in *ad hoc* fashion even by those using the term, typically without examining the notion. The NLR notations on English development had been no exception. Here we had lacked the conceptual clarification, and comparative foundations, necessary to establish what was distinctive about it. A condition of further enquiry was clearly a critical reflection on the category of bourgeois revolution itself. The first part of the book ends with a stock-taking of this problem, from the mid seventies.

Meanwhile, the intellectual situation in which the original NLR theses had been developed was undergoing fundamental changes. Two of these were of particular significance. On the one hand, there was the rapid growth of a more conceptually alert historical scholarship in Britain, after the ferment of the sixties. This was a period that marked a high tide of Marxist influence in reconstructions of the national past, the work of a number of generations of creative historians. But it saw, too, many of the same problems addressed from rival theoretical standpoints, often under their stimulus. The result was the accumulation of a large body of empirical knowledge, focused from different angles on many of the issues that had concerned us, and transforming subsequent understanding of them. On the other hand, these years also produced an important second reception of Gramsci within the political culture of the Left, distinct from the first.[7] The central figure in this development was Stuart Hall; the journal which became associated with it was *Marxism Today*. The starting-point of this programme of work lay in Gramsci's reflections on popular culture, rather than state forms. Its most striking product was to be Hall's prescient analysis of the ideological rise of the new Right in Britain at the end of the decade, which then evolved into a famous account of the hegemonic project of Thatcherism in the eighties.[8] Around this nucleus, a cluster of gifted

7. There is now a excellent critical survey of the whole history of these receptions in David Forgacs, 'Gramsci and Marxism in Britain', *New Left Review* 176, July–August 1989, which is notable for the balance of its judgements.

8. The major texts from 1978 onwards are now collected in Stuart Hall, *The Hard Road to Renewal: Thatcherism and the Crisis of the Left*, London 1988.

writers extended discussion of the Conservative regime in other directions – social and institutional – in the pages of *Marxism Today*. Eventually, in what became a third wave of influence, mediated through the French regulation theorists, Gramsci's vision of Fordism set off an ambitious series of theorizations of post-Fordism, as the emergent forms of capitalist production and consumption, culture and communications in the nineties.[9] The naturalization of his thought has now gone very far.

The second part of the book reflects this altered context, in which there was both a large body of new historical scholarship on the English past, and a lively array of conjunctural analyses of British politics and society on the Left. It starts with a reconsideration of our original account of these, whose aim is to separate the valid from the invalid arguments of those days by setting them against the evidence of the most recent research, and within the context of a wider sense of the range of national routes to advanced capitalism. This was the longer historical side of the first essay. But our theses were also subject to another kind of test – the actual development of the United Kingdom since we had first spoken of its crisis. What was the balance-sheet of twenty years of official endeavours to reverse its decline? 'The Figures of Descent' appeared at a moment when Britain's economic renaissance and the Thatcher Revolution were being widely hailed, even outside the area of ordinary government support. Its judgement of that miracle can be left to stand.

The essay that follows, 'A Culture in Contraflow', looks at what has happened since in the intellectual fields scanned in the sixties. Formally similar in design, as a comparison of initial suggestions with later outcomes, its argument runs in the opposite direction – underlining the contrasts rather than the continuities between the pattern of the two periods. The reversal here was sufficiently striking to warrant interest, even had it not been registered in the political sphere – as in fact it pointedly was. But it could still be thought that the cultural circuit discussed in this text, as in its antecedent, is too specialized and remote to weigh significantly in the scales of hegemony. The more typical focus for analysis of this has been, in recent years, popular rather than learned culture. Gramsci's conception, of course, included both. If the unity and complexity of his own vision are so rarely reproduced today, the

9. See Stuart Hall and Martin Jacques, eds, *New Times: The Changing Face of Politics in the 1990s*, London 1989. The original impetus to ideas of post-Fordism came from Christian Palloix in the early seventies, somewhat before the rise of the Regulation School.

reason lies partly in the transformations of the two levels he found no difficulty in joining. The Italy of the twenties was still a society in which folklore was more important than film, and whose leading philosopher was a leisured rentier. The characteristic worlds of the mass media and of the modern academy, and the chasm between them, had not yet arrived. Their real entrenchment dates only from the post-war period, when the industrialization of commercial entertainment and the bureaucratization of university research acquired their present moulds. For all the institutional distance between these, the motifs of high and low culture themselves have, however, never been simply segregated. The interbreedings between them in the social imaginary have, indeed, given rise to the most dazzling of all frescoes of contemporary sensibility at large, in Fredric Jameson's *Postmodernism*. Its field is the cultural logic of capital in general.

In the case of Britain, Tom Nairn's study of national identity as it has been constructed by monarchy, in *The Enchanted Glass*, affords a quite different, but no less striking, capture of a fusion of elite and folk ideological forms. But its theme – the displacement of the more familiar phenomenon of popular nationalism by Ukania's pulp-royalism – indicates another, more specific difficulty in applying a Gramscian grid to British culture. A central category in Gramsci's analyses of hegemony was the 'national–popular', signifying all those symbolic forms that condensed and projected the role of the people in the creation of the nation. In Britain, however, the organizing definition of the national was inescapably imperial – the 'British' people, strictly speaking, emerging as an artefact of the empire-state, from the various island nationalities. The ostensible nation here was overwhelmingly the creation of its rulers, and no popular movement was ever able to mark it with a strong alternative imprint, as the Garibaldian Risorgimento or the Northern Resistance did in Italy. The political dissociation of the national and the popular in Ukania is no doubt one of the reasons why the two programmes of Gramscian research indicated above could be so different: one essentially concerned with the first, the other with the second. So too in the cultural field, views from above and below – each necessary – have proved hard to combine. The conglomerate that gives its name to the state lacks other forms of historical substance. It is partly for this reason that the title of this book avoids reference to it. In the text, 'Britain' and 'England' and their adjectives often alternate without distinction, as they do in casual usage which it remains pedantic to scout altogether. In the title, however, the dominant reality it is *bon ton* to be discreet about today is given its due relief.

The volume ends by looking at the recent evolution of Labourism, as the traditional form of opposition to Conservative hegemony in Ukania. The concluding essay tries to set the particular cast of the party within the more general development of European social democracy in this period. Certain common features in the fate of the Northern movements of the continent emerge, and other very specific traits of the British variant, confronting problems of a morbid economy and state that are refracted through its own body. What the future will bring to this nexus of party and society, only time can tell. Like all the writing collected here, this final text is situated midway between the historical and the political – an attempt to mediate some of the requirements of scholarship, and others of partisanship, without satisfying either entirely. Interventions of this kind must always be provisional, aware of their inevitable fallibility. If they still seem worth attempting, it is because neither the academic nor the journalistic are best suited to the kind of political conjecture they involve. The example set by Gramsci is still compelling here, however distant we are now from his universe. I have set down my view of his hopes, and what we can make of them today, elsewhere.[10] Their trace is evident in these pages, which start in a time of insurgency and end in one of restoration. In the depths of his own defeat, Gramsci's strength of mind was to bring moral resistance and political innovation together. In related circumstances, this is the combination needed today.

10. See the concluding chapter of the companion volume to this, *A Zone of Engagement*, London 1992.

PART ONE

1

Origins of the Present Crisis

British society is in the throes of a profound yet cryptic crisis, undramatic in appearance, but pervasive in its reverberations. So much everyone agrees. But what kind of crisis is it? What kind of outcomes to it are likely? Anyone who looks for an answer to these questions in the spate of recent books on the 'condition of England' is likely to be disappointed. By and large, they offer not so much an analysis of the crisis as an account of its symptoms. Most of these works – by Shonfield, Shanks, Sampson, Hartley, or Macrae[1] – are ephemeral because they lack any historical dimension. Shonfield, whose book is the earliest and best of the genre, devotes five pages out of three hundred to an explanation of the secular decline of the British economy he discusses in the rest of his book; and he is unique in offering any structural explanation at all.

If one turns to socialist critics of the Right or the Left, the same blankness is striking. Crosland's *Conservative Enemy* is in many ways an eloquent and intelligent work; it is certainly far more serious than the vulgar run of books whose theme – the 'stagnation' of Britain – is the same. Yet Crosland, too, attacks 'conservatism' in every reach and level of British society without providing a line of explanation of the malady he deplores. No socialist writer stands in greater contrast to Crosland than Raymond Williams, whose *Culture and Society* and *Long Revolution* certainly represent the most original body of thought to have been produced on the Left since the war. Apparently, *Culture and Society* is a historical work; but for all its merits, it is so in a strictly limited sense – for what it offers, in fact, is a purely immanent critique

1. Respectively – *British Economic Policy since the War* (1958); *The Stagnant Society* (1961); *Anatomy of Britain* (1962); *A State of England* (1963); *Sunshades in October* (1963).

of a set of ideological traditions, abstracted for the purpose from the broader movement of history. The title of *The Long Revolution* promises a directly historical perspective, but the actual achievement of the book is a theoretical rather than historical one. The concluding discussion of 'Britain in the Sixties' starts *ex nihilo*, after the philosophical and cultural analysis which precedes it. The unity of the book deliberately lies elsewhere. Yet it is surely significant that neither the 'technical' (Crosland, Shonfield) nor the 'ethical' (Williams) criticisms of British society today are founded historically.

Does the available corpus of history and sociology make this unnecessary? By no means. We must be unique among advanced industrial nations in having not one major structural study of our society today; but this absence follows from the lack of any serious global history of British society in the twentieth century. The limits of our sociology reflect the nervelessness of our historiography. Marxist scholars, whose works are only now beginning to consolidate each other, have so far mainly confined themselves to the heroic periods of English history, the seventeenth and early nineteenth centuries. Most of the eighteenth and all of the twentieth remain largely unexplored. Thus no attempt has so far been made at even the outline of a 'totalizing' history of modern British society. Yet until our view of Britain today is grounded in some vision of its effective past, however misconceived and transient this may initially be, we will continue to lack the basis for an understanding of the contradictory movements of our society, which alone could yield a strategy for socialism. The present conjuncture, which offers obvious opportunities to the Labour Party, was neither created nor foreseen by it. If the Left is to take advantage of the present situation, the first prerequisite is a serious attempt to analyse its real character. To do this involves a consideration of the distinctive overall trajectory of modern British society since the emergence of capitalism. The remarks which follow will, inevitably, be extremely simplified and approximate notations. But their essential focus – the global evolution of the class structure – must be the anchorage of any socialist theory of contemporary Britain. The present crisis can, in effect, only be understood in terms of the differential formation and development of British capitalist society since the seventeenth century. The crude schema offered below is intended only to start discussion at the point where it might properly begin.[2]

2. To avoid making the text unwieldy, substantiating references will generally be omitted.

1. History and Class Structure: Trajectory

Capitalist hegemony in England has been the most powerful, the most durable and the most continuous anywhere in the world. The reasons for this lie in the cumulative constellation of the fundamental moments of modern English history.

(1) *England had the first, most mediated and least pure bourgeois revolution of any major European country.* The Civil War of 1640–49 remains the most obscure and controversial of all the great upheavals which led to the creation of a modern capitalist Europe. Never was the ultimate effect of a revolution more transparent, and its immediate agents more enigmatic. The view that the conflict of the 1640s was a simple struggle between a rising bourgeoisie and a declining aristocracy is clearly untenable. The current alternatives – that the Civil War was the work of a *fronde* of discontented squires or that it was a sudden, transcendent condensation of 'faith and freedom' (Puritan and constitutional) in the clear air of Stuart England – are still less convincing; the one is trivial, the other naive. Who made the Revolution? What kind of a Revolution was it? It can, perhaps, be said that it was a clash between two segments of a landowning class, neither of which were direct crystallizations of opposed economic interests, but rather were partially contingent but predominantly intelligible lenses into which wider, more radically antagonistic social forces came into temporary and distorted focus. Furthermore, the ideological terms in which the struggle was conducted were largely religious, and hence still more dissociated from economic aspirations than political idioms normally are. Thus, although its outcome was a typically bourgeois rationalization of state and economy, and its major direct beneficiary was a true bourgeoisie, it was a 'bourgeois revolution' only by proxy. The main protagonists on both sides were a rural, not an urban class. The conflict between them revolved round the economic, political and religious role of the monarchy. It is clear that the inefficient, would-be feudal Stuart monarchy was threatening by its economic exactions to cripple the expansion of the rationalized agrarian and commercial capitalism which had been maturing in England for a century before 1640. It is probable, but not proved, that a majority of those landowners who were dynamic and investment-oriented sided with Parliament, and that a majority of routine and rentier landlords sided with the King; it is, however, certain that the most economically progressive regions of England were Parliamentarian, and the most backward Royalist. At the

same time, the nature of the allies flanking each side magnified and clarified the logic of the division between them: at one extreme the archaic clan society of northern Scotland; at the other mercantile capital, particularly in the City of London. This last formed a crucial component in the bloc which finally won the Civil War, providing the indispensable financial reserves for the victory.

The Revolution, once under way, followed a classic course of radicalization. When military victory was won, the artisans and yeomen recruited to the New Model Army increasingly intervened to inflect the Army to the left, thus effectively severing it from the Parliamentary Right; but when their pressure began to threaten the franchise privileges of the landowning class itself, the landed officer elite crushed them. The military apparatus was thereafter alone in a void. The Revolution had overshot the political intentions of its agrarian initiators (execution of the King), but had been halted as soon as it threatened their economic interests. It was in this ambiguous vacuum that mercantile capital, the only true bourgeois kernel of the Revolution, inherited the fruits of victory. The economic policy of the Commonwealth did more for its interests than for that of any other group. This anomalous outcome was the culminating product of the complexly refracted and mediated character of the Revolution. The fact that it was primarily fought within and not between classes meant that while it could and did destroy the institutional and juridical obstacles in the path of economic development left by feudalism, it could not alter the basic property statute in England. But it could do so – decisively – abroad. The violent rationalizing 'charge' of the Revolution was detonated overseas, in the economic legacy of Commonwealth imperialism (Irish conquest, Navigation Acts, Dutch and Spanish Wars, seizure of Jamaica). Mercantile capital was its beneficiary. When political anarchy threatened after Cromwell's death, it was the City that triggered the Restoration – and a general settlement that confirmed it in its enhanced position. There followed a progressive stabilization and consolidation of the long-term gains of the Revolution: essentially, the development of a dynamic capitalist agriculture and the rise of a mercantile imperialism, in a period of great economic boom.

Thus the three major idiosyncrasies of the English Revolution which have determined our subsequent history can be summed up as follows. First, the Revolution shattered the juridical and constitutional obstacles to rationalized capitalist development in town and country: monopolies, arbitrary taxation, wardships, purveyance, selective enclosure, etc. The effect of this was a dramatic quickening of the whole economy in the latter half of the century. In this sense, it was a supremely successful capitalist revolution. At the same time, however, it left almost the entire social structure intact.

Second, it achieved this by profoundly transforming the roles but not the personnel of the ruling class. No social group was evicted or displaced by the Revolution;[3] rather one section of a class fought another and by its victory converted the whole class to a new type of production. For the next hundred years the British aristocracy proceeded to perfect the ruthless and richly rewarding system of capitalist landlord, tenant farmer and landless agricultural labourer, which eventually destroyed the English peasantry and made Britain the most agriculturally efficient country in the world. But no career open to talents, no enlarged franchise, no weakening of the principles of heredity and hierarchy, followed this. Landed aristocrats, large and small, continued to rule England.[4]

At the same time, mercantile capital expanded on a new and imperial basis. It had not been the leading military or political force in the Revolution; it was its most direct economic heir. But it was never subsequently able to constitute itself as an internally compact or autonomous political force. Despite their rapidly increasing wealth, bankers and merchants remained a subaltern group within the ruling system, an 'interest' and not a class. There was a constant haemorrhage of its profits and pioneers towards the countryside, as successful traders abandoned their background, investing in estates and becoming members of the landed class. Conversely, landowners had from the outset of the Revolution (and earlier) participated in colonial and trading ventures (Pym, Hampden). There was thus a permanent partial interpenetration of the 'moneyed' and 'landed' interests, which simultaneously maintained the political and social subordination of merchant capital, and gave the City the aristocratic coloration it has retained to this day.

Finally, the ideological legacy of the Revolution was almost nil. Its most militant creed, radical Puritanism, was the great loser from the Restoration Settlement. Henceforth it went into a profound spiritual recession, losing its fiery intramundane activism and becoming the repressed private creed of a disestablished minority. The religious

3. A section of the smaller Royalist landowners, who did not regain their estates after the Restoration, forms the only exception.

4. Throughout this essay, the term 'aristocracy' is used to designate, not the titled nobility, but the landowning class as a whole. This use blurs the important distinction between the large agrarian magnates and the gentry, but space precludes discussion of this secondary division here.

beliefs which had seen divine intervention justifying the Rebellion in the hour of its success, also – and irrevocably – saw providence condemning it when the Republic collapsed. Because of its 'primitive', pre-Enlightenment character, the ideology of the Revolution founded no universal tradition in Britain. Never was a major revolutionary ideology neutralized and absorbed so completely. Politically, Puritanism was a useless passion.

The eighteenth century sailed forward into an era of unparalleled stability. The landed aristocracy had, after a bitter internecine struggle, become its own capitalist class. The mercantile bourgeoisie was contained and decanted into an honourable ancillary status. No ferment of ideas or memories remained. By a classic process of psychological suppression, the Civil War was forgotten and its decorous epilogue, the Glorious Revolution of 1688, became the official, radiant myth of creation in the collective memory of the propertied class.

(2) *England experienced the first industrial revolution, in a period of counter-revolutionary war, producing the earliest proletariat when socialist theory was least formed and available, and an industrial bourgeoisie polarized from the start towards the aristocracy.* The Revolution of 1640 had made possible the transformation of the body of landowners into a basically capitalist class with powerful mercantile auxiliaries. It was precisely this 'mix' which, after a hundred years' maturation, set off the Industrial Revolution: agrarian capitalism provided the economic and human surplus for industrialization, depopulating the countryside to provide investment and labour for the towns. Mercantile imperialism, dominating Asia, Africa and Latin America, provided the markets and raw materials. The cotton industry, based squarely on control of the world market, from India (calico) to West Africa (slaves), to the Caribbean (raw cotton), launched the take-off. The industrial concatenation which followed inevitably produced its own, new bourgeoisie – the manufacturing middle class of Manchester and the North. Yet the condition of its appearance in England was the prior existence of a class which was also capitalist in its mode of exploitation. There was thus from the start no fundamental, antagonistic contradiction between the old aristocracy and the new bourgeoisie. English capitalism embraced and included both. The most important single key to modern English history lies in this fact.

A period of intense political conflict between the nascent industrial bourgeoisie and the agrarian elite was, of course, inevitable once the manufacturers began to aspire towards political representation and power. But this clash itself was profoundly affected, and attenuated, by the context in which it occurred. The French Revolution and Napoleonic expansion froze propertied Europe with fright. For twenty panic-stricken years the new English manufacturing class rallied to the aristocracy; in that time it developed habits and attitudes it has never lost. A whole era of war against the French abroad and repression against the working class at home marked the years of its emergence. Two decades after the fall of the Bastille, it celebrated its entry into history by cutting down working-class demonstrators at Peterloo.

When the fear of the early years of the nineteenth century receded, the industrial bourgeoisie at last began to mass its strength to secure incorporation into the political system. It was almost overtaken by a radicalized working class which had developed in isolation from it during the relentless years of reaction. But with considerable belated skill, it forced an extension of the franchise including itself and excluding the proletariat, nicely demarcating the new ruling bloc from the populace beneath it. The traditional mercantile bourgeoisie had never achieved direct political representation in Parliament; because of its peculiar situation and composition it had always been content to delegate its 'interest' to a section of the (Whig) aristocracy. The Reform Bill of 1832 secured the change which it had never managed – or needed – to effect. Commercial capital too now entered Parliament for the first time, behind its industrial successor, in the breach the latter had made.

The next – and last – victory of the new middle class was the repeal of the Corn Laws in 1846. Convinced that cereal protection favoured landowners at its expense by limiting the markets for manufactures at home and abroad, the industrial bourgeoisie mounted a second triumphant campaign for its abolition. This sectional conflict concluded the independent role of the industrial middle class in British history. It was its – brief and inglorious – high-water mark. The aftermath was illuminating. Fired by the success of the Anti-Corn Law League, its greatest spokesman, Cobden, launched a campaign against 'the eleventh commandment' of primogeniture as a key to aristocratic control of the land. The call for 'free trade not only in corn but in land' aimed directly at the social power of the aristocracy. The bourgeoisie, its fighting spirit gone, refused to follow it. Henceforth it was bent on integrating itself into the aristocracy, not collectively as a class, but by individual ascent.

Even after 1832, it was noticeable that the new middle class used its vote to elect Members of Parliament not from among its own ranks, but from those of the aristocracy, thus reproducing the relationship between its predecessor and the landed elite even after it had won the power to do otherwise: as late as 1865, over 50 per cent of the House of

Commons were linked by intricately extended ties of kinship. Thus for a period one can speak of a delegation of power by one distinct social class to another. But this phase was relatively short. It was followed by a systematic symbiosis of the two classes, effected above all by the arrival of a common educational institution: the new public schools, designed to socialize the sons of the – new or old – rich into a uniform pattern that henceforth became the fetishized criterion of a 'gentleman'. The reforms of the universities, and more particularly of the civil service (1854), instituting a rationalized but hierarchic recruitment based on prior induction into the public schools, complemented this central mechanism of assimilation. Meanwhile, as industrial accumulation proceeded and the relative weight of the agrarian sector declined, an increasing horizontal intertwining of landed, commercial and industrial capital took place. Agrarian magnates opened up mines and invested in railways, captains of industry purchased estates and formed special relationships with merchant bankers. The end result of these convergent mutations was the eventual creation of a single hegemonic class, distinguished by a perpetually recreated virtual homogeneity and actual – determinate – porousness.[5] The second generation of any parvenu bourgeois family could henceforward automatically enter the 'upper class' via the regulating institutions of assimilation. Thus it was that by a singular paradox of Victorian capitalism, the aristocracy became – and remained – the vanguard of the bourgeoisie.

For the first five decades of the century – the heroic age of the English proletariat – the working class evolved in a diametrically opposite direction to that of the middle class. Counter-revolutionary war abroad was accompanied by social siege at home (more troops mobilized to suppress the Luddites than to fight the concurrent Peninsular War). Repression circumscribed the working class and cut it off from the rest

5. In other words, what Sartre calls a 'detotalized totality'. The dominant bloc in England can be envisaged as a narrow, highly structured hegemonic class, with, beneath it, a large, diffuse, polymorphous reservoir – the entrepreneurial, professional and salaried 'middle classes'. The rigorous structure of the one radically destructures the other, as access is always open to the select few from the 'middle' to the 'upper' class: thus the middle classes in England have never produced institutions and culture of anything like a comparable distinctiveness and density to those of the upper or, for that matter, working class. The device of the two-party system has, of course, also powerfully acted to inhibit the emergence of a clear corporate identity in the middle class, by denying it expression at the political level. England has never known an independent political movement of the petty bourgeoisie of any serious dimensions, in contrast to the other major West European countries. The special nature of the dominant bloc in England has undoubtedly contributed to preventing this.

of society. Plunged in its own racked and famished world, it fought bitterly for an alternative human order for itself. It was the first proletariat ever to suffer industrialization: it had to invent everything – tactics, strategy, ideas, values, organization – from the start. It achieved no victories, but its defeats were astonishing. In 1819 it organized the first national political campaign of the post-war period, so scaring both the bourgeoisie and aristocracy that it provoked a massacre and exceptional legislation. In 1831–32 it formed the great heaving swell of the Reform Movement, constantly threatening to capsize the bourgeois groupings adroitly navigating on its surface. From 1829 to 1834 it produced in Owenism the first, mass socialist movement of the century. When this was crushed by 1836, it rose again in an independent working-class movement for Reform. Chartism, its supreme effort, lasted for a decade. In the end, crippled by the weaknesses of its leadership, it collapsed without a fight. With it disappeared for thirty years the élan and combativity of the class. A deep caesura in English working-class history supervened.

The tragedy of the first proletariat was not, as has often been said, that it was immature; it was rather that it was in a critical sense premature. Its greatest ardour and insurgency coincided with the least availability of socialism as a structured ideology. Consequently it paid the price of the forerunner. The division of culture in the nineteenth century meant that the development of socialist thought was bound in the main to be the work of non-working-class intellectuals. (The utopian socialism of Owen was, of course, just this.) Thus everywhere it tended to come to the proletariat from outside. But it took fifty years of the experience of industrialization over a whole continent for it to develop, and the timing of its impact was crucial. It is no surprise that the youngest proletariats, of Italy and Japan, should have become most generally attached to Marxism; or that the oldest, those of England and Belgium, have rather similar political parties and consciousness. In England, in contrast to countries that industrialized afterwards, Marxism came too late: the *Communist Manifesto* was written just two months before the collapse of Chartism.

(3) *By the end of the nineteenth century, Britain had seized the largest empire in history, one qualitatively distinct from all its rivals, which saturated and 'set' British society in a mould it has retained to this day.* Late-nineteenth-century imperialism was the climax of three centuries of plunder and annexation. It was the most self-conscious and belligerent phase of British imperialism; but it was not the most profoundly formative for British society. The mercantile imperialism of the seven-

teenth and eighteenth centuries, which provided the preconditions for the economic take-off of the early nineteenth century, and the diplomatic–industrial imperialism of the mid nineteenth century, whose enforcement of international Free Trade had created British world economic supremacy, were both more decisive. The lasting contours of British society were already visible before the rise of the military–industrial imperialism of the 1880s.[6] Yet it was this ostensible apotheosis of British capitalism which gave its characteristic *style* to that society, consecrating and fossilizing to this day its interior space, its ideological horizons, its intimate sensibility. It is, above all, from this period that the suffocating 'traditionalism' of English life dates.

The multiform impact of militant imperialism on the economy and society of Britain can only be suggested here. It is clear that the existence, maintenance and constant celebration of the Empire affected all classes and institutions in Britain; it could not have done otherwise. Equally obviously, its effects varied greatly from group to group. The main single effect of the new imperialism in the period from 1880 to 1914 was probably to clinch the preternaturally hierarchical character of the traditional social order, and in particular of its typical *model of leadership*. It has been argued that the imperialist expansion of this epoch (scramble for Africa, penetration of China) was an 'atavistic' phenomenon, the product of 'pre-capitalist' aristocratic and military residues in the industrialized states of Europe. This view is manifestly indequate; imperialism was an inevitable climax of pre-Keynesian capitalism, the product of a massive investment surplus and a limited internal market. But Schumpeter's imaginary cause was a true effect. The reflux of imperialism at home not merely preserved but reinforced the already pronounced personality type of the governing class: aristocratic, amateur, and 'normatively' agrarian. Originally this ideal was naturally secreted by a leisured landowning elite. But by the second half of the nineteenth century the English aristocracy was rapidly becoming as factually 'bourgeois' as the English bourgeoisie was becoming 'aristocratic'. Moreover, with the agricultural depression of the 1870s, the traditional economic base of the landed oligarchy collapsed. Thus, just at the moment when the 'atavistic' values of the

6. By 'diplomatic–industrial imperialism' is meant the economic subjugation of other nations, usually secured by the threat of force, rather than by outright annexation. 'Military–industrial imperialism' proceeded by straight conquest; it was a product of the fear of rival European imperialisms, in particular of Germany, whose shadow haunted the extreme patriots of the period. It thus marks the moment at which British world supremacy was no longer unquestioned.

country's aristocracy were gravely threatened, imperialism rescued and refortified them. In doing so, it bequeathed to twentieth-century England the governing class which has at length found its final, surreal embodiment in the fourteenth Earl of Home.

The major impact of imperialism was almost certainly on the character and ethos of the ruling bloc. But its feedback was not limited to this. A general internalization of the prestations and motifs of Empire undoubtedly occurred. Its most prominent expression was, of course, the new religion of monarchy which marked the late Victorian era – inaugurated, predictably, by the creation for the Queen of the title of Empress of India. The Durbar, and its domestic derivative the Jubilee, became the symbol of a whole society present to itself, celebrating its own plenitude. The 'manifest' function of the monarchy was (by assertion) to unify the nation; its 'latent' function was (by example) to stratify it. The two were equally important. Probably at no period in peacetime history was English society so suffused with chauvinism and so glutted with rank.

These implicit normative patterns were no doubt the lasting imprint of imperialism on English life. Its explicit ideological expressions, although virulent at the time, were ultimately more transient. Their omnipresence in this period merely serves to suggest how deeply acclimatized English culture became to the ambience of Empire. All political groups – Conservatives, Liberals and Fabians – were militantly imperialist in aims; each differed only in its programme of implementation. The nascent socialist movement shared in the general jingoism. Webb, Hyndman and Blatchford – Fabian, 'Marxist' and ILP supporter – respectively the most influential, the most 'advanced' and the most popular spokesman of the Left, were all in their different ways vocal imperialists. This did not necessarily mean that the working class became in any direct sense committed to imperialism. It is very doubtful whether industrial workers in this period benefited materially from colonial exploitation, although they did indirectly from the difference in productivity between the British economy and its overseas possessions. Politically, the emigration which drained off many of the most vigorous and independent members of the working class, as well as forestalling excess population pressures, was probably throughout the nineteenth century a more important safety-valve for English capitalism than colonial super-profits. However, the primary impact of imperialism on the working class – as throughout British society – was at the level of consciousness. British workers were not in any deep sense mobilized *for* imperialism; to this extent, the options of many of their leaders were of little moment. But they were, undeniably, deflected *from* undistracted engagement with the class exploiting them. This was the real – negative – achievement of social–imperialism. It created a powerful 'national' framework which in normal periods insensibly mitigated social contradictions and at moments of crisis transcended them altogether. The unquestioning participation of most of the Left in the First World War was the logical outcome of decades of national–imperial mystification.

However, for the working class too, the zenith of imperialism saw in essence only a consolidation of morphological changes which had occurred long before it. The debacle of Chartism finally broke the morale of the early proletariat; a state of shock and retreat followed. For thirty years the English working-class movement went through a kind of prolonged catatonic withdrawal. The most insurgent working class in Europe became the most numbed and docile. Ambitious attempts to create single national unions, audacious schemes for an autarkic co-operative economy, mass campaigns for universal suffrage – gave way to cautious, *bien-pensant* insurance clubs and wavering support for the Liberal Party. The major formal goal of Chartism, votes for the working man, was partially granted by a Conservative Government in 1867. But far from being an autonomous victory of the labour movement, this tactical manoeuvre of Disraeli's in a sense only revealed its absorption and defeat. The vote was extended into the working class since there was no longer any danger that it would use it as some of the Chartists had threatened to do, for the transformation of the social system. The Conservative Government's attention was almost purely devoted to outflanking the Liberal opposition; it cared so little about the substance of its bill that it let it be amended indefinitely by a handful of Radicals in Parliament.

No great change followed the Second Reform Act. For well over another decade the working class continued to play an innocuous and subordinate role in the British political system. Artisans and home-industry workers increasingly gave way to a factory proletariat. The rapidly increasing surplus of the economy, after the first period of capital accumulation, allowed substantial increases in wage-levels to be granted by employers, providing the economic basis for the reformism of the period. It was not until the 1880s that labour began to recover from the traumatic defeat of the 1840s. By then the world had moved on. In consciousness and combativity, the English working class had been overtaken by almost all its continental opposites. Marxism had missed it, developing precisely in the years of the British proletariat's amnesia and withdrawal. While in France, Germany or Italy, Marxism was taking root in the working class, in England, everything was against it: the wounds of the past, the diffidence of the present, the national culture of past and present. In 1869 the German Social Democratic Party was founded; in 1876 the Parti Ouvrier in France; in 1884 the Socialist Party in Italy; in 1889 the Social Democratic Party in Sweden. In England, the first socialist *sect*, the Social Democratic Federation, was only formed in 1884 – and the first working-class *party*, the Labour Representation Committee, only in 1900; over twenty years later than in France or Germany. The SDF did not succeed in making a lasting ideological impact on the labour movement. The Labour Party, itself created primarily as a defensive measure to reverse the effects of the Taff Vale decision, included no major Marxist component from its early years onwards. The lateness of its formation was an index of the degree of subordination of the working-class movement within British capitalist society. The crescendo of imperialism which coincided with the rise of the modern labour movement only confirmed changes which had preceded it.

(4) *Alone of major European nations, England emerged undefeated and unoccupied from two world wars, its social structure untouched by external shocks or discontinuities.* The victories of 1918 and 1945 were the last of the special graces granted by history to English bourgeois society. War and invasion have been perhaps the greatest catalysts of change in modern Europe – even the early English Revolution being precipitated by Scottish incursion. In the First World War, collapse on the Eastern Front set in motion the Russian Revolution; defeat on the Western Front produced the Spartacist rising in Berlin, the Bavarian soviet republic, and Social Democratic parentage of the Weimar Republic. In the Second, the occupation of France and fighting in Italy threw up resistance movements with Socialist–Communist majorities. In each case the general advance of the Left was checked or reversed – by fascism between the wars, by anti-communism afterwards. But at some point the whole social order had nevertheless been fissured and challenged, and the restabilization which followed, brought on by the international pressures of Depression and Cold War rather than by internal changes, was distinct from the status quo ante.

No comparable turmoil disturbed the placid waters of British social history. Even won, however, the two world wars were the only serious forcing-periods of social change in English history in the twentieth century. The outbreak of the 1914–18 War providentially aborted a potentially explosive situation in Britain, when the propertied class was deeply split (on an imperial issue, Ireland) and working-class militancy threatened to escape the control of a faltering trade-union leadership (syndicalism). The long-term effect of the Great War, however, was to increase the weight and strength of working-class organizations. Between 1914 and 1919 TUC membership doubled and the Labour vote increased fivefold. The Labour Party, previously a small pressure group on the flank of the Liberals, emerged after the War as the main opposition and five years later as a (minority) government. Simultaneously, the traditional political pattern of the ruling bloc underwent a permanent mutation. The vortex of the War smashed the flimsy barriers between Conservative and Liberal Parties, temporarily producing a fluctuating disorder, out of which eventually emerged a unified political organization of the Right – the Conservative Party. The survival of the Conservative rather than the Liberal Party was conditioned both by factional divisions within the Liberal Party and by the obvious desuetude of Free Trade doctrines in the Depression years. But in a more important sense, it revealed the continuing ascendancy of the patrician segment of the dominant social bloc. It was in the logic of the previous fifty years. Neither party had ever been a simple crystallization of distinct strata within this bloc – precisely because its nature precluded sharply differentiated levels or layers within it. But the Liberal Party had always tended towards a more bourgeois admixture; the Conservative Party towards one with a greater aristocratic component. The ideologies of the two parties had usually, although not always, over-expressed this difference. The eclipse of the one and the triumph of the other signified the final 'feudalization' of the ideology and protocol of the dominant bloc.[7] The Liberal Party, despite its greater initial proximity to the centre of gravity of future parliamentary politics, lost because its identity was finally so much weaker. When real danger threatened and a single party of the Right became necessary, proto-reformist velleities were no match for centuries of aureoled tradition.

By the twenties, the parliamentary system had for the first time in its long and *trompe l'œil* history become the arena of a genuine class confrontation. Under post-war conditions the attractive power of Labour swiftly increased. Its seats in the House of Commons increased from 60 in 1919 to 191 in 1924, when it formed its short-lived first minority government, and then – after losses in the election of that year – to 287 in 1929, when it formed its second government, also in a minority but this time as the strongest party. Within two years this Labour Government collapsed – more completely and ignominiously

7. 'Feudal' only metaphorically, of course.

than any other Social Democratic government has ever done. Vast Conservative majorities dominated the next decade. The first cycle of the Labour Party's history was brought to an end by the outbreak of the Second World War.

The 1939–45 War opened the second cycle, which reproduced with remarkable similarity the timing and movement of the first. Again the tremendous pressures of the War effected a sudden, qualitative leap forward in British history. For the first and only time in this century, an appreciable redistribution of income took place, secondary education was generalized, and the foundations of the Welfare State were laid. The 1945 election confirmed these changes, when the Labour Party won a large absolute majority in the Commons. This time its electoral strength and its legislative achievements (creation of the National Health Service, socialization of fuel and transport, etc.) were much greater than those of its ephemeral governments after the First World War. Its development may thus be more accurately described as spiral, rather than as truly cyclical. But at a higher level, much the same sequence was repeated. The period of upsurge was brief and rapidly dissipated. The Labour Government fell in 1951, on the twentieth anniversary of the disaster of 1931, in renewed circumstances of economic crisis, political division and ideological demoralization. The result was, once again, an uninterrupted decade of Conservative rule. In fifty years, such was the total change since the advent of political democracy, in a country where the manual working class constitutes an overwhelming sociological majority of the population.

The distinctive facets of English class structure, as it has evolved over three centuries, can thus be summed up as follows. After a bitter, cathartic revolution, which transformed the structure but not the superstructures of English society, a landed aristocracy, underpinned by a powerful mercantile affinal group, became the first dominant capitalist class in Britain. This dynamic agrarian capitalism expelled the English peasantry from history. Its success was economically the 'floor' and sociologically the 'ceiling' of the rise of the industrial bourgeoisie. Undisturbed by a feudal state, frightened by the French Revolution and its own proletariat, subdued by the prestige and authority of the landed class, the bourgeoisie won two modest victories, lost its nerve and ended by losing its identity. The late Victorian era and the high noon of imperialism welded aristocracy and bourgeoisie together in a single social bloc. The working class fought passionately and unaided against the advent of industrial capitalism; its exhaustion after successive defeats was the measure of its efforts. Henceforward it evolved, separate but subordinate, within the apparently unshakeable structure of British capitalism, unable, despite its great numerical superiority, to alter the fundamental nature of its society.

2. History and Class Consciousness: Hegemony

The preceding schema is a crude and preliminary attempt to pose some of the developmental problems of British capitalism. It remains to complete its arguments with some consideration of the structural order produced by this history. Again, the subject is of a magnitude and complexity that permits only the most general suggestions here. But even very partial and inexact definitions may be better than none, if they invite correction and discussion.

The power structure of English society today can be most accurately described as an elastic and all-embracing hegemonic order. Hegemony was defined by Gramsci as the dominance of one social bloc over another, not simply by means of force or wealth, but by a wider authority whose ultimate resource is cultural. This is an imperative order that not merely sets external limits to the aims and actions of the subordinated bloc, but shapes its internal vision of itself and the world, imposing contingent historical facts as necessary co-ordinates of social life itself. The hegemonic class is the primary determinant of consciousness, character and customs throughout the society. Such tranquil and unchallenged sovereignty is a relatively rare historical phenomenon. In England, however, the unparalleled temporal continuity of the dominant class has produced a striking example of it. The peculiar morphology of this class has resulted in often apparently bizarre or absurd, but in reality effective and explicable, forms of hegemony:

(1) *Social Relations*. British society is notoriously characterized by a seemingly 'feudal' hierarchy of orders and ranks, distinguished by a multiplicity of trivial insignia – accent, vocabulary, diet, dress, recreation. This set of stations corresponds neither to the primary reality of a system divided into economically based classes, nor to the secondary reality of limited individual mobility within the system. It is, however, the projective image of society naturally held and propagated by a landowning class. The deferential pattern of social relations in the countryside, at the height of this group's economic power, lingered on as a normative reference after industrialization, because of its continued political leadership. If the mythologies of rank captivated the

middle class, producing a notorious social-climbing and craving for titles, they also powerfully mystified real social relations for the working class as well. For although British workers themselves continued instinctively to use a bi-polar language ('us' and 'them') to describe their situation, labour leaders moving in an overlapping zone, in constant contact with representatives and institutions of the dominant bloc, tended to absorb false, 'feudal' consciousness. Hence the protests in *The Future Labour Offers You* today against 'outdated social distinctions', 'snobbery' as major social evils. In this way, the divorce between relations of production and social consciousness that is always essential to capitalism percolates into declared opponents of the system. In general the hierarchical, pseudo-feudal coloration of English society, expression and instrument of the hegemony of an (ancestrally agrarian) aristocracy, operates as perhaps the most successful of all camouflages of class structure: by simultaneously intensifying and displacing class consciousness, it tends to render it politically inoperative and socially self-perpetuating.

(2) *Ideology*. The hegemony of the dominant bloc in England is not articulated in any systematic major ideology, but is rather diffused in a miasma of commonplace prejudices and taboos. The two great chemical elements of this blanketing English fog are 'traditionalism' and 'empiricism': in it, visibility – of any social or historical reality – is always zero. Traditionalism – veneration for the Monarchy, the Church, the Peerage, the City, etc. – was the natural ideological idiom of the landed class as soon as its monopoly of political power was threatened. It emerges, in fact, with Burke's polemics against the French Revolution at the end of the eighteenth century. Empiricism, on the other hand, faithfully transcribes the fragmented, incomplete character of the English bourgeoisie's historical experience. It did not have to overthrow a feudal state in the nineteenth century, and it did not succeed in becoming sole master of the new industrial society. Thus it never went through a truly egalitarian phase and so never struck at the ideological rationale of the aristocracy. Traditionalism and empiricism henceforward fuse as a single legitimating system: traditionalism sanctions the present by deriving it from the past, empiricism binds the future by fastening it to the present. A comprehensive conservatism is the result, covering society with a pall of simultaneous philistinism (towards ideas) and mystagogy (towards institutions), for which England has justly won an international reputation.

(3) *Leadership*. As already suggested, the major sociological legacy of

imperialism was its consecration of the style of leadership peculiar to the hegemonic class. The administration of an empire comprising a quarter of the planet required its own special skills. Imperialism automatically sets a premium on a patrician style: as a system of alien domination, it always, within the limits of safety, seeks to maximize the existential difference between the ruling and the ruled race. Domestic domination can be realized with a popular and egalitarian appearance, colonial never: there can be no plebeian pro-consuls. In an imperial system, the iconography of power is necessarily aristocratic. The aristocrat is defined not by acts which denote skills but by gestures that reveal character: a too specific training or aptitude would be a derogation of nobility. The famous amateurism of the English 'upper class' has its source in this ideal. Traditionally contemptuous of exclusive application to 'trade' or 'letters', the businessman or the intellectual, the rulers of England were also – uniquely – neither professional politicians nor bureaucrats nor militarists. They were at different times all of these, and so finally and splendidly none of them.

(4) *Rejects.* The industrial bourgeoisie of the nineteenth century did produce one articulated ideology with universal claims: utilitarianism. This played an important role in the early decades of industrialization, as a militant creed of capital accumulation and cultural nihilism. But it never achieved a truly hegemonic status. In part, this was due to the historic inability of the class which was its bearer to win political dominance. But its failure was also due to its own limitations: a fanatically bleak materialism was ill suited to creating that cultural and value system which is the mark of a hegemonic ideology. Utilitarianism in the end became a sectional rationale of the workings of the economy, that never penetrated the legitimation of the system as a whole. A slightly later product of the rise of the bourgeoisie was liberalism as such, both refining and diluting the original virulence of utilitarian doctrine. A more contradictory and wayward phenomenon, it inspired the sporadic enthusiasm for good causes abroad which distinguished the enlightened middle class of the time (Cobden); but despite the distinction of spokesmen like Mill, it was prevented from becoming a serious claimant for domestic ascendancy by the objective structure of British imperial society, negating its avowed norms – hence its tendency to find refuge in altruistic international campaigns.

* * *

Capitalist hegemony bears crucially on the working class in a specific, historically determined way in Britain. A combination of structural and conjunctural factors in the nineteenth century produced a proletariat distinguished by an immovable corporate class consciousness and almost no hegemonic ideology. This paradox is the most important single fact about the English working class. If a hegemonic class can be defined as one which imposes its own ends and vision on society as a whole, a corporate class is conversely one which pursues its own ends within a social totality whose overall determination lies outside it. A hegemonic class seeks to transform society in its own image, inventing afresh its economic system, its political institutions, its cultural values, its 'mode of insertion' into the world. A corporate class seeks to defend and improve its own position within a social order accepted as given. The English working class has been characterized since the mid nineteenth century by the disjunction between an intense consciousness of separate identity and a continuous failure to set and impose goals for society as a whole. In this disjunction lies the secret of the special nature of the labour movement in England. The very intensity of its corporate class consciousness, embodied in a distinct, hermetic culture, has blocked the emergence of a universal ideology in the English working class. It has not been lack of class consciousness but – in one sense – excess of it which has been the obstacle to the spread of socialism. It is this paradox that is the foundation both of the immobile reformism of the Labour Party and of the failure to convert it to neo-liberalism, in imitation of the Bad Godesberg alteration of German Social Democracy.

Historically, the reasons for this complex form of consciousness lie at the origins of English capitalism. The structural context has already been indicated: in the social world fashioned by the hegemonic class, *all* classes had to appear and to see themselves as natural 'estates', defined by a fixed station and way of life – the working class no less than others. At the same time, the primary conjunctural influence was undoubtedly the harsh repression and segregation which the working class suffered in its formative years, which drove it inwards on its own resources, to create a separate moral universe. This siege experience fixed an attitude to the outside world which has persisted to this day. The early years of the working class were also, of course, the period in its history when it rose directly against capitalist society – but in the confusions of the time, the defeats it suffered were almost unconditional. Armed with a more systematic vision, it would no doubt still have been defeated, but its struggles would have entered an enduring tradition, capable of informing the future. The actual result was that the experience of fifty years was not cumulative, and played little role in the later development of the working class. Conversely, the fully fledged emergence of socialism as an ideology in the second half of the century came at a moment when the labour movement in England was at its lowest and least receptive ebb.

A second influence on the particular form taken by working-class consciousness was the failure of any significant body of intellectuals to join the cause of the proletariat until the very end of the nineteenth century. The reasons for this disconnexion, whose consequences bear heavily on the Labour Party today, lie partly in the sociological moorings of the English intellectuals of the Victorian period, and partly in the more general history of the time. Aristocratic rule had never allowed the formation of an independent intellectual enclave within the body politic of landed England. As early as the sixteenth century, the gentry had averted the possibility of a secular intelligentsia emerging as a successor to the clerical intelligentsia (recruited from the humbler classes) of the mediaeval period, by dispatching its offspring to educational institutions once relatively restricted to the latter. Thereafter it produced its own intellectuals, mainly from the lesser, professional reaches of the class. The eventual result was to be the English phenomenon of a body of intellectuals which was at once homogeneous and cohesive and yet not a distinct intelligentsia, because its unity was mediated less through ideas than through kinship. Whereas in France intellectuals became a more or less autonomous group, integrated vertically by their relationship with their predecessors to form a continuous, internally unified community, in England their bond lay in an external insertion into their class.

This is not to say that they showed consistent political conformity. Victorian intellectuals did, in fact, in their own way produce a remarkably far-reaching critique of Victorian capitalism – the tradition, mainly but not exclusively of Romanticism, which forms the subject of *Culture and Society*. But this critique, containing many insights close to the philosophical premises of Marx, was nevertheless for good sociological reasons fatally divorced from the realities of economic structure and political conflict. At the same time, the French Revolution chilled most of these intellectuals as much as it did their class. Hence the tradition often foundered in ideological confusion and ultimately – in the twentieth century – was in political terms to become predominantly conservative. Thus the major intellectual critique of capitalism in the nineteenth century failed to encounter the major social force capable of challenging capitalism. The tradition of Romanticism and its sequels remained politically naive and became reactionary. The working-class movement, after its repression and long retreat, was to fall prey to the progeny of the most stunted bourgeois ideology of all – utilitarianism.

It is a general historical rule that a rising social class acquires a significant part of its ideological equipment from the armoury of the ruling class itself. Thus the universal axioms of the French Revolution were turned by the working class in France against the bourgeoisie which first proclaimed them, founding a revolutionary ideology directed against the initiators of the revolution. In England, a supine bourgeoisie produced a subordinate proletariat. It handed on no impulse of liberation, no revolutionary values, no universal language. All it transmitted were the deadly germs of utilitarianism, from which the Labour Party has sickened in the twentieth century. For the first sizeable group of intellectuals which finally joined political struggle on the side of the working class were the Fabians.[8] The intellectual descent of the Webbs and their companions was candidly avowed: they saw themselves as the successors of Bentham and Spencer. No more leaden legacy could have been left the working-class movement. Confusion of influence with power, admiration for bureaucracy and disdain for equality – all the philistine narrowness of the Webbs and their associates became imprinted on the mentality of the Labour Party in later years. Even in its original form as a doctrine of the bourgeoisie, the limitations of utilitarianism had prevented it from achieving widely persuasive force. Shorn of its youth and fire, and diluted with paternalism, it was never, in its Fabian form, a serious challenge to the hegemony of the dominant bloc.

Fabianism was not, of course, the only ingredient in the early outlook of the Labour Party, although it was in the end the most important. The other component of classic 'Labourism' was the genuine working-class radicalism that stemmed from the ILP (symbolized initially by Keir Hardie). It was this which gave the Labour Party its unshakeable social character and stopped it from ever becoming a simple party of middle-class reform. But the ideological expressions of this current never achieved the coherence of Fabianism, remaining a heteroclite mixture of adulterated Marxism, transposed Methodism and inherited Liberalism. In the early years of the party's existence, the last element was of some importance, as it passed on a tradition of internationalism and partial anti-imperialism to a section of the Labour leadership (MacDonald's refusal of the First World War). Its importance subsequently dwindled.

By and large, then, it can be said that the one distinctive and coherent

8. Morris's thought was, tragically, too isolated to become a major influence on the movement.

ideology which took root in the labour movement in this century was tributary to the one distinctive, coherent and unsuccessful bourgeois ideology of the last century. Yet this movement was never captured or turned into a purely adaptive political machine. It can, indeed, be argued that its real historical substance was not in the main articulated ideologically at all, but rather institutionally. In a famous passage, Raymond Williams has written: 'The culture which it [the working class] has produced, is the collective democratic institution whether in the trade unions, the co-operative movement or a political party. . . . When it is considered in context, it can be seen as a very remarkable creative achievement.'[9] This idea represents a strong version of one of the two contrasting poles of socialist accounts of the working class, in which the practices of the labour movement prefigure the form of the society it seeks to create. In Hegelian terms, this is a conception of 'proletarian positivity' – as opposed to the idea of the working class as a 'negativity' of history, whose end is to abolish class society and so effectively itself. The reality of any empirical movement involves a variable mixture of both moments – since, pure positivity, no working class could project any general change, and, pure negativity, it would be immolated in a perpetual uprising. In England, there is no doubt which moment has dominated. The dense, object-invested universe described in *The Uses of Literacy* is a monument to the positivity of the oldest working class in the world.[10] Too much so: the weakness of Williams's argument is that it lacks a distinction between corporate and hegemonic institutional forms. The very density and specificity of English working-class culture has limited its political range and checked the emergence of a more ambitious socialism in England. Williams attempts to resolve the difficulty by attributing an indefinite capacity for extension to working-class, but not to bourgeois institutions. The claim, however, apart from any factual weakness, skirts the conflicts between them. The truth seems to be that the spirit of working-class culture has been much as Williams describes it, but that the will to universalize it, to make it the general model of society, which he tacitly assumes to be a concomitant, has only rarely existed.

---

9. *Culture and Society*, London 1958, p. 327.

10. For the debate on negativity and positivity, see Georg Lukács, *Histoire et Conscience de Classe*, Paris 1960; Jean-Paul Sartre, 'Les Communistes et la Paix', *Les Temps Modernes* 81, 84–85, 101, July and October–November 1952, April 1954; Maurice Merleau-Ponty, *Les Aventures de la Dialectique*, Paris 1955; and Lucio Magri, 'Problemi della Teoria Marxista del Partito Rivoluzionario', *Critica Marxista*, no. 5–6, 1963. In England, Hoggart's striking phenomenology has been the major contribution. Marx's work emphasizes both moments.

Thus, at whichever level one choses to look, the same basic paradox reappears. In Britain, the working class has developed over a hundred and fifty years an adamantine social consciousness, but never a commensurate political will.[11] The very name of its traditional political party underlines this truth. Alone of major European working-class formations, it is called neither a Social Democratic nor a Socialist nor a Communist Party; it is the *Labour* Party – a name which designates not an ideal society, as do the others, but an existent interest.

* * *

By way of illustration, it will suffice to recall three historical moments at which the nocturnal structure of hegemony has been suddenly and vividly lit up by the lightning of a major political crisis:

(i) In 1926 the General Strike saw the most direct collision of class forces in this century. Can its defeat be attributed simply to 'betrayal', as in standard accounts on the Left – was victory ever conceivable? The answer is surely that the Strike could not but fail, for there never existed the political will to carry it through. Cole's description of the contrast between the two camps says everything: 'When the moment came, however, it was the workers who drew back. The inherent constitutionalism of the main body of the labour movement never asserted itself more plainly than in the great "unconstitutional" movement known as the "General Strike". On the other hand, the readiness of the defenders of law and order to force the issue when the crisis came, rather than meet the Trade Union leaders' evident will to come to terms, showed a very different temper. The pacific General Council and the bellicose Mr Winston Churchill, the mild *British Worker* and the furious *British Gazette*, presented a contrast no less instructive than ironic. . . . From the first the strikers' only real chance of success lay in frightening the government into surrender or persuading it into compromise. The temper of the government throughout the dispute excluded the latter solution, which the strike leaders would, of course, have welcomed. The struggle therefore became one of morale – it was a question of waiting to see which side would crumple up first. But with Winston Churchill in command and thoroughly enjoying the "scrap", the

11. Parliamentarism, often held to be the root vice of the Labour Party, is thus only an expression of a deeper failure.

government was not likely to crumple up. . . . All things considered, the strikers from the first had little real chance of winning.'[12]

(ii) In 1931 the disintegration of the Labour Cabinet, under the pressure of a run on the pound, ended in the worst catastrophe to overtake any government in British history, with the collective desertion of most of the top echelon of the party in power to the opposition, resulting in a near-annihilation of the party at the succeeding election. Was this disaster the inevitable outcome of the Depression? Tawney's verdict on the Labour Party a year later was this: 'It is the author, the unintending and pitiable author, of its own misfortunes. It made a government in its own image; and the collapse of that government was the result neither of accident – though that played its part – nor of unfavourable circumstances – though luck was against it – nor least of all, it must be repeated, of merely personal feelings. It was in the logic of history. . . . In spite of the dramatic episodes which heralded its collapse, the Government did not fall with a crash, in a tornado from the blue. It crawled slowly to its doom, deflated by inches.'[13]

(iii) In 1951 the next Labour Government fell, amidst a balance-of-payments crisis and splits in the Cabinet. What had happened to the parliamentary landslide of 1945? Had Labour over-reached itself in office – was its exit foredoomed? In fact, the Attlee Government had soon lost the initiative, and by the end of its term had no idea where to go. Its final departure was virtually a voluntary abdication, as Crossman's retrospect makes clear: 'Why was Hugh Dalton able to reveal . . . that by 1947 – only two years after the electoral triumph – the government was manifestly losing both its coherence and its sense of direction? . . . What was it that so rapidly deflated the public demand for social change that had swept the party into power in 1945? . . . When the 1951 election came, there was no violent anti-socialist swing of public opinion. On the contrary, the party made headway in the country – polling the highest vote in its history. . . . If only Mr Attlee had held on, instead of appealing to the country in the trough of the crisis, he would have reaped the benefit of the 1951 recovery, and Labour might have stayed in power for a decade. . . . An independent critic is . . . [likely] to find that the electoral losses in 1950 were quite

12. G.D.H. Cole, *A Short History of the British Working-Class Movement 1789–1947*, London 1952, pp. 383, 419.

13. R.H. Tawney, 'The Choice before the Labour Party', *The Political Quarterly*, July–September 1932, pp. 326, 323.

unnecessary, and that the precipitate decision to resign a year later was not an inevitable result of the crisis, but a consequence of physical exhaustion and loss of nerve.'[14]

The history of hegemony in twentieth-century Britain is tersely indicated in these three comments, by sympathetic critics loyal to mainstream traditions of Labour itself.

* * *

It remains to suggest the way in which the hegemonic system works as an overall order, delimiting and defining the roles of antagonistic social classes within it. For this purpose, the crucial moments are those at which the working-class party has won overt political power and formed a government. The analytic problem can be posed simply as follows: what is the invisible barrier between the formal control of unlimited state power (enshrined in the sovereignty of Parliament) and the actual implementation of qualitative social change (enshrined in the party's constitution)?

An answer must start from the obvious fact that power in advanced capitalist societies is polycentric. If the official mythology that it is located uniquely in the site of political democracy, Parliament, is plainly false, it cannot be said that the Left has developed a substantial or sophisticated theory of the distribution of power in late capitalism to replace it. The lack here illustrates a more general atrophy in analysis of the *mediations* of capitalist rule. In the long run, to be sure, power coincides with control of the means of production, as traditional exegesis insists. But at any particular moment of history, this will not necessarily be true. Rather than abstract reassertions of the truism that power ultimately derives from the pattern of ownership in a society, what is needed is a concrete typology of the different modalities of power in history. For it is clear that a whole spectrum of possibilities exists, realized in different societies at different epochs. In the short run, power can be predominantly military, bureaucratic, economic, ideological, even – as a limiting case – purely political; it can be crystallized directly in the means of violence (Nazi Germany), the means of administration (Confucian China), the means of production (company-states like Honduras or Katanga), the means of communication (increasingly, Western societies), or the means of legislation (which would be socialism). Of course, no power structure in any

14. Richard Crossman, 'The Lessons of 1945', *New Statesman*, 19 April 1963.

society – capitalist or pre-capitalist – is ever limited to a single dimension: all involve institutional mixtures. But these do not preclude meaningful distinctions both in and between different patterns of such power. In modern Britain, at any event, there is a very specific configuration, the product of a particular historical and geographical situation.

Schematically, three main idiosyncrasies of this structure of power stand out: the relative insignificance of bureaucratic or military forms, the unusually immediate striking-capacity of economic forms, and the ultimately crucial importance of ideological and cultural forms. Together this combination may be defined in terms used first by Hegel and then by Marx, as the supremacy of civil society over the State. Each element in the constellation corresponds to a fundamental moment in the history of the dominant bloc. Despite their manifest class character, neither the armed forces nor the civil service are of such directly political importance in the United Kingdom as in most other advanced capitalist countries (France, until recently Germany and Japan). The profile of the army in England is the result of a long dialectical history: the late Middle Ages saw the worst over-militarization of the countryside in Europe during the Wars of the Roses, leading to the radical demilitarizing policies of the Tudor monarchy; then when the monarchy itself attempted to build up a standing army (James II), the landowning class prevented it as a threat to its independent power in the countryside; while the geographical isolation of England removed the need for permanent external defence. The absence of a major state bureaucracy corresponded to the local and molecular character of original gentry control of the countryside, when the unpaid, spare-time JP combined economic, social and political power in his physical person; attempts to create a centralized bureaucratic machine from above (Charles I) foundered on this obstacle. The success of agrarian capitalism, followed by the spontaneous outbreak of the first industrial revolution, then joined the anti-bureaucratic traditions of landlord politics with those of laissez-faire economics (where industrialization was later, more deliberate and imitative, as in Germany, the State by contrast became one of the main engines of the Industrial Revolution). The modern civil service dates only from 1854: it is more significant as a column of power than the army, and has undoubtedly had a braking influence on the Labour Governments of this century – but it has never been powerful enough to derail them.

By contrast, direct economic power in England is exceptionally great. Just as the relative modesty of the military and bureaucracy in the structure of hegemony is a product of the original dominance of agrarian capitalism, so the massive weight of business stems from the subsequent pattern of industrial capitalism in England. If 'economic power' is often invoked on the Left, it is rarely analysed as it needs to be in the variety of its component forms: labour decisions (dismissals), investment decisions (dividend-levels), price decisions (tax transfers to the consumer), publicity decisions (subsidies to political parties), and so on. Here it is necessary only to stress that the aggregate power of capital in England is at once unusually formidable and structurally excitable, because of the international exposures of the British economy. The ultimate sanction of economic power faced with a hostile government is flight of capital. In England, the organization of the Sterling Area has made this a permanent possibility rather than an emergency temptation, since the vulnerability of the pound to overseas speculation constantly threatens turbulence in the English capital market itself. Labour governments face the daily danger of losing the confidence of international investors, and suddenly confronting huge financial outflows which the Sterling Area, closing the circle, makes it abnormally difficult to control. In Britain, these movements operate above and beyond the normal discretionary power of capital to act in what it may choose to regard as an emergency.

Finally, the extreme importance of cultural institutions in the British pattern of hegemony follows from the historical developments traced above. In modern times, control of the systems of education (public schools, universities) and of communication (oligopoly of press) has been central to the reproduction of the dominance of the 'upper class'. In each case these institutions derive from, and conform to, the larger character of the field of power. The peculiar salience of Oxbridge and the public schools in the culture of privilege corresponds to their role as educational summits outside the state system, in contrast with the normal situation on the Continent. The unparalleled concentration in ownership of the press, and its virtually saturation levels of readership, in turn reflect the degree of commercial centralization and national integration which marks the oldest major capitalism in the world.

This triangular topography is the true sociological 'setting' of parliamentary democracy in Britain, whose operative character can only be understood in terms of it. In a sense, the remarkable formal aspect of parliamentarism in England is the absolute sovereignty vested in the legislature. From one point of view, it could be thought that this would be a devastating weapon for any radical government: no other modern capitalist state has ever taken the risk of dispensing with a written constitution (many have even had the sanctity of private property written into their constitutions, besides severe checks on the legislature). This singularity of the British political system is historically intelligible enough. The House of Commons was for centuries a one-class institution: there was always a sociological guarantee of its predictability that made juridical safety-rails unnecessary. Subsequently the upward pressure of the bourgeoisie and then the working class was accommodated within the same framework, by gradual extensions of the franchise. The famous parliamentary democracy which eventually emerged was, looked at from one angle, the most enduring achievement of the working class. But it was also a necessary adjustment of traditional forms of social domination to a new historical situation: from this angle, democracy was the ransom of hegemony. Faced with the rise of the middle and then of the working class, the rulers of the country had either to break with their tradition and try to retain exclusive power by military or bureaucratic coercion; or they had to yield entry into the political system to these new social forces, and neutralize their efficacy within it by powerful extra-parliamentary means, which were consonant with the strategic style of its past. They chose, of course, to do the latter. The manufacturing bourgeoisie was culturally contained within a still largely aristocratic framework, into which it was then selectively co-opted. The new unified bloc then turned to confront labour. There was no possibility of dissolving this as a class, but the incorporation of industry into the established order supplied a substitute second weapon, in the organizational strength of massed capital.

Thus today, Parliament, the formal site of political power, is two quite different 'places' according to which party holds office. Its role in the power system is analytically distinct in each case. When a Conservative Government is in office, it is an integral part of a continuous landscape which extends in a smooth, unbroken space around it. When a Labour Government holds office, it is an isolated, spotlit enclave, surrounded on almost every side by hostile territory, unceasingly shelled by industry, press and orchestrated 'public opinion'. Each time it has in the end been overrun.

Of course, the actual balance of forces is more complex than an image of this kind suggests. In theory, the power of the trade unions could provide very strong support for a Labour Government outside Parliament, although this has so far never really occurred. However, the customary assertion that the working-class movement possesses 'countervailing power' under democratic capitalism evades the real question, which is not: are there two sets of forces? but: what is the final balance of forces? The countervailing power invoked by Galbraith or Strachey scarcely amounts to more than the ability of the industrial working class to prevent the relative depression of its standards of living in an expanding economy.

In reality, two unequal forces are in perpetual shock against each other, pushing the point of collision between them now in one direction and now in another, but over a period of time establishing a *relatively stable equilibrium* at a point favourable to one and unfavourable to the other. This partially stabilized equilibrium, neither total victory nor drawn combat, but permanent net superiority of the hegemonic class, is the reality of social peace and political democracy in England today. A reforming Labour Government like that of 1945 can shift the equilibrium to the left, as it did with the enlargement of welfare provision and of the public sector, so that the band of its future oscillations is situated more favourably for the working class. Successful pressures from the Right may then, as in the present period, roll the point of equilibrium some way back along the distance it has come (inversion of income redistribution, denationalizations, etc.). The present balance of forces in Britain remains a crushingly capitalist one, with inequalities which rival or outdistance those anywhere in the capitalist world: one per cent of the population owns two-fifths of the fixed property of the country, while half of the Cabinet comes from a school of a thousand pupils, in a population of fifty million. The narrow area in which at any given period the equilibrium moves back and forth can be defined as the elasticity of the hegemonic order at that conjuncture.

3. Increasing Entropy

The character of the present crisis, and the way in which labour stands in relation to it, can now be resumed. This crisis is a general malady of the society, infrastructure and superstructure alike – not a sudden breakdown, but an increasing entropy. For the conditions which constituted the unique good fortune of the ruling bloc in the nineteenth century have turned against it. The 'law' of uneven development has produced one of its dialectical reversals, with a vengeance. Today Britain appears an archaic society, trapped in past successes, now for the first time aware of its lassitude, but as yet unable to overcome it. The symptoms of decline have been catalogued too frequently to need much repetition here: stagnant industries, starved schools, run-down cities, demoralized rulers, parochial outlooks. All these sores of the present have their origins in advantages of the past. This past is not merely that of the imperialist era, as so many socialist – and capitalist – critics now repeat. It extends both backwards and forwards well beyond the late nineteenth century. The major single cause of the present crisis is, of course, the protracted international decline of the economy that started during the period in which Britain's world empire was being completed, when exports of capital surged, while investment fell short and technological innovation flagged at home. The quantitative returns of imperial and overseas investment long masked a qualitative deterioration in the country's competitive position, but their legacy ended by exacerbating it. The exigencies and constraints of the Sterling Area have at length become the *bête noire* of the advanced bourgeois publicists of the day, as the chief culprit of the ills of the British economy in our time. Yet this last form of empire is dominated by the first historical nucleus of British imperialism, the City of London, whose origins go back not to the nineteenth but to the seventeenth century. Aristocratically connected as no other department of urban capital has been, the City is now socially the most revealing, and sectorally the most significant, determinant of the shape of the economy. In the palimpsest of interests within the dominant order, the industrialists who in their prime merged with the ruling landowners have over time become corroded in the union, as the practices of the amateur and the nepotist spread from the councils of state to the boardrooms of industry. By the fifties, the most efficient firms in Britain were found to be mainly enterprises which were either started by foreigners (refugees) since 1940, controlled by minorities (Quakers, Jews), or branches of international corporations (mainly American). The conquering entrepreneurs of the mid nineteenth century had become mediocre executives in the mid twentieth.

In the same period, the State came to reveal complementary weaknesses. The Treasury became, after the City, the second great albatross round the neck of English economic growth. What was once a historic achievement of the English governing class in all its metamorphoses, its long maintenance of the supremacy of civil society over the State, is now undermining it. Today, as the giant international corporation increasingly emerges as the basic unit of capitalism, the State intervenes ever more universally in the national economy to steer and control it in the interests of the system as a whole. The indicative planning typical of this neo-capitalism demands technocratic skills and a powerful administrative apparatus. In England, the traditions of the governing class have not provided for this. Its virtues were those of the squire and the mill-owner. If these are gone, the vices of an anachronistic economic liberalism are left. Predictably, in post-war conditions the Treasury came to display what one critic has called the 'apotheosis of dilettantism' – with fatal results for the success of the Conservative regime of the fifties. For in this period, the final good fortune of British capitalism, its victory in two World Wars, also became a factor in its decline. Never forced by mass physical destruction of its plant to renew its capital stock radically, it fell drastically behind the rates of growth of those countries which had to re-equip their industries after defeat in war – Germany, France, Italy, Japan. Now, belatedly, slogans of 'planning', 'growth' and 'efficiency' resound in government speeches, and the need to rationalize the composition and direction of the economy is pressed in every journal of the Right.

Socially, too, the triumphs of the past have become the bane of the present. The English bourgeoisie had never been outstanding for its devotion to technological or scientific education: the slow, epochal maturing and sudden 'natural' blossoming of the Industrial Revolution originally rendered unnecessary the official creation of a widespread system of technical training, like that which so greatly assisted industrialization in Germany. But this fortuitous advantage was soon cast in a more deliberate mould. In the mid nineteenth century, the burgeoning middle class sold its birthright for the accent of a gentleman. The public schools which sealed the pact between landowners and manufacturers reduced the norms of the two classes to a common denominator, and imprinted it on the following generations. If the bourgeoisie contributed least to the new public school ideal (repression and philistinism), and the aristocracy most (arrogance and amateurism), in either case science and technique went by the board. The ruling bloc was trained to rule, and did so; but a century later its skills had often become mere manners, and its manners, increasingly, affectation.

In the fifties, the large capital-intensive corporations belatedly began to endow the public schools (and universities) with science blocks and laboratories. But by now it was too late to save the educational system as a whole from challenge, as the state sector, ill-financed and underprivileged as the English form of capitalist hegemony required that it should be, was not even fulfilling its menial role of providing the necessary intermediate and lower echelon skills for the economy. Today, private and public sector alike are put in question by the most reputable spokesmen of the ruling order, and the 'unprecedented' expansion of education advocated by recent Reports is everywhere greeted as an imperative necessity. Indeed, public reaction against traditional social hierarchies has reached a point where Macmillan, in the final days of his premiership, could call a Conservative Conference to battle in the following terms: 'This country has got to be prepared for change. . . . We are all more or less planners today . . . we are still as a nation too set in our ways, too apt to cling to old privileges, too unwilling to abandon old practices that have outlived their usefulness . . . there are too many demarcation lines, social and industrial – one might almost say a sort of caste system.' The Conservative Party as a whole has not, of course, been converted to the new talk of efficiency and 'equality'. One section believes it, another demagogically uses it, another rejects it altogether. In alarm after Macmillan's resignation, despite the obvious requirements of the moment, the party obeyed its oldest and deepest instincts and chose as its leader a caricature of its past aristocratic eminences. But for all that, it is significant that for the first time some kind of ostensible egalitarianism has become inscribed on the banner of the English bourgeoisie.

It is in the political field, of course, that the present crisis has produced its most visible – if also often superficial – manifestations. Failures of economic policy, fiascos of military ambition, collapse of diplomatic ventures, urban blight and sexual scandal: in their variety of symptoms, these have been the signs of the disarray of a governing class confronting a world that had passed it by. Its real moment of truth had come in 1958, and it had not seen it. When the Conservative regime refused to sign the Treaty of Rome, it threw away its one chance of renovating British capitalism without a major political and social crisis at home. With fatal hubris, it thought England was still a nation apart, as the apex of a worldwide Commonwealth that guaranteed it an eminence above Europe. Four years later it realized its error, but the Fifth Republic was now firmly installed, and the gates clanged shut as it turned to the Community for refuge.

In retrospect, the famous flavour of the Conservative decade takes on an eerie significance. Under Macmillan's aegis, a neo-Edwardianism reigned and high politics in England became more aristocratic than they had been in the time of Chamberlain. The Edwardian era was, of course, the last period in which the imperial paramountcy of the British governing class was still intact. In the late fifties, it was as if, by an unconscious, instinctive mimetism, the same class was re-enacting its former role down to its most trivial details, in the hope of somehow recreating the confidence of the last unchallenged epoch of the past in order to face the perils and – soon – the disasters of the present. The crisis, then, is a logical outcome of the long pilgrimage of British capitalism from its origins to its present precarious position within the world of the second half of the twentieth century. As a result of it, the dominant bloc in Britain today must, if it is to preserve its hegemony, undergo yet another metamorphosis. Re-enacting the past has not restored it: the ruling order now, in the main, realizes that it must change once again. The international pressures of contemporary capitalism require a radical adaptation. The unfinished work of 1640 and 1832 must be taken up where it was left off.

The opportunity this crisis offers the labour movement is correspondingly great. It is clear from the preceding, or any, analysis of its history and ideology that it is incapable of tabling a socialist transformation in any immediate future. For that Labour would have to transform itself into a socialist party first. But between this perspective and the role of executor of bourgeois reform and stabilization, which some socialists are already predicting for it, there lies a wide gamut of choices. What will these choices be, and which forces will fight to determine them, are the questions which will dominate the coming years.

1964

2

Components of the National Culture

A significant student movement has not yet emerged in Britain. But it may now be only a matter of time before it does, since this is the last major industrialized country which has not produced one. The issues that are the natural focus for a student revolt that seeks a workers' alliance are obvious enough: challenges to authoritarianism at home, and solidarities against imperialism abroad. There is, however, another front to be opened: against the reactionary culture inculcated in universities and colleges, which it is one of the functions of British higher education to instil in students.

Louis Althusser has recently written that within the general system of higher education 'the true fortress of class influence' is 'the very knowledge students receive from their teachers'.[1] A scaling of this fortress is a necessary condition for the take-off of a student movement, as the example of the SDS in Germany makes clear. One of the main reasons for the lateness of any student unrest in England is the lack of revolutionary traditions within the local culture, for it is only where these are freely available – forming part of the daily environment – that large numbers of students are likely to stir. Hitherto they have been quiescent here, not primarily because of their class origins (which are somewhat more democratic than in many countries with violent upheavals), but more importantly because of their cultural formation. It is not social recruitment which distinguishes British from German, Italian or French students, but intellectual heritage. To unblock traditional attitudes towards university and society, a critique of established British culture is needed – not as a substitute for practical struggles in institutions of higher education and the society of which they are a part, but as their accompaniment. Where is such a critique to be found? The

1. 'Problèmes étudiants', *La Nouvelle Critique* 152, January 1964, pp. 88–89.

natural source for it would be the political Left. Unfortunately, any emergent student movement will not find much immediate assistance there.

Britain, the most conservative major society in Europe, now has a culture in its image: mediocre and inert, within any larger context. But it is a culture of which the Left has usually been a passive spectator, at times a prisoner, rarely questioning a national inheritance that for the most part has been made against it.[2] That task awaits any socialist movement in Britain that may emerge from the debris of the past. Without revolutionary theory, ran Lenin's famous dictum, there can be no revolutionary movement. Gramsci added, in effect, that without a revolutionary culture, there will be no revolutionary theory. A politics capable of overcoming capital could only emerge from a culture that contested its intellectual sway across the board and offered effective alternatives. It is enough to say this to be reminded that in Britain, at present, there is virtually no test of arms of any kind, along this front. We do not even have an elementary cartography of the terrain to be disputed. The most influential socialist work of the past decade was called *Culture and Society*. Yet if the British Left has few analyses of the structure of its society, it lacks any of the pattern of its culture.

The aim of the present essay is to begin an inventory of the problems involved in considering the overall 'set' of this culture, and its meaning for socialists. Given the mutism of the past, any such initial attempt will inevitably suffer from errors, elisions and omissions. But since discussion of the subject is a condition of progress on campuses and beyond them, a start must be made somewhere. The risks of haste are obvious; but the fact is that we are suffering from the results of years of delay.

1. Culture

In speaking of culture here, what do we mean by the term? The concern of this argument will not be with the anthropological conception – culture as the sum of social customs and symbols in a given society. This sense of the notion was central to much of the thinking of the Left

2. In recent years a number of critiques of different intellectual disciplines have appeared, one after the other: Gellner's *Words and Things*, Carr's *What is History?*, Robinson's *Economic Philosophy* and Leach's *Rethinking Anthropology*. All of these express an awareness of stagnation, and make effective criticisms of existing orthodoxy. But written from the standpoint of a consequent liberalism, rather than from the left, they have not achieved a cumulative effect.

in the fifties, and was responsible for important insights into British life. This was, so to speak, the moment of Richard Hoggart's *Uses of Literacy*. What this usage does not bring into focus, however, is the specificity of the complex formed by a society's original thought and art.

The remarks below will be concerned with this. But their range will be limited by two exclusions from the superstructural range considered. These are the natural sciences at one extreme and creative art at the other. The reasons for this restriction follow from the point of departure. In effect, the culture that is most central and internal to any politics is that which supplies our basic concepts of humanity in society. These form, by definition, essential premises of public action. Thus the disciplines which are most obviously relevant and amenable to the kind of analysis at issue here are history, sociology, anthropology, economics, political theory, philosophy, aesthetics, literary criticism, psychology and psychoanalysis. The natural sciences and creative arts are, of course, also intimately linked to the institutional order of society, and the class relations which underpin it. But the articulations are qualitatively different. The problem is a large one in its own right, which cannot be discussed here. It may be enough to say, very approximately, that the dose of 'objectivity' in the natural sciences and 'subjectivity' in the arts is symmetrically greater than either in the social sciences delimited above, and they therefore have correspondingly more mediated relationships to the social structure. They do not, in other words, directly provide our basic concepts of humanity in society – the natural sciences because they forge concepts for the understanding of nature, not *society*, and the arts because they treat of humanity in society, but do not provide us with their *concepts*. The autonomy of the three spheres, and the 'central' intercalation of the first, is traceable in the fate of socialism itself. Russia in the thirties, during the darkest years of Stalin's rule, witnessed the atomic physics of Kapitza and the lyrical poetry of Pasternak. But it was on the whole devoid of advance in the social or human sciences. The combination was no accident. The strategic band of culture for twentieth-century politics – central redoubt of the 'class fortress' – is the segment that lies between creative art and physical science. For procedural convenience, and the sake of compression, this will be the scope of the culture discussed here.

2. Structure

When confronted with particular social disciplines, one impulse of rebellion has been to take aim at reactionary distortions in the content of their current instruction. This is a necessary exercise, but if it accepts the distribution of these fields, it falls short of a critique of the culture as such. That requires a more structural analysis. According to Lévi-Strauss, a structural method in the study of social facts is characterized by examination 'not of the terms [in a system], but of the relationships between the terms'.[3] In this sense, the structure of the culture in question here is to be located essentially in the interrelations between the disciplines which compose it, rather than within each discipline. In other words, it is not the content of the individual sectors that will principally determine the character of each so much as the ground-plan of their distribution. Of course, the former will tend to relay the latter in their own space. The aim of a map should be to trace the articulation of the system as a whole.

This, at any rate, will be the form of the analysis below. It is obvious that a full immanent account of each sector – given the span of disciplines – is impossible for any one critic. The illusion that this would be necessary is doubtless partly responsible for the silence of the Left on the topic. In fact, no such universal competence is required, once the aim is not to assess the corpus, but to capture the structure of British culture, in the sense indicated. This, of course, requires some consideration of the character of each sector within it – enough, that is, to establish its specific articulation with the others into a system. But no attempt will be made to give a comprehensive account of any one discipline. The analysis will thus be deliberately incomplete and open.

3. The Absent Centre

Where should such a survey begin? An appropriate starting-point will be any observed irregularities in the field of British culture, viewed internationally – that is, features which contradict expectation from comparative experience and so seem to call for special explanation. These may prove to furnish a key to the general nature of the system.

If we survey the disciplines listed above, and consider them in a European perspective, is there any obvious anomaly among them? History, economics, anthropology, philosophy, aesthetics, political theory, psychology, or literary criticism – none of these presents anything abnormal in Britain by comparative standards. All are repre-

3. *Le Nouvel Observateur* 115, 25–31 January 1967.

sented by departments in universities, which teach courses legitimated by decades of tradition. The local pedigree of each is respectable; the leading practitioners enjoy a certain external reputation, if only (frequently) in the English-speaking world. There is, however, one evident exception: sociology. A trivial, if significant index of the disjuncture between it and the other 'terms' of the system is the lack of any chair in sociology at Oxford or Cambridge, the traditional summits of British higher education, and the lack of any course at either (both have part-time papers). The case seems to be unique among the world's major universities. This institutional aspect, however, is merely the remote consequence of a more original and fundamental historical fact.

Britain – alone of major Western societies – never produced a classical sociology. Events that fail to happen can be more important than those which do, but they are naturally more difficult to see. Nothing is so familiar as the absence of an English Durkheim, Pareto or Weber, and yet so little noticed. But the failure of a body of classical sociology to emerge in England, and its consequence, the withered half-life of the subject to this day, were of large intellectual moment. For the development of sociological enquiry was one of the great achievements of European bourgeois culture at the end of the last and beginning of the present century. Its classical figures emerged at virtually the same time in Germany with Weber, France with Durkheim and Italy with Pareto. It was these three thinkers who founded the tradition later dynamically recapitulated by Parsons in *The Structure of Social Action* – the heir to this lineage, whose work shows that sociology was in no fashion destined to be a merely 'continental' phenomenon, after its origins. For Britain not merely failed to participate in the arrival of the new social science in Europe before the First World War.[4] It also proved unresponsive to its development in North America, which took the lead from the thirties onwards. British universities have remained impervious to Parsonian theory to this day. The UK thus missed both major moments in the growth of the discipline. The lack of any great mind of the order of Weber, Durkheim or Pareto is not the only tell-tale sign. A glance at the secondary figures who contributed to what the standard volume on the subject – Stuart Hughes's *Consciousness and Society* – calls 'The Reorientation of European Social Thought

4. Parsons explains why Spencer may not be regarded as a classical sociological thinker. Indeed, his book opens with the words: 'Who now reads Spencer?' His laconic answer: 'Spencer is dead.' He who worshipped at the shrine of evolution was its victim, when scientific theory evolved elsewhere. *The Structure of Social Action*, New York 1937, p. 3.

1890–1930' shows that of some twenty lesser thinkers listed, not one is English. The gap remains to be filled. To this day, despite the recent growth of sociology as a formal discipline in England, the record of listless mediocrity and wizened provincialism is unrelieved. The subject is still largely a poor cousin of 'social work' and 'social administration', the dispirited descendants of Victorian charity.

What is the meaning of this spectacular fault in the English intellectual landscape? Is it an isolated fissure, or does it have wider implications? Classical European sociology was a discipline of social synthesis. In that lay its critical innovating importance. Weber's sociology of religion, law and the market, Durkheim's study of suicide and social solidarity, Pareto's theory of elites, aimed beyond discrete 'economics', 'psychology' and 'history' at a grasp of societies as totalities. The most distinguished English social thinker of this generation was Alfred Marshall. But as Parsons argues, his eventual impasse may be seen as due to his failure to generate the categories necessary to integrate his neo-classical framework within a wider theoretical ensemble (Marshall's problem of 'activities' beyond rational economic egoism). Sociology, in this sense, came into existence as a science which sought an overall reconstruction of social formations.[5] This was its *differentia specifica*. It is quite logical that it should later have produced the monumental architectonic of Parsonian action theory, embracing every dimension of social existence in a single schedule of classificatory concepts. Whatever the concrete outcome of this enterprise, the ambition to provide such an overall synthesis was written into its programme from the start.

Sociology, however, was itself largely (not exclusively) a response to a previous totalizing system. The extent to which it emerged as a reaction to Marxism on the Continent is well known. Weber's hostility to the doctrines of the labour movement in imperial Germany was unyielding; Pareto set out to combat the primitive 'mob-rule' of socialism by writing a violent attack on Marx; Durkheim sought to domesticate it within the reformist perspectives of French positivism. A profound fear of mass politics and premonition of social disorders haunts the work of all three.

Marxism had preceded classical sociology by fifty years, as synthesis of discrete disciplines on an even more potent scale. In Lenin's traditional formulation, Marx's thought had brought together German philos-

5. For this history, see Parsons's *Structure of Social Action* and his recent essay 'Unity and Diversity in the Modern Intellectual Disciplines: The Role of the Social Sciences', in *Sociological Theory and Modern Society*, New York 1967.

ophy, French politics and English economics. The new conception of history developed from a critical appropriation of each, showing the limits of Hegel's theory of State and civil society, of Proudhon's understanding of the market, of Ricardo's conception of production. The sequence of these critiques led to the revolutionary theory of the mature Marx. Its concept of totality is distinct from that at work in Weber or Durkheim. For this is a 'complex' totality of different levels, not to be reduced to each other, but 'loaded' by the greater weight of one level within it, such that dynamic contradictions are generated by discrepancies between them.[6] This notion involved a break with the Hegelian idea of totality, to which Weber, inspired by German idealism, later effectively returned. For Weber's social whole is a tacitly circular set of determinations, whose elements – religious ethics or economic practice – express and condition each other in reciprocal parity. Not that classical sociology was to be unaware of contradiction. But its conceptions of it were significantly different. Weber's work on bureaucracy and charisma as the two dominant poles of political order is a constant meditation on their instability, and tendency to capsize into each other. Pareto's theory of power posited a continual overthrow of elites, from 'lions' to 'foxes' and back again, in an interminable circular movement. Durkheim's account of the development from mechanical to organic solidarity, primitive to industrial societies, produced the concept of anomie – the unceasing reproduction of subjective rulelessness by a society that is defined by its ensemble of objective rules. In every case, a notion of contradiction is at the core of the work. But it is always a 'degraded' contradiction, that is cyclical rather than dialectical in its movement, reproducing and not transforming itself. If this kind of contradiction is a possible by-product of an idealist totality, it is not a necessary one. Its presence in classical sociology betrays the disquiet of its founders, and the impending disasters of the epoch of the Great War. Parsons was later to develop an absolutely integrated totality, in which contradictions as such have disappeared: there is only 'tension-control' and 'pattern-maintenance'. This is the main difference between action theory and classical sociology; it indicates the distance between the forebodings of a European civilization on the eve of its international civil war, and the optimism of American capitalism in the epoch of its world supremacy.

If Marx's thought, meanwhile, was sufficiently ahead of its time to be

6. See Louis Althusser's account in 'Contradiction and Overdetermination', *New Left Review* 41, January–February 1967, pp. 15–35; included in the English translation of his *Pour Marx* (*For Marx*, London 1977).

generally unassimilable within polite culture until the end of the century, when the political rise of the labour movement started to make it difficult to ignore, it then set in train not only the reactions of classical sociology or marginalist economics, but also a second kind of historical materialism itself. In their different ways, Lenin, Lukács and Gramsci were the dominant figures of this phase, out of which flourishing Marxist cultures eventually rose in every important continental country. Through many political vicissitudes and theoretical bombardments, these survived to leave a lasting imprint on the post-war scene. Today, the serious social science of these countries has developed either against or within the heritage of Marx.

Britain was solitarily exempt from this tension. Marxism, in fact, was all but unknown as a significant influence until the thirties, when the experience of the Depression and the rise of fascism suddenly drew a generation of intellectuals towards the Communist Party. If it is still difficult to assess the decade fairly, through the screen of later myth and cliché, the general outline of this episode is clear. A spontaneous radicalization within traditionally dormant milieux was cut short after a few years by the Nazi–Soviet Pact and the Second World War.[7] The majority of those who had briefly been on the Left in due course swung to the Right, and the traditional tenor of English cultural life was effectively restored. Thirties fever was for most of those affected the product of a political conjuncture, and lacked much of an intellectual dimension. Marx's own work and the later developments of his theory, contrary as they were to established modes of thought, received little sustained attention from rebels who by and large were not historians, sociologists or philosophers, but littérateurs or scientists.[8] But if the

---

7. There were two moments in English cultural history when something like a collective defection looked as if it might create a dissident intelligentsia. Both were snapped off before they had time to develop. The precursor of the thirties was the nineties of the last century, when bohemianism as a significant phenomenon finally arrived in England – sixty years after its advent in Paris. Art Nouveau and the aesthetic socialism of Wilde were its products. Events dealt as summarily with this revolt as with its successor: 1895, Wilde's trial; 1898, Beardsley's death; June 1899, MacKintosh's Exhibition; October 1899, Boer War. Mafeking submerged the memory of the nineties, much as the Molotov–Ribbentrop Pact gave the quietus to the thirties.

8. For poignant examples of what could happen when poets or physicists tried to apply their formal beliefs, see Neal Wood, *Communism and British Intellectuals*, London 1959, pp. 108–113 and 138–144 (Spender and Bernal). The context of the decade is well presented in Alexander Cockburn, 'To and From the Frontier', *The Review* 16. Towards the end of it there germinated, of course, the group of historians who were eventually to produce the kind of Marxist work the thirties never saw. Christopher Hill's first essay on the English Revolution dates from 1940, a year when Eric Hobsbawm and Raymond Williams were undergraduates together producing a pamphlet defending the Russian invasion of Finland.

typical impact of Marxism in the thirties was superficial, the general post-war reaction against it, going with the grain of prior wisdom, was not. The net effect of the thirties was to vaccinate British culture against an alien virus. The resistances built have survived largely intact to this day. The fifties and sixties saw the multiplication of Marxisms elsewhere; Adorno in Germany, Della Volpe in Italy, Althusser in France all founded important and divergent schools. England remained unaffected. Marxist thought in this sense had never become naturalized.

Britain, then, may be defined as the European power which – uniquely – never produced either a classical sociology or a national Marxism. British culture was consequently characterized by an absent centre. For both historical materialism and classical sociology, in their different variants, were totalizing enterprises – attempts to capture the 'structure of structures', the articulation of the social whole itself. Britain has for more than fifty years lacked any significant form of such undertaking. This has been a cultural configuration determined – and dislocated – by a void at its centre. Before looking at the many consequences of this phenomenon, it needs to be asked: what were its proximate causes?

4. The Sociology of No Sociology

Mannheim proposed a sociology of knowledge; what is called for here is a sociology of ignorance. Why did Britain never produce *either* a Weber, a Durkheim, a Pareto *or* a Luxemburg, a Lukács, a Gramsci? The peculiar destiny of the nineteenth-century industrial bourgeoisie contains the genesis of this pattern. The class which led the great technological transformations of the time never achieved a political or social revolution in England. It was checked by a prior capitalist class, the agrarian aristocracy which had matured in the eighteenth century, and controlled a State formed in its image.[9] There was no insuperable contradiction between the modes of production of the two classes. Northern manufacturers, mindful of the French Revolution and fearful of the nascent working-class movement, were not disposed to risk any overturn of the dominant landowners, and never evicted them from control of the political order – rather melding with them in a composite ruling order after mid century. From this history there emerged no

9. For remarks on this history, see Tom Nairn, 'The British Political Elite', and Perry Anderson, 'Origins of the Present Crisis', chapter 1 above.

insurgent body of thought comparable to the Enlightenment. The culture of the English middle class included powerful sectoral disciplines – notably the economics of Ricardo and Malthus. It made revolutionary breakthroughs in the natural sciences – above all the evolutionist biology of Darwin. But it did not give rise to any general theory of society, or any philosophical synthesis of compelling dimensions. The one *sui generis* creed it produced, Benthamism, was a crippled parody of such an ideology, with no chance of becoming the official justification of the Victorian social system. The hegemonic ideology of this society was a much more aristocratic combination of 'traditionalism' and 'empiricism', intensely hierarchical in emphasis, accurately reiterating the history of the dominant agrarian class. The British bourgeoisie on the whole assented to this archaic legitimation of the status quo, and sedulously mimicked it.[10] After the the amalgamations of the later nineteenth century, it became second nature to the collective propertied class.

What was the result of this history? From the outset, the British bourgeoisie forwent any large questioning of society as a whole. A deep, instinctive aversion to the very category of the totality came to mark its characteristic outlook.[11] It never had to recast society as a whole, in a concrete historical practice. It consequently never had to rethink society as a whole, in abstract theoretical reflection. Empirical, piecemeal intellectual disciplines corresponded to humble, circumscribed social action. Nature could be approached with speculative audacity: society was treated as if it were an immutable second nature. The category of the totality was renounced by the British bourgeoisie in its acceptance of a comfortable, but secondary station within the

10. See Raymond Williams's comments on the 'mellow dusk' in *The Long Revolution*, London 1961, p. 319.

11. A century later, H.B. Acton – official philosopher and editor of *Mind* – celebrated its instinct with these revealing words: 'It is not without interest, perhaps, in this connection to mention that in 1857, two years before Marx published his *Critique of Political Economy*, a body was founded known as the National Association for the Promotion of Social Science. . . . The sort of topics discussed in each section may be seen from the following examples, one from each section, taken from the first Volume of the Transactions: Judicial Statistics; An Inquiry on Early Withdrawal from School in Swansea and its Neighbourhood; Crime and Density of Population; Houses for Working Men – Arrangement, Drainage and Ventilation; the Early Closing Movement. . . . The notions employed are seldom so general as "society", "capitalism", "revolution", etc. but are rather of the relative particularity of "convictions", "sentences", "bankruptcies", "adulteration of food", "drainage" and "penny banks". . . . This would seem to be the sort of approach to social science that is most likely to ensure that its exponents know what they are talking about': *The Illusion of an Epoch*, London 1962, pp. 185–86.

hierarchy of early Victorian capitalism.[12] In this first moment of its history, it did not need it. Because the economic order of agrarian England was already capitalist and the feudal State had been dismantled in the seventeenth century, there was no indefeasible necessity for it to displace the previous ruling class. A common mode of production united both, and made their eventual fusion possible. The cultural limitations of bourgeois reason in England were thus politically rational: the *ultima ratio* of the economy founded both.

Superfluous when the new bourgeoisie was fighting for integration into the ruling order, the notion of the totality became perilous once it achieved it. Forgotten one moment, it was repressed the next. For once the new hegemonic class had coalesced, it was naturally and resolutely hostile to any form of thought that might put the social system as a whole in question. There were social critics of Victorian capitalism, of course: the distinguished line of thinkers studied by Williams in *Culture and Society*. But this was a literary tradition that never generated a cumulative conceptual system. The preoccupations that produced Weber, Durkheim or Pareto were foreign to this world. One important reason for this, of course, was that the political threat which had so hastened the birth of sociology on the Continent – the rise of socialism – did not materialize in England. The British working class failed to create its own political party throughout the nineteenth century. When it eventually did so, it was twenty years behind its continental opposites, and was still quite untouched by Marxism. The dominant class in Britain was thus never forced to produce a counter-totalizing body of thought by the danger of a revolutionary socialism. Both the global ambitions and the secret pessimism of Weber or Pareto were alien to it. Its hardened parochialism was proof against any foreign influences or importations. The curious episode of a belated English 'Hegelianism', in the work of Green, Bosanquet and Bradley, provides piquant evidence of this. Hegel's successors in Germany had rapidly used his philosophical categories to dispatch theology. They had then plunged into the development of the explosive political and economic implications of his thought. The end of this road was, of course, Marx himself. Sixty years after Bruno Bauer and Ludwig Feuerbach, however, Green and Bradley innocently adopted an aqueous Hegel, in their quest for philosophical assistance to shore up the traditional Christian piety of the Victorian middle class, now

12. For the purposes of definition: a totality is an entity whose structures are bound together in such a way that any one of them considered separately is an abstraction – it is not an aggregated sum of parts.

threatened by the growth of the natural sciences.[13] This anachronism was naturally short-lived. It merely indicated the retarded preoccupations of its milieu, a recurring phenomenon. Two decades earlier, George Eliot had solved her spiritual doubts by borrowing Comte's 'religion of humanity' – not his social mathematics. These importations were ephemeral, because the problems they were designed to solve were artificial. They simply acted as a soothing emulsion in the transition towards a secular bourgeois culture.

In a panorama empty of profound intellectual upheaval or raging social conflict, British culture tranquilly cultivated its own private concerns, at the end of the long epoch of Victorian imperialism. In 1900, the harmony between the hegemonic class and its intellectuals was virtually complete. Noel Annan has drawn the unforgettable portrait of the British intellectuals of this time. 'Here is an aristocracy, secure, established and, like the rest of English society, accustomed to responsible and judicious utterance and sceptical of iconoclastic speculation.'[14] There was no separate intelligentsia.[15] An intricate web of kinship linked the traditional lineages which produced scholars and thinkers to each other and to their common social group. The same names occur again and again: Macaulay, Trevelyan, Arnold, Vaughan, Strachey, Darwin, Huxley, Stephens, Wedgwood, Hodgkin and others. Intellectuals were related by family to their class, not by profession to

---

13. See Melvin Richter, *The Politics of Conscience*, London 1964, pp. 36 and passim.

14. 'The Intellectual Aristocracy', in J. Plumb, ed., *Studies in Social History, A Tribute to G.M. Trevelyan*, London 1955, p. 285.

15. The historical reasons for this phenomenon were complex and overdetermined. Hexter's famous essay 'The Education of the Aristocracy in the Renaissance' (in *Reappraisals in History*, London 1961) shows how the aristocracy captured public schools and universities in the sixteenth century, preventing the development of a separate clerisy within them. The absence of Roman law in England was also of importance. On the Continent, the legal faculties of such university centres as Bologna and Paris taught abstract principles of jurisprudence, whereas in England legal training was controlled by the guild of practising lawyers and was based on the accumulation of precedent. Weber wrote of the precepts of English law: 'They are not "general concepts" which would be formed by abstraction from concreteness or by logical interpretation of meaning or by generalization and subsumption; nor were these concepts apt to be used in syllogistically applicable norms. In the purely empirical conduct of [English] legal practice and legal training one always moves from the particular to the particular but never tries to move from the particular to general propositions in order to be able subsequently to deduce from them the norms for new particular cases. . . . No rational legal training or theory can ever arise in such a situation': *Law in Economy and Society*, Cambridge USA, 1954, p. 202. The intellectual consequences of such a system are evident. Ben Brewster has pointed out that the Scottish Enlightenment may, by contrast, be partly traced to the tradition of Roman law north of the border: *Cambridge Forward*, no. 40.

their estate. 'The influence of these families', Annan comments, after tracing out their criss-crossing patterns, 'may partly explain a paradox which has puzzled European and American observers of English life: the paradox of an intelligentsia which appears to conform rather than rebel against the rest of society.'[16] Many of the intellectuals he discusses were based in Cambridge, then dominated by the grey and ponderous figure of Henry Sidgwick (brother-in-law, needless to say, of Prime Minister Balfour). The ideological climate of this world has been vividly recalled by a latter-day admirer. Harrod's biography of Keynes opens with this memorable evocation: 'If Cambridge combined a deep-rooted traditionalism with a lively progressiveness, so too did England. She was in the strongly upward trend of her material development; her overseas trade and investment were still expanding; the great pioneers of social reform were already making headway in educating public opinion. On the basis of her hardly won, but now solidly established, prosperity, the position of the British Empire seemed unshakeable. Reforms would be within a framework of stable and unquestioned social values. There was ample elbow-room for experiment without danger that the main fabric of our economic well-being would be destroyed. It is true that only a minority enjoyed the full fruits of this well-being; but the consciences of the leaders of thought were not unmindful of the hardships of the poor. There was great confidence that, in due course, by careful management, their condition would be improved out of recognition. The stream of progress would not cease to flow. While the reformers were most earnestly bent on their purposes, they held that there were certain strict rules and conventions which must not be violated; secure and stable though the position seemed, there was a strong sense that danger beset any changes.'[17] Such was the solid, normal world of the English intelligentsia before 1914.

5. The White Emigration

Occupation, civil war and revolution were the continuous experience of continental Europe for the next three decades. Hammered down from without or blown from within, not a single major social and political structure survived intact. Only two countries on the whole land-mass were left untouched, the small states of Sweden and Switzerland. Elsewhere, violent change swept every society in Europe, from Oporto

16. Annan, op. cit.
17. *The Life of John Maynard Keynes*, London 1951, pp. 2–3.

to Kazan and Turku to Noto. The disintegration of the Romanov, Hohenzollern and Habsburg Empires, the rise of fascism, the Second World War, the arrival of communism in Eastern Europe, followed each other uninterruptedly. There was revolution in Russia, counter-revolution in Germany, Austria and Italy, occupation in France and civil war in Spain. The smaller countries underwent parallel upheavals.

England, meanwhile, suffered neither invasion nor revolution. No basic institutional change supervened from the turn of the century to the era of the Cold War. Through all the turmoil in Europe, the stability and security of British society were never seriously ruffled. It is this continuity, which seems so natural to the English and so exceptional to others, that has given its peculiar shape to the evolution of the national culture since the Great War. If one surveys it at mid century, what is the most prominent change that had taken place since 1900? It is so obvious that it has been generally overlooked. The phalanx of local intellectuals portrayed by Annan has been eclipsed. In this intensely provincial society, foreigners suddenly become omnipresent. The formative influences in the arc of culture with which we are concerned are now, again and again, émigrés. Their quality and originality vary greatly, but their collective role is indisputable. The following list of *maîtres d'école* gives some idea of the extent of the phenomenon:

	Discipline	*Land of Origin*
Ludwig Wittgenstein	Philosophy	Austria
Bronislaw Malinowski	Anthropology	Poland
Lewis Namier	History	Poland
Karl Popper	Social Theory	Austria
Isaiah Berlin	Political Theory	Russia
Ernst Gombrich	Aesthetics	Austria
Hans-Jürgen Eysenck	Psychology	Germany
Melanie Klein	Psychoanalysis	Austria
(Isaac Deutscher	Marxism	Poland)

The two major disciplines excluded here are economics and literary criticism. Keynes, of course, commanded the former; Leavis the latter. But literary criticism – for evident reasons – has been the only sector unaffected by the phenomenon. For at the succeeding level, the presence of expatriates is marked in economics too: the most practically influential today is perhaps Nicholas Kaldor (Hungary), and the most original Piero Sraffa (Italy). The number of leading intellectuals of continental origin who have left their mark since the War is legion: Von Hayek, Elton, Plamenatz, Gellner, Wittkower, Wind, Lichtheim, Steiner and others.

The contrast with the 'intellectual aristocracy' of 1900 is certainly arresting. But what is its meaning? Britain is not traditionally an immigrants' country, like the USA. Nor was it ever host, in the nineteenth century, to European intellectuals rising to occupy eminent positions in its culture. Refugees were firmly suppressed below the threshold of national intellectual life. The fate of Marx speaks for itself. The very different reception of these expatriates in the twentieth century says something about the nature of the emigration itself – and of the condition of the national intelligentsia.

The wave of emigrants who came to England in this century were by and large seeking refuge from the instability of their own societies – that is, the proneness of most of continental Europe in this period to unpredictable, violent, fundamental change.[18] England epitomized the opposite of all this: tradition, continuity and orderly empire. The island's culture was consonant with this special history. A process of natural selection occurred, in which those intellectuals who had some elective affinity to English modes of thought and political outlook gravitated here. Those refugees who did not went elsewhere. It is noticeable that there were many Austrians among those who chose Britain. It is perhaps significant that few important Germans did so, with the exception of Karl Mannheim, by origin Hungarian. The German emigration, coming from a philosophical culture distinct from the parish-pump positivism of interbellum Vienna, generally avoided England. The Frankfurt School of Marxists – Marcuse, Adorno, Benjamin, Horkheimer, and Fromm – went to France and then to the USA. Neumann and Reich (after a time in Norway) followed. Lukács went to Russia, Brecht went to Scandinavia and then to America. This was a 'Red' emigration, unlike that which arrived here. If it did not settle in England, it was because of mutual incompatibility.[19]

The intellectuals who came to Britain were thus not just a chance collection. They tended to be a 'White', conservative emigration. The individual reasons for their arrival were inevitably mixed. Namier

18. Some dates: Klein was born in 1882 in Vienna. Malinowski 1884 in Cracow. Namier 1888 near Lvov. Wittgenstein 1889 in Vienna. Popper 1902 in Vienna. Deutscher 1907 near Cracow. Berlin 1909 in Riga. Gombrich 1909 in Vienna. Eysenck 1916 in Berlin.

19. Adorno spent two years in Oxford working on Husserl, unnoticed, before he went to America. A number of the greatest names of modern art spent a similar brief and obscure sojourn here before crossing the Atlantic to a more hospitable environment: Mondrian, Gropius, Moholy-Nagy and others.

came from the powder-keg of Polish Galicia under the Habsburgs. Malinowski chose England, like his countryman Conrad, partly because of its empire. Berlin was a refugee from the Russian Revolution. Popper and Gombrich were fugitives from the civil war and fascism of post-Habsburg Austria. Wittgenstein's motive in finally settling for England is unknown. Whatever the biographical variants, there was a general logic to this emigration. England was not an accidental landing-stage on which these intellectuals found themselves unwittingly stranded. For many it was a conscious choice, as the antithesis of everything they rejected. Namier, who was most lucid about the world from which he had escaped, expressed his hatred of it most deeply. He saw England as a land built on instinct and custom, free from the ruinous contagion of Europe – general ideas. He proclaimed 'the immense superiority which existing social forms have over human movements and genius, and the poise and rest which there are in a spiritual inheritance, far superior to the thoughts, will or invention of any single generation.'[20] *Rest* – the word conveys much of the underlying trauma of this emigration. The English, Namier thought, were peculiarly blessed because, as a nation, 'they perceive and accept facts without anxiously enquiring into their reasons and meaning.'[21] For 'the less man clogs the free play of his mind with political doctrine and dogma, the better for his thinking.'[22] The theme is repeated, in different guises, by thinker after thinker; one might say that it is the hallmark of this emigration. Namier tried to dismiss general ideas by showing their historical inefficacy; Popper by denouncing their application to society as moral iniquity ('holism'); Eysenck by reducing them to personality traits; Wittgenstein by undermining their claims to conceptual alteration altogether.

Established English culture naturally welcomed these unexpected allies. Every insular reflex and prejudice was powerfully flattered and enlarged in the mirror they presented to it. But the remarkable dominance of the expatriates in these decades is not comprehensible by this alone. It was possible because they both reinforced the existing orthodoxy, and exploited its weakness. For the unmistakable fact is that the traditional disciplines, having missed the stimulus of the synthesizing impulses in Europe, were suffering from inanition. English culture had progressively lost impetus since the Great War. Already by the turn of the century, the primacy of James and Conrad, Eliot and Pound – three

20. *Vanished Supremacies*, London 1962, p. 26.
21. *England in the Age of the American Revolution*, London 1961, p. 13.
22. *Personalities and Power*, London 1955, p. 5.

Americans and a Pole – in the great national literary forms foreshadowed later and more dramatic dispossessions. The last great products of the English intelligentsia matured before the First World War: Russell, Keynes and Lawrence. Their stature is the measure of the subsequent decline. After them confidence and originality seeped away, as if the cumulative absence of new historical experience in England had deprived much of the culture of its energies. The ascendancy of the émigrés is to be understood against this background. Their qualities were, in fact, very uneven. Wittgenstein, Namier and Klein were brilliant originators; Malinowski and Gombrich honourable but limited pioneers; Popper and Berlin fluent ideologues; Eysenck a popular publicist. The very heterogeneity of these individuals underlines the sociological point: no matter what the quantum of talent, any foreign élan was an asset in the local doldrums, and might make an intellectual fortune.

The relationship between the new arrivals and the old traditions they encountered was not a simple adaptation. British empiricism and conservatism was on the whole an instinctive, *ad hoc* affair. It shunned theory even in its rejection of theory. It was a style, not a method. The expatriate impact on this syndrome was paradoxical. For what the émigrés typically did, in effect, was to systematize refusal of system. Characteristically they created tighter codes out of the slovenly habits of the past. Empiricism was elevated in their hands, if also paradoxically rendered more vulnerable. The transition from Moore to the early Wittgenstein exemplifies this movement. Wittgenstein's later philosophy reflects an awareness of the pitfall, and an attempt to retreat back to a non-systematized empiricism, a guileless, unaggregated registration of things as they were, in their diversity. On the political plane, Popper's shrill advocacy of 'piecemeal social engineering' lent a somewhat mechanistic note to the consecrated processes of British parliamentarism, while Hayek's polemics against any kind of social planning were deprecated as themselves somewhat too planned by Oakeshott, as a native conservative. This aside, however, the tremendous injection of life that émigré vigour and intelligence bestowed upon a fading British culture is evident. The famous *morgue* and truculence of Wittgenstein, Namier or Popper expressed their inner confidence of superiority. Established British culture rewarded them amply, with the appropriate honours: Sir Lewis Namier, Sir Karl Popper, Sir Isaiah Berlin and (perhaps soon) Sir Ernst Gombrich.

This was not just a passive acknowledgement of merit. It was an active social pact, as can be seen from the opposite fate of the one great expatriate intellectual that Britain harboured for thirty years who was a revolutionary. The structural importance of emigration in the pattern of conventional British thought is confirmed by the symmetrical salience of a foreigner within its Marxist antithesis. Isaac Deutscher, the greatest Marxist historian of his time, was the only major contributor of his generation to that international system of thought resident in Britain. A larger figure than his compatriot Namier, Deutscher was ignored by the academic world throughout his life, and never secured the smallest university post. British culture accepted and promoted what confirmed its fundamental set: it put to the margin what departed from it. If the White emigration accentuated and enhanced its pre-existent bent, it did not significantly alter it.

6. Configuration of Sectors

What was the intellectual constellation thus produced? Two significant anomalies of the British scene have so far been indicated – the central absence of a classical sociology, and the dominant presence of a White emigration. We can now ask: in a cultural system specified by these co-ordinates, what are the relations between the different sectors which make it up? In other words, what is its structure? The suggestions below are only a pilot project. Their aim is to show that an inter-sectoral analysis is possible, not to constitute a model of one. They will consciously omit and select material, making no attempt at a comprehensive account of any given discipline. A recent essay on English historiography by Gareth Stedman Jones furnishes an exemplary analysis of this type.[23] Here, by contrast, the focus will be on the general cultural nexus of which each discipline is a part. To control the span of material, the method adopted will be to discuss only a single dominant thinker in each sector, and the themes of their work which relate it to what is viewed as the overall configuration. Such an approach can cast one, specific light on its subject; not explore it at all fully. That would be the task of more hands than this.

7. Philosophy

Since the War English philosophy has been dominated by the influence

23. 'The Pathology of English History', *New Left Review* 46, November–December 1967, pp. 29–43.

of Wittgenstein. In his youth, Wittgenstein was a philosopher who sought a one-to-one fit between a reducible language and a fragmentable reality: basic propositions mirrored atomic facts. This was in effect a monist theory of language, which implicitly excluded 'metaphysical' statements from the realm of the intelligible, because they lacked correspondence with verifiable, molecular entities. After the *Tractatus*, the Vienna Circle proceeded to a much bolder and cruder attack on all forms of discourse which did not conform to the prescriptive model of the physical sciences or mathematics. Any propositions not verifiable by their procedures were written off – not as mistaken, but as meaningless. The distance from logical atomism to logical positivism was – despite the abandonment of Wittgenstein's notion of granular 'facts' – a short one. The nihilist implications of the latter, however, were too comprehensive to be acceptable to any established order, with its need for some consecrated morality or macro-ideology. The social antinomy here reflected an epistemological one. Empiricism pushed to this extreme was subversive of the very experience it should have underwritten: the criterion of verifiability was itself notoriously unverifiable.

Wittgenstein's *Philosophical Investigations* provided an elegant and delphic solution to these problems. In his later work, Wittgenstein constantly asserted that language was a heteroclite collection of games with discrete rules governing them. No 'absolute' standpoint outside of them was conceivable. Each game was separate and valid in its own right; the great intellectual error of philosophers was to confuse them, by misapplying a rule for one in the context of another. The meaning of a concept was its conventional use, and the true philosopher was the guardian of conventions. Formally, this doctrine conceded the possibility of 'metaphysics' (i.e. the traditional concerns of philosophy) as one game among others – if an esoteric one.[24] In practice, significantly enough, only religion was ever substantially accorded this status. The main effect of Wittgenstein's later philosophy was simply to underwrite the commonplaces of ordinary parlance. The anodyne assertion that no external purchase on existing language was possible (attack on ideal languages) was coupled with the implicit assumption that existing

---

24. Popper had foreseen this possibility already in the early Wittgenstein, and had taken alarm at it: 'Wittgenstein's method leads to a merely verbal solution and must give rise, in spite of its apparent radicalism, not to the destruction or to the exclusion or even to the clear demarcation of metaphysics, but to their intrusion into the field of science, and to their confusion with science': *The Open Society and Its Enemies*, vol. 2, London 1952, pp. 296–99.

language was effectively a complete sum of usages, in which any internal elimination or addition of one game by another was precluded. The duty of the philosopher, on the contrary, was to ensure the identity and stability of the set, by preventing unorthodox moves within it. The effect of this doctrine was to extend a more or less undifferentiated affidavit to the conceptual status quo. Its predictable outcome was a mystique of common sense, and the ordinary language which reflected it. Wittgenstein, a thinker of genuine – if narrow – integrity and originality, despised the 'impotence and bankruptcy of *Mind*' and castigated Oxford as a 'philosophical desert'.[25] But Oxford was to be the home of the philosophical school inspired by him.

Linguistic analysis after Wittgenstein put behind it the traditional vocation of philosophy in the West. General ideas about humanity and society had been cultivated by virtually every major philosopher of the past, whatever their inspiration. Hume no less than Kant, Locke no less than Spinoza, Descartes no less than Leibniz, Mill no less than Hegel, wrote ethical or political works as well as logical or epistemological treatises, as part of their enterprise. English philosophy after the Second World War suspected any such intellectual innovations. Wittgenstein had written: 'Philosophy may in no way interfere with the actual use of language; it can in the end only describe it. For it cannot give it any foundation either. It leaves everything as it is.'[26] The eventual outcome of this credo was to be Austin's exquisite classifications of syntax. His famous address to the Aristotelian Society, *A Plea for Excuses*, presents their justification: 'Our common stock of words embodies all the distinctions men have found worth drawing, and the connexions they have found worth marking, in the lifetimes of many generations; these surely are likely to be more numerous, more sound, since they have stood up to the long test of the survival of the fittest, and more subtle, at least in all ordinary and reasonably practical matters, than any you or I are likely to think up in our armchairs of an afternoon.'[27]

The social import of such a doctrine is obvious enough. If, as Gramsci once wrote, common sense is the practical wisdom of the dominant class, the philosophical cult of it says something about the role of linguistic analysis in England. The philosophy of ordinary language has functioned as an anaesthetic ideology, blotting out mental

25. Norman Malcolm, *Ludwig Wittgenstein: A Memoir*, London 1958, pp. 36 and 58.
26. *Philosophical Investigations*, Oxford 1953, p. 49.
27. *Proceedings of the Aristotelian Society*, 1956–57, p. 8.

alternatives: 'philosophy begins and ends in platitude', wrote Wittgenstein's pupil Wisdom. The intellectuals who issued such endorsements of the categories of the ongoing society have been aptly described by Gellner: 'We have here a sub-group consisting of people who belong to, or emulate, the upper class in manner; who differentiate themselves from the heartier rest of the upper class by a kind of heightened sensibility and preciousness, and, at the same time, from the non-U kind of intelligentsia by a lack of interest in ideas, argument, fundamentals or reform. *Both* of these *differentiae* are essential to such a group, and both are conspicuously present.'[28] The assiduous praise of ordinary language and aversion for technical concepts paradoxically produced a purely technical philosophy, entirely dissociated from the ordinary concerns of social life.

The technicism of contemporary English philosophy has thus necessarily also enjoined philistinism. Wittgenstein himself knew virtually nothing of the history of philosophy, was devoid of sociological or economic culture, and possessed only a limited repertoire of literary reference. A vague religiosity and naive moralism form the barren backdrop to his work, as his memorialists show: wistful yearnings for Tolstoy mingled with echoes of Schopenhauer. The intellectual life of the twentieth century by and large passed him by. Wittgenstein's outlook is well summed up by his friend Paul Engelmann, who writes of 'his loyalty towards all legitimate authority, whether religious or social. This attitude towards all *genuine* authority was so much second nature to him that revolutionary convictions of whatever kind appeared to him throughout his life simply as "immoral".'[29] Such conformity suggests a bemused peasant of Central Europe, not a critical philosopher. Wittgenstein's successors were on the whole no more enlightened, as the strange intellectual void surrounding their idea of language shows. This was a timeless view; inspired by the *Investiga-*

28. *Words and Things*, London 1959, pp. 241–42. All criticism of English philosophy is indebted to Gellner's classic study, which has never been answered by linguistic orthodoxy, and so panicked its official representatives that discussion of it was forbidden in *Mind*. Linguistic philosophy wrote its own sociology in this episode. In a later essay Gellner has argued that this school must be seen partly as a displaced reaction to the success of the natural sciences, which have threatened the traditional role of the discipline: 'The Crisis in the Humanities and the Mainstream of Philosophy', in J.H. Plumb, ed., *Crisis in the Humanities*, London 1964. This explanation, however, seems to fail a comparative test: the impact of the natural sciences is universal, but linguistic philosophy is essentially an Anglo-Saxon phenomenon. Gellner has recently been concerned to cut back parasitic creepers from linguistic philosophy onto the social sciences – 'Enter The Philosophers', *Times Literary Supplement*, 4 April 1968.

29. *Letters from Ludwig Wittgenstein with a Memoir*, Oxford 1967, p. 121.

tions, it effectively presupposed an unchanging corpus of concepts and a constant set of contexts governing them.[30] Only a radical historical amnesia could produce such an illusion. The intellectual evolution of Western societies has consisted in little but a process of concept-formation and rejection. No extra-terrestrial, absolute standpoint is needed to establish the inter-temporal contingency of language. The truth is rather the opposite. It was Wittgenstein who evacuated time from language, and thereby converted it into an ahistorical absolute. Lacking any sense of the contradictions within a culture, he was closed to the obvious process of linguistic change in which incompatibilities between different usages give rise to new concepts under specific historical pressures. This has been the theme of that French philosophy which has explored the conditions of appearance of new concepts – just the problem English philosophy is designed to avert. It supposes an idea of language as neither a seamless unity, nor a segmented plurality, but as a complex system traversed by tension and inconsistency. In this spirit, Canguilhem and Bachelard studied the emergence of the concepts which gave rise to the modern sciences of life and matter. Such an enquiry moves in the opposite direction from the drift of Wittgenstein's philosophy, and indicates its parochialism. To emphasize the social nature of language, as he did, is not enough: language is a structure with a history, and it has a history because the frictions and discrepancies within it are determined by other levels of social practice. The

---

30. David Pole's lucid book *The Later Philosophy of Wittgenstein* (London 1958) develops the same criticism as that advanced here: 'It is clearly possible to change existing linguistic practice; and one can sensibly claim that the innovation is better than the accepted form. Wittgenstein's account seems to allow no appeal beyond existing practice, and we must ask how it is to accommodate this possibility I speak of. Ultimately, I believe, it cannot; it splits, I shall maintain on this rock . . . [Wittgenstein] has explicitly laid it down that our ordinary expressions are "in order as they are", and has forbidden philosophers to tamper with them. But the difficulty goes deeper. His own system makes no provision for the adoption of any new way of speaking in conflict with existing practice' (p. 57). Pole himself contends that it is rational argument and agreement that produces new forms of language. This is an evidently idealist solution. Who decides what is 'rational'? Pole's formulation virtually admits its own deficiencies: 'The essence of rational discourse is the search for agreement. Wittgenstein's failure to take account of it, I suggest, prejudices his whole picture of language. . . . Clearly to call a statement rational is not to assert that all men ever will, or even might, agree about it; for some are always too stupid or too prejudiced. It is to assert, we may tautologously say, that all men would agree, supposing they were rational' (p. 59). The naive psychologism of 'some are always too stupid or too prejudiced' is no aberration, but characteristic of contemporary English philosophy. So much for the epoch-making turmoil of the Renaissance, the Reformation or the Enlightenment! The obvious fact is that important conceptual disputes have nothing to do with psychological differences – they are grounded in the given structure of knowledge at any moment of time and in social conflicts.

magical harmony of language assumed by English philosophy was itself merely the transcript of a historically becalmed society.

8. Political Theory

An atemporal philosophy consorts with a disembodied political theory. Berlin, a contemporary and intimate of Austin, gravitated towards the study of political ideas early in his career. His conviction of their importance, anomalous in his professional milieu, perhaps derived from family experience of the Russian Revolution. At all events, his concern was largely prophylactic. Philosophers, he argued, ought to criticize political doctrines. If they do not, these ideas 'sometimes acquire an unchecked momentum and an irresistible power over multitudes of men.'[31] The dangers of such 'fanatically held social and political doctrines' could only be conjured by philosophical vigilance. Berlin thought that his colleagues, preoccupied by 'their magnificent achievements' in analytic philosophy, tended to 'neglect the field of political thought, because its unstable subject-matter, with its blurred edges, is not to be caught by fixed concepts, abstract models and fine instruments suitable to logic or to linguistic analysis.'[32] Thus the difference between his method and theirs was merely one of the degree of precision of their respective objects. Ordinary language, in this curious argument, was stable and exact; political concepts were, alas, unstable and vague. Hence study of the latter would be a looser variant of the analysis of the former. Nothing else changed. Political theory became a timeless elucidation of concepts, separated from any historical or sociological context. The *locus classicus* of this procedure is Berlin's essay *Two Concepts of Liberty*, the most influential text of this kind. Here Berlin counterposes two hypostatized constructions: negative freedom – the ability to act without interference, and positive freedom – the achievement of self-determination by the subject. The argument proceeds by imputing a developmental logic to these ideas, which can largely dispense with anything so mundane as quotation. The result is two opposed lineages, which function somewhat like genealogies in the Bible. The idea of negative freedom is attributed to Bentham, Mill, Constant and de Tocqueville; the ideal of positive freedom to the Stoics, Spinoza, Kant, Rousseau, Fichte, Hegel, Marx and Green. Neutrality between the two is momentarily affected: 'The

31. *Two Concepts of Liberty*, Oxford 1958, p. 4.
32. Ibid.

satisfaction that each of them seeks is an ultimate value which, both historically and morally, has an equal right to be classed among the deepest interests of mankind.'[33] The true intention, however, is not long hidden. A few pages later, Berlin writes: 'Negative liberty . . . seems to me a truer and more humane ideal than the goals of those who seek in the great, disciplined authoritarian structures the ideal of "positive" self-mastery by classes, and peoples, or the whole of mankind.'[34] Such self-contradiction belongs to the intellectual method itself. For the same ideal which inspires 'Kant's severe individualism', we are told, informs 'totalitarian doctrines' today. Why is such a captious genealogy necessary? The point of the exercise is to discredit a prefabricated notion of 'positive freedom' – responsible for modern dictatorship and the extinction of liberty by its separation of the concept of self-determination from the empirical attitudes of the individual. But the very insubstantiality of this entity is what summons the unlikely amalgam of thinkers alleged to have fathered it: the accumulation of names is all that lends the illusion of substance.

Political theory, thus conceived, extrapolates ideas from history and transforms them into weightless counters that can be manipulated at will in the space of ideology. The end-product is typically a mythical genealogy in which ideas generate themselves to form a manichean morality tale, whose teleological outcome is the present: struggle of the free world against totalitarian communism. On a much vaster canvas, Popper exemplifies the same procedure in *The Open Society and Its Enemies*. The problematic and its answer are the same; only the tone and terminology differ. The dualism of 'negative' and 'positive' freedom is repeated in that of the 'open' and 'closed' society. The latter culminates, predictably, in 'modern totalitarianism', which itself is 'only an episode within the perennial revolt against freedom and reason'[35] – a law of human nature that is mysteriously exempt from Popper's strictures against the formulation of historical laws. The same suprahistorical conflation is used: Plato, Aristotle, Hegel and Marx are all enemies of the same Open Society. *The Poverty of Historicism* is dedicated to the 'countless men and women of all creeds and nations' who were victims of 'the fascist and communist belief in Inexorable Laws of Historical Destiny'. Who are the philosophical culprits of this historicism? The method produces the same disconcerting results as with Berlin. Much of this work dedicated to the victims of fascism and

33. Ibid., p. 52.
34. Ibid., p. 56.
35. *The Open Society and Its Enemies*, vol. 2, p 80.

communism is devoted to attacking – John Stuart Mill. The *reductio ad absurdum* indicates the vacuity of Popper's conception of historicism itself. This he defines as follows: 'I mean by "historicism" an approach to the social sciences which assumes that historical prediction is their principal aim.'[36] Hegel, of course – the arch-historicist for Popper – refused all historical prediction. Historicist prophecies are said by Popper to include belief in absolute laws in history, whereas scientific predictions are based on trends. Tendencies of social development, not absolute laws, were what Marx or Lenin more than once said they analysed.[37] Popper's innocence of the sociology he championed as an antidote to historicism was equally arresting. His advocacy of methodological individualism (all statements about society are reducible to statements about individuals) shows no awareness of the classic texts in the discipline: Durkheim's discussion of social facts in *The Rules of Sociological Method* and Parsons's account of emergent properties in *The Structure of Social Action*.

A professional philosopher of science, Popper was an amateur in political theory, even of the English variety, with fewer than ordinary inhibitions. His discussion of Hegel is a memorable example. The German philosopher was a 'paid agent', a 'servile lackey', a 'charlatan', a 'clown', whose works were a 'farce', written in 'gibberish' that was a 'despicable perversion of everything that is decent'.[38] The paranoia here was genuine: it produced its own pathological imagery. 'The Hegelian farce has done enough harm. We must stop it. We must speak – even at the price of soiling ourselves by touching this scandalous thing.'[39] The significance of the diatribe is the limiting case it provides of the possibilities of a dehistoricized political theory. Its wildness was to be meticulously shown by a fellow liberal, Walter Kaufmann.[40] This, however, was in the rather different philosophical conditions of the United States. In England, it was never challenged for a decade, because it was so natural to the methodological framework of native political theory.

The extrapolations of the discipline have not, meanwhile, been merely from political or social history. They have also, and crucially, been from the social science most adjacent to political thought, and

36. *The Poverty of Historicism*, London 1957, p. 3.

37. See 'Technology and Social Relations', Georg Lukács, *New Left Review* 39, September–October 1966, pp. 32–33.

38. *The Open Society and Its Enemies*, vol. 2, pp. 27–80.

39. Ibid., p. 79.

40. Walter Kaufmann, 'The Hegel Myth and its Method', in *The Owl and the Nightingale*, London 1959.

traditionally so integrated with it as often to have been inseparable – economics. Berlin mentions the word 'property' just twice in his address on liberty, and it plays no role in his conceptual analysis. Yet the variety of different theories of liberty cannot be dissociated from concomitant conceptions of property. The demonstration of this came from a Canadian shortly afterwards, when Macpherson's *Political Theory of Possessive Individualism* showed the extent to which the meaning of freedom in Hobbes or Locke was connected with their notions of ownership – liberty as property in one's person. Macpherson's procedure was not to put such thinkers back into their social class and interpret their work in the light of it, but to put their ideas back into the context of their intellectual assumptions as a whole, thereby illuminating their relation to the class society of the time. Later work on political liberalism and neo-classical economics has further illustrated the importance of 'economic assumptions in political theory'.[41] The discipline is potentially being redrawn here. But the prevailing cast of English political theory is proof against solitary or alien dissent. It continues to abstract political ideas from economic premises, not to speak of political or economic history.

9. History

Ideas divorced from history are matched by a history voided of ideas. Namierism is the obverse of English political philosophy. In this case, however, a powerful and original intelligence produced genuinely new knowledge. The very inability of his disciples to reproduce Namier's achievements is testimony to their novelty – one that was never systematized by Namier, who studded his own thought with cultural and political curios.

Namier was an expatriate in England who became a super-patriot. He believed in the paramount attainments of the English and expressed a general contempt for other peoples and cultures. Thus he could write of 'German political incapacity and deadness',[42] 'French ideas, adaptable in their rootless superficiality'[43] and Austria, where 'Vienna has never produced anything truly great or creative'.[44] A functionary in

41. See 'Post-Liberal Democracy?', *Canadian Journal of Economics and Political Science*, November 1964, pp. 485–498.
42. *Vanished Supremacies*, p. 49.
43. *England in the Age of the American Revolution*, p. 39.
44. *Vanished Supremacies*, p. 28.

the Foreign Office during the First World War, he vigorously advocated the liquidation of Austro–Hungary and the elimination of German influence from Eastern Europe. 'The future of the white race', he wrote, 'lies with Empires, that is those nations which hold vast expanses of land outside Europe.'[45] These attitudes were not accidental or tangential to his work. They determined its distinctive dual structure. One half of it was devoted to a meticulous and reverent study of the power structure of landed England in the eighteenth century. The other half was devoted to brilliant and acrid reflections on the history of continental Europe in the nineteenth and twentieth centuries. Namier's studies of the epoch of George III were a milestone in English historiography, because they were the first to offer a structural approach to the oligarchy of the time. Dispatching the legend of two antagonistic political parties divided on social–ideological lines, he showed the class unity of eighteenth-century parliaments, and the immediate material interests – of corruption or clientage – which governed political fortunes and allegiances within it. This was a history which virtually ignored chronology. On the whole, Namier disdained the babble of narrative. His stony edifices were acceptable to British historians, because of their infrastructure of detail: his empirical standards were above reproach. Namier's structural method was well adapted to the largely tranquil social order of eighteenth-century England. He saw his adopted country as a society which had miraculously achieved a territorial nationality,[46] based on freedom from foreign invasion and the gradual growing together of different ethnic and linguistic communities made possible by it. Namier thought that only such a territorial nationality could produce liberty. This he identified with parliamentary sovereignty. Parliamentary institutions in turn demanded a hierarchical social structure. England was uniquely blessed in possessing these conditions of freedom, and the eighteenth century saw the birth of the political system which was the token of this privilege.

Nineteenth- and twentieth-century Europe provided a diametric contrast to this idyllic picture. Namier analysed the whole movement of continental history from 1789 to 1945 as the deleterious triumph of nationalism and democracy. He regarded both as the enemy of liberty. All the terms of his argument were reversed in Europe, where territorial nationality on English lines was absent. There was first the dynastic, denationalized State that was the multifarious property of its ruler – the

---

45. *Germany and Eastern Europe*, London 1915, p. 128.

46. It is odd that there has been so little awareness of the central role of this concept in Namier's historical thought.

Habsburg Empire, *par excellence*. Then there was its no less pernicious opposite – the linguistic and racial nation preached by Mazzini, Kossuth and the German Parliament of 1848. This idea was the historical content of nationalism, and it was indissolubly linked to democracy. Democracy for Namier was 'a levelling of classes' and not 'constitutional growth'. Social equality he believed to be flatly incompatible with political liberty. 'Oligarchy is of the essence of Parliament, which requires an articulated society for basis. Elections presuppose superiorities.'[47] The insistence that 'acknowledged superiorities there must be' naturally produced a vision of modern European history as an unrelieved process of decline. Namier's analyses of the France of Louis Napoleon, the Germany of the Hohenzollerns, the Austro–Hungary of the Habsburgs, the Europe of Versailles, are all equally mordant and sombre. An inexorable deterioration sets in after the French Revolution, which works its effects in Europe until, at the end of the Second World War, Namier thought the concept itself had disappeared: 'Indeed,' he finally asked, 'what remains of Europe, of its history and its politics?'[48]

Namier executes this fresco with the greatest artistry. But what is striking about it is that it records a decline that it never explains. Namier was not mystified about the existence of classes or the conflict of their interests: indeed his awareness of them was the core of his analysis of the power structure of eighteenth-century England, and his candid appraisal of the social character of British parliamentarism. But he lacked any dynamic theory of historical movement. This was a consequence of the peculiar character of his materialism. The charge that he 'took the mind out of history' was one that he proudly accepted. It meant that he radically devalued the importance of ideas in promoting historical change. A mindless history complements a timeless philosophy: there is a mediate symmetry in the legacy of Wittgenstein and Namier, in which the work of a thinker like Berlin provides the middle term. It is what Namier substituted for 'mind' that is significant here. 'What matters most is the underlying emotions, the music, to which ideas are a mere libretto, often of very inferior quality; and once the emotions have ebbed, the ideas, established high and dry, become doctrine, or at best innocuous clichés.'[49] Ideas were thus reduced to emotions. The ultimate instance of history is psychology. Namier thought that his work was inspired by his appreciation of Freud, but in

47. *Vanished Supremacies*, p. 79.
48. Ibid., p. 209.
49. *Personalities and Powers*, p. 4.

fact he showed little knowledge or understanding of Freud's work, and never made any serious application of it to his historiography. His credo was actually a vulgar psychologism – as Gareth Stedman Jones has pointed out, much more akin to Nietzsche's notions of the base motive behind the lofty sentiment. Such a psychologism necessarily supposes a fixed human nature, and is therefore quite inoperative as a principle of change. Hence the curious paradox of Namier's passionate belief in psychology. It is both central to his theory and quite marginal to his practice. For by underlying everything, it explains nothing. It is consequently only introduced as a banal coda, when the work of concrete analysis is done: 'I refrain from inquiring into the sense of the envenomed struggles we have witnessed; for such an inquiry would take us into inscrutable depths or into an airy void. Possibly there is no more sense in human history than in the changes of the seasons or the movements of the stars; or if sense there be, it escapes our perception.'[50] The absence of meaning in history, underlined here, has a dual signification. For Namier its sense is that purposive human action, controlled by ideas, does not govern the course of events: 'there is no free will in the thinking of the masses, any more than in the revolutions of the planets, in the migrations of birds, and in the plunging of hordes of lemmings into the sea.'[51] But it also indicates that Namier, once he had adopted the premise of an immutable substratum of irrational emotions and passions, had no principle of explanation available to him. Thus the gathering avalanche of nationalism and democracy in Europe after 1789 was depicted and denounced by Namier: but it was never rendered causally intelligible. In this sense, the dictum that 'history has no meaning' is a translation of the fact that Namier's history had no *motor*. The distance between this materialism and that more properly called historical needs no emphasis: Marx's theory accommodated the importance of ideas within social relations, its account of change including the disjunctures between them.

In Namier's European writings, time exists only as dilapidation. His insights persist: but their context has altered. His great structural examination of the Austro-Hungarian Empire closes with its disintegration. His secular account of the geopolitical pattern of European diplomacy – a *tour de force* arising from the sharpness of his perception of the State as a historical entity – ends with the submergence of Europe. Namier's legacy to English historiography was thus equivocal.

50. *Vanished Supremacies*, p. 203.
51. *England in the Age of the American Revolution*, p. 41.

His structuralism was rapidly suppressed from memory. The two best-known historians today divide his minor bequests. Trevor-Roper inherited Namier's acute sensitivity to the State as a material complex of power and prebends. He used this to sketch perhaps the most coherent general interpretation of the crisis of the Renaissance State.[52] Elsewhere, his writings are erratic and eclectic. Namier's main self-proclaimed disciple has been Trevor-Roper's adversary in controversy. Taylor inherited Namier's philistinism about ideas, and his xenophobia, but converted the microscopic study of structures into its opposite – a conventional, often trivial narrative: the apparent accumulation of minutiae links the two, as if Namier had merely produced a census. Few disciples have ever guyed their master so completely. Namier's political outlook was frankly regressive, but in England his approach to history was intellectually advanced. Its virtues have generally been forgotten, and its faults exaggerated. A new school of history has in the last decade emerged on the Left, quite outside his tradition – but this is another subject. Within the dominant orthodoxy that followed Namier, history without ideas slowly became a drought of ideas about history.

10. Economics

The insulation of political theory from economic thought duplicated an earlier division: the emergence of 'economics' out of the disappearance of 'political economy'. This time, the shift was general, in all Western countries. The advent of marginalism marked the birth of an economic science ostensibly free from political or sociological variables. What this meant, of course, was that they were pushed outside the conscious focus of the system, to become its silent preconditions. Conventional equilibrium theory, as it became the new orthodoxy, purported to represent a pure logic of the market – while in fact ideologically underwriting it by relegating the notion of monopoly to a special case and excluding the notion of planning. Neo-classical doctrine rationalized laissez-faire at the very historical moment that it was being superseded, with the new economies of the age of imperialism; and after the Great War it proved incapable of providing any solution to the crises of Western capitalism. It was the great merit of Keynes to see that in these conditions the system of neo-classical categories needed to be

52. *Religion, the Reformation and Social Change*, London 1967, pp. 46–89.

recast. At first prompted by simple political pragmatism, he merely advocated practical measures to stabilize British capitalism: then, a decade later, he provided the theory for them. The intellectual advance of *The General Theory of Employment, Interest and Money* was to integrate two conceptual planes that had previously been separate into a new synthesis. Monetary theory and employment theory were regarded by neo-classical economics as distinct topics, without intrinsic connection between them. Only three years before the publication of *The General Theory*, Pigou had written his *Theory of Unemployment* without seriously discussing the problem of investment at all. Keynes's achievement was a 'retotalization' of his field. He was well aware of this: 'When I began to write my *Treatise on Money* I was still moving along the traditional lines of regarding the influence of money as something so to speak separate from the general theory of supply and demand. This book, on the other hand, has evolved into what is primarily a study of the forces which determine changes in the scale of output and employment as a whole; and, whilst it is found that money enters into the scheme in an essential and peculiar manner, technical monetary detail falls into the background. A monetary economy, we shall find, is essentially one in which changing views about the future are capable of influencing the quantity of employment and not merely its direction. But our method of analysing the economic behaviour of the present under the influence of changing ideas about the future is one which depends on the interaction of supply and demand, and is in this way linked up with our fundamental theory of value.'[53] This synthesis in turn produced its own concepts. The ideas of liquidity preference and the multiplier were not simply additions to the existing canon. They reformulated the whole system, by knocking away the assumption of a stationary equilibrium. For both concepts, of course, presuppose a dynamic framework. In developing them, Keynes thus effectively reintroduced time into orthodox economic theory. In this lay the greatness of his thought – but also its ambiguous limitation. For

---

53. *The General Theory of Employment, Interest and Money*, London 1964, pp. vi–vii. The limitation of Keynes's synthesis was, of course, that he substituted a new partition for the old, by introducing what became the distinction between micro-economics and macro-economics. 'The division of Economics between the Theory of Value and Distribution on the one hand and the Theory of Money on the other hand is, I think, a false division. The right dichotomy is, I suggest, between the Theory of the Individual Industry or Firm and of the rewards and the distribution between different uses of a given quantity of resources on the one hand, and the Theory of Output and Employment as a whole on the other hand.' *The General Theory*, p. 293. It is this division that is rejected in works like Baran and Sweezy's *Monopoly Capital*, where the theory of the firm and of the economy are not separated.

the Keynesian temporality is a very restricted one. It is brief and cyclical: 'In the long run, we are all dead.' Keynes accepted capitalism, but without zeal or sanctimony. He was mainly concerned with assuring its immediate stability, not justifying it *sub specie aeternitatis*. This prevented him both from ever becoming an official ideologue of the status quo like so many economists, and from developing a deeper and longer dynamic perspective. His contemporary Kalecki, who unlike Keynes was familiar with the work of Marx, achieved some of the same countercyclical insights, albeit in fragmentary form, but saw the ulterior implications of them. By reinserting Keynesian categories into a rudimentary political economy, he was able to predict what he called the 'political trade-cycle', which has since become the principal economic contradiction of advanced capitalism: the conflict between full employment and stable prices.

After Keynes, it was no longer possible to develop economic theory within the old equilibrium framework. The temporal dimension he introduced was there to stay. The next step was logically the emergence of growth theory as such. Here, however, the inherent limits of economic formalism checked its path. The preoccupation with growth which was the distinguishing feature of post-Keynesian economics should logically have returned it to the tradition of political economy that had concluded in Marx (among whose central concerns was the reproduction of capital). But political economy raised uncomfortable questions about the socio-economic system as a whole. The result was that growth theory developed on an essentially *ad hoc* basis, with an accretion of hypotheses abstracted as far as possible from the property regime. This is particularly clear in its initial formulation by Harrod. He simply added technical invention – the least social variable available – to the Keynesian model, to produce an equation for progress.[54] Subsequent demonstrations that technology does not determine the rate of capital accumulation merely scattered the arena into divergent piecemeal claims, which have never been unified into any general theory. In this respect time now haunts orthodox economic theory, but it is unable to dominate it. Graphic evidence of the failure to move from Keynes's short-run economics to a true long-run economics is the

54. 'An Essay in Dynamic Theory', *Economic Journal*, March 1939, pp. 14–33. The role of technique is implicit, not explicit in Harrod's formula. It is assumed to check the diminishing rate of return on investment, and thereby render output per unit of capital constant. The ostensible focus of Harrod's essay is propensity to save, but variations of this are not explained within the model. Hence the determinant role effectively reverts to technique, which is taken as autonomous.

impotence of British economic orthodoxy to provide any coherent theory of Britain's present economic crisis. The national predicament has obsessed public debate for five years now, all political discussion revolving round it. In that time, innumerable unrelated or contradictory explanations for the crisis have been advanced by British economists. The most influential has doubtless been Kaldor's, which attributes Britain's post-war economic decline to a shortage of cheap labour from the primary sector, due to the uniquely rationalized English agriculture of the last century.[55] There is little need to labour the general inadequacy of these accounts. It is plain that British economic decline has more than one major cause; that these causes are both likely to be interrelated and unlikely to be of equivalent weight; and that they extend into the sociopolitical structure of the country. But orthodox economics has proved quite unable either to develop a model of causal hierarchy (not mere plurality), or to broach a sociology of the crisis. The co-option of so many economists – Kaldor, Balogh, Neild, Seers and *tutti quanti* – into a foundering government has merely underlined these deficiencies. The crisis persists, unabated.

For all its formal advances in mathematization, contemporary economics in England has been unable to grapple with the practical issues which confront it. Retrospectively, Keynes's magnitude has grown. He was perhaps the last great social thinker produced by the English bourgeoisie, with all the largeness and generosity of a once-confident liberalism. His theoretical system was validated practically; yet he never became a fanatic advocate of the society to whose temporary salvation he contributed so much. He never hesitated to pronounce outside his subject, on a gamut of topics which recalls that of his contemporaries, Russell and Lawrence. It is characteristic that Keynes could write a brief memoir of them which situates that trio perhaps better than any work of cultural history since.[56] He was an intellectual in a classical tradition.[57]

If Keynes's international reputation lent British economics a peculiar

---

55. *Causes of the Slow Rate of Economic Growth in the United Kingdom*, Cambridge 1966. Kaldor explicitly discounts such other factors as the balance of payments or the rate of investment (pp. 16 and 25). It is perhaps not surprising that the most cogent account of the crisis is the work of an economic historian, not an economist, Eric Hobsbawm's *Industry and Empire*, London 1968.

56. 'My Early Beliefs', in *Two Memoirs*, London 1949.

57. Keynes was very conscious of his sociological ancestry. He wrote in *Essays in Biography*: 'I have sought . . . to bring out the solidarity and historical continuity of the High Intelligentsia of England, who have built up the foundations of our thought in the two and a half centuries since Locke, in his *Essay Concerning Human Understanding*, wrote the first modern English book': p. viii.

status among its fellow-disciplines, it was unable to enhance it after him. His own definition of the qualities necessary to be a great economist is a standing indictment of his successors: 'The master-economist must possess a rare combination of gifts. He must reach a high standard in several different directions and must combine talents not often found together. He must be mathematician, historian, statesman, philosopher – in some degree. He must understand symbols and speak in words. He must contemplate the particular in terms of the general, and touch abstract and concrete in the same flight of thought. He must study the present in the light of the past for the purposes of the future. No part of man's nature or his institutions must be entirely outside his regard.'[58] This statement of faith has been quietly forgotten. Today, routine and mediocrity have settled over most of the discipline. Its superior pedigree has not enabled it to produce so much as a Galbraith – an average economist bold enough to formulate some general propositions about the structure and tendency of monopolized capitalism. Sraffa, its most unusual mind, has been ignored. Technique has become a substitute for theory: without bearings in political economy or history, British economics has visibly stagnated.

11. Psychology

Namier believed that ideas were merely rationalizations of emotions. Political ideas, in particular, were the camouflaged expressions of unconscious attitudes and passions. This reductionism was faithfully reproduced, quite independently, in the discipline of psychology itself. Eysenck, its presiding spirit since the War, sought to classify political beliefs by relating them to psychological attitudes. The result of this programme, *The Psychology of Politics*, is a monument to crude psychologism that opens with the credo: 'Psychology so conceived has one advantage over other disciplines which makes it of particular interest and importance. Political actions are actions of human beings; the study of the direct causes of these actions is the field of the study of psychology. All other social sciences deal with variables which affect political behaviour indirectly. . . . The psychologist has no need of such intermediaries; he is in direct contact with the central link in the chain of causation between antecedent condition and resultant action.'[59] Here, more bluntly stated than in any other field, is one of the most

58. *Essays in Biography*, London 1933, p. 170.
59. *The Psychology of Politics*, London 1954, pp. 9–10.

widespread convictions of this culture: the belief in a fundamental psyche which is prior to social determinations, and may therefore be considered the immediate pivot of political action.

Eysenck constructed an attitude chart destined to show the emotional convergence of extremisms (left or right) and counterpose them to a solid centre of moderation. The effect of this, of course, was to establish an identification between fascism and communism – contrasted with democratic creeds such as conservatism or liberalism: a typical enterprise of the period. The specially designed categories of 'tough-mindedness' and 'tender-mindedness' were superimposed on those of 'radicalism' and 'conservatism' to achieve this result. Totalitarians of all persuasions proved, of course, to be 'tough-minded'. Dwelling at length on the similarity of test-scores between communists and fascists, which showed the temperamental peculiarities of the two, Eysenck dedicated his work to the hope of 'a society more interested in psychology than politics'. The declaration is a self-definition. Eysenck is a special case in the gallery of expatriates. All the others show some intellectual distinction. Eysenck has never been of the same category. A crusading publicist, he has dominated his subject more by prolific output than unanimous acclaim. But this should not lead to an underestimation of his historical importance. After the War Eysenck developed the use of factor analysis in England, a basic methodological tool of experimental psychology, thereby rapidly achieving prestige and influence. In these years, Eysenck became the symbol of a new, aggressive scientism. The success generated by the initial lack of any serious challenge to him bore fruit in an ample range of works, pronouncing on the psychology not only of politics, but of crime, intelligence tests, mental illness, smoking and numerous other topics. No other psychologist in England can rival a fraction of this output.

In the course of its production, however, Eysenck undoubtedly overreached himself. Today, his works have been subjected to criticism by colleagues even in this positivist discipline *par excellence*. The erosion of his relative immunity started, appropriately enough, with a devastating exposé by three Americans – Rokeach, Hanley and Christie – of *The Psychology of Politics*. Subjecting it to scrupulous statistical, methodological and conceptual checks, they concluded that Eysenck had misinterpreted his data, miscomputed his statistics, and misconstrued his results. In particular, they decided that there was no similarity between communists and fascists, even on Eysenck's own unscientific evidence. 'Eysenck arbitrarily lumps Communists and Fascists together in an attempt to indicate their similarity. . . . It is clear that Eysenck's Communist samples are neither "tough-minded" nor "authoritarian" when the data produced as evidence by Eysenck are carefully examined.'[60] The very concept of tough-mindedness was fictive – a product of Eysenck's arbitrary statistical procedures. 'Our analysis leads us to the conclusion that tough-mindedness/tender-mindedness, as conceived and measured by Eysenck, has no basis in fact. It is based on miscalculations and a disregard for a significant portion of his data. It conceals rather than reveals the attitudinal differences among existing groups.'[61] Eysenck's replies did not convince his critics. Christie's restatement of his judgement is memorable. *The Psychology of Politics* contains: 'Errors of computation, uniquely biased samples which forbid any generalizations, scales with built-in biases which do not measure what they purport to measure, unexplained inconsistencies within the data, misinterpretations and contradictions of the relevant research of others, and unjustifiable manipulation of the data. Any one of Eysenck's many errors is sufficient to raise serious questions about the validity of his conclusions. *In toto*, absurdity is compounded upon absurdity, so that where, if anywhere, the truth lies is impossible to determine.'[62]

The Psychology of Politics, however, is an expression of the discipline from which it emerged. It is symptomatic that Eysenck's book was eventually put to rest, not by English colleagues, but by American psychologists.[63] Criticisms of other aspects of his work followed. But Eysenck's public renown in England – built on innumerable broadcasts, articles and paperbacks – has been virtually unaffected. To a greater extent than any other of the émigrés discussed here, he is popularly identified with his subject. There is good reason for this. Despite various reservations about Eysenck's writings, no English psychologist has yet written a critique of his work as a whole. Scattered objections do not constitute a considered intellectual rejection. Eysenck thus continues, from his chair at the Maudsley, to symbolize psychology and preach psychologism in England. His very defects are part of his significance: the quality of his work is an index of the readiness of the culture to accept its assumptions.

60. Richard Christie, 'Eysenck's Treatment of the Personality of Communists', *Psychological Bulletin*, vol. 53, November 1956, pp. 425, 427.

61. Milton Rokeach and Charles Hanley, 'Eysenck's Tender-mindedness Dimension: A Critique', *Psychological Bulletin*, vol. 53, March 1956, p. 175.

62. Richard Christie, 'Some Abuses of Psychology', *Psychological Bulletin*, vol. 53, November 1956, p. 450.

63. There is a parallel here with Kaufmann's exposure of Popper.

12. Aesthetics

Within the field of experimental psychology, the study of perception has yielded the most rapid and reliable scientific results, and has consequently exerted a general influence on the orientation of the discipline. In England, however, a significant reprise has occurred, for here the dominant work in visual aesthetics has been derived from the psychology of perception: Gombrich's erudite and intelligent *Art and Illusion*. Gombrich may be said to dominate the theory of pictorial art today as his companion thinker Popper has done the theory of the natural sciences.

This influence is not self-explanatory. The history of art has been an enclave in British culture more completely colonized than any other by expatriates. Given the predominance of literary over visual values in the intelligentsia described by Annan, this is not particularly surprising. The great majority of scholars who have produced serious works on painting, sculpture or architecture in England have been Germans or Austrians: Saxl, Wittkower, Wind, Antal, Pevsner and others. The primacy enjoyed by Gombrich is not explicable merely by reason of his undoubted merits. Here too a filtering mechanism has been at work, in which the traditional culture has selected what is congenial and disregarded what is not. Antal, a social historian of Florentine painting, was kept outside the university world. Gombrich, associate and admirer of Popper and Hayek, has been canonized at large.

The general reason for this success is that Gombrich's theory of art is a variant of the psychologism that patterns the culture as a system. To say this is not to deny the sophistication of this work, which certainly represents the most rewarding example of the phenomenon, one with real achievements on its own terrain. Gombrich's central problem has been the relation of perception to painting. Basing himself on findings of experimental psychology, he showed that perception itself is predetermined by stable schemata. There is thus nothing natural in naturalism, as a practice in painting. An increasingly accurate transcription of reality was historically a long and difficult achievement, never a spontaneous or unreflective gift. In Gombrich's account the difference between one age of painting and another is primarily a question of techniques, whose development permits an ever closer approximation to mirror-like representation, via innumerable rectifications of the perceptual schemata that govern the painter's vision.

In the course of his argument, Gombrich unfolds many acute local demonstrations. But the theory as a whole is vitiated by the narrow horizons of its discussion. The problem of any psychologism is to account for historical change, since the initial assumption is a self-contained, universal psyche. Gombrich solves the dilemma for his theory of art by use of the pregnant notion of technique. Technical progress is, in effect, the minimum dose of history available here, for it is the most easily conceived as an asocial movement. In Gombrich's account of the development of painting or scuplture, what it denotes is a continual amelioration in the perceptual equipment of the individual artist, abstracted from the social conditions of artistic production. The result is in its own way a radical de-historicization of art. It is one matter to show that Ancient Egyptian art was not an intentional refusal of faithful naturalism, but preceded the very capacity for it. It is another to explain the specific conventions that 'distorted' representation in Ancient Egypt. Gombrich, indeed, is at a loss to comprehend them. For the principles of any such explanation lie outside his range of concepts. Why is Ancient Egyptian art so different from Ancient Chinese art? Only the structure of the historical society in which each was produced could yield the elements of an answer. Gombrich himself is obliged to have recourse to *ad hoc* sociological explanations to block in the gaps in his scheme. Thus Ancient Egyptian art was perhaps influenced by the priesthood, and Ancient Greek by the rise of trade. Hypotheses of this kind, external to the theory, are thrown in to buttress its incoherence where it most evidently fails to account for the specificity of a form of art. Gombrich's chronological study of his subject is called *The Story of Art*, not its history: the narrative of successive styles is confined to description rather than explanation. At most, vague action–reactions of fashion and generation are evoked, as in the literary criticism of fifty years ago. Here Gombrich resorts to commentary of this kind: 'We remember the feeling of uneasiness created by the brilliant messiness of impressionist "snapshots" of fleeting sights, the longing for more order, structure and pattern that had animated the illustrators of the Art Nouveau with their emphasis on decorative simplification, no less than such masters as Seurat and Cézanne.'[64] The vapid circularity of such observations, and the futility of their psychologism ('feeling of uneasiness', 'longing for more order' and so on), are revealing in a writer of this authority. *The Story of Art* is a popular rather than a scholarly work, but it conveys the narrowness of Gombrich's substantive theory.

Early in his career, Gombrich was more uncomfortably aware of the inadequacy of his psychological problematic. He admitted the validity

64. *The Story of Art*, London 1950, p. 433.

of Vasari's famous definition of the task of the art historian: to investigate the causes and roots of style – *le causi e radici delle manieri*. He had to confess a general blankness here: 'We have no theory of style which might account for its stability or its changes. . . . Psychology alone can never suffice to explain the riddle of history, the riddle of particular changes. . . . For me, at least, the enigma of style is wrapped in a thrilling mystery.'[65] But no sooner had he said this than he suppressed the thought, and a moment later was dismissing Vasari's classical query as by definition unanswerable: 'I do not think we can ever hope to produce a final explanation of this type of problem.'[66] In its place, he proposed the theme which was to become the programme of *Art and Illusion*: 'the role of skill, of the learning process involved' in art; 'the individual and particular works of art as the work of skilled hands and great minds in response to concrete demands'.[67] The transition from one position to another eventually produced an unconscious regression to the very belief which he had once formally rejected. A few years later, he was tranquilly writing of 'the shifting urges, the psychological pulls and counter-pulls that result in changes of taste and style within the context of civilization'.[68] This is exactly the formula for the vacant undulations in *The Story of Art*. In the closed space of his later preccupations, the psychology which was once exorcized is a revenant which necessarily returns to rule.

Theory and history have a different relationship in a true aesthetics: Vasari's question insistently demands an answer. The iconology of Erwin Panofsky approached the problem much more closely through its focus on the meaning of paintings and sculptures, rather than simply their means.[69] For the rules of perception and the march of technique – the individual psyche and its immanent evolution – are insufficient to

65. 'Art and Scholarship', in *Meditations on a Hobby-Horse and Other Essays on the Theory of Art*, London 1963, pp. 117–18.

66. Ibid.

67. Ibid., pp. 117, 119.

68. Ibid., p. 43.

69. Thus Panofsky wrote: 'The art historian will have to check what he thinks is the intrinsic meaning of the work, or group of works, to which he devotes his attention, against what he thinks is the intrinsic meaning of as many other documents of civilization historically related to that work or group of works, as he can master: of documents bearing witness to the political, poetical, religious, philosophical and social tendencies of the personality, period or country under investigation.' *Meaning in the Visual Arts*, New York 1955, p. 39. Panofsky's discussion of the contrast between Egyptian and Greek forms is, as might be expected, much more illuminating than that of Gombrich. See 'The History of the Theory of Human Proportions as a Reflection of the History of Styles', in *Meaning in the Visual Arts*, pp. 55–107. Panofsky's recent death passed all but unnoticed in Britain.

differentiate the art of any society or epoch from another. The very schemata which Gombrich correctly insists govern perception are not alignable on a linear time-track. Their origin must be sought in the diverse societies in which they existed, and which themselves are amenable to no mono-evolutionary classification. Gombrich's psychologism – the construction of a theory of art based on the psychology of perception plus the accumulation of technique – simulates time more than it recovers it. If the art of the late twentieth century has baffled it, in the fading of representation, this is because it has abstained from the sort of history necessary to render a change of this kind intelligible. At the end of the story, the 'psychology' of art becomes an interdiction of its meaning.

13. Psychoanalysis

The disciplines so far discussed have formed an interconnecting and self-confirming circuit. A verification of their character can be found *a contrario* in the fate of the one quite new area to emerge within the traditional space of the human sciences. This was psychoanalysis. In Britain, it did not escape the general rule of expatriate dominance. Melanie Klein, an Austrian who came to London after working in Berlin, formed a school which after the War became the distinctively British contribution to the international development of psychoanalysis. Klein's powerfully original work developed Freud's legacy beyond the limits of what he had thought possible. For she pioneered a theory and a therapy to capture the psychic structures of infancy – the aboriginal first months of life which precede and found the experience of childhood theorized by Freud. In this radicalization of the scope of psychoanalysis, Klein arrived at one of the first coherent answers to a fundamental problem left unresolved by Freud. His clinical revolution was to render the conduct of neurotics – previously regarded as a physical pathology, without meaning – intelligible as significant human action. Freud, however, never provided a comparable general theory of the psychoses. He insisted on the categorical difference between the two disorders, but beyond a brilliant sketch of a case of paranoia (the Schreber affair), he never formulated an inclusive theory establishing the respective bases of neuroses and psychoses, leaving his inheritors at most some cryptic signposts. The Kleinian bathysphere into the submarine recesses of infancy unexpectedly produced a *sui generis* solution. By developing the concepts of successive 'paranoid' and 'depressive' positions, universally experienced in the course of infancy,

Klein was able to reunite psychoses and neuroses along an evolutionary axis. Psychosis became a reversion to the paranoid position, which the patient had never properly passed; neurosis to the depressive position. Plausible criticisms can be made of this evolutionism: there is no doubt that it represents a 'naive' synthesis. Glover and Anna Freud subjected Klein's work to a violent environmentalist criticism in the forties, much of which was formally justified.[70] Klein's capacity for stringent formulation was not equal to her intellectual courage and practical intuition, and any linear genetic account of psychological disorders has obvious weaknesses. The objective merit of Klein's work, however, was to re-table the question of a unified theory. Today the work of Laing, Cooper and Esterson represents a step towards an understanding of 'intelligibility' in schizophrenia which makes no concession to evolutionism. This is an uneven development, accompanied by a silence on Freud which has precluded any general theory: but the preconditions of excentric progress here derive from the problematic generated by Klein.

Psychoanalysis in Britain has thus in no fashion been a mediocre or infertile phenomenon. On the contrary, Klein's pupils and associates – Winnicott, Isaacs, Bion, Rosenfeld and Riviere – form one of the most flourishing schools in the world; not to speak of separate cases such as Laing or Cooper. But if we ask what has been the impact of psychoanalysis on British culture in general, the irony is that it has been virtually nil. Psychoanalysis has been sealed off as an esoteric enclave: a specialized pursuit unrelated to mainstream 'humanistic' concerns. In America, Germany or France – three very different examples – Freud's work belongs to a common intellectual inheritance, whose effects can be seen in such contrasted figures as Parsons or Ricoeur, Adorno or Lévi-Strauss. There is no comparable English thinker who has been similarly touched. A minor sign of the larger situation here has been the availability of Freud's texts themselves. The English *Standard Edition* is the best in the world, its twenty-four volumes the model for all other scholarly editions. Naturally, its circulation is very limited. The converse of this specialist undertaking has been the virtual absence of any of the major works of Freud in paperback form – while millions of copies of them are sold to American or European publics. To some extent, the isolation of psychoanalysis in England was historically self-imposed. Jones and Glover, the two men most responsible for its institutionalization, were determined to prevent the confusion and

70. See Edward Glover, 'Examination of the Klein System of Child Psychology', in *The Psychoanalysis of the Child*, Volume 1, London 1945, pp. 75–118, and the references there to the discussion of 1943–44.

vulgarization of Freud's thought they felt had occurred elsewhere. One consequence, of course, was a very limited diffusion of Freud's ideas and writings outside the professional milieu. More important for its isolation, however, was the intellectual context which confronted psychoanalysis in England, and to which it eventually adapted.

Freud often compared his discovery to that of Copernicus, and Althusser has recently enlarged on the parallel: 'It was not in vain that Freud sometimes compared the critical impact of his discoveries with the upheaval of the Copernican revolution. Since Copernicus, we know that the earth is not the centre of the universe. Since Marx, we know that the human subject, the economic, political or philosophical ego is not the centre of history – we even know, against the Enlightenment and against Hegel, that history has no centre, but possesses a structure without a centre. . . . Freud has shown us in his turn that the real subject, the individual in his singular essence, does not have the form of an I centred on the "ego", "consciousness" or "existence" – that the human subject is decentred, constituted by a structure which itself has no centre.'[71] The implications of this alteration for the social sciences were and are very large. There is nothing surprising in the fact that elsewhere it has so widely affected sociology, anthropology, aesthetics or philosophy. The resistance of British culture to any serious impingement can be seen from the reactions of the last. The English brand of linguistic analysis has characteristically flown from the emergence of new concepts, seeking to align philosophical truth with the conventions of ordinary speech. It so happens that psychoanalysis is one of the most radical modern examples of the way in which a conceptual revolution can contradict the rules of everyday discourse. The dethronement of the cogito bespeaks the end of a straightforward usage of the first person, as the unconscious generates a language at variance with the ego-centred syntax of everyday speech. 'I' is no longer I in the metonymic *double entendre* of Freud's patients, their roles governed by a script that escapes them. No appeal to the conventions of understanding in drawing-room conversation can controvert the meaning of the parapraxes disclosed on the couch. Taken seriously, psychoanalysis strikes at the basis of Oxford philosophy.[72]

What has been the reaction of English philosophers to it? By and

71. 'Freud et Lacan', *La Nouvelle Critique*, 1964, 161–62, December 1964–January 1965, p. 107.

72. As it also undermines the plausibility of certain forms of literature, like the traditional novel of character, without so far, however, yielding alternatives that are more than experimental.

large, they have ignored it. None has confronted psychoanalysis as a central issue for this philosophy. A few have tried to deal with it as an anomaly or special instance. Austin, after declaring (as we saw) that: 'Our common stock of words embodies all the distinctions men have found worth drawing, and the connexions they found worth marking, in the lifetimes of many generations',[73] went on to admit two special 'source-books' – law and psychology – whose concepts might be additional to those of ordinary language. His formulation of the problem is, in fact, particularly clear: 'Some varieties of behaviour, some ways of acting or explanations of the doing of actions, are here noticed and classified which have not been observed or named by ordinary men and hallowed by ordinary language, though perhaps they often might have been so if they had been of more practical importance. There is real danger in contempt for the "jargon" of psychology, at least when it sets out to supplement, and at least sometimes when it sets out to supplant, the language of ordinary life.'[74]

Austin illustrates his comment with the technical concepts of 'compulsion' and 'displacement', for which he admits there are no equivalent adverbial expressions in colloquial speech. How, then, is the ideology saved? By means of the simple device of proclaiming this class of phenomena of no 'practical' importance. Ordinary language 'embodies the inherited experience and acumen of many generations of men. But then, that acumen has been concentrated primarily upon the practical business of life. . . . Compulsive behaviour, like displacement behaviour, is not in general going to be of great importance.'[75] The candour of such philistinism is almost admirable. No attempt is made at an intellectual argument: the mere invocation of the 'practical business of life' (the cramped routines of any *bien-pensant* bourgeois) is enough to dispatch the problem. Freud's concepts were explicitly formulated to capture normal and abnormal behaviour in their contradictory unity (neuroses are the obverse of perversions): they represent a general theory of the unconscious, not a pathology of special cases. Even on Austin's own terms, the lack of any attempt to *relate* the concepts of

73. Feyerabend has commented aptly on this notion: 'The firmness, the solidity, the regularity of usages are a function of the firmness of the beliefs held as well as of the needs that these beliefs satisfy: what is regarded linguistically as the "firm ground of language" and is thus opposed to all speculation is usually that part of one's language that is closest to the most basic ideology of the time and expresses it most adequately. That part will then be regarded as being of great practical importance.' 'Problems of Empiricism', in Robert Colodny, ed., *Beyond the Edge of Certainty*, New York 1965, p. 188.

74. *Proceedings of the Aristotelian Society, 1956–57*, p.15.

75. Ibid., pp. 11, 30.

ordinary language to those of 'psychology' (when does the latter not merely 'supplement' but 'supplant' the other?) is remarkable. Instead of significant connexions, there is only a mindless summation of different 'sources'.

Wittgenstein's pupil Wisdom has assayed another type of solution. Here the concepts of psychoanalysis are integrated wholesale into the philosophy of ordinary language, despite their incompatibility with it, by the ingenious device of dubbing them 'paradox' and then asserting that paradox is a special but legal language-game.[76] This latitudinarian position – both use and misuse of language are significant – has been devastatingly criticized by Gellner. It represents the classic antinomy of this empiricism, where it becomes an all-purpose permissiveness, thereby cancelling itself. Another approach to the problem has been tried by Hampshire. His Ernest Jones lecture of 1960 is avowedly concerned to build the shortest possible 'bridge' between everyday language and psychoanalysis.[77] For this purpose, Hampshire selects the concept of memory, and argues that psychoanalysis posits a total memory, the greater portion of which becomes unconscious and thereafter generates repressed motives and purposes. No new concepts are therefore needed: the existing notion of memory merely needs to be 'extended'. What is striking here is the open and *a priori* assumption that the task of the philosopher is to provide the easiest possible reconciliation of new concepts with common sense. It is this extraneous goal which determines the analysis of psychoanalytic theory, not the internal necessity of the object. Banalization becomes the public vocation of philosophy. Hampshire's text is in many respects an astonishing document. He actually says: 'It would be an intellectual disaster if theoretical discussion of psychoanalysis were to be confined to clinical contexts, and if at this stage the philosophy of mind went on its old path unheeding.'[78] Fifty years after the advent of Freud, an English philosopher suddenly discovers that it would be an 'intellectual disaster' if his work 'were' to be forgotten by philosophy! What retrospective description is possible, then, for the intervening half-century, since the maunderings of Moore in *Principia Ethica*? Hampshire solemnly adds: 'The substitution of a scheme of explanation depending on an extended concept of memory for explanation by causal laws will not be

---

76. 'Philosophy, Metaphysics and Psychoanalysis', in *Philosophy and Psychoanalysis*, Oxford 1957.

77. 'Disposition and Memory', *International Journal of Psycho-Analysis*, January–February 1962, pp. 59–68.

78. Ibid., p. 68.

fully understood and evaluated by philosophers for many years.'[79] The tranquil ignorance of the profession is thus assured an indefinite respite. These avowals, by one of the most liberal ornaments of the school, are a suitable epitaph for it. They suggest as much of the fate of psychoanalysis as of the character of philosophy in Britain.

14. Anthropology

Across the panorama surveyed so far, the traditional disciplines have lacked any salient conception of totality, in a culture which itself, however, has revealed marked systemic traits. But the notion of totality can never be entirely absent from an advanced industrial society. If it is suppressed in its natural sites, it is likely to emerge in abnormal or paradoxical habitats. So it has been in Britain.

If modern British society was distinguished by its failure to produce any classical sociology, there was a no less arresting obverse of this phenomenon. For the same society produced a brilliant and flourishing anthropology. It is true that the decisive 'founder' of this anthropology was yet again an expatriate, Bronislaw Malinowski, a Polish aristocrat from the Galician *szlachta*. ('Rivers is the Rider Haggard of anthropology: I shall be its Conrad', he said.) But his contemporaries and pupils were to constitute one of the strongest and most influential schools in any Western country. Radcliffe-Brown, Evans-Pritchard, Fortes, Firth and Leach all won worldwide reputations. Their distinction throws into yet greater relief the anonymity of British sociology. This strange contrast has been generally unremarked. But it evidently calls for some explanation. The career of Durkheim, who was the most powerful foreign source of inspiration for British anthropology in its formative decades, serves as a reminder of how anomalous the British situation was. Durkheim's work was equally and inseparably 'sociological' (*Suicide*) and 'anthropological' (*The Elementary Forms of Religious Life*): the division did not exist for him. Why did it hold, as a virtually absolute datum, in England?

The answer is to be found, not in the aims and methods of the two disciplines, but in their objects. British culture never produced a classical sociology largely because British society was never challenged as a whole from within. The dominant class and its intellectuals consequently had no interest in developing a theory of its overall

79. Ibid., p. 67.

structure, for it would necessarily have been an 'answer' to a question which to their ideological advantage remained unposed. *Omnis determinatio est negatio* – the very demarcation of a social totality places it under the sign of contingency. The British bourgeoisie had learnt to fear the meaning of 'general ideas' during the French Revolution: after Burke, it rarely forgot the lesson. Hegemony at home required a substantial moratorium on them. By the end of the nineteenth century, however, this class was master of a third of the world. English anthropology was born of this disjuncture. British imperial society *exported* its totalizations onto its subject peoples. There, and there only, it could afford scientific study of the social whole. 'Primitive' societies became the surrogate object of the theory proscribed at home. British anthropology developed unabashedly in the wake of British imperialism. Colonial administration had an inherent need of cogent, objective information about the peoples over which it ruled. The miniature scale of primitive societies, moreover, made them exceptionally propitious for macro-analysis; as Sartre once remarked, they form 'natural' significant totalities. British anthropology was thus able both to assist British imperialism, and to develop a genuine theory – something sociology in Britain was never able to do. The class core of this contrast is not an arbitrary construction. The least suspect of sources has innocently admitted it. MacRae, symbol of British sociological orthodoxy ('a rather splendid amateurism'), writes: 'British social anthropology has drawn on the same intellectual capital as sociology proper, and its success, useful to colonial administration and dangerous to no domestic prejudice, shows at what a high rate of interest that capital can be made to pay. . . . The subject . . . unlike sociology, has prestige. It is associated with colonial administration – traditionally a career for a gentleman, and entrance into the profession and acceptance by it confers high status in Britain.'[80] Useful to colonial administration and dangerous to no domestic prejudice – the formula is brief and exact. These were the twin conditions of existence of British anthropology, as it developed.

The scholars themselves, of course, were nearly always liberal within the paternalist framework of their vocation. But the sensibility nevertheless produced by it is vividly conveyed by Evans-Pritchard, whose classic study of the Nuer contains this calm aside, after a lengthy and often lyrical account of Nuer life: 'In 1920 large-scale military oper-

80. *Ideology and Society: Papers in Sociology and Politics*, London 1961, pp. 36 and 9.

ations, including bombing and machine-gunning of camps, were conducted against the Eastern Jikany and caused much loss of life and destruction of property. There were further patrols from time to time, but the Nuer remained unsubdued. . . . From 1928 to 1930 prolonged operations were conducted against the whole of the disturbed area and marked the end of serious fighting between the Nuer and the Government. Conquest was a severe blow to the Nuer.'[81] Needless to say, the passing reference to this brutal war is quite dissociated from the analysis of Nuer society itself. Later developments often lessened the role of outright violence in colonial rule. But the context of anthropological work had not changed greatly twenty years later, when a volume of tributes to Radcliffe-Brown, edited by Fortes, could include the following contribution on the uses of anthropology to more 'modern' notions of imperial control: 'It is only after months or years of administration, and sometimes not even then, that a Military Government officer or colonial administrator learns the virtues of "opposition face". By this is meant that the native leader or appointed official must be allowed some leeway to oppose the occupying administration for the purposes of his public, in order that he may the more successfully carry through the main and essential necessities of government for the maintenance of law and order. This is simply good political horse sense. One good reason for giving native leaders some sense of responsibility (not necessarily for policies but rather for methods and procedures of carrying them out) is to avoid too much paternalism. The latter is stutifying and may lead to complete lack of co-operation on the part of the people. A reasonably alert and satisfied population is amenable in terms of labour procurement and any other problem of administration requiring the co-operation of the people.'[82]

This, then, was the practical historical setting of the growth of imperial anthropology. What were its theoretical achievements? The formidable research carried out by two generations of scholars was integrated under the canons of functionalism. Radcliffe-Brown provided the most coherent theoretical explanation of this doctrine, but was himself more influential in the USA than in Britain. It was the original author of the notion, Malinowski, who formed a generation of English anthropologists. The basic idea of functionalism was that the diverse parts of society – economy, polity, kinship or religion – form a consistent whole, unified by the interconnecting functions of each. Functionalism

81. *The Nuer*, Oxford 1940, p. 131.
82. John Embree, 'American Military Government', in Meyer Fortes, ed., *Social Structure: Essays Presented to A.R. Radcliffe-Brown*, Oxford 1949, p. 220.

represented the notion of an immediate and simple totality. As such, it was an enormous advance over the atomized empiricism of domestic British thought, and naturally produced a social science of incomparably greater force and insight: to this day, British anthropology towers above its stunted sibling. The limitations of functionalism, however, became increasingly evident with time. Malinowski's founding version of it was a variety of psychologism – the recurring motif discernible throughout this cultural pattern. The function of the different institutions which made up a society was to serve the psychological needs of the population, which Malinowski believed were innate. Parsons has written the critique of this theory; it did not survive Malinowski.[83] But the deeper limit of functionalism persisted. It was a totalization without contradictions. Having posited the compact integration of social institutions, it was at a loss to deal with structural antagonisms. Where conflicts were considered at all, they tended to be treated as actually conducive to ultimate order (Gluckmann). Hence a progressive loss of impetus once the pioneering work of Malinowski's pupils was done. No renewal was possible within this framework, which represented the outer limit of a totalizing theory whose vector was a stable British imperialism.

The Second World War provoked the crisis of this imperial system. The emergence of new tendencies within British anthropology coincides with this crisis. The material for the work which represented a new departure was gathered while its author was an officer in the Burmese campaign. Leach's *Political Systems of Highland Burma* was explicitly an attack on the equilibria assumptions of previous British functionalism. The focus of its analysis of Kachin society are the inherent contradictions of a political system perpetually veering between a hierarchical and an egalitarian pole, without achieving stabilization at either – the hierarchical model cancelling kin relations and thereby producing revolt, the egalitarian model fostering privileged lineages and thereby reproducing hierarchy. Logically enough, Leach invoked Pareto as his inspiration. For, indeed, this was a cyclical contradiction – just the kind that had been the concern of classical sociology. If the criticisms that may be made of it are the same, Leach himself supplied a potential corrective, when he noted a significant asymmetry in the contradiction – the precondition of the hierarchical, unlike the egalitarian, model was the production of a reasonable

83. 'Malinowski and the Theory of Social Systems', in Raymond Firth, ed., *Man and Culture*, London 1957, pp. 53–70.

economic surplus. Leach's study, moreover, firmly integrated the imperial administration into the anthropological analysis itself, showing how British colonial ideology had insisted that there was only 'one' model of Kachin society – the hierarchical – because colonial practice repressed the other as subversive, while accentuating autocratic features of Kachin hierarchy for the purposes of indirect rule. Here political awareness was the condition of scientific progress.

Leach's subsequent development confirmed this radical start. He was the first British anthropologist to register the significance of the work of Lévi-Strauss, using it aggressively to criticize the methodological procedures of the discipline as a whole in *Rethinking Anthropology*. More recently he has produced a powerful structural analysis of myth in *The Legitimacy of Solomon*, whose theme is once again an endemic contradiction – the need for the Jews in Palestine to claim endogamy for the purpose of religious unity, while practising exogamy for the purpose of political alliances.[84] Reading the Old Testament as a set of genealogical myths that transform this contradiction into a maze of binary oppositions that work to reconcile the two demands, Leach in effect reinstates a classical conception of ideology as an imaginary resolution of real contradictions. This is, in its object and its method, an exercise in iconoclasm. The displacement which was at the origin of British anthropology has continued to bear fruit. Both its earlier functionalism and the structuralism of Leach's later work are anomalies for what became of English empiricism. Anthropology has formed a deviant sector within British culture, because its application has lain outside it. The exception here can be termed a corollary of the rule.

15. Literary Criticism

The second displaced home of the totality was to be literary criticism. Here no expatriate influence ever became dominant. Leavis commanded his subject within his own generation. With him, English literary criticism conceived the ambition to become the vaulting centre of 'humane studies and of the university'. English was 'the chief of the humanities'.[85] This claim was certainly unique to England: no other country has produced a critical discipline with these pretensions. They should be seen, not as a reflection of megalomania on the part of Leavis, but as a symptom of the vacuum at the centre of the culture.

84. *Archives Européennes de Sociologie*, vol. 7, no. 1, 1966, pp. 58–101.
85. *Education and the University*, London 1943, p. 33.

Driven out of any obvious habitats, the notion of the totality found refuge in the least expected of studies. The peculiar status of literary criticism, as conceived by Leavis and his pupils, underlines the global anomaly of the system. One might say that when philosophy became 'technical', a displacement occurred and literary criticism went 'ethical'. The two thereafter stood in a curious relation of inverted complementarity. English philosophy, with Wittgenstein, abandoned ethics and metaphysics for the neutral investigation of language; English criticism, with Leavis, assumed the responsibility of moral judgement and metaphysical assertion. Across the Channel, France exhibited the opposite pattern – a technical, hermeneutic criticism (Poulet or Richard) and an ontological or moral philosophy (Merleau-Ponty or Sartre).

Leavis's personal achievement as a critic was outstanding, his rigour and intelligence establishing new standards of discrimination. *Revaluations* and *The Great Tradition* permanently altered complacent traditional receptions of English poetry and the English novel. But the paradox of this great critic is that his whole *œuvre* rested on a metaphysic which he could never expound or defend. Empiricism here found its strangest expression. Leavis, whose work transcended the rut of English philistinism so militantly (and was so hated for it), used its most extreme form to evade open debate of his ideas. His was a metaphysic which refused to justify itself. Wellek, in his famous letter to Leavis in 1937, wrote: 'I could wish that you had stated your assumptions more explicitly and defended them more systematically.' Declaring that he shared most of these assumptions, he went on: 'But I would have misgivings in pronouncing them without elaborating a specific defence or a theory in their defence . . . I would ask you to defend this position more abstractly and to become conscious that large ethical, philosophical and, of course, ultimately also aesthetic choices are involved.'[86] Leavis's reply was a considered refusal: 'Ideally, I ought perhaps to be able to complete the work with a theoretical statement'[87] – but in practice he declined to do so, on the grounds that a critic does not judge a work by any external philosophical norm, but first achieves a complete internal possession of it and then adjusts for the sense of its relation to other works. 'We were empirical and opportunist in spirit', he later wrote.[88] Wellek had pointed out the constancy with which certain key formulations and epithets – 'healthy',

86. René Wellek, 'Literary Criticism and Philosophy', *Scrutiny*, March 1937, p. 376.
87. 'Literary Criticism and Philosophy – A Reply', *Scrutiny*, June 1937, p. 62.
88. *Scrutiny: A Retrospect*, vol. XX, Cambridge 1963, p. 4.

'vital', 'plain vulgar living', 'actual' and others – recurred in Leavis's writings, forming the systematic substructure of his works. The most important, and notorious, of these was the idea of 'life' that was central to Leavis's criticism. His book on Lawrence, his most extended intellectual statement, exemplifies with particular clarity the paradoxes of an insistently metaphysical vocabulary combined with a truculently positivist methodology. '*The Daughters of the Vicar*, I say, is profoundly representative of Lawrence, and class-distinctions enter as a major element into its theme. . . . The part they play in the given tale is a sinister one, and the theme is their defeat – the triumph over them of life. It is one of the difficulties of criticism that the critic has to use such phrases as that last. It is one of the advantages of having such a creative achievement as *The Daughters of the Vicar* to deal with that the phrase gets its force in the tale, the movement and sum of which define "life" in the only way in which it can be defined for the purposes of the critic: he has the tale – its developing significance and the concrete particulars of its organization – to point to.'[89] The circularity of the argument is repeated again and again: 'We are made to judge that she has chosen life. The sense in which she has done so it takes the tale to define, and in defining it the tale justifies that way of describing her decision.'[90]

How did Leavis justify this logical circle? The answer is that his criticism did contain a very specific epistemology, which in its turn implied a particular interpretation of history. When challenged for the rationale of his critical statements, Leavis always replied that they did not properly speaking have an affirmative, but an interrogative form. The latent form of all literary criticism was: 'This is so, is it not?' Thus Leavis wrote that his method in *Revaluations* was to get his readers 'to agree (with, no doubt, critical qualifications) that the map, the essential order of English poetry seen as a whole did, when they interrogated their experience, look like that to them also.'[91] The formal circularity of the criticism of a text was the elliptical sign of a substantive exchange between its readers.

The central idea of this epistemology – the interrogative statement – demands, however, one crucial precondition: a shared, stable system of beliefs and values. Without this, no loyal exchange or report is possible. If the basic formation and outlook of readers diverge, their experience will be incommensurable. Leavis's method presupposed, in other words, a morally and culturally unified audience. In its absence, his

89. *D.H. Lawrence: Novelist*, London 1955, pp. 75–76.
90. Ibid., p. 93.
91. 'Literary Criticism and Philosophy – A Reply', p. 62.

epistemology disintegrates. This is surely the reason for the pervasive nostalgia in his work for an 'organic community' of the past. The illusory nature of this image – its character as myth – has been often criticized, and rightly so. But its function within his work has not been properly understood. It is not a whimsical ideal, but a validating reference for the actual operation of the criticism. For nothing was less obvious or to be taken for granted in Leavis's day than a stable, shared system of beliefs. Indeed, his very epistemology is the explanation of Leavis's own famous inability to understand or sympathize with either avant-garde or foreign literature (with a very few exceptions, such as Tolstoy). His incomprehension of these was built into his method: it should not merely be attributed to arbitrary traits of his personality. For once time (avant-garde) and place (country) changed, the cultural basis for a shared interrogation collapsed. Prejudice and bafflement were predictable products of the ensuing disorientation.

Leavis's epistemology was necessarily accompanied by a philosophy of history. The organic community of the past, when there was no division between popular and sophisticated culture, died with the Augustan age: Bunyan was among its last witnesses. Thereafter, history for Leavis traced a gradual decline. The Industrial Revolution finally swamped the old rural culture. But it did not initially undermine the existence of a cultivated elite, the minority that created and responded to literature. The nineteenth century produced such Romantic poets as Keats or Coleridge and the great tradition of the English novel – Eliot, Conrad and James. With the twentieth century, however, the inexorable tide of industrialism began to invade the very precincts of humane culture itself. Leavis saw the new media of communication – newspapers, magazines, radio, cinema and television – as menacing bludgeons of commercialism and Benthamism. They threatened to obliterate in a new barbarism every critical standard on which the existence of culture depended. The duty of the literary critic was to fight without compromise or pause against any dilution or degeneration of these standards. Defying every convention of the British intelligentsia, Leavis lent a violent zeal and fury to this role.

The pages of *Scrutiny* are pervaded by an immense pessimism: a sense of inexorable cultural atrophy, and of a dwindling minority aware of it. This is the memorable and unifying theme of the journal. Article after article laments an increasing deturpation of literary standards and a triumph of the meretricious. Leavis's commination of the corruptions of the new media, and of the metropolitan world of letters, became more strident with every year. But this was only one of *Scrutiny*'s two main ideological concerns. The other was anti-

Marxism. Leavis is the only intellectual in this survey to have been significantly affected by Marxism. This will appear a paradoxical statement to those who only know his latter-day reputation. But *Scrutiny* was in fact born in close proximity to a certain Marxist influence – its predecessor, *The Calendar of Letters*, was edited by a communist – and it developed in a permanent tension with it thereafter. Leavis wrote in its first year: 'I agree with the Marxist to the extent of believing some form of economic communism to be inevitable and desirable.'[92] Antagonism rapidly grew after this, when the metropolitan literary world was suddenly seized with radicalism, and Marxism became fashionable among young writers, often only lightly acquainted with it. This became one of the social and intellectual poles against which *Scrutiny* then defined itself. Leavis and his colleagues constantly attacked the shallowness of a vulgar leftism over which they had no difficulty in establishing their superiority. By the end of the decade, this modish literary leftism had virtually disappeared. In *Scrutiny*, Leavis wrote its obituary: 'Marxist the decade decidedly was. It was also, in literature, a very barren decade.'[93]

The rout of this opponent did not alleviate Leavis's general cultural diagnosis. If anything, his forebodings deepened after the Second World War. Leavis saw himself as the spokesman of traditional humane values, a critic determined to safeguard the great heritage of English literary culture and the classical English university. Yet he himself was rejected by the very institutions he exalted. Cambridge, model of his idea of a university, rebuffed or ignored him. Isolated in this hostile environment, *Scrutiny* finally drifted to a halt in the fifties. The retrospect that Leavis wrote ten years later is an extraordinary document. In it, Leavis defines his relations both to Marxism and to Cambridge. 'We were anti-Marxist – necessarily so (we thought); an intelligent, that is real, interest in literature implied a conception of it very different from any that a Marxist could expound and explain. Literature – what we knew as literature and had studied for the English Tripos – mattered; it mattered crucially to civilization – of that we were sure. It mattered because it represented a human reality, an autonomy of the human spirit, for which economic determinism and reductive interpretation in terms of the class war left no room. Marxist fashion gave us the doctrinal challenge. But Marxism was a characteristic product of our "capitalist" civilization, and the economic determinism

92. 'Restatements for Critics', *Scrutiny*, March 1933, p. 320.
93. 'Retrospect of a Decade', *Scrutiny*, June 1940, p. 71.

we were committed to refuting practically was that which might seem to have been demonstrated by the movement and process of this. The dialectic against which we had to vindicate literature and humane culture was that of the external or material civilization we lived in. "External" and "material" here need not be defined: they convey well enough the insistence that our total civilization is a very complex thing, with a kind of complexity to which Marxist categories are not adequate.

'Cambridge, then, figured for us civilization's anti-Marxist recognition of its own nature and needs – recognition of that, the essential, which Marxist wisdom discredited, and the external and material drive of civilization threatened, undoctrinally, to eliminate. It was our strength to be, in our consciousness of our effort, and actually, in the paradoxical and ironical way I have to record, representatives of that Cambridge. We were, in fact, that Cambridge; we felt it, and had more and more reason to feel it, and our confidence and courage came from that. . . . Only at Cambridge could the idea of *Scrutiny* have taken shape, become a formidable life and maintained the continuous living force that made it hated and effective. It was (to deepen the emphasis) a product, the triumphant justifying achievement, of the English Tripos. I express, and intend to encourage, no simple parochial enthusiasm or loyalty in dwelling on these truths. I had better, in fact, add at once the further testimony that *Scrutiny* started, established itself and survived in spite of Cambridge.'[94]

This passage contains the core of Leavis's intellectual position: it is a precise, binary exposition of its structure. Marxism is the 'doctrinal challenge'. It is rejected because it partakes of the very society which it claims to condemn: it is materialist and therefore a 'characteristic product of capitalist civilization'. Against it, Leavis proclaims 'literature and humane culture' which are essential to 'civilization', but which are factually negated by its 'external and material drive'. The essence of civilization becomes inner and spiritual; it is represented supremely by Cambridge, and Cambridge is represented supremely by – indeed coincides with – *Scrutiny*. 'We were Cambridge.' But the actual Cambridge – inner and spiritual essence of civilization – negated *Scrutiny*, which only survived 'in spite of Cambridge'. Reality becomes completely volatilized in this multiple regression towards the ideal. The logical structure of the argument reveals the intolerable strain that Leavis's actual experience imposed on his preconceptions. It becomes a vertigin-

94. *Scrutiny: A Retrospect*, p. 4.

ous spiral of antinomies, in which the flight from one merely produces another which in turn reproduces another. Marxism seems to be a critique of capitalist civilization; in fact it is merely an exemplification of it. This civilization seems to confirm economic determinism; in fact, only its external and material drive does, not its spiritual essence. The inner spirit of civilization seems to be exemplified in Cambridge, and Cambridge in *Scrutiny*; in fact Cambridge systematically rejected *Scrutiny*, which was created against it.

What was the meaning of these desperate and impossible syllogisms? What they point to is the final impasse in Leavis's thought. Alone of the thinkers in this survey, he felt acutely aware that something had gone wrong in British culture. But he was unable to explain the decline he denounced. The fate of humane culture was attributed to the drive of 'mass' civilization and the corruption of modern literati. Against these enemies, Leavis posed older ideals – Cambridge: but then Cambridge itself was complicit with them. The fixations on trivial targets which came to assume such disproportionate importance for him – the British Council, Bloomsbury or the *Times Literary Supplement* – can be seen as aberrant symptoms of his failure to locate the causes of the decline. Intellectually blocked, his insight became a displaced acrimony and monomania. Leavis correctly sensed a cultural landscape of much mediocrity and conformity. This was not, however, an inevitable product of either industrial civilization or capitalism, but had its origins in a much more specific local history, which explains why the sanctum into which Leavis sought to withdraw refused him. For the unity of British culture naturally included it: Bloomsbury and Cambridge were not antipodes but twins, as Forster or Strachey were there to show.

Insisting to the end on a meta-Cambridge, Leavis was ultimately trapped in the cultural nexus he hated. His empiricism became banally reactionary in old age. Like many thinkers, he survived himself to his detriment. But the importance of his achievements remains. It was not by chance that the most significant work of socialist theory of the fifties, Raymond Williams's *Long Revolution*, should have emerged out of literary criticism, of all fields.[95] It was from this tradition that Williams was able to develop a vision of British society as a whole – connecting work, politics, culture, nurturance – that broke with the

95. Its idealist traces owe something to Leavis, who believed that 'to say that the life of a country is determined by its educational ideals is a commonplace': 'Scrutiny: A Manifesto', *Scrutiny*, May 1932, p. 6.

Fabian forms of Labour's own empiricism. The origins of that move in the outlook formed by *Scrutiny* are an appropriate tribute to its legacy.

16. Summary

The arguments of this survey can now be briefly resumed. The culture of British society is organized about an absent centre – an overall account of itself, that could have been either a classical sociology or a national Marxism. The particular path taken by English social structure, which never produced a revolutionary challenge from below, is the explanation of this arrested development. Two results followed, the visible index of a vacuum. A White emigration rolled across the flat expanse of English intellectual life, capturing sector after sector, until this traditionally insular culture became dominated by expatriates, of heterogeneous calibre. Simultaneously, there occurred a series of structural distortions in the character and connections of the inherited disciplines. Philosophy was restricted to a technical inventory of language. Political theory was thereby cut off from history. History was divorced from the exploration of political ideas. Psychology was counterposed to them. Economics was dissociated from both political theory and history. Aesthetics was reduced to psychology. The congruence of each sector with its neighbour came to form something like a closed system, in which elements incompatible with the dominant pattern, like psychoanalysis, were quarantined. Suppressed in every obvious sector at home, thought of the totality was painlessly exported abroad, producing the paradox of a major anthropology where there was no such sociology. In the general vacuum thus created, literary criticism usurps ethics and insinuates a philosophy of history. Logically enough, it finally became the one area to generate a synthesizing socialist theory.

The void at the centre of this culture generated a pseudo-centre – the timeless ego whose metempsychosis in discipline after discipline we have encountered in this survey. The price of missing sociology, let alone Marxism, was the prevalence of psychologism. A culture lacking the instruments to conceive the social totality typically fell back on the nuclear psyche, as first cause of society and history. This invariant substitute is explicit in Malinowski, Namier, Eysenck or Gombrich. The general result was to put change out of reach. Time exists at best as intermittence (Keynes), at worst as decline (Leavis) or oblivion (Wittgenstein). Ultimately (Namier, Leavis or Gombrich), the twentieth century itself, with its political or cultural revolutions, becomes an impossible object.

The chloroforming effect of this configuration is general. Silently underpinning the social status quo, it stifles intellectual questioning of the existing order and deprives political opposition on the Left of the resources needed to understand its society, the condition of changing it. History has tied this knot, and only history can undo it. A revolutionary culture is not for tomorrow. But a socialist practice within culture is possible today: the student struggle is its initial form.

1968

3

The Notion of Bourgeois Revolution

Among the concepts traditionally associated with historical materialism, few have been so problematic and contested as that of bourgeois revolution. There are good reasons why its position within the Marxist legacy should be at once so central and so controverted. The starting-point for a reflection on them today is to note an initial paradox. Marx, to whom the paternity of the idea of 'bourgeois revolution' is conventionally attributed, was himself the contemporary of – that is, lived through and observed – what subsequent generations of Marxist historians have often seen as a crucial cluster of bourgeois revolutions, on a world scale. He was a participant and critic, after all, of the Spring-Time of the Peoples, the wave of popular insurrections which broke out across continental Europe in 1848. These uniformly failed to replace the old royal or absolutist orders against which they rose – whether in Germany or France, Italy or Hungary, Austria or Romania – with any civic republican regime. Marx and Engels wrote extensively on this experience, in some of their most famous writings – *The Class Struggles in France*, *The Eighteenth Brumaire*, *Revolution and Counter-Revolution in Germany*. So much is familiar enough. What has been less noticed, however, is that from the late 1850s to the turn of the 1870s, Marx and Engels were witnesses to a broad wave of successful overthrows, by armed violence, of pre-capitalist or absolutist political structures, not only in Europe but also in North America and even the Far East. This was the period that saw the triumph of the Risorgimento in Italy; the Unification of Germany under Bismarck; the victory of the industrial North over the slave-holding South in the American Civil War; and the destruction of the Tokugawa Shogunate in Japan, which has gone down in history as the Meiji Restoration. All these momentous upheavals of the second half of the nineteenth century have retrospectively come to be regarded, by particular Marxist historians of the countries concerned – Italy, Germany, the USA and Japan – as the decisive chapters of the bourgeois revolution in their respective nations; and even by non-Marxist or anti-Marxist colleagues as – regardless of labels – the beginnings of the modern state structure in these societies, which include the three largest economies today. It would be difficult to minimize the overall historical significance of the great international turbulence of these dramatic fifteen years or so.

Yet – it is a striking fact – very little of this wide turmoil was analysed, much of it scarcely even registered, by Marx or Engels themselves. There is nothing surprising, of course, in their ignorance of events in the secluded empire of Japan, of which few Europeans of any kind were aware.[1] Their relative indifference to, and incomprehension of, the Italian Risorgimento – all too visible, for example, in Engels's unhappy brochure on *The Po and the Rhine*, virtually siding with Austrian reaction in the peninsula[2] – are much more curious. Equally, if not yet more, disconcerting is the blankness with which they met the unexpected process of Unification in their own country, Germany: about which Marx left us no significant text at all, even if Engels did – some time after the event – produce one acute essay on it, *The Role of Force in History*.[3] Finally, while Marx and Engels took a close and passionate interest in the American Civil War – unlike any other of the three conflicts – it cannot be said that their judgements of it were distinguished by any great political acumen or historical insight: it is sufficient to think of the wholly uncritical encomia addressed to Lincoln, hailed by Marx as 'the strong-minded, iron son of the American working class',[4] a title which – whatever other merits might be ascribed to this quintessentially bourgeois politician – he least of all deserved. Basically, we might say, the significant fact is that Marx and Engels never took real cognizance of the actual political revolutions of

---

1. Marx had a good idea of the general character of the Tokugawa countryside: 'Japan, with its purely feudal organization of landed property and its developed small-scale agriculture, gives a much truer picture of the European Middle Ages than all our history books': *Capital*, vol.1, London 1976, p. 878; but knew nothing of its reorganization under the Meiji oligarchs.

2. Marx–Engels, *Werke*, vol. 13, Berlin 1964, pp. 225–268: views strongly coloured by hostility to Napoleon III, in early 1859. Engels warmed to Garibaldi's exploits later on.

3. His final judgement of the process of Unification was categorical: 'Bismarck understood the German civil war of 1866 for what it was, namely a *revolution*, and he was prepared to carry it through with revolutionary means – and so he did.' *Werke*, vol. 21, Berlin 1962, p. 432.

4. *Werke*, vol. 16, Berlin 1968, p. 19: reduced to 'single-minded' in the American translation (Marx–Engels, *The Civil War in the United States*, New York 1961, p. 281).

their time that inaugurated a new epoch in the life of capital, preoccupied as they were with the prospects for another kind of revolution, one that would usher in the rule of labour but which did not in fact materialize.

If we look at the body of Marx's theoretical work as a whole, we can see perhaps in part why it was so difficult for him to take the measure of these contemporary upheavals. For, contrary to what is often believed, the notion of 'bourgeois revolution' that subsequent Marxists were to apply to them is scarcely to be found as such, *en toutes lettres*, in his writing at all. We can search in vain for it, for example, in the text where above all we might expect to find it – *The Communist Manifesto*. The *Manifesto* is in many ways a veritable hymn to the revolutionary vocation of the bourgeoisie on a world scale. But the upheavals ascribed to it are seen in terms of the economic impact of large capitalist industry and the expanding world market, not in terms of a political assault by the bourgeoisie on the Anciens Régimes of the late feudal order. The occasions on which Marx directly uses the expression 'bourgeois revolution' are very rare, and confined to early texts;[5] Engels did so somewhat more frequently, but without any attempt at a theoretical systematization.

The idea proper, in fact, does not become truly current within the vocabulary of historical materialism until the end of the nineteenth and the beginning of the twentieth century. It was the Russian revolutionary movement that gave it for the first time an established status within Marxist vocabulary, above all through the writings of Plekhanov and Lenin. The notion crystallized in the Russian labour movement for essentially political and strategic reasons. Plekhanov and Lenin had to distinguish the revolution that was approaching in the Tsarist Empire from the projections of the Narodniks, who advocated an outright socialist revolution in the belief that Russia could leap over any phase of capitalist domination, to reach a more or less peasant communism directly from existing feudal conditions in the countryside. Against this conception, Plekhanov and Lenin insisted that the coming revolution would be bourgeois, even if the working class came to play the leading

5. The principal text in which Marx does use the term 'bourgeois revolution', referring directly to the English Civil War, the French Revolution and the coming struggles in Germany, is 'Die moralisierende Kritik und die kritisierende Moral. Beitrag zur deutschen Kulturgeschichte' of late 1847: *Werke*, vol. 4, Berlin 1959, pp. 338–43, 350–53, in which he argued that the German workers 'can and must accept the *bourgeois revolution* as a condition of the *workers' revolution*'.

role in it – a scenario which, as we know, history was not going to confirm.[6]

The important point for our purposes, however, is that the first extended usages of the concept of bourgeois revolution were the product of a debate centred on the prospects of a proletarian revolution, the governing concern of the leading minds of the RSDLP. The idea of bourgeois revolution thus emerged essentially as the *negative* of proletarian revolution, not for what it was itself. The consequence was that the concept never really became a theoretical object in its own right. Rather, it was essentially constructed through a retro-projection whose model was the proletarian revolution, implying the idea that the structure of bourgeois revolutions would be homologous with what was known – or thought to be known – of proletarian revolutions. In other words, there was no independent conceptualization of the phenomenon.

This was an epoch which expected the coming socialist revolutions to be played out between a manufacturing bourgeoisie and an industrial proletariat, in a bilateral shock of these two classes against each other. By analogy, then, the bourgeois revolution was conceived as a similarly direct collision between a class of feudal landowners and a rising industrial bourgeoisie. Such was, more or less, the prevailing interpretation of the concept during the golden age of classical Marxism before and during the First World War. It is important to note that in this epoch there still did not exist any professional Marxist historiography as such, in the modern sense. It was only from the fourth and fifth decades of this century onwards that schools of Marxist historians *stricto sensu* started to emerge. But when they did so, they typically focused precisely on investigations of the episodes in their national past that could be taken as the bourgeois revolutions in their own countries. Such was the case, for example, of the work of Christopher Hill in England, Albert Soboul in France or the Rono-ha historians in Japan.[7]

When these historians started to study the English Civil War, the French Revolution or the Meiji Restoration, they could not but register

---

6. The first test of these projections came, of course, in the upheavals of 1905, which Plekhanov firmly reasserted was and could only be a bourgeois revolution: see Samuel Baron, *Plekhanov. The Father of Russian Marxism*, London 1963, pp. 263 ff. Martov was equally definite: Israel Getzler, *Martov*, Melbourne 1967, pp. 101 ff.

7. Christopher Hill, *The English Revolution 1640*, London 1953; Albert Soboul, *The French Revolution 1787–1799*, London 1974; for the Rono-ha view of the Meiji Restoration, see George Beckmann and Genji Okubo, *The Japanese Communist Party 1922–1945*, Stanford 1969, pp. 135 ff.

a whole series of anomalies or deviations from the presumptive model of what a bourgeois revolution should be. In particular, it proved very difficult to locate an unequivocally bourgeois class, direct carrier of an ascendant capitalist mode of production, as the central subject of these upheavals. One result was that their non-Marxist colleagues or anti-Marxist adversaries found it relatively easy to question or reject the interpretations of these episodes by Marxists. The classic occasions of these *fins de non recevoir* are familiar enough. In the case of England, Hugh Trevor-Roper was famously to deny any pertinence of the term 'bourgeois revolution' to the Civil War of the seventeenth century, insisting that the leading role in that conflict was played by a stratum of declining rural gentry – indeed that it was inappropriate to speak of a 'revolution' in the period at all, of whatever character.[8] In the case of France, Alfred Cobban, François Furet and Denis Richet have dismissed any validity to the idea that a bourgeois revolution was set in motion in 1789, pointing to the lack of manufacturers or industrialists in the leading ranks of the Convention, and to the slow rates of French capitalist growth after the fall of the monarchy.[9] Marxist historians have not, on the whole, so far succeeded in making a convincing reply to this type of objection.

To escape from the impasse in which much Marxist literature on this subject has found itself, it may be worth suggesting an alternative approach. Instead of first looking at specific national upheavals and then trying to match these against a pure model of what a bourgeois revolution is assumed to be, inevitably concluding with the registration of a whole range of anomalies and discrepancies in each case, let us for the moment adopt an exactly inverse procedure. That is to say, it may be more sensible to start by trying to establish the formal structures and limits of any possible 'bourgeois revolution' *before* passing to the study of any specific scenario; in other words, to attempt to construct the theoretical concept before exploring its historical incarnations. If we do this, we may discover that the specificities of the chain of great upheavals that Marxists came to call bourgeois revolutions are not a mere sum of anomalies or discrepancies such as mark the distance between concept and reality in an empiricist epistemology, but are rather intelligible variations within a common field.

It must, of course, immediately be added: the procedure suggested is

---

8. H.R. Trevor-Roper, *The Gentry 1540–1640*, Cambridge 1953; 'The Social Causes of the Great Rebellion', *Historical Essays*, London 1957, pp. 195–205.

9. Alfred Cobban, *The Social Interpretation of the French Revolution*, Cambridge 1964; François Furet and Denis Richet, *La Révolution Française*, Paris 1973.

no dispensation from a scrupulous and detailed examination of the historical facts themselves – that is, the concrete course of any given process denominated a 'bourgeois revolution', in all the particularity and complexity of the evidence for it. That evidence constitutes both the immediate point of enquiry and the ultimate court of appeal for any serious historical theory. But a theory will only be such – that is, a meaningful general framework for the interpretation of the past – if it possesses in the first instance a clear and coherent set of concepts. It is these that will be explored here, and tested against the major political upheavals which are generally accepted – independently of their categorization – as watersheds in the emergence of the modern state in the leading capitalist societies of our own time. Any list of these must include, in chronological order, the Revolt of the Netherlands in the sixteenth century; the English Civil War of the seventeenth century; the American War of Independence and the French Revolution of the eighteenth century; and the Italian Risorgimento, Unification of Germany, American Civil War and Meiji Restoration in the nineteenth century. Our question will be whether there is any conceptual framework compatible with Marxist assumptions that could hold together these hugely differing episodes, stretching across four centuries, as a common historical set.

We can begin by asking the question: within the general parameters of historical materialism as a theory, are there any formal structures that could be said to delimit the space of any imaginable bourgeois revolution? The answer, on reflection, is surely that we can identify at least four, *a priori*. Borrowing a term from Louis Althusser, but without any commitment to his use of it, we shall speak of this quartet as the *necessary* – not contingent – 'overdetermination' of any process that could be designated a bourgeois revolution.[10] Let us enumerate them.

First there is the familiar fact that the specific character of the feudal mode of production was such as to permit a certain degree of capital accumulation and enlarged circulation of commodities within its own economic order. Capitalism, as a new economic system, could grow in the urban interstices of feudalism, as well as out of its rural relationships of rent; just as the municipal bourgeoisie, as a new social class, could rise within the framework of post-mediaeval monarchies. In Marxist terms, the relationship between feudalism and capitalism is fundamentally distinct in this respect from the – projected – relation-

10. Louis Althusser, *For Marx*, London 1971, pp. 87–128.

ship between capitalism and socialism. For according to the conceptions of Marx and Engels, socialism could have no determinate historical existence as a mode of production, prior to the achievement of political power by the working class. The objective basis of the coexistence, for a long historical epoch, of feudalism and capitalism within transitional social formations was their common definition as systems of private property. Of course, feudal property and capitalist property were themselves quite different forms, but the crucial point for our purposes is that there never existed between them the divide that separates private property – whether feudal or capitalist – from socialized property. Thus in the process of any transition from feudalism to capitalism, there was always the possibility of a scale of mutually advantageous transactions – up to 'organic' compromise – between the nobility and bourgeoisie as social classes, that were excluded from the range of equivalent relations between bourgeoisie and proletariat in Marx's vision of them. We could call this the overdetermination of bourgeois revolutions from above.

Second, the transition from feudalism to capitalism never involved simply a bipolar relationship between an aristocracy on one side, and a bourgeoisie on the other. This too was no contingent fact. For the feudal mode of production requires the existence of a large non-possessing class of peasants in the countryside, whose exploitation yields the rents from which any landowning aristocracy derives its wealth and social power. On the other hand, capitalism as a mode of production requires the existence of propertyless wage-earners, whose surplus labour yields the profits that assure the wealth and social power of bourgeois employers. The co-presence of both rural and urban masses below the line of noble–bourgeois contradictions was thus inherent in the social conflicts unleashed by the growth of capitalism. In consequence no revolutionary crisis could ever be a simple duel between a nobility and a bourgeoisie, since its formal structure always involved a three- or four-sided relationship. In other words, the pervasive presence of popular classes – whether of town or countryside – in the political convulsions of the transition is neither accidental nor external: it is inherent in their very nature, which all but precluded the schema of a simple opposition between the two possessing classes. We could call this the overdetermination of bourgeois revolutions from below.

Let us now consider the central protagonist of the process, as it was classically conceived – the bourgeoisie itself. If this is defined as the class of capitalists that owns the principal means of production, it has always been a small social group. For Marx it was axiomatic that the private ownership of manufacturing or industrial means of production always tends in the direction of concentration – that is to say, to become the attribute of an increasingly restricted stratum, as the process of capital accumulation itself progresses. In this sense, the pure circle of capital proper is virtually always too narrow to act alone as class force: to enter on the political scene, it must endow itself with another gravitational weight, a *masse de manœuvre* in some measure exterior to it. This mass is typically composed, on the one hand, of the gamut of professional, administrative and technical groups that enjoy life-conditions analogous to capitalists proper – everything customarily included in the broader term 'bourgeoisie' as opposed to 'capital'. On the other hand, this same bourgeoisie will normally lack a clear-cut frontier with layers of the petty bourgeoisie below it, for the difference between the two in the ranks of the small employer is often quantitative rather than qualitative. All this very clearly sets the bourgeoisie apart, as a historical class, from either the nobility before it or the working class after it. For all the important differences within each of these contrasting classes, their homogeneity is structurally greater: the aristocracy was typically defined by a legal status combining civil titles and juridical privileges, while the working class is massively demarcated by the condition of manual labour. The bourgeoisie possesses no comparable internal unity as a social group; it forms by nature a more heteroclite structure. We can call this the overdetermination of bourgeois revolutions from within.

Fourth, and finally, capitalism as a mode of production has historically required a national state to impose its stable reproduction over a given territory. So long as this necessity obtained, every bourgeoisie would tend to emerge in potential rivalry with other possessing classes abroad, feudal or capitalist, in struggles between these states. What this means is that every original revolution of capital contained *ab initio*, as part of its logic, a dynamic towards some confrontation and conflict with its external environment. There was unlikely to be any major episode of upheaval in which the presence and pressure of these outer forces was not felt within the process of inner transformation itself. This could be termed the overdetermination of bourgeois revolutions from without.

Everything said so far has been purely formal. But preliminary considerations of this kind make it clear why none of the great turbulences of the transition to modernity has ever conformed to the simple schema of a struggle between a feudal aristocracy and industrial capital of the sort presupposed in the traditional Marxist vocabulary. The porous pattern of feudalism above, the unpredictable presence of exploited classes below, the mixed disposition of the bourgeoisie within, the competitive pressure of rival states without, were bound to defeat this expectation. In that sense, one could say that it was in the nature of 'bourgeois revolutions' to be denatured: these transformations could never have been the linear project of a single class subject. Here the exception was the rule – every one was a bastard birth.

But if this is so, it is also possible to understand as logical and not arbitrary those features of them on which anti-Marxist historians have most insisted. Here we may schematically mention just a few. At their head can come the pervasive presence of agrarian rather than urban classes in the leadership of so many revolutions that Marxists have called bourgeois. For in effect the English, North American, Italian, German and Japanese revolutions were all in different ways dominated by different landowning classes. The hegemonic force in the English Civil War were gentry; the leaders of the American War of Independence were mostly planters and farmers; German Unification was steered by junkers; the Meiji Restoration was led by samurai. The character of these agrarian classes varied widely, of course. The English gentry was in a process of mutation towards a relatively advanced form of rural capitalism by the outbreak of the Civil War; the American colonial landowners a century later were commercial farmers in one region, but more substantially slaveowners in another; the Prussian junkers were rapidly modernizing their estates after the Reform Era, while retaining certain feudal labour controls; the Japanese samurai who led the Meiji Restoration depended on mediated seigneurial dues, but were divorced from any direct part in rural production. In each case, the central role of these agrarian classes of pre-capitalist origin was founded on the evolution or conversion of one type of private property into another. In not one of these upheavals did there ever occur an expropriation of noble lands by the bourgeoisie. No aristocracy ever lost all its wealth or power through the changes they brought; this was, of course, true even of the French Revolution which was not directed, even if it was in part initiated, by the nobility, and which moved decisively against them.

Secondly, these upheavals were characteristically marked by an objective interference of lower classes in the overall interplay of forces. In France, it was the spontaneous peasant rising of 1789 that unexpectedly heaved the whole revolution forward, and the support of the peasantry that provided the mass basis for Napoleon's stabilization; in Japan, village tumults and widespread unrest accelerated the downfall of the Shogunate. In the Low Countries, the unemployed driven by hunger who smashed icons in Flanders set off the train of violence that engulfed Spanish rule. It was the labouring poor in the sansculotte crowds who gave force to the *enragés*, and demanded the Law of the Maximum. The independent organization of the German proletariat in the 1860s critically influenced the option of the industrial bourgeoisie for a bloc with the junker class. In the American Civil War, abolition was finally adopted because of the need to rally a war-weary working class.

Beyond these effects, of course, there was the recurrent phenomenon of an uncontrolled 'petty-bourgeois' radicalism outflanking the aims of more substantial proprietors and temporarily twisting the course of events in its direction: the soldiers and artisans of the New Model Army who demanded the Leveller franchise and legal reforms in England; the shopkeepers and notaries of the Jacobin regime that installed terror and price controls in France; the guild-masters and craftsmen whose Councils of Ten confiscated enemy goods in the Netherlands. In America, the recruits of the Stamp Riots or the Tea Party were deftly mobilized from above; in Italy, students, journalists and small lawyers supplied a commando that always threatened to upset the careful trajectory of the Piedmontese Moderates, although it never finally did so.

The obverse of these multiple tensions and displacements was the curiously decentred or marginal role of capital itself in the pattern of these revolutions. The City in the English Civil War, New England merchants in the War of Independence, the National Liberals in Germany, some of the *chonin* houses in Japan, played key parts in their respective upheavals: but not lead, let alone solo, roles. Paradoxically, the only original revolution firmly and unequivocally dominated by an urban bourgeoisie was the first, that of Holland, which was the earliest and least advanced of all. This was also the only one to produce an exclusively bourgeois state after its victory, although this bourgeoisie was anything but industrial. If we include the American Civil War as a subsequent episode in the chain of these upheavals, then there is one other case of a bourgeoisie, this time truly industrial, which led a revolutionary struggle – not against a noble class or feudal order, however, but against another form of capital which threatened the unity of the existing state; while the results of Northern victory did not even include general relations of free wage labour, let alone more democratic political structures, in the South.

Lastly, we may note the universality of national conflict and imperial expansion in all these processes. The Revolt of the Netherlands was born as a rising against Spanish rule and ended with the conquest of a colonial empire in Asia; the English Republic consolidated itself in the conquest of Scotland, colonization of Ireland, war against Holland,

and seizure of Jamaica. The American Revolution was a struggle for independence against England; the French Revolution unleashed twenty years of warfare against the continental monarchies and English empire; the Unifications of Germany and Italy were accomplished through wars with Austria and France; the Meiji Restoration was triggered by the intrusion of Western powers, and reacted as imperial rival to them, with the annexations of Formosa and Korea.

If we turn from the agents to the accomplishments of these revolutions, what is their balance-sheet? In conventional terms, their achievements were all strikingly incomplete. The only historical task fully realized by them was the construction of a national state. There was no major revolution which did not accomplish this, though with the single exception of the Risorgimento the winning of national independence was always accompanied by the subjugation of other peoples. Socially, no feudal aristocracy was ever destroyed by an ascendant urban class. The Netherlandish squires lived on unmolested in the United Provinces; the English peerage and gentry became the country's premier capitalist class; the bulk of the French nobility either survived the Revolution or was indemnified after it; the Sicilian barons shared power in the New Italy; the Prussian junkers dominated the army and much of the bureaucracy of the Reich; the Japanese *daimyo* became rentier magnates while the samurai seized the helm of the State. The Southern planters alone suffered genuine expropriation, when slavery was abolished without compensation; yet they were merely replaced by parvenu successors. The common fate of the previous ruling classes was not sudden eviction from their property, but a gradual blending with newer bourgeois groups in a common bloc, in which specifically agrarian interests became progressively less important and distinct as industrialization proceeded.

Politically, the spectacular overthrow of traditional forms of rule did not therewith generate characteristically modern ones. The immediate upshot of these can often look modest in retrospect. The Revolt of the Netherlands did not broaden the suffrage or produce a unitary state. The Civil War in England did not redistribute property, extend the franchise or reform the legal system. The first American revolution did not touch slavery; the second achieved no political equality in the South. The French Revolution issued into military dictatorship and monarchical restoration. The overturns in Germany, Italy and Japan created differing types of authoritarian state which passed over in a subsequent epoch, without internal rupture, into fascism. Even the modest proposal of founding a Republic was not respected in the majority of cases. Only the Dutch and American revolutions successfully got rid of monarchies, but in each case the dynasties concerned were foreign rather than local. The last revolutions, in Germany, Italy and Japan, were actually conducted under royalist banners, with an intensification rather than diminution of monarchist ideology.

That declension raises a final issue. The upheavals under discussion can be analysed and compared as a set of disparate, separate cases. But they were, of course, historically interrelated, and the sequence of their connexions enters into the definition of their differences. Their order was constitutive of their structure. At one level, the linkages between them are obvious enough. Each revolution was in some measure a condition or inspiration of the next. The Dutch Republic provided the base for the English Revolution of 1688 which overthrew James II, when an army from the United Provinces stabilized the post-Civil War settlement. The Glorious Revolution ensured the kind of colonial development that issued into the American Revolution. The costs of assisting its War of Independence were the immediate cause of the financial crisis that produced the French Revolution. The Second Empire, declaring its fidelity to the ideals of the First, gave the Risorgimento its first military successes. The threat from Italy divided Austrian armies, contributing to Prussian victory at Sadowa; while the sequel at Sedan yielded Rome to Italy. The American Civil War, meanwhile, distracted US penetration from Japan, helping to create the breathing-space in which the Shogunate could be overthrown; Bismarck's experts advised on the shape of the new Japanese state.

Beneath these surface dependences, however, a structural divide can be discerned. There were in effect two temporalities in the series of these upheavals. In a first cycle, stretching from the sixteenth century to the eighteenth, capital remains predominantly mercantile or agrarian. The time of the Dutch, English, American and French Revolutions belongs to an epoch prior to the Industrial Revolution. In this period commercial landowners or bourgeois notables could usually rally particular popular classes – tenants or traders or artisans – to themselves without insuperable difficulties. Political alliances against the old order mingling proto-capitalist and pre-capitalist forces, in town or country, stamp these upheavals. The French Republic saw the culmination of this type of movement, of which the most radical form became the Jacobinism that left the dreadful warning of the Year II. This first wave of revolutions was generally marked by a spontaneous social turbulence, as successive layers of *menu peuple* erupted into political life from below, without institutional controls, and with unforeseeable consequences. Ideologically, nearly all the great themes of bourgeois liberty and equality were developed in the crucible of this experience.

Why was this so? The answer seems to lie in an underlying connexion between what was still the relative economic weakness of capitalism in its early stages, and the kinds of political violence and social radicalism that in different ways marked these conflicts. One could say that everything happens as if a frontal *political* assault against the old order was necessary precisely because there was still no irresistible *economic* dynamic, capable of carrying all before it, on the part of the capitalist mode of production itself.

With the arrival of the Industrial Revolution in the nineteenth century, a second temporality starts. From the ranks of property there now increasingly emerged industrial capitalists in the strict sense of the term; while beneath them came into being a new working class of factories, docks and mines. Therewith a chasm started to open up between capital and labour which had not existed in the previous epoch: the social antagonism between the possessors and the dispossessed became increasingly less bridgeable. The great convulsion of 1848 failed precisely because it was a last attempt to repeat a traditional scenario, now rendered anachronistic. The Jacobin formula of an insurgent alliance between propertied and popular classes was no longer viable. The memory of 1794 was in all minds, and the effects of industrial change were visible in every large town. The labouring crowds in the cities could now only too easily be seen as a potential threat to the very existence of the bourgeoisie as a class. In France, the July massacres were its response. The continental defeat of 1848–49 marks the watershed between the two 'times' of the revolutionary series. The decade of the fifties saw the first great international boom of industrial capitalism, and set the stage for the second cycle. The subsequent capitalist revolutions in Germany, Italy and Japan – this holds good too for the second instalment of the American Revolution – reveal a quite distinct pattern. The epoch of revolutions from above produced no new political ideas, and minimal popular turmoil. They were not, of course, exempt from violence, but this was now the regimented and manipulated violence of great regular armies, equipped with industrialized means of warfare. Its monuments are the battlefields of Magenta, Antietam or Sedan, with their unprecedented number of dead. The improvised exploits of Garibaldi's Legion are a last, moving memento of another epoch amidst this scenery of organized carnage – just as are the republican and democratic ideals that went down to defeat in the Risorgimento. The dominant ideology of all these episodes was national rather than social: there was no further evolution or significant development of the classical values of the earlier revolutions. What these transformations brought was in many ways a contraction or regression from them. Instead of the banners of Liberty, Equality and Fraternity, the new elites drove conscript masses under the signs of Nationality and Industry.

For while the ideological stress of this cycle fell ever more heavily on the bonds of nationalism, its deeper thrust corresponded to the economic force capitalism itself had now acquired. The massive superiority of machinofacture was a daily demonstration by the second half of the nineteenth century. It was thus the world *economic* strength of the capitalist mode of production – its spontaneous power of social transmutation – which rendered possible the limited *political* thrust of these revolutions. Modern industry had arrived, with all the power of its self-expansion through the world market, and all the advantages – of mechanized means of coercion and communication – it conferred on the high commands of army and state alike. The artillery of commodities could act as a substitute for the promises of the Tennis Court. No deep awakening of popular energies or radical shock against the old order, of the kind witnessed in the first cycle of upheavals, was any longer necessary. In this sense the parabola of what the Marxist tradition has theorized as bourgeois revolutions traces a descending – not an ascending – curve, until at the end of the nineteenth century the cycle of these convulsions appears to be concluded, and the circle of leading capitalist states is provisionally closed.

1976

PART TWO

4

The Figures of Descent

The debates aroused by a number of theses on Britain, published in *New Left Review* some twenty years ago, had at their centre a dispute over the character of the dominant class in Hanoverian and Victorian England, and the nature of the state over which it presided. These were the historical issues most hotly contested at the time, and since. If it seems an appropriate moment to reconsider them today, it is necessary to begin with a reminder. The set of hypotheses then developed in this journal had a clearly stated purpose. They were designed to offer an explanation of the pervasive crisis of British society in the mid sixties. Intellectually, the *explanandum* was the malady of the capitalist order in the UK. The agrarian and aristocratic stamp of English rulers in the era of the Pax Britannica, the subordination of bourgeois manufacturers and mill-owners to them, with all the consequences – economic, political and cultural – that followed from the cadet role of industrial capital in the Victorian age, were the *explanans*. In the controversies set off by these claims, the structure of the argument itself often tended to be forgotten.[1] Thus Edward Thompson roundly rejected the picture of the hegemonic bloc within English society in the epoch of its world supremacy that we had drawn, and sketched in his own alternative to it – just as he no less vigorously refused the image of the subordinate class

1. The principal texts at issue were Tom Nairn, 'The British Political Elite', NLR 23, January–February 1964; Perry Anderson, 'Origins of the Present Crisis', Chapter 1 above; Nairn, 'The English Working-Class', NLR 24, March–April 1964; Nairn, 'The Anatomy of the Labour Party', NLR 27 and 28, September–October and November–December 1964. Sequels included Anderson, 'Socialism and Pseudo-Empiricism', NLR 35, January–February 1966, and 'Components of the National Culture', of 1968, Chapter 2 above; Nairn, 'The British Meridian', NLR 60, March–April 1970, and 'The Twilight of the British State', NLR 101, February–April 1976.

to be found in our essays, in favour of another vision of them.[2] But he did not address himself to the central problem at stake – the origins of the present crisis – at all. It is this continuing question, however, which forms the real testing-bed for a review of our successive surmises today. How far are these compatible, not only with the historical evidence of the time, but with the contemporary pattern of events since?

We wrote as Marxists. Our critics replied to us as – better – Marxists. That was true, for example, of Nicos Poulantzas, as much as of Edward Thompson.[3] In point of orthodoxy, there seemed little doubt as to which side possessed the proper credentials. England was, after all, the classical laboratory of *Capital*. If the industrial bourgeoisie was not the triumphant master of the world of Peel and Gladstone, when British capitalist society soared above all others, where else could it fulfil the destiny of the *Manifesto*? It was consequently assumed that Marx's own view of the matter could be taken for granted – it was also, after all, that of a previous liberal consensus as well. Against this background, our interpretations could appear a heterodox foible without pedigree or prospect, as scant in fact as they must be short in life.

In reality, however, they had precedents of some significance. The problem of the nature of the dominant class and the state of Victorian England was a crux with a long history behind it. Paradoxically, it can be traced nowhere so clearly as in the writings of Marx and Engels themselves. For on the one hand, they did indeed repeatedly insist that the new industrial bourgeoisie of the nineteenth century – manufacturers, millocrats, or middle classes generally – was the true regnant power of the age. At the outset of their encounter with Britain in 1844, Engels asked himself: 'Who then actually rules England?', and replied: 'To the extent that the influence of the actual middle class is on the whole much greater than that of the aristocracy, to that extent the middle class does indeed rule.'[4] When Marx arrived in London in 1850, he was equally prompt to assert that the 'new, more colossal bourgeoisie' that had arisen from the Industrial Revolution 'becomes so omnipotent that even before the Reform Bill puts direct political power into its hands, it forces its opponents to pass laws almost exclusively in its interests and

2. 'The Peculiarities of the English', *The Socialist Register 1965*, republished in slightly fuller version in *The Poverty of Theory*, London 1978, pp. 35–91.

3. See Nicos Poulantzas, 'Marxist Political Theory in Great Britain', NLR 43, May–June 1967, pp. 57–74.

4. 'The Condition of England II. The English Constitution', article written for *Vorwärts* in September 1844, Marx–Engels, *Collected Works*, vol. 3, London 1975, pp. 497–8.

according to its needs.'[5] Commenting on the background to the Ten Hours Bill in the same year, Engels concurred: 'The manufacturers have virtually secured their ascendancy' – 'the landlord and the shipping interests have been sacrificed to their rising star.'[6] If the Whigs were now triumphant over the Tories, Marx remarked two years later, it was as 'the aristocratic representatives of the bourgeoisie, of the industrial and commercial middle class'.[7] But they would soon be eliminated in their turn by the radical Free Traders, 'the official representatives of modern English society', as 'the part of the self-conscious bourgeoisie, of industrial capital', whose objectives were 'the complete annihilation of Old England as an aristocratic country', with its monarchy, army, colonies, church and legal system, and the installation of a rational laissez-faire republic in its stead.[8]

Yet these forthright judgements typically sat side by side with qualifications and counter-indications that were not easily reconcilable with them. Thus Engels in 1844 had also stressed the immense wealth of the English aristocracy, and the power it exercised through its control of the House of Commons, based on a dependent rural electorate.[9] In 1855 Marx was no longer claiming 'direct political power' for the new industrial class, but rather describing the British Constitution as 'an antiquated, obsolete, out-of-date compromise between the bourgeoisie, which rules not officially but in fact in all decisive spheres of civil society, and the landed aristocracy which governs officially', and sought to fix the relationship between the two in a contrast between the policies and the apparatuses of the Victorian State – industrialists determining the former, and so functioning 'politically as the ruling class', while 'the entire system of government in all its detail, i.e. the actual making of laws in both Houses of Parliament, remained safely in the hands of the landed aristocracy'. Marx concluded: 'The aristocracy, subject to certain principles laid down by the bourgeoisie, rules supreme in the Cabinet, in Parliament, in the Administration, in the Army and Navy.'[10] Later Marxists – Poulantzas

---

5. Review of Guizot's '*Pourquoi la Révolution d'Angleterre a-t-elle Réussi? Discours sur L'Histoire de la Révolution d'Angleterre*', written in February 1850, *Collected Works*, vol. 10, London 1978, p. 255.
6. 'The Ten Hours Question', February 1850, in *Collected Works*, vol. 10, p. 274.
7. 'The Elections in England – Tories and Whigs', August 1852, in *Collected Works*, vol. 12, London 1979, p. 330.
8. 'The Chartists', August 1852, *Collected Works*, vol. 12, pp. 332, 333.
9. 'The Condition of England', *Collected Works*, vol. 3, pp. 495–6.
10. 'The British Constitution', March 1855, in *Collected Works*, vol. 14, London 1980, pp. 53, 54.

among them – often tended to take this variant of Marx's verdicts as canonical: the idea of a delegation of power by the bourgeoisie to the aristocracy, to do its governing for it.[11]

But the very text that sets out this idea most fully also contains a curious, casual subversion of it. For in the next sentence, Marx goes on to speak of the aristocracy as 'relatively the most important section' of the British nation.[12] Amidst the disasters of the Crimean War, however, he thought that this landowning class would finally have to sign its death warrant and 'admit under the eyes of the whole world that it no longer has the calling to govern England'.[13] In the event, the 'relatively more important' component of the dominant bloc did not dwindle away in military defeat or economic eclipse, in the subsequent estimates of the founders of historical materialism. Already in 1854, a year earlier, Marx had scathingly noted how well the 'splendid brotherhood of fiction-writers', Dickens and Thackeray, Miss Brontë and Mrs Gaskell, depicted 'the cramped and narrow sphere' in which 'every section of the middle class' moved, 'servile to those above and tyrannical to those beneath them'. Fearful of the working class beneath it, the English bourgeoisie imitated and tried to link itself to the aristocracy. 'The consequence is that the feudalism of England will not perish beneath the scarcely perceptible dissolving processes of the middle class; the honour of such a victory is reserved for the working classes.'[14]

This judgement – irreconcilable with either of the prior two – was no mere isolated shaft of ill-humour. It came to form the predominant emphasis of nearly all the later evaluations of the character and role of the British bourgeoisie by Engels and Marx alike. In 1861 Marx was remarking that since the Glorious Revolution of 1688 'the aristocracy has always monopolized the direction of foreign affairs in England' – scarcely a minor dimension of the political life of the largest Empire in the world – and caustically registering its consequence, a state of affairs which 'emasculated the general intellect of the middle-class men by the

---

11. 'The fact that the "aristocracy" in England appears to be in control of a state with marked feudal features is explained by Marx and Engels as a "delegation of power" by the bourgeoisie to the landowning aristocracy which is "objectively" the "representative" of the political interests of the bourgeoisie': Poulantzas, 'Marxist Political Theory in Britain', pp. 65–66. Poulantzas himself expressed the same notion rather more curtly. For him 'the aristocracy was merely the "clerk" of the bourgeoisie, both in the power bloc and in relation to the State', p. 70.

12. 'The British Constitution', *Collected Works*, vol. 12, p. 54.

13. Ibid.

14. 'The English Middle Class', August 1854, in *Collected Works*, vol. 12, London 1980, pp. 664–5.

circumscription of all their energies and mental faculties within the narrow sphere of their mercantile, industrial and professional concerns'.[15] Seven years after the Second Reform Bill, Engels commented that with the defeat of Gladstone's government in the elections of 1874, 'the new Parliament represents big landed property and money capital even more exclusively' than before.[16] Economically, English capitalism had triumphed completely; but no commensurate political advance by industrial capital had followed. In 1889, on the contrary, Engels could see, in its typical failure to abolish the anachronistic superstructures of the old order, 'the political decline and abdication of the English bourgeoisie'.[17]

Behind these discrepancies, there lay a solid historical grasp of the original compact of 1689 that had laid the foundations of all later development. The Glorious Revolution had created 'a persisting alliance of the bourgeoisie with the majority of the big landowners', a class which was 'not in contradiction with the conditions of existence of the bourgeoisie, but, on the contrary, in perfect harmony with them', for 'in actual fact their landed estates were not feudal but bourgeois property'.[18] Initially, the merchant oligarchy of the City alone was included in the compromise. William III ushered in 'the epoch of the association of the landed aristocracy with the financial aristocracy': ever since 'we find privilege bestowed by blood and privilege bestowed by gold in constitutional equilibrium'.[19] With the 'consolidation of the constitutional monarchy' there began the 'large-scale development and transformation' of English society that culminated in the transition from manufacture to industry, when a new industrial bourgeoisie emerged to claim in turn its political inheritance.[20] The oscillation in Marx's and Engels's outlook starts precisely at that point. In their writings can be found three distinct and disparate evaluations of the political power of the English bourgeoisie thereafter: (i) that this class was itself directly in command of Victorian state and society; (ii) that it was mediately dominant, through the representation of its interests by

15. 'The London Times and Lord Palmerston', October 1861, in *Collected Works*, vol. 19, London 1984, pp. 21–22.

16. 'Die Englische Wahlen', February 1874, in Marx–Engels, *Werke*, vol. 18, Berlin 1962, p. 496.

17. 'Die Abdankung der Bourgeoisie', October 1889, in *Werke*, vol. 21, Berlin 1962, pp. 383–7, apropos passive capitalist acceptance of the medieval City regulation of London's docks.

18. Review of Guizot, p. 254.

19. 'Palmerston', in *Collected Works*, vol. 14, p. 53.

20. Review of Guizot, p. 225.

fractions of the aristocracy; (iii) that it was self-limiting and subordinate in its actions and aspirations. There is a recurring slippage from one to another of these incompatible positions, especially though not exclusively between the first two. But over time, as Marx and Engels lived through the long Victorian stabilization, the accent unmistakably shifted towards the last.

The dilemmas of judgement here neither appeared nor disappeared with Marx and Engels. They can be traced in many of their Victorian contemporaries. Cobden, the apostle of Manchester free trade, excoriated the servility of the industrial bourgeoisie he championed: 'We have the spirit of feudalism rife and rampant in the midst of the antagonistic development of the age of Watt, Arkwright and Stephenson. Nay, feudalism is every day more and more in the ascendant in political and social life. So great is its power and prestige that it draws to it the support and homage of even those who are the natural leaders of the new and better civilization. Manufacturers and merchants as a rule seem only to desire riches that they may be enabled to prostrate themselves at the feet of feudalism. How is this to end?'[21] A few years later Arnold, scourge of the creed of 'material progress' propagated by Cobden, yet more than half convinced of the force of the crusading liberalism he represented, was nevertheless voicing much the same complaint, lamenting the self-satisfied inertia of the philistine middle class from which he came, under governors from a class of landowners he deemed barbarian. 'A Barbarian often wants the political support of the Philistines', he noted, but 'when he flatters the self-love of Philistinism, and extols, in the approved fashion, its energy, enterprise and self-reliance, he knows that he is talking clap-trap.'[22]

The same tensions and contradictions of characterization have been echoed by subsequent scholars and critics down to the present. No student of nineteenth-century Britain has proposed bolder claims for the Victorian manufacturers than Harold Perkin, a historian averse to any sort of Marxism, in his well-known work *The Origins of Modern*

21. Cobden wrote these lines in 1863, shortly after negotiating the Anglo–French Trade Treaty. His biographer John Morley, transcribing them a generation later, added glumly: 'It is too early yet to say how far our feudal society will ultimately be recast. So far, plutocracy shows a very slight gain upon aristocracy, of which it remains, as Cobden so constantly deplored, an imitation, and a very bad imitation.' *Life of Richard Cobden*, London 1908, vol. 2, pp. 480–90. Cobden's view of the British bourgeoisie was constantly pessimistic. 'Our mercantile and manufacturing classes,' he wrote, 'are often timid and servile in their conduct towards the aristocracy and we must wink at their weaknesses if we are to keep them political company': see ibid., pp. 392–3, 342–3.

22. *Culture and Anarchy*, London 1889, p. 77, pages in which Arnold rains down sarcasms on the aims and ideals of Victorian liberalism.

English Society. Its central theme is the 'triumph of the entrepreneurial ideal' after the conclusion of the Napoleonic Wars, realized through a wholesale transformation of morality, education and the state that bent each to the norms and interests of the bourgeoisie which had arisen from the Industrial Revolution. In sustaining this case, Perkin employs virtually the same arguments as Marx himself. For 'the entrepreneurial class ruled, as it were, by remote control' – 'through the power of its ideal over the ostensible ruling class, the landed aristocracy which continued to occupy the main positions of power down to the 1880s and beyond': formulae where, symptomatically, the term 'power' undergoes a curious movement of dissociation and duplication. But the sense of Perkin's account is clear enough: 'It was by persuading the rest of society, or the great majority of it, to accept the ideal of a class society based on capital and competition, not by personally capturing the institutions of government, that the capitalist middle class was able to achieve its aims: free trade in nearly everything from commerce, through land, labour, and appointments under the State, to education and religion.' Hence 'neither contemporaries nor historians have doubted that the capitalist middle class were the "real" rulers of mid-Victorian England.'[23] That would seem to be as categorical and authoritative a conclusion as could be asked for. Yet here too, it proved very difficult to hold steady. By the end of his book, Perkin's tone had changed. For in late Victorian and Edwardian England, he decided, 'the old, virile, ascetic and radical ideal of active capital was submerged in the still older, supine, hedonistic and conservative ideal of passive property.' In an apparent loss of will, 'the entrepreneurial ideal had triumphed only to throw in its lot with the seemingly defeated aristocratic. This belated capitulation, which was from the first in the logic of the entrepreneurial position with its ambivalent emulation of the landed aristocracy, goes far to explain why Britain, the first to experience the Industrial Revolution, should remain the most traditional and aristocratic of industrialized societies.'[24]

Whatever the coherence of these judgements, they rested on a chronology. But a few years later, Perkin's emphases started to list and slide more steeply – unsettling the early and mid-Victorian periods

23. Harold Perkin, *The Origins of Modern English Society 1780–1880*, London 1969, pp. 271–2. Perkin's version of the argument differs only in the mild culturalist twist he gives it – since here it is bourgeois 'ideals' rather than 'interests', as in Poulantzas, that prevail behind an aristocratic façade. But such ideals are in themselves only the medium through which the practical 'aims' of the middle class are imposed.

24. Ibid., p. 436. Note the parallelism again with the declensions of Engels's judgements.

themselves. Far from contemporaries unanimously acknowledging that the middle class were the real rulers of nineteenth-century Britain, Perkin now concluded that 'the myth of middle-class rule had no foundation in contemporary middle-class opinion'. The *Westminster Review* (1833), Bright (1848) and Mill (1871) were all cited to the very opposite effect – on the power of the landed aristocracy over them. 'At all three dates the middle class was vociferously aware that the landowners were the ruling class, and most of them deplored it.'[25] Its weakness could be gauged from its inability, rather than its ability, to achieve free trade in land – where merchants and manufacturers would not follow the agitation of Bright and Cobden, 'the two Gracchi of Rochdale'. The economic decline of the agrarian aristocracy was 'more apparent than real', as 'the big landowners, contrary to popular opinion, grew richer rather than poorer', becoming in the decades between 1890 and 1920 'an integral part of the capitalist plutocracy': 'it would be wrong to underestimate their influence down to and beyond 1940.' Politically, it is 'one of the more surprising quirks of modern British history' that 'it should have been the Conservatives, the traditional party of the majority of landowners, rather than the Liberals, the party (notwithstanding its landowning wing) of the majority of Victorian businessmen, which survived into the twentieth century as the party opposed to Labour.'[26] In other words, the glissade in Marx and Engels has been more or less faithfully reproduced in these pronouncements, based on all the resources of modern scholarship, a century later.

The factual character of the hegemonic class in Victorian Britain was one of the critical areas of contention in the debate over the NLR theses in the sixties. There was a second, however, logically separate but insufficiently distinguished: the exceptional nature we attributed to it. For not only did we argue that landowner predominance was a political and cultural reality from the Civil War onwards; we also suggested that this was a *differentia specifica* of England among major capitalist societies. There were general reasons why that presumption was wrong, as it related to the structural form and historical record of the original 'bourgeois revolutions' themselves, in each principal country of capitalist development. These have been schematically indicated elsewhere.[27] At the other end of the time-span at issue, moreover, there

25. Harold Perkin, 'The Structured Crowd', *Essays in Social History*, Brighton 1981, p. 104.
26. Ibid., pp. 90, 95, 123–4.
27. See Chapter 3 above.

now exists a formidable empirical demonstration of agrarian paramountcy in the ruling orders of every European power down to the First World War itself – Arno Mayer's work *The Persistence of the Old Regime*, which has drastically redrawn the conventional portrait of the Belle Epoque. Mayer not only shows how universal was the political power and cultural prestige of landed or nobiliary strata at the turn of the twentieth century – whether in Germany or France, Italy or England, Austro–Hungary or Russia, for all their other differences. The real force, and novelty, of his survey is its analysis of the economic underpinnings of this durability.[28] Agriculture remained far the largest employer of labour in every country save Britain. Land typically generated the larger part of the revenue of the propertied classes. Industry generally remained small in scale, its principal trades traditional consumer goods – textiles, food or furniture. Modern capital-goods sectors nowhere dominated equity, output or employment in manufacturing. It was on these at best semi-industrialized foundations that the superstructures of aristocratic or notable politics retained their extensive material pedestal.

Looked at, then, with what Mayer calls a 'wide-angle lens', the position of the English landowning class as we had depicted it took its place in a much wider European panorama. This continental context, however, if it has made our descriptions more readily plausible, also leaves their explanatory function apparently more questionable. For if every European capitalism was dominated by social echelons of estate-owning or title-bearing aspect down to the First World War, how could the particular decline that eventually overtook British capitalism – setting it apart from the rest – be even indirectly connected with the traditionalist cast of the English ruling class? The problem of the historical sources of the British crisis in the mid twentieth century then remains intact. How is it to be resolved? The answer must be sought, logically, *at a lower level of individuation* than where we previously located it: that is to say, not in the general phenomenon of landowner persistence, or mercantile association with it, but in the particular patterns taken by these – or other forces and factors – in Britain. Our original theses did include elements of just such a specification: above all, in everything we wrote of the meaning of Britain's maritime Empire for the character of the possessing classes that presided over it. But this dimension of the analysis was never integrated into an adequately

28. See the first chapter of *Persistence of the Old Regime. Europe to the Great War*, New York 1981, pp. 17–79.

comparative perspective as a whole, which would have allowed the nature of the English state and English capital to be more precisely seized. In what direction, today, would a renewed enquiry lead? In my view, the historical evidence that has accumulated over the twenty years since Edward Thompson debated with us strongly vindicates the thrust of our initial intuitions, once these are more firmly situated at the level of particularization they require. To use his own famous metaphor, the conventional verdict of the time[29] – Thompson upheld – appears to have been consequentially overturned in the courts of appeal. To see why this is so, we need to glance at some major findings about the collective dramatis personae whose relative importance and character were in dispute. These will, in their turn, permit a closer approach to the question of what really delineated the figures of the leading social classes in Britain. In a brief overview, all that will be attempted here are a few capsule definitions in each case.

1. Landowners

Traditional agrarian classes either led or survived every major political upheaval that opened the way to the modern capitalist state, not only in Europe but in North America and Japan as well. What distinguished the English aristocracy and gentry in this respect from their counterparts elsewhere? First, this was the landowning elite with the longest consecutive history as a capitalist stratum proper. The English estateholders had no rival in this regard. The divorce of the direct producers from the means of production in the countryside had started to occur much earlier and more thoroughly than anywhere else in Europe, as an unforeseen result of the class struggles on the land in the later Middle Ages.[30] The consequence was the emergence of a capitalist farming geared to the market, employing wage-labour and registering marked increases in productivity, already in the course of the sixteenth century.

---

29. For representative opinions, reflecting the consensus of at any rate the local Left, see Richard Johnson, 'Barrington Moore, Perry Anderson and English Social Development', *Cultural Studies* 9, Spring 1976, pp. 7–18; Keith Nield, 'A Symptomatic Dispute? Notes on the Relation between Marxian Theory and Historical Practice in Britain', *Social Research*, vol. 47, no. 30, Autumn 1980, pp. 479–506, a communiqué reporting 'total victory' on the empirical battlefield for an 'infinitely more accurate' Thompson. The famous passage in which Thompson likened historical to legal enquiry is in *The Poverty of Theory*, pp. 236–7.

30. See Robert Brenner, 'Agrarian Class Structure and Economic Development in Pre-Industrial Europe', and 'The Agrarian Roots of European Capitalism', in T.H. Aston and C.H.E. Philpin, eds, *The Brenner Debate*, Cambridge 1985, pp. 46–9, 292–7.

By the time of the Civil War, gentry agriculture was well on the way to the generalization of this pattern. The full Agrarian Revolution, with the introduction of High Farming techniques and the spread of enclosures, thereafter coincided with the conquest of world commercial hegemony, and predated the Industrial Revolution by a hundred years. The legatees of this good fortune were a unique formation by mid-Victorian times. Their degree of both continuity and closure as a social group, given their economic bases in market competition, was astonishing: its core comprising families that controlled the same county seats over six generations or more. Perhaps less than 10 per cent of major landowners in the 1870s were newcomers since the 1780s; 90 per cent of the largest owed their wealth to ancestral accumulations prior to the coming of industry. An aggregation of advantages, across the board, was the hallmark of these English agrarians. 'They were capitalists although rentiers, innovators although patricians, and, although subject to a heavy land tax, were willing to pursue an aggressive naval conquest of overseas markets. Until the late nineteenth century, they managed to have the best of all worlds: the profits of the entrepreneur and the prestige of the aristocrat; the policies of commercial expansion and the prerequisites of political power; the convenience of a banking system and a monied interest and the protection of Corn Laws and Game Laws.'[31]

There were other, highly successful classes of rural exploiters that also accomplished a conversion from feudal to capitalist agriculture and presided over a spectacular expansion of the state. Prussian junkers and Japanese samurai were the outstanding cases, known and often admired in England by the end of the nineteenth century. But the decisive changes in the life-history of each came later, and their resultant power was more brittle and partial. The Prussian nobility was jolted out of manorial custom and servile labour only by defeat in the Napoleonic Wars. Its Reform Era preceded the beginnings of German industrialization by scarcely more than a few decades. The growth in output and productivity of the corn estates of East Germany between the Congress of Vienna and the Austro–Prussian War, once markets in land and labour were freed, was very fast. But from mid century onwards the rise of the Ruhr was yet more rapid. By the time Bismarck had forged the Second Reich under Prussian domination, the class he represented was not two generations away from its provincial and

31. Lawrence and Jeanne Fawtier Stone, *An Open Elite? England 1540–1880*, Oxford 1984, p. 286. For the statistics of stability, see p. 206, and J.V. Beckett, *The Aristocracy in England 1600–1974*, Oxford 1986, pp. 79, 87.

seigneurial past, and confronted industrialists and bankers manifestly superior to it in capitalist dynamic enterprise. In Japan, the South-Western samurai who created the Meiji state introduced capitalist agriculture at the price of cutting off their class from the countryside altogether, and allowing a new stratum of village landlords to consolidate itself in their stead. Their entry into modernity was much more compressed even than that of the Prussian junkers – just as their origins were yet more regional. In neither case was there anything approaching the long national maturation of English landowners in the ways of capital and the means of hegemony. The Virginian planters of the age of Jefferson were politically and culturally closer to these. But if they lacked feudal ancestry altogether, sharing a yet more undiluted Lockean outlook, they were also tied to slavery – an asset that became an incubus as industrialization proceeded, costing them the federal primacy they had once enjoyed, and pitching them into marginalization and defeat in the Civil War. The British elite stands out from all of these in its protracted and unforced command, over two centuries, of the secrets of improving cultivation and rationalizing rents.

There was a second difference, related to this. The Hanoverian and Victorian landowning class was not only the most stable in Europe. It was also the wealthiest. In Hungary or Russia, Southern Italy or Spain, there were agrarian magnates whose estates could match or surpass those of the largest English peers in size. But even before Emancipation or agrarian reform, the proportion of land controlled by the nobility was smaller, because it coexisted with a traditional peasantry that was absent in England. There the degree of concentration was without equal. In the 1870s, no less than 80 per cent of private real estate in Britain was controlled by 7,000 persons. Some 360 magnates holding estates upwards of 10,000 acres owned a quarter of the land in England. An agrarian elite whose least affluent rung was defined at estates of 1,000 acres accounted for 55 per cent of English soil.[32] By contrast, its French counterpart controlled only 20 per cent in the early nineteenth century, with a lower boundary of 300 acres. In Prussia, too, large estates were reckoned to start at 375 acres, yet their owners controlled no more than 40 per cent of the land at mid century, when the average *Rittergut* was well under half the size of the median gentry

32. F.M.L. Thompson, *English Landed Society in the Nineteenth Century*, London 1963, pp. 27–28, 31, 112–14, who comments: 'We have, then, the seeming paradox of a landed aristocracy which was increasing in material strength, in terms of the balance of property, and in social cohesion, in terms of the expansion of the nobility, in the period from 1790 to the 1880s': p. 44.

estate in England. The Kaiser was to own less farmland than the Duke of Devonshire. In Spain, land-holdings were considered big that were four times smaller than the minimum in Britain, in a territory four times as large – and even so covered perhaps just over half the soil, with major concentrations confined to the South. In late-nineteenth-century Russia, there were some 150 magnates with average estates of 270,000 acres – the most immense tracts of noble land in the continent. But half the nobility owned less than 270 acres, and the aristocracy as a whole controlled only about 14 per cent of the territory of European Russia.[33] In the United States, capital values of the land held by the Southern planter class in the post-Jackson era started at levels that were somewhat less than the rental income of the smaller gentry in England.[34]

The pre-eminence of the British landlord stratum lay not just in the extensive scale of this agrarian property; it also enjoyed an intensive advantage for most of the century. Net yields were 60 per cent above those of any other European country, as late as 1880.[35] The greater productivity of English farming in turn helped to ensure that the rental value of agricultural land was higher than anywhere else in this period. Nor did the good fortune of the English aristocracy end there. Britain was the largest coal-producer in Europe throughout the nineteenth century, and its mines fell predominantly within the estates of major agrarian proprietors, capable of making initial investments in them, and then of securing advantageous leasing arrangements to industrial venture capital. Most significantly of all, the English aristocracy played a role in urban development which had no equivalent anywhere on the Continent. Entrenched in London ever since seasonal residence in the capital became customary in the eighteenth century, and long habituated to provincial spas, landowners in the nineteenth century cornered a lion's share of speculative profits from middle-class urbanization, utilizing the peculiar form of the leasehold estate to extend the West End or develop brand-new suburbs or seaside resorts

33. David Spring, ed., *European Landed Elites in the Nineteenth Century*, Baltimore 1977, pp. 2–6; the richest man in early-nineteenth-century France appears to have been the Duc de Crillon, who left a mere £400,000 at a time when the Duke of Sutherland was worth five to ten times as much.

34. Only the top 15 per cent of Southern estates were worth upwards of $5,000, or £1,000: James Oakes, *The Ruling Race. A History of American Slaveholders*, New York 1982, p. 38. Labour, of course, was more valuable than land to the slaveowner, so that average revenue of the small elite of wealthy planters with fifty slaves or more, at some $7,500, was comparable to that of the English squire.

35. Paul Bairoch, 'Agriculture and the Industrial Revolution', in Carlo Cipolla, ed., *The Industrial Revolution*, London 1973, p. 472.

like Edgbaston or Eastbourne.[36] 'There is no country in the world', remarked the century's leading statistician, 'in which the value of house property to population is so high as in England.'[37] In sum, a landlord class controlling a superior measure of more productive countryside and more expensive cityscape was economically – both on average, in its middle ranks, and at the top of its scale, where mineral and urban rents could swell ducal incomes to colossal proportions – stronger and better endowed than either the ramshackle aristocracies of Eastern and Southern Europe, typically polarized between a princely few and a semi-indigent mass, or the more homogeneous but also more modest nobilities of Northern and Western Europe.

The most important economic fact for understanding the role of the agrarian elite of Victorian society was, however, not so much its strength in comparison with a range of estate-owners abroad, as its elevation over the run of manufacturers at home. The fortunes of the greatest aristocrats towered over those of the most successful industrialist. There were also many more of them. During the first half of the nineteenth century, virtually all those with property proved at over £500,000 were landowners. Until about 1880 these still comprised over half the ranks of the very wealthy in Britain.[38] Indeed, down to the 1920s, no businessmen millionaires ever equalled the opulence of the richest landed magnates. The unfaltering succession of aristocratic Cabinets and landlord Parliaments which dominated British politics for a full century after the advent of the Industrial Revolution was thus no mere cultural quirk or institutional anachronism. It reflected certain real and continuing disparities of material situation. These were, of course, not just to do with income. It was also the case that the peculiar form of English capitalist agriculture, with its triad system of landed proprietor, tenant farmer and rural labourer, typically freed its beneficiaries from detailed or direct estate management, if they were so minded, for easy and often precocious participation in local and parliamentary politics. The Victorian landowners possessed the advan-

---

36. Of 261 provincial towns surveyed by a commission in 1886, no fewer than 103 were largely owned by peers. For the building patterns involved, see David Cannadine, *Lords and Landlords: the Aristocracy and the Towns 1774–1967*, Leicester 1980, *passim*.

37. 'Nor any,' he concluded drily, '(except Russia) where it is lower than Ireland': Michael Mulhall, *The Dictionary of Statistics*, London 1909, p. 590.

38. W.D. Rubinstein, *Men of Property*, London 1981, pp. 60–61. Rubinstein's work on probate records has transformed our knowledge of the patterns of wealth in Victorian and Edwardian Britain.

tages of the rentier over the entrepreneur in this respect.[39] Few industrialists could afford to be so disengaged from the pressures of business; public careers were rarer and started later. Here too, in fact, the position of the British gentry was peculiarly privileged. In the absence of an equivalent intermediate layer of farmers responsible for the organization of capitalist production on the land, East Elbian squires or Deep South planters had to devote more of their energies to the management of output and labour. In England, land meant leisure, and leisure afforded politics, more than elsewhere. A comparison of the House of Commons with the Prussian Landtag at mid century, let alone the French Chamber of Deputies or the US Congress, is revealing. The massive preponderance of landowners at Westminster was not matched in Berlin, where up to half the deputies were civil servants, while in Washington or Paris lawyers already predominated. The parliamentarism of Britain's agrarian rulers was in its turn related to the absence of any longstanding militarism.[40] The English Empire had been won overwhelmingly at sea. There was no tradition of a major land army at home, the principal bulwark of aristocratic interest and influence on the Continent. The military establishment of the state consequently formed an outwork of landlord power rather than a central citadel of it: vital for the maintenance of colonial dominion abroad, relatively marginal for the structure of paramountcy at home. Symptomatically, career officers often tended to come from the neediest and least reputable branch of the class, its Anglo–Irish extension, which provided most of Britain's leading commanders down even to a century later, in a line stretching from Wellington to Roberts, Kitchener

---

39. The role of the landlord was, of course, not simply a passive one in the English countryside: it could involve considerable investment, and always necessitated some measure of mediated estate-management. For a sketch of these activities, see Beckett, op. cit., pp. 142–56, 179–80, 203–4 – a study which takes a compendiously benign view of its subject.

40. Schumpeter, who saw more lucidly than any other observer of his generation the central role of landowning classes in the structures of European power during the epoch of high industrialization, thought it 'best exemplified by the English case.' But paradoxically his general explanation of it applied least to England, for he attributed it largely to the feudal military inheritance of the nobility, 'that ability and habit to command and to be obeyed that carried prestige with all classes of society and in every walk of life.' No fighting glamour attached to business, by contrast – 'the Stock Exchange is a poor substitute for the Holy Grail': the bourgeoisie was thus always at a disadvantage in the arts of political rule. 'Economic leadership of this type does not readily expand, like the medieval lord's military leadership, into the leadership of nations. On the contrary, the ledger and the cost calculation absorb and confine.' *Capitalism, Socialism and Democracy*, London 1943, pp. 136–7. Pertinent though such reflections were, they neglected the material – as well as cultural – reasons for aristocratic predominance in England.

to Alanbrooke, Montgomery to Templer. In the Victorian epoch, the regionalism of the barracks corresponded to the exclusivism of the Chamber, 'the most fashionable debating-club in Europe', as Engels called it. Patrician rule was civilian; its centre of gravity lay in the sovereignty of Parliament.

2. Merchants, Bankers, Manufacturers

Capital's first historical incarnation in England was agrarian. Its second was mercantile. When the landowners themselves had split in the seventeenth century, in the Civil War that sealed their conversion to capitalist forms of development, it was merchants who helped to tilt the balance to their parliamentary wing, frustrating the consolidation of an English Absolutism. The Revolution of 1688 which then secured the predominance of Parliament in the State also led to the creation of the Bank of England and the Stock Exchange, and therewith laid the modern foundations of the City. Hitherto the London merchant community had been a classical trading interest, its activities revolving essentially around the import and export of luxury or bulk commodities. For a century its principal rivals in international commerce had been the more powerful Dutch. The War of the Spanish Succession, allying England and Holland against the threat of French hegemony, transformed the relationship of forces between the two. The United Provinces were drained by the military struggle, while Britain emerged from the Treaty of Utrecht as the world's premier commercial and naval power. Further and ampler colonial conquests followed in India, North America and the Caribbean. Amidst the general boom of the Atlantic economy, London had become by the mid eighteenth century the largest centre of international trade, and its merchants the most prosperous in Europe. Acceptance and discounting houses now lubricated the exchange of physical commodities by advancing credit through 'bills on London'. At the same time the overhead costs of English imperial expansion escalated throughout the century, far exceeding the traditional fiscal resources of the landowner state. The sale of government stock covered the gap. The burgeoning National Debt in turn generated an intense secondary market in these securities, finance and commerce intertwining in a quite new configuration, into which large numbers of gentry investors were drawn. The Hanoverian epoch thus saw an increasingly intimate connexion between the dominant landed and moneyed interests, even if this never extended to social fusion. For all its prosperity, trading wealth did not usually succeed either in buying its way into the ranks of estate-owners, or in stabilizing itself durably into merchant dynasties of its own.[41]

London was the first port and warehouse of the world by the time of Walpole. But it was not yet the hub of international finance. Amsterdam retained this role down to the eve of the French Revolution. Dutch commercial capital, increasingly deprived of its traditional outlets as native exports declined, switched into financial intermediation on an imposing scale in the eighteenth century. Its accumulated reserves and technical experience gave it a critical edge in merchant banking, currency exchange, and speculative operations. When the American War of Independence broke out, over 40 per cent of the English National Debt itself was owed to Dutch investors. As late as 1763, all payments in Anglo–Russian trade had to be routed through Amsterdam, because no exchange rate was quoted between London and St Petersburg.[42] It took the second great contest between Britain and an ascendant France to end the financial primacy of the *Beurs* in Amsterdam, as the first had broken its commercial dominance. The Napoleonic Wars lifted the National Debt in Britain to vertiginous heights – £860 million by the end of hostilities; interest payment on it in the aftermath absorbing 70 per cent of state expenditure. More decisively, however, the combination of the Industrial Revolution at home and the destruction after Waterloo of any barrier or competition to English global hegemony overseas brought into being a quite new form of world economy, in which British manufacturers possessed overwhelming preponderance amid generalized international free trade. As the density of commercial exchanges multiplied between ever more states and regions drawn into a common network, the functional necessity for a central switchboard to direct its flows grew steadily. The regular reproduction of multilateral transactions, in a world economic space segmented into independent political units, depended on the

41. 'For reasons which are still not clear, successful merchants in England did not form a parallel, hereditary, town-based elite, like those of Amsterdam, Lyons or Genoa': Lawrence and Jeanne Stone, *An Open Elite?*, p. 256, who suggest partible inheritance and demographic attrition as possible reasons for the lack of a continuous urban patriciate in Britain.

42. C.H. Wilson, *Anglo–Dutch Commerce and Finance in the Eighteenth Century*, Cambridge 1941, pp. 65–87. Wilson believed that Dutch and English development were quite dissimilar, in that Britain's capital exports in the nineteenth century 'enabled her to sell her industrial surplus abroad' whereas Holland's foreign investment was simply 'a permission to utilize Dutch credits in other countries' – hence 'while finance in England became the handmaid of industrial revolution, in Holland it was to become the mistress of a plundered and bankrupt household': pp. 199–300, 188. The image of the handmaid, as will be seen, is scarcely the most apposite.

existence of at least one major clearing-house of universal scope.[43] English industry and the English navy ensured that there would be only one. Amsterdam, isolated and sidelined by the Continental System, never recovered from the wartime blockade. With the submergence of Holland and the defeat of France, London had no possible rival.

The resumption of gold payments in 1821 laid the basis for sterling to perform the role of a stable world currency, while the Huskisson reform of warehousing in the early 1820s freed London to become ever more the physical as well as financial pivot of international trade. In the first half of the nineteenth century, as the Industrial Revolution gathered pace in the North, the City witnessed a concurrent growth. But although the export dominance of British manufacturers helped to secure the commercial hegemony of the City – which would scarcely have been thinkable if the world's leading industrial complex had been located elsewhere at this stage – the actual mechanisms of the latter did not depend directly on it. For the main weight of the City's development continued to lie in its two principal pre-industrial activities: traffic in government securities, and discounting and insurance of foreign trade – regardless of its origin or destination. There was a disjuncture from the start between this set of interests and those of nascent domestic industry, but little or no immediate contradiction. The City did not raise venture capital for investment in provincial manufacturing. Its strictly banking functions were effectively divorced from the accumulation of industrial capital, whose firms typically remained small in size, and met their financial needs from internal savings or local banks.

From mid century onwards, the City moved increasingly into overseas investment, in a pattern that duplicated its domestic operations – portfolio holdings dominated by government bonds. By this stage, provincial joint-stock banking had evolved to a point where it could provide most of the investment funds for Victorian industry. Two economic sectors thus grew up side by side under the Pax Britannica, without intrinsic structural connexion other than a common imperial framework. At best, the City's export of capital – some of it in reality

43. This is the central thesis of Geoffrey Ingham's succinct and fundamental work *Capitalism Divided? The City and Industry in British Social Development*, London 1984, perhaps the most important single contribution – at once historical and theoretical – to a better understanding of the British fate to have appeared in the eighties: for an appreciation of its significance, see Colin Leys, 'The Formation of British Capital', NLR 160, November–December 1986.

re-export – helped finance foreign imports of British goods, mainly in the underdeveloped world, while its invisible earnings covered the trade deficit. The latter was the more important function, and threw into sharp relief the relations between industrial and commercial capital in Victorian England. For between 1820 and 1870, the heyday of the 'workshop of the world', London's commercial and financial revenues alone – setting aside any investment income earned overseas – grew at a steadily faster rate than the export of manufactures. City profits were 30 per cent of the total value of exports in 1820: by 1880 the figure had risen to 50 per cent.[44]

The result of this two-track development of capital was a marked division within the propertied middle class. As Rubinstein has shown, the bourgeoisie of London was commercial and financial in character, clustered round brewing, stock-jobbing, merchanting, warehousing, retailing and shipping, as opposed to the manufacturing and mining that dominated the North. It was probably more numerous than that of all provincial cities put together, and was certainly wealthier per capita. Generally Anglican and Conservative in outlook, except for its immigrant enclaves, it always furnished the great majority of the largest fortunes outside land – the Morrisons, Loders, Rothschilds and others.[45] By contrast, Northern industrialists were typically smaller figures. Making history and making money were by and large two different things: most of the concerns which helped to reshape British society yielded a good deal less profit for their entrepreneurs than others which tended to reproduce it. Manchester produced a mere handful of millionaires, fewer than Liverpool with its ship-owners, merchants and bankers. Even within the manufacturing sector itself, it was not the pioneering industries – textiles, railways, chemicals – that generated the major dynasties, but those closer to pre-industrial activities: above all, food, drink and tobacco. Thus, just as there were good economic reasons for the political prominence of landowners in the Victorian age, so there were too for the social modesty of manufacturers, separated from the former by a substantial layer of mercantile wealth a station above them. It was not just that 'England's role as the clearing-house of the world preceded its emergence as workshop of the world': much more arrestingly, 'even during the mid-day of Victorian

44. Ingham, *Capitalism Divided?*, p. 97.
45. Rubinstein, *Men of Property*, pp. 62, 68–69, 106–107.

prosperity, it predominated over it'.[46] The contrast with America was marked already by this date. There, heavy industry – railroads, steel, later petroleum, auto – generated fortunes incomparably larger than any agrarian wealth and overtopping those of the richest financiers as well. In absolute size, after the Civil War, the greatest US industrialists had left their British counterparts well behind; by the Gilded Age they dwarfed them. In Germany too, the summits of capital were uncompromisingly industrial, commanded by the Ruhr giants Krupp, Thyssen and Stinnes. It was the absence of figures like these which distinguished the Victorian economy.

3. State

From the Younger Pitt to the elder Gladstone the British State was a logical creature of this triangular constellation of land, trade and industry. The Georgian monarchy was not a mutant of European Absolutism, but a machinery of convenience issuing from the English revolution against it. The Hanoverian State born in 1714 was always oligarchic and corrupt, founded on faction and patronage. But it represented landowner and merchant interests with tranquil assurance and stability, presiding over an expanding agrarian economy and overseas empire for the better part of a century. It was not until its defeat at the hands of the American Revolution – thrown up by a capitalist order in advance of it – that public agitation for reform really gained impetus in Britain, in the 1780s. Such pressures – part bourgeois, part plebeian – were brought to an abrupt halt by the far greater challenge to England's rulers represented by the French Revolution, and the political repression and patriotic mobilization that was their response to it. Yet the Napoleonic Wars – the supreme test of the unreconstructed landlord regime – also witnessed the self-liquidation of the larger part of Old Corruption, and the rationalization of the aristocratic state at its own behest, under military emergency. Patronage was reduced in the offices of government, and paternalism dismantled in the regulation of the economy, with the abolition of sinecures in the one and wage and guild controls in the other. The

46. W.D. Rubinstein, 'Wealth, Elites and the Class Structure of Modern Britain', *Past and Present* 76, August 1977. This was the seminal essay that first announced many of Rubinstein's findings. For comparative observations, see 'Introduction', W.D. Rubinstein, ed., *Wealth and the Wealthy in the Modern World*, London 1980, pp. 9–46.

formal principles of public administration and political economy advanced together. They could do so, with such little fuss, because of the nature of the Ancien Régime itself. There was no major standing army, nor any Absolutist bureaucracy. The machinery of government rested in the localities on unpaid justices of the peace, and at the centre on a minuscule cadre of permanent officials. In 1797, the state possessed some 16,000 civilian employees in all, the majority of them collecting customs and excise. The Ministries themselves had tiny staffs – 26 clerks at the Home Office, 24 at the Foreign Office, 12 at the Colonial Office: nearly half of the grand total of 1,500 central government officials was supplied by War, Ordnance and Navy.[47] There was no huge parasitic outgrowth of office-holding to cut back, contrary to radical rhetoric at the time. The transition towards a modern departmental structure and a more professional civil service could thus be initiated without commotion between 1780 and 1820, before the industrial bourgeoisie was a major force on the political scene. Similarly, it was the landowner Parliament that effectively deregulated wages during the Napoleonic Wars and a Tory Cabinet that liberalized foreign trade after them. The Corn Laws represented the single outstanding derogation from the imperatives of laissez-faire in these years. But as a concession to sectional interest they were of less lasting importance than the return to gold and reform of the Bank of England, which were to entrench the priorities of the City permanently in the Treasury's steerage of the state.

The industrial bourgeoisie forced its entry into the political system with the Reform Bill of 1832, and middle-class radicalism achieved a number of significant goals in its wake. But no major structural change was needed in the state for the purposes of mill-owners or manufacturers. The basic design transmitted by laissez-faire landlords proved eminently adaptable and suitable to the needs of the first Industrial Revolution. The tensions between aristocratic and bourgeois politics within the post-Reform framework did not coincide with any conflict over the role of the state in the common capitalist economy. Just as each social group was programmatically committed to the liberalism of Smith and Ricardo, so each was pragmatically willing to advocate doses of interventionism, as the occasion and interest arose, in a criss-crossing pattern. The Factory Acts were carried by Tory Radicals: the inspiration of the New Poor Law and Public Health Acts was

47. E. Cohen, *The Growth of the British Civil Service 1780–1939*, London 1941, pp. 34–35.

Benthamite. Contradictions such as these were local responses to particular problems within a shared conception of state in society.

That conception was indeed minimalist, by the international standards of the age. The stabilized Victorian State was exceptional in the austerity of its means, and the simplicity of its functions. In absolute figures, overall public expenditure registered nil growth between 1830 and 1850, actually falling in per capita terms. Thereafter it rose a mere 20 per cent per capita over the next forty years – at a time when public outlays more than doubled in France, and trebled in Germany and the United States. By the last decade of the century, the Third Republic and Second Empire were collecting tax revenues at a rate nearly half as high again as Her Majesty's Government.[48] The physical size of the administrative apparatus reflected these disparities. At mid century, the Victorian civil service numbered just under 40,000 – a figure which had fallen to 31,000 by 1861, or little more than the level of 1821. If local government is included, the absolute size of English officialdom did not much exceed 60,000 when Palmerston died. The French bureaucracy of the same period was four times as large – 250,000. By 1881 the British civil service, central and local, had risen to 80,000: by then its German counterpart numbered 450,000.[49] The peculiar profile of the English state owed its origins to the interdiction of a royal Absolutism in the seventeenth century. The creation of an extensive corps of office-holders, heavily but not exclusively recruited from the nobility, laid the foundations for the subsequent emergence of a permanent professional bureaucracy in the continental monarchies. The victory of decentralized gentry rule, through a landowner parliament and unpaid justices of the peace, blocked this path towards a modern state in England.[50] One of the reasons why an Absolutist consolidation failed had been the lack of any collective need for powerful defence forces on land in insular conditions. This strategic determinant, however, continued to operate long afterwards – preventing any militarization of the Hanoverian oligarchy, whose external power remained essentially naval. Thus neither a major army nor a bureaucracy was bequeathed by the pre-history of agrarian power in nineteenth-century Britain. Nor, on the other hand, did the industrial upheaval that now occurred substantially

---

48. Michael Mulhall, *The Dictionary of Statistics*, London 1909, pp. 257–60.

49. These are the approximate figures calculated by Herman Finer, *The Theory and Practice of Modern Government*, vol. 2, London 1932, pp. 1294–5, 1167, who excluded the armed forces, judiciary, police and teachers from his estimates.

50. For a discussion of this point, see the excellent recent study by M.L. Bush, *The English Aristocracy, A Comparative Synthesis*, Manchester 1984, pp. 203–205 ff.

alter the traditional parameters of the state. Just because industrialization came as a spontaneous, molecular process, after a long prior build-up, there was no occasion for official intervention to promote or guide it from above: at most to buffer some of its side-effects.

The result of these cumulative circumstances can be seen most clearly in a threefold absence that separated the Victorian State from its European counterparts. It played no role in the development of the basic grid of physical communication in the new age, the railway system – in every continental society a key infrastructural field for the state, in Britain privately financed. It ignored conscription as a means of mass mobilization for citizenship and war, unlike its principal rivals, relying on pauper recruiting for its garrisons. It deferred any public education long after universal elementary schooling had become established elsewhere. The last of these abstentions was in part the product of an initially favourable stock of popular literacy and skill, at the outset of the Industrial Revolution – one rapidly eroded, however, as a more thorough education spread abroad; but more essentially a result of the confessional division which pitted Anglican and Dissenting brands of obscurantism against each other, to the detriment of any unitary lay school system. Only after 1870 – more than half a century later than Prussia – was there any general provision at all for elementary education in England; and even this did not become compulsory until another decade had passed, when the United Kingdom lay behind every West European country in the proportion of its children in school save Spain, Italy and Portugal. State secondary education had to wait till 1902.

Exonerated from economic, military and cultural tasks that fell to its contemporaries and helped to mould them, the British State devoted itself to the most limited range of traditional duties. Within the budget first place was occupied by interest and redemption payments on the national debt, which accounted for 40 per cent of total outgoings in the half-century between 1837 and 1889. Military expenditure came next, absorbing some 36 per cent of public spending. All the civil functions of government combined received no more than 25 per cent – a residue within which law and justice remained the major items.[51] The key functions of the state reflected this allocation of resources: they were largely imperial. A standing army a little over a third of the size of the French, or later German, was preponderantly assigned to colonial occupation duties: three-quarters of British infantry were stationed

51. Mulhall, *The Dictionary of Statistics*, pp. 231, 260.

overseas. The Admiralty spent as much as the War Office, on a navy that always had double the tonnage of any continental power. But although these were the principal coercing and spending Ministries, they were not the controlling centre of the state structure as a whole.

That role was played in England, uniquely, by the Treasury. Here alone bureaucratic supremacy was identified with, and realized through, financial stringency. From the epoch of Gladstone onwards the doctrine of 'Treasury control' made the Exchequer the real nerve-centre of the state, the dominant department of government enforcing its discipline on all others. But this dominance was not that of a specialized elite; and its spirit was anything but cameralist. Traditionally, the higher reaches of the civil service had been recruited informally from branches of the landed connexion, with no specific training for their posts, within a loose patronage framework. The Northcote–Trevelyan reforms proposed at mid century, but implemented only in the 1870s, groomed rather than displaced this gentlemanly intake. Characteristically inspired by the exigencies of colonial rule in India, they were not intended to democratize the civil service at home so much as to safeguard gentry grip on it, by assuring upper-class privilege more modern credentials.[52] What these amounted to was a superior general culture of literary inspiration, principally drawn from the classics, rather than any particular professional skills in public administration, let alone economic or civil engineering expertise. The purest expression of the state cadre so formed became the archetypal Treasury official.

4. Parties, Intellectuals

The political system girding this social and state order was an institutional descendant of late Stuart arrangements. Until the last decades before the Civil War, election to Parliament had normally been an uncontested affair, a single candidate emerging from self-selection among leading county families. With the religious and constitutional conflicts of the mid seventeenth century, the gentry divided into

---

52. See the remarkable analysis by Peter Gowan, 'The Other Face of Administrative Reform', *New Left Review* no. 162, April–May 1987. A pointed comparison with the Prussian civil service reforms can be found in Hans-Eberhard Mueller, *Bureaucracy, Education and Monopoly, Civil Service Reforms in Prussia and England*, Berkeley–Los Angeles 1984, who concludes that 'civil service reform appeared in a very different light to the contemporary actors' – 'To the Prussian middle-class careerists, it meant gaining administrative power. To the English gentlemen administrators it meant holding on to it': p. 233.

ideologically and politically opposing wings. After the upheavals of Commonwealth and Restoration, something like the same fault-lines reappeared – now taking more self-conscious factional form, as two relatively continuous 'parties' contending for office. The Tories rallied more backward country squires and conservative noblemen in the cause of the Anglican Church and an anointed monarch, the Whigs a grandee layer with connexions to the City, and gentry more inclined to tolerance of Dissent and suspicion of royal power. The long Whig dominance petered out in the final decades of the eighteenth century when urban and popular unrest at home coincided with the threat of the French Revolution abroad, propelling the great bulk of the landed class over to the party of militant reaction as natural organizer of the struggle to defeat Robespierre and Napoleon.

It was thus a Tory regime that presided over the Industrial Revolution breaking through at home during the Napoleonic Wars, and then confronted the insurgent forces of protest and change unleashed by it after Waterloo. After fifteen years or more of pressure and agitation from below, a Whig administration was finally formed willing to introduce an electoral reform. In 1832 the new manufacturing bourgeoisie secured its entry into the political system. But not merely was the working class it had tactically utilized against the old order excluded from the settlement; so was at least half of the middle class itself, in a franchise which was only increased by perhaps 300,000 over a previous half million, and was carefully skewed towards county and small borough seats.[53] The decisive feature of the Reform Act was its limitation of potential urban representation below the threshold at which an autonomous bourgeois party, with a popular following, could enter the parliamentary arena on its own terms. In its origins, the simple plurality rule for electing MPs was a natural procedure in a one-class political system with two parties. But once a second class was admitted, if it could not muster enough strength to win at least half the total electorate, it was effectively forced to throw in its lot with one of the prevailing landowner interests. A handful of Radicals held out against this logic, but the bulk of middle-class reformers were rapidly absorbed by the Whig Party. The founding moment of independent bourgeois representation was missed.

The consequence was a fundamentally unaltered aristocratic ascendancy in English politics. Between 1818 and 1900 there was no increase

53. The total reformed electorate amounted to about 14 per cent of adult males: Norman Gash, *Aristocracy and People*, London 1979, p. 132.

at all in the number of commoners in British Cabinets.[54] When the manufacturing interest did mobilize against agrarian protection, the Anti-Corn-Law League was an extra-parliamentary organization without any direct purchase in the political system. Repeal of the Corn Laws, when it came in 1845, was prompted more by the Irish Famine than by the agitation of the League, and was implemented by a Tory government concerned to prevent the isolation of the landed class, in its own interests, and persuaded that the spread of High Farming would in any case absorb its effects on average rents. Peel's decision split his party, returning the Whigs to power for twenty years. His free-trade policies notwithstanding, manufacturing capital had always felt a greater affinity for the rival party, and settled down easily with the Whig regimes of the 1850s and 1860s under the unmolested leadership of Russell and Palmerston – the time when Marx first observed Victorian politics. Industrialists did not leave the seats of power to landowners out of some historical inadvertence, while effectually imposing their will on them. They remained junior partners in the natural order of things, without compelling economic motives or collective social resources to transform it.

On the other hand, their presence at the Whig side was not an indifferent matter for the balance of the party system. If landowner politics continued to be divided between two traditional contestants, the one that could attract manufacturing and commercial capital was likely to win the upper hand. Not only would the specific weight of urban capital within economy and society inevitably tend to grow as industrialization proceeded; but also much of the new middle class would be better placed, by reason of both region and religion, to enlist a working-class electorate behind it once the suffrage was extended further. This was, indeed, what started to happen once a more modern Liberalism emerged from the Whig chrysalis. Northern industry and non-conformity proved critical in winning the bulk of the workers enfranchised by the Second Reform Bill of 1867 for Gladstone. By the turn of the seventies it looked as if the Conservatives, lacking this bourgeois admixture, might be condemned to semi-permanent minority status within parliament.

In fact, the last quarter of the nineteenth century reversed the position of the two parties. Although there were dramatic economic and social changes in England in this period, these were not – significantly – what triggered the transformation of the political balance.

54. M. Bentley, *Politics without Democracy*, London 1984, p. 23.

That was Home Rule. Just as Tory hegemony had disintegrated with Catholic Emancipation in 1830, and Whig dominance was the outcome of the Famine of 1845, so Ireland once again became the arbiter of British party fortunes once Gladstone was converted to autonomy for Dublin in 1885. By then Disraeli had already demonstrated that Conservatism could gain a middle-class and popular following by adopting the kind of overseas grand-standing that had been Palmerston's speciality. But the dividends of such chauvinism could pass: it took the colonial question within the United Kingdom itself to convert them into a permanent premium. Once Ireland commanded the parliamentary stage, with the rise of local nationalism, the prospect of the Liberal Party consolidating a national dominance, and the industrial bourgeoisie entering into eventual inheritance of it, disappeared. The logic of landlord politics and an imperial state broke Liberalism apart, as Whigs and Chamberlainite Radicals, for their different reasons – landowner solidarity and colonial ideology – bolted to the Conservative Party. The ensuing dependence of Gladstone on the continuing loyalty of a too largely working-class electorate made Liberalism even more suspect to the Anglican sectors of the middle class in the South. The result was the long Unionist ascendancy of Salisbury and Balfour that consummated the century.

This political finale reflected social shifts within the propertied classes as a whole. The late Victorian epoch saw the emergence of an increasingly integrated plutocracy of landed magnates, financiers and brewers. Beneath it spread a prosperous villa Toryism of the suburbs and Home Counties, centred on London. Here an earlier commercial bourgeoisie was joined by an enlarged professional middle class, which played a critical mediating role in the cultural bonding of the dominant bloc. This was the stratum that furnished the bulk of the country's intellectuals. From mid century onwards, the public schools had provided a common education – not to speak of intensive inter-socialization – for sons of the gentry and upper bourgeoisie alike. The values of this education were markedly anti-industrial from the outset: a training for rule, not for trade. Subsequent university reforms at Oxford and Cambridge reinforced these, generating an academic ethos in which the disinterest of the scholar mingled and blurred with that of the aristocrat, and ideals of service subliminally associated the profession of rule with the rule of the professions. The civil service reform nurtured by Jowett was an expressive product of this milieu, organically linking an administrative elite of English intellectuals to the state. In their wider role within civil society, the majority of these intellectuals now articulated the ideology incomparably depicted by Martin Wiener in his study

English Culture and the Decline of the Industrial Spirit. A certain disdain for commerce had been a normal literary, as gentlemanly, stance in the eighteenth century. A fierce hostility to the Industrial Revolution was typical of the early Romantics. But these traditions always had their ambiguities – was their target corruption or trade? industry or capitalism? – which could give them a sharply radical edge. They also possessed their counterpoints – Defoe or Bentham – which might be no less robust and influential. What was new in the late nineteenth century was the secretion of a deeply conformist and conservative cult of countryside and club, tradition and constitution, as a predominant outlook among the intelligentsia, repudiating bourgeois origins and miming seigneurial postures in a synthetic gentility and ruralism extending far into the twentieth century. 'In no country', commented Arnold mordantly, 'do the professions so naturally and generally share the cast of ideas of the aristocracy as in England.'[55] If the patterns of office reflected the distribution of wealth, the bias of culture followed the lines of power in the long Victorian evening.

5. From Sedan to Berlin

Meanwhile a world economic depression had set in after 1873, and an acute agricultural slump after 1882, putting the first sharp strains on the British capitalist order. The effect of the recession was to disclose the limits of the Victorian compromise within which the advances of industry were encased. For it was now that English manufacturing started to lose ground against its major overseas competitors, the United States and Germany – two powers whose simultaneous rise, announced by Northern victory in the Civil War and Prussian triumph over France, was the decisive international fact of the time. Each possessed substantially larger populations – hence internal markets – than the UK, and newer stocks of fixed capital. As rates of accumulation in the Midlands fell below those of the Ruhr or Pennsylvania, and technical initiative passed to North American or German combines, British exports came under increasing pressure in the richer Atlantic markets. Productivity growth in the UK stagnated in the two decades to 1890, and declined thereafter.[56] There was neither spontaneous indus-

55. Martin Wiener, *English Culture and the Decline of the Industrial Spirit 1850–1980*, Cambridge 1981, pp. 16, 47–49.

56. M.W. Kirby, *The Decline of British Economic Power since 1870*, London 1981, pp. 2–3.

trial concentration, nor concerted state counteraction in response. Trusts and tariffs alike remained absent from the English scene, where small and medium business continued on the whole to operate on traditional lines. The country with the most concentrated agrarian capital in the world preserved one of the most fragmented manufacturing capitals. Steel, chemical and electrical industries failed to match US or German sizes of plant or levels of output. Instead of organizational or technological renovation, British industry drew on the assets of empire, settling into an easy reliance on customary and (in the case of India) captive markets. This turn in the pattern of trade was accompanied by a surge of overseas investments. After 1870, capital exports regularly surpassed capital formation at home; by the last years before the First World War, their volume was twice as large. The value of UK holdings abroad in 1913 – no less than 41 per cent of the world total – was probably greater than that of US corporations in 1973.[57] This enormous outflow generated rentier revenues that for a brief Edwardian spell even exceeded the City's commercial and financial earnings. Yet the latter were the real prize of the *fin-de-siècle* economy. The dominance of London within the networks of international exchange binding the world market together increased as Britain's national performance within it slipped.

The prosperity of the City, in its turn, cushioned the crisis of aristocratic incomes when the agrarian depression struck in the 1880s, as an increasing interpenetration of persons and fortunes for the first time occurred at the highest levels of wealth. Protection of British agriculture was not restored, cereal cultivation contracted, and this time lesser landowners were hard hit. But the maintenance of cheap grain imports, while it helped to keep the wage costs of manufacturing down, was mainly determined by the electoral necessities of low food prices for the masses. There was also the general advisability of preserving the good name of British economic liberalism at a time when the balance of payments depended ever more on London's ability to capture transaction profits on international trade. This was not so much a significant victory for industry, which had to pay its own price for the openness of the economy, as a sign of the suzerain influence of commerce and finance. At a time when every other major capitalist state was protecting farms or promoting factories in the interests of national power – the age of Méline and Crispi, the Solidarity bloc, the McKinley tariff – the British State remained true to form. The priorities

57. Ibid., p. 14.

of the Salisbury–Balfour regime lay elsewhere. Non-interventionist *par excellence* in agriculture and manufacturing at home, it reserved its energies for interventions abroad – moving actively enough to seize its share in the division of Africa, and to pacify rural unrest in Ireland. The plane of international competition on which it took its stand was colonial, not industrial.

By the first decade of the twentieth century, the deterioration of British performance in world manufacturing markets had become all too clear. The result was a belated revolt of the newer sectors of Midlands industry based on the metal trades against the official laissez-faire consensus. A mounting campaign for import duties ensued. When Chamberlain captured the Conservative Party for Tariff Reform in 1905, the political hour of heavy industry seemed finally about to strike. But precisely at this point Conservative ascendancy crumbled. Both above and below, there proved to be an insufficient base for the politics of protection. Crucially, the industrial bourgeoisie itself split on the issue. The three principal export branches were still relatively sheltered from the full blast of foreign competition. Textiles (accounting for half of total exports as late as 1914) had the tightly controlled Indian market; coal was not yet challenged in third markets by a German and American output absorbed by domestic demand; shipbuilding, an industry relying on a montage of specialized skills rather than standardized mass production, was directly linked to the blue-water requirements of Admiralty strategy. These older complexes stretching out along the Tyne and Clyde, Mersey and Lagan, formed a Northern industrial pole distinct from the Midlands engineering more oriented to the home market, and remained loyal to Free Trade. So too naturally, and even more resolutely, did the City.[58] National protectionism was anathema to its interest in global intermediation. But it was the popular defection from Unionism that was most decisive of all, in giving back to the Liberal Party its last spell of power. For Tariff Reform in England was not just a straightforward protectionism designed to shield British manufactures from foreign competition. It also involved Imperial Preference, or the promotion of agricultural imports from the colonies. That was its Achilles heel as a political

58. For these issues, see the classical discussion in Bernard Semmel, *Imperialism and Social Reform*, London 1960, pp. 146-8. Why did the City nevertheless remain politically Conservative? Perhaps partly because it reckoned it could neutralize real protectionism if Chamberlain regained office; but mainly because it felt especially acutely the widespread aversion of the propertied world in London for the suspect popular retinue of turn-of-the-century Liberalism.

programme. In Germany or America, modern heavy industry could impose high tariffs not only because it had greater weight in the economy as a whole, but also because protection could either be extended directly to rural producers as well, or combined with a competitive export agriculture – the Bloc of Iron and Rye, or Gilded Age Republicanism. Chamberlain's scheme, by contrast, had appeal only for high-cost colonial farmers. There was no rural electorate at home that could compensate for the urban unpopularity of increased food prices. The cause of industry was thus compromised by the connexions of empire in a way that occurred nowhere else.

Instead of a redressment of the position of British manufacturing, the end of the Belle Epoque consequently witnessed the apogee of rentier returns on overseas investment, and commercial profits on all-purpose world trade. The City, without abandoning its Conservative attachments, prospered under the Liberal restoration as never before. Its banking regime largely ignored the problems of domestic industry, where lead sectors of the future – motor cars or electrical engineering – were stunted for lack of major issue-capital or stable credits. Just as the political sway of landowners in the nineteenth century was a European pattern, but took on a quite distinct conformation in Britain, so the economic dominance of banks was a general rule in the West in the early twentieth century – yet it too assumed a quite special meaning in England. Paradoxically, the capital of world finance never witnessed the world of finance capital, in the Marxist sense of the term. Hilferding himself noted, in his classical work on the subject, how far London departed from the German or Austrian, French or American phenomenon of a fusion of financial and industrial capital, under the control of powerful investment banks.[59] Characteristically, the Asquithian State

59. 'It is sheer dogmatism', Hilferding wrote, 'to take the organizationally backward English banking system, with its division of labour between deposit and merchant banks, as an ideal to be attained', for 'the English system is an outmoded one and is everywhere on the decline because it makes control of loaned-out bank capital more difficult.' He also perceived the connexion between the specific character of British banking and the faltering of British industry. 'There can be no doubt that the different course of development taken by the banking system in England, which gives the banks far less influence over industry, is one cause of the greater difficulty of cartelization in England, and of the fact that when cartels have been formed, they have in most cases involved loose price agreements which achieved extraordinarily high prices during periods of prosperity and then collapsed in a depression. Improvements in the organization of English industry, particularly the growth of combinations in recent years, are due to American and German competition. English industry has been retarded by its monopoly on the world market.' *Finance Capital*, London 1981, pp. 293, 408. Hilferding was much more attuned to the historical differences between the leading capitalist economies than his contemporaries Luxemburg and Lenin, or *a fortiori* Marx: see, e.g., pp. 306–307.

that presided over the very different florescence of City interests, and their predominance within the British economy at large, bestirred itself to confront foreign rivals with real energy only in an accelerated Dreadnought programme to preserve English naval supremacy.

The First World War, when it came, unmasked the real correlations of imperialist power that had emerged by the turn of the century. The Great War was won by the Entente only because Britain ultimately secured the alliance of the stronger of the two rivals to its global hegemony against the weaker – American entry from the West finally trumping German victories in the East. The casting of this die was virtually inescapable for England's rulers.[60] The strategic exigency shielding a maritime empire from America's potential sea-power, the economic linkage of longstanding investments in the US, the cultural ties of a common language and elite descent, the paramount advance of transatlantic industry, all pointed in the same direction. But the price of the long-term option was high, and payment started soon. The war forced a certain state-led modernization of economic sectors essential to the military effort – electricity, chemicals, machine-tools. But the value of British overseas holdings contracted sharply, principally to pay off debts to US suppliers, while American (as also German) industry grew far faster. Peace thus brought balance-of-payments difficulties for the first time, and left the competitive weaknesses of British industry more exposed, without restoring earlier conditions of unhampered world trade. Yet now, as after the Napoleonic Wars but in far more unfavourable circumstances, London reinstated gold as the standard of exchange, overvaluing sterling against the dollar to the detriment of the bulk of UK manufacturers. The vice in which the economic policies of the state were held by the pressures of the City and the Bank thus actually tightened during the twenties.

It took the devastating blow of the World Depression to relax this traditional grip. The advent of the Slump finally forced Britain off the gold standard, and out of unrestricted free trade. By 1932 Chamberlain's programme was in posthumous operation, with high industrial tariffs and Imperial Preference for primary commodity imports. The gradual economic recovery that followed only showed how limited its effects would ever have been, in the absence of a much more thoroughgoing reconstruction of state and industrial society in Britain. Behind

---

60. The option for the United States as ally, and Germany as enemy, is rightly described by Andrew Gamble as a 'momentous choice', comparable in significance to the retention of free trade for the course of British history thereafter: see his admirable *Britain in Decline*, London 1981, pp. 58–63.

the barriers of protection, and with some intermittent encouragement from the Treasury, a wave of amalgamations brought the scale of a number of key manufacturing firms for the first time up to more advanced international standards, creating most of the modern corporations of today. But these benefited neither from any important reorientation of banking capital towards domestic industry – the City essentially redirecting its flows to finance Dominion deficits in the Sterling area rather than into the United Kingdom itself – nor from any great technological or organizational leap forward. The West Midlands and South-East saw the emergence of a new consumer-durable complex. Auto and electrical goods became mass-production industries for the first time. But both remained internationally uncompetitive, lagging far behind their US counterparts, and still constituted only a modest share of total output – less than the declining forces of textiles and shipbuilding. The motor of the relative upswing after 1934 was rather a housing boom that called for little competitive drive, the building trades remaining fragmented and tradition-bound. Even where the giant firm did emerge in British industry, it typically lacked the efficient multi-divisional structure of the American corporation – remaining organizationally a generation or more behind it.[61] The core heavy industries of the economy failed abysmally to overhaul their capital stock or to maintain their export markets. By 1939 British coal, whose productivity had been steadily falling even during its halcyon years before the First World War, was less efficient than Polish or Dutch – let alone German – and had lost a third of its share of world exports. British blast furnaces had not even attained the average output levels of US pig iron prior to the Great War. British shipyards had fallen to about half their part of world tonnage after the Armistice.

Politically the inter-war period was one of renewed Conservative dominance, at its height more complete than ever before. But there was no return to traditional strategic priorities. The Versailles settlement had enlarged the territory of the British Empire in Asia and Africa, and endowed the UK with unprecedented rights of veto and intervention in continental Europe. Yet these imperial gains soon proved illusory. The Great War, itself largely a consequence of the international disequilibrium created by Britain's relative loss of power, had in turn weakened the real foundations of English capitalism further. The economic sinews for martial claims on the old scale had disappeared. The

61. D.F. Channon, *The Structure and Strategy of British Enterprise*, London 1973, p. 68.

Washington Conference brought this brutally home. Under US displeasure England was forced to abandon its alliance with Japan in Asia, without any counterpart, and to accept naval ratios that formally codified its reduction to parity with America.[62] The Far East was the most distant of imperial theatres. But in Europe itself, a second round of German expansionism met only emollience and retreat – inspired partly by class solidarity with the new order in Berlin, and partly by Treasury fears for the financial consequences of rearmament, but above all prompted by the collective apprehension of the authorities in London at the prospect of what another global conflict would bring for the Empire. While New Deal and Nazism were transforming the economic role of the state with public works programmes and deficitary budgets, the Baldwin–Chamberlain regime was distinguished mainly by the highest levels of social insurance in the West: crabbed welfare, amidst mass unemployment, rather than directed growth. Only in the final countdown to hostilities did the British State muster the will to start to reorganize the aircraft industry – its sole interventionist initiative of significance in twenty years.

The Second World War, so long foreseeable, repeated the experience of the First at a lower loop down the same spiral. England escaped defeat in 1940–41 thanks, once again, to its compact with the United States. But the military struggle with Germany revealed, now far more starkly than ever before, the calamitous state of much of the equipment and organization of British industry. Total manufacturing output actually rose less than 5 per cent during the War – while the rate of German increase was at least sixfold higher: a differential that widened to tenfold in the engineering industries. Even in the enormously expanded aircraft industry, on which Britain's defence above all depended, peak productivity was a fifth below that of Germany, and less than half that of the United States. It was, indeed, American patronage alone that allowed the reconversion of the British economy for an effective war effort at all. In 1940–41 shipments of US machine-tools to the UK ran at half the volume of native production; two years later imports of American radio equipment were reckoned to equal four-fifths of local output, in a vital industry where pre-war British productivity had been less than a quarter of its transatlantic counter-

62. For a savage critique, from imperial assumptions, of the whole inter-war logic that led from the Washington Conference to the arrival of Lend-Lease, see Corelli Barnett, *The Collapse of British Power*, London 1972, esp. pp. 250–73, 188–93, a philippic without equal in the whole literature on British decline.

part.[63] But US technology and matériel came at a crippling price. Washington fine-tuned its aid with more or less cold calculation to shore Britain up as a forward barrier against German domination of Europe, yet whittle it down as an economic and territorial competitor in the world at large. As London's financial reserves were expended and its overseas assets liquidated, and it was forced to pledge an end to imperial preference, economic autonomy drained away and present alliance became future subordination. Russian entry into the War, which eventually overthrew the Third Reich, could not alter the basic terms of the relationship henceforward set between the Anglo-Saxon powers. The compact was one between capitalisms: the emergence of a formidable anti-capitalist power would only reinforce it.

Politically, however, the decisive fact for British society was nevertheless the simple survivor – if not victor – status of the United Kingdom itself, as Soviet troops entered Berlin in 1945. For peace brought with it a record that was truly unique in the ranks of all the major capitalist powers. Among them, Britain alone had now never experienced a modern 'second revolution', abruptly or radically remoulding the state inherited from the first. For between the initial bourgeois revolution that breached the old order and the final completion of bourgeois democracy as the contemporary form of the capitalist state, there typically lay violent intervening convulsions that extended the work of the original upheaval and transformed the political framework of the nation. In that sense, the notion of 'bourgeois revolution' can neither be confined to a single primordial episode, nor made coeval with a continuous evolutionary process. Rather, the historical genesis of the modern bourgeois state has normally taken the pattern of a series of successive ruptures with the existing settlement, concentrated in their rhythm and coercive in their impact, remedying the omissions or reversing the defeats of their predecessors.

The English revolution was no exception. The Great Rebellion, cancelled by the Restoration, was followed within a generation by the Glorious Revolution. The singularity of the British case lay simply in the rapidity and finality of the sequel, a century before the advent of industrial capitalism itself. After 1688 the state was never again

63. Corelli Barnett, *The Audit of War*, London 1986, pp. 60, 146, 159, 170; for the pre-war record in coal, iron and steel and ship-building, pp. 71, 921, 111. Barnett's latest work constitutes the most detailed and devastating panorama of the misery of British industry yet to have appeared, and the most radically wounding to national illusions. It is composed at a historical depth that makes previous treatments seem indulgent sketches by comparison.

formally altered, nor was a new Constitution ever proclaimed. Rather, piecemeal reforms of suffrage or administration, in homeopathic doses, slowly modified the structures of traditional power and privilege, without ever radically redrawing them at a stroke. The experience of every other major capitalist state was very different. Two centuries after the Revolt of the Netherlands, an ossified magistrate oligarchy was evicted by the Batavian Republic. The French Revolution was followed by the Parisian risings of 1830 and 1848, putting an end to the Restoration and the July Monarchy, and by the military defeat and popular insurrection of 1870–71 which ushered in the Third Republic. The American War of Independence found its completion in the far bloodier Civil War a century later. The Bismarckian monarchy disintegrated in the November Revolution. Then, in the vortex of the Second World War, not only Germany but Japan and Italy, France and Holland, all saw their states smashed by foreign invasion and occupation. Allied victory brought agrarian reform to Japan, partition to Germany, the republic to Italy, universal suffrage to France. The final clearance of the social and institutional landscape that had prevailed down to the First World War – the whole scenery surveyed by Mayer – was only accomplished in the Second. The general significance of these 'revolutions after the revolution' was everywhere the same. They were essentially phases in the modernization of the state, which thereby permitted a reinvigoration of the economy. The most conservative or regressive social elements of the ruling order – Dutch regents, Southern slaveowners, French legitimists, Japanese landlords, Prussian junkers, Italian latifundists – were eliminated, amidst a drastic recomposition of the dominant bloc. Something like a fresh historical start occurred, at the summit of society. Britain alone was exempt from this process, throughout the whole epoch of industrialization which it pioneered. In a Paretian vocabulary, it was bound in the long run to suffer from its poor circulation of elites. In the post-war epoch, the still aristocratic tone and origins of its hegemonic stratum were an anachronism in a world in which its German or Japanese equivalents, once a good deal more feudal or patriarchal than England's rulers, had become pure business classes, bourgeoisies without vacillation or varnish. States whose pedigrees went no further back than the Declaration of Casablanca were to have a decided advantage over one that traced its ancestry to the Bill of Rights. No 'gale of creative destruction' had blown through the creaking political timbers of the United Kingdom for nearly three centuries when the victorious powers met at Potsdam.

6. Workers

Just at this moment, as Germany was being divided, the election of a majority Labour Government brought a new entrant onto the scene. The principal party of the British working class now for the first time took undivided charge of the affairs of the state. Labour's platform appeared to hold out the prospect of a deliberate and wide-ranging transformation of British capitalism. The advent of the Attlee administration was the culmination of a long prior history, the particular experience of the workers' movement in Britain since the Industrial Revolution. What was the character of that movement by the mid twentieth century, as a candidate for altering the direction of the country?

The early English proletariat of the first half of the nineteenth century was socially still composed in the main of hand-workers and artisans, in industries where the machine-driven factory was the most advanced rather than the most typical unit. Economically it was subjected to the harshest tyrannies of the first industrial capitalism – dispossessed of its skills and deprived of its traditional ways of life, packed into urban slums, pitched into violent depressions and cyclical unemployment. Politically it was excluded from representation, without vote or legal purchase on the state. Culturally it pre-existed modern socialist ideology, which its struggles helped to bring into being. Successive popular revolts, each different in form and broader than the last, broke unavailingly against the ruling order: from Jacobin conspiracy to Luddite anger, from Owenite cooperation to Chartist insurgency, when working-class radicalism finally – all too briefly – joined together rejection of constitution and of capital in a movement explosively close to a political socialism. Armed repression and patriotic mystification, civic tradition and material concession, combined in varying admixtures at different moments, wore down these challenges in the end. The English 1848 closed a history. This first working class, not only in Britain but in the world, left a great memory but little organizational legacy behind it.

It was the second half of the nineteenth century that saw the emergence of a labour movement, as distinct from a proletarian identity, with some institutional stability and continuity. By now the weight of factory labour was more central in the class a whole, even if still far from preponderant. A stratum of skilled workers had emerged, enjoying enough material and social privileges to separate their outlook from the mass of the labouring population. Average wages rose above the level of previous decades, as capital accumulation acquired broader bases in the mid-Victorian boom. These socio-economic changes in the composition and condition of the working class were accompanied by its limited admittance to the political system, when the suffrage was extended first in 1867 and then in 1884 to its more prosperous sections. The formation of a relatively self-enclosed proletarian culture followed. By the turn of the century much of the basic cast of the modern British labour movement was set.

Two features, above all, characterized it. On the one hand, it achieved a degree of industrial organization ahead of its counterparts elsewhere. This never embraced the majority of unskilled or casual labourers. British trade unions were originally craft associations of skilled workers; and even after the emergence of industrial and general unions, these long remained the centre of gravity of the movement. Workplace organization was strong, in an economy whose typical enterprise units were still small, and bargaining was decentralized. The labour process became a terrain of class contention and customary entrenchment at a technological stage prior to the coming of the mass-production industries of the second industrial revolution.[64] At the point of production, capital lost unfettered control over the disposal of plant and workforce before it had reached the age of electricity and petroleum, across much of British manufacturing. By 1914, after the upsurge of a new syndicalist militancy, nearly a quarter of the workforce was unionized – about double the proportion in Germany or the USA, and four times that in France; in a country where the working class, in the absence of peasants or farmers, was itself a much larger proportion of the total population.[65] This was a qualitative difference in economic strength, making British trade unionism one of a kind in the final years before the First World War.

On the other hand, the political projection of labour was exceptionally weak. By the end of the 1870s, Britain had the most restricted franchise of all the major capitalist powers: no more than 60 per cent of adult males possessed the suffrage as against universal masculine

64. This basic point is made most clearly by A. Kilpatrick and T. Lawson, 'On the Nature of Industrial Decline in the UK', *Cambridge Journal of Economics*, vol. 4, no. 1, March 1980, pp. 85–102. They emphasize, correctly, that it was not just the early implantation but also the evolutionary continuity of British unionism – uninterrupted by any equivalent of fascism, occupation or American Plan – which was critical to its effects on industry. But they tacitly overstate the causal importance of these on the overall trajectory of the British economy, by isolating them from the organization of capital.

65. G.S. Bain and R. Price, *Profiles of Union Growth: A Comparative Statistical Portrait of Eight Countries*, London 1980, pp. 37, 88, 133, 142.

entitlement in Germany or France, and in the USA (soon restricted again to Whites). Even after the Third Reform Act in 1884, less than half the working class – excluding women – could vote. This gradual and only partial inclusion into the constitutional order was a resultant of both pressure from below and calculation from above. Its effect was to filter the most advantaged and respectable layers of the working population from the rest of the poor and exploited. The combination of higher wages associated with imperial power, and civic freedoms identified with a national heritage prior to landlord or capitalist rule, had already quietened impulses of popular rebellion by the time of the Great Exhibition. The subsequent integration of the upper levels of the working class into an electoral system in which a pair of traditional parties vied under first-past-the-post rules thus simply allowed the more bourgeois of the two to acquire a proletarian ballast. Politically, British labour as an organized force was a captive client of the Liberal Party down to the end of the century, even if a sizeable section of the working-class electorate persistently voted Conservative. This peaceable submission to the parties of the ruling bloc was equally singular for the age, as Marx and Engels frequently and sharply pointed out. 'No real labour movement in the Continental sense of the word exists here', Engels noted in 1879.[66] Fifteen years later, his verdict was much the same: 'These English workers with their sense of imaginary national superiority, with their essentially bourgeois ideas and viewpoints, with their "practical" narrow-mindedness, with their leaders steeped in parliamentary corruption, can really drive one to despair.' Even if, he thought, things were by now moving forward somewhat, it was still the case that 'the "practical" English will be the last to arrive'.[67] By then Germany and France, Italy and Sweden, Belgium and Austria all had independent socialist parties with a mass following. Even in the United States, where industrial struggles were far more numerous and volcanic than in Britain in the late nineteenth century, but working-class politi-

66. Letter to Bernstein, June 1879, in *Werke*, vol. 34, Berlin 1966, p. 378. 'Hence I do not think you will miss much if for the present you do not receive any report of the activities of the trade unions here.'

67. Letter to Plekhanov, May 1984, in *Werke*, vol. 39, Berlin 1968, p. 248. British delusions of self-importance nevertheless started early on the Left, as Engels was aware. 'For your entertainment – Mr Sidney Webb, Professor of Political Economy at the Workingmen's College, who has also refuted Marx's theory of value, said: "We are only 2,000 socialists in England, but we are doing more than all the 700,000 socialists in Germany" ': Letter to Liebknecht, April 1889, in *Werke*, vol. 39, p. 186.

cal action was very limited, New York nearly elected a socialist mayor at a time when London was a fief of triumphalist Toryism.[68]

It was a shift in the dispositions of the dominant bloc above more than any autonomous movement below that eventually disrupted the attachment of British labour to the established order. Following the Liberal split over Ireland and general drift of commercial and financial capital to the Conservatives, Salisbury rallied the bulk of the possessing classes on a platform of confident reaction. It was the industrial repercussions of this political change which eventually led to an independent labour politics. After a decade of Conservative consolidation, employers launched a broad attack on the unions' strength in the 1890s, culminating in the defeat of the engineers' strike of 1897 and the government-inspired Taff Vale decision of 1901 rescinding union legal rights. Denied parliamentary alternation by the Liberal eclipse, and threatened with industrial constraint by Tory belligerence, the TUC finally moved to set up a Labour Representation Committee of its own – though still as a modest outrider of Liberalism, negotiating for a few seats with it. There was to be no mention of socialism. In 1906 a handful of working-class MPs were elected amidst a Liberal landslide: 'The new Labour Party had arrived on the political scene not as the grave-digger of Liberalism, but as an integral part of a great Liberal revival.'[69]

The New Liberalism, rendered more responsive than the old to mass poverty and insecurity by its years in the wilderness, advocated state intervention to contain social unrest. The Asquith governments, while refusing any departure from free trade to contend with economic competition from abroad, inaugurated a bureaucratic insurance scheme and modest welfare measures to stabilize the labour force at home. The Labour Party was inducted into national politics under this dual aegis. It accepted the Liberal reforms uncritically, including their clipping of popular autonomies, and did not even demand extension of a suffrage that still excluded a large majority of the population. By 1914, after eight years of docile acquiescence in the politics of Asquith, Churchill and Lloyd George, the Party had only just come round to the idea of electoral independence from the Liberal machine – while most

68. Between 1885 and 1910 Unionism dominated over two-thirds of the parliamentary constituencies in London: Henry Pelling, *The Social Geography of British Elections 1885–1910*, London 1967, pp. 26–59.

69. James Hinton, *Labourism and Socialism*, Brighton 1983, pp. 74–75: the finest synoptic account of the modern British labour movement, and its relations with the wider working class, that we now have.

of the unions still hankered for its patronage. Yet the same years had seen the most turbulent upsurge of industrial militancy in national history. The British working class down to the First World War thus remained, in a sense, the mirror opposite of the German. In the Second Reich, the general weakness of union organization in heavy industry, toughly policed by more intransigent employers, was compensated by the massive strength of the SPD in the electorate:[70] by 1903, the largest single party in the country. In Edwardian England, a tiny Labour Party without even a nominal socialist commitment coexisted with a union movement firmly embedded in the structures of a more decentralized production. The political subordination of British labour stood out in any comparative perspective. In the United States itself, there was a mass Socialist Party with 120,000 members and a million voters.

The First World War transformed this situation. Once again, however, the fundamental change that it produced in the prospects of labour occurred without its volition, in the sphere of bourgeois politics above it. During the War the unions were coopted without difficulty into the military effort, their numbers growing as employment expanded in the arms industries. The Labour Party never deviated from social patriotism, eventually joining the Conservatives themselves in the Lloyd George Coalition. But the War destroyed the Liberal Party, in a second split which removed it permanently from the scene as a major force in British politics. The consequence of its sudden demise was that post-war Labourism inherited the space left by Liberalism, without ever having to engage in a direct contest with it. This circumstance was in the long run to be much more crucial for the character and course of Labourism than the immediate conjuncture in which the party acquired a new constitution and programme in 1918. By then shop-steward resistance to wartime wage controls and labour 'dilution' had broadened into a more widespread radicalization, as official militarism fell into discredit. Against a background of increasing industrial turmoil, the Labour Party now formally committed itself to the goals of Clause Four and emerged as the main challenger to the post-war Coalition regime. At the same time, however, its new constitution formally ratified the absolute dominance of the unions inside the party with a voting structure unlike that of any European social democracy, which effectively neutralized the admission of individual members. The organizational nexus tying the trade-union and parliamentary institutions

70. See the pertinent remarks of David Blackbourn and Geoff Eley, *The Peculiarities of German History*, Oxford 1984, pp. 107, 268. In 1903, when the Free Trade Unions still numbered fewer than a million members, the SPD gained 31.7% of the national vote.

of labourism together did not mean any practical unification of industrial and political struggles. Quite the reverse: they were rigidly separated in the ideology of the movement, each wing defining its arena of activity as off-limits to the other – in the familiar duo of economism and electoralism that came to define Labourism.

The result was a dialectic of desynchronization in popular experience itself in the inter-war period. The great industrial upsurge after the Armistice, which had seemed at moments to threaten the very basis of the social order, was rolled back by 1922. In the aftermath of its defeat, a first minority Labour Government was elected in 1924 – only to be ousted within a few months. Two years later the General Strike broke out in solidarity with the miners' fight against wage reductions. After it had been crushed by Baldwin and Churchill, a second Labour administration was formed in 1929 – only to split in 1931 over cuts in unemployment benefit resisted by the unions, amidst the Great Depression. From the mid thirties onwards the Labour Party and the TUC alike recovered to pre-slump levels of strength, but there was no resurgence of militancy on the shopfloor nor any electoral breakthrough in sight. The balance-sheet between the Wars was very limited. About a third of the workforce was now unionized, and about a third of the electorate voted Labour. The party's polling strength was still largely restricted to the older industrial regions of the North, although London was captured in 1934. Two ephemeral Labour administrations had failed to leave any mark, the second exhibiting a paucity of response to the Slump that made Liberal politics look heterodox. There had been no equivalent of the German or Austrian experience of constitution-making; the Swedish programme of public works; or the French introduction of the forty-hour week and paid holidays. The main achievements of British labour remained indirect and defensive. The beginnings of social security designed by Lloyd George were extended by Chamberlain: concessions that mitigated the depth of the Depression and the harshness of Conservative rule. But gains such as these were also prophylactic measures that redounded to the benefit of their sponsors. Half the working class still voted Conservative by the end of the thirties, and a third consecutive electoral victory for the Tories was impending when the Second World War broke out.

Military defeat in Norway brought Labour into government as a junior partner in a comprehensive coalition under Churchill. The five years of wartime administration that followed were Labour's real baptism in office. Cocooned within a nationalist concert, it acquired credentials of safety and reliability it had hitherto never possessed, however moderate its policies. Control of the Ministry of Labour allowed it to promote unionization and collective bargaining, while maintaining a close restraint on wage struggles. Otherwise its policy contributions were very limited. The Churches had more influence on a feeble and belated Education Act, which did nothing to remedy Britain's international deficiencies. Yet just as Labour had profited from the break-up of Liberalism as a governing party during the First World War, it now benefited from the fall-out of Liberalism as an intellectual force. The two key innovations of the war years were both the work of major Liberal thinkers strategically placed within the state machine: the reformed budget designed by Keynes for the Treasury in 1941, based on new-style national income accounting, and the report on Social Security produced by Beveridge in 1942, promising minimum public standards of material provision for all citizens. The twin foundations of the post-war political settlement – counter-cyclical demand management and a welfare state – were thus laid independently of Labour, in a civil-service-initiated consensus.[71] In the more egalitarian social climate created by the military struggle against fascism, however, the potential advantages of these changes naturally tended to go in the direction of the Left.

The Second World War thus transformed Labour's position within British society in two fundamental ways. Each came, not as the fruit of conscious purpose or collective struggle, but as a historical windfall. The party was initiated into power without having to mobilize for it; and it acquired a programme for government without having to originate the ideas behind it. Moreover, Labour in 1945 inherited a popular radicalization it had done little directly to stimulate, before which it could present itself as the responsible continuator of the social changes the War had put on the national agenda. The result was to lift the electoral barriers that had held it to a minority position in the inter-war period. Not only the bulk of the working class but also a significant section of the lower middle and professional classes rallied to Labour for the first time – a change noticeably reflected in its parliamentary delegation. The Party's share of the total vote – 48 per cent – was below the peak levels achieved by the Norwegian or Swedish labour movements of the time, but the electoral system gave it the largest parliamentary majority – 61 per cent of seats – ever enjoyed by a social

71. Paul Addison, *The Road to 1945*, London 1975, remains the outstanding exploration of the gradual bureaucratic metabolism behind the Attlee experience. Addison speaks of Labour's 'dual mandate', from above and from below, when it took office, and rightly stresses the legacy of wartime nationalism for the climate that annealed them: pp. 16, 276.

democratic party to date.[72] The 'lag' in the political record of the British working class had been made good with a vengeance.

What use did the Labour Government make of its victory? Its priorities were social welfare and economic reconstruction. The most significant achievements of the Attlee administration were the creation of a National Health Service that went somewhat beyond the limits projected by Beveridge, within a social security system whose conceptions were otherwise uncritically adopted from him; and the maintenance of near-full employment with a series of Keynesian budgets, facilitated by the establishment of a public sector that mainly comprised declining or deficitary industries. There was little ruling-class opposition to most of these measures. Their most significant long-term effect was to consolidate the bargaining power of British trade-unionism, in tight labour markets with a social wage. The defensive strength of the working class within British capitalism was considerably increased, even if the unions themselves were leashed by the Labour Government in the name of a necessary austerity. The general configuration of British capitalism itself, however, was left essentially untouched. No major redistribution of income occurred. Wartime controls were switched *ad hoc* from arms production to an export drive which scored early short-term successes as continental Europe lay devastated. But there was neither overall planning nor state action to increase the volume of investment in British industry, which in key sectors actually fell behind pre-war levels. The stock of undestroyed capital which gave Britain its international advantage underwent no thorough renovation, of the sort imposed elsewhere. The whole effort of Labour's rule was not to transform the historic structures of Britain's imperial economy, much less state, but to restore them.

Restoration, after the gigantic costs of the World War itself, necessarily meant diminution. To achieve it, two fundamental changes had to be accepted. American tutelage – a 'special relationship' with the USA which at once guaranteed and controlled the UK's role in the world at large – was the first and far the most decisive. Latent during the fighting itself, when sentiment and self-deception helped to obscure its reality for Churchill, it became overt immediately after the conclusion of hostilities, when Truman peremptorily terminated Lend-Lease. The ensuing financial crisis then forced London to accept an American loan secured by Keynes; the price was the abandonment of Imperial

72. A figure never approached till the Spanish Socialists won 58 per cent of the Congress of Deputies in 1982, with 48 per cent of the vote.

Preference. The second change was the loss of India, whose independence was now strategically unavoidable, given the balance of military and political forces in the sub-continent. Labour was better suited than the traditional Conservative custodians of empire to negotiate the rapid conclusion of both these transformations. Within the shrunken framework they set, however, British pretensions were by no means abandoned. The Attlee regime was an active initiator of the Cold War against Russia in Europe, playing a central role in the creation of NATO – a brainchild of Ernest Bevin. At the same time it sought military autonomy within the new Atlantic Alliance by the development of its own nuclear arsenal. Where colonial wars could still be won, they were fought – as in Malaya, far the most profitable single possession of the pre-war period. But the limits of British overseas action were now much narrower. In Palestine, in Greece and in Iran the baton of command and counter-revolution had to be passed, more or less reluctantly, to the United States. The underlying reality was that the principal condition of Britain's continued empire after the Second World War was its glacis function for US global domination. Its cost, on the other hand, was to be the frustration of any chance that the UK economy would keep its conjunctural competitive edge. Just as the period began with the abrupt cancellation of Lend-Lease, so it ended with the imposition of massive rearmament for war in Korea – a region in which England had no traditional or strategic interest whatever. In effect, decisions in Washington opened and closed the cycle of reformism in London. In 1950 Britain's engineering industry and Labour's political unity were alike sacrificed to the role of imperial subcontractor by the Attlee administration.[73] The first majority Labour government expired under a military budget so large it had to be pruned by the Conservative administration that succeeded it.

How little Labour had modified the basic coordinates of British capitalism was shown by the smoothness of the transition back to a decade and more of Conservative rule. The traditional governing class, personified by the Prime Ministers of the time – Churchill, Eden, Macmillan, Home – returned to the helm of the state, placidly accepting welfare and full employment as consensual goals of the post-war settlement. Industrial controls – already semi-dismantled by the end of the Attlee era – were abolished, as the UK entered the slipway of the world boom of the fifties and sixties. Far the most important change of

73. For the economic consequences of Korean rearmament, see Sam Aaronovitch, Ron Smith, Jean Gardiner and Roger Moore, *The Political Economy of British Capitalism*, London 1981, pp. 70, 77.

the Conservative years, however, was the revival of the City after its hibernation during the War. The mechanisms of the Sterling Area provided the dollar deposits, extracted from Commonwealth exports, necessary for the maintenance of the pound as an international reserve currency. But a recovery of the City's historic role required liberalization of its transactions as a world commercial and financial centre. In 1951, the foreign exchange markets reopened in London; soon followed by the gold and commodity markets. In 1958 sterling regained full convertibility. Britain's invisible earnings could once again acquire pride of place under Macmillan. The Bank recovered its role as conductor to the City, and the Treasury reinforced its dominance within the state. The result, at a time when the defeated powers of World War Two were rapidly renewing their capital stock and coming back into the world market in force, was to penalize British manufacturing as the exigencies of sterling – a high and stable exchange-rate – were translated into the vagaries of a credit control erratically expanding and contracting domestic demand in response to pressures on the external account.

Yet amidst historically unprecedented rates of international accumulation, as Fordist industry spread outwards from the USA under the Pax Americana, the growth of the British economy was rapid by nineteenth-century standards. The result was a domestic prosperity that consolidated both Conservative electoral ascendancy and trade-union industrial strength. Traditional elites and financial earnings flowered above, while shop stewards multiplied in numbers and wage drift followed below. The arrival of mass consumption of durables brought with it a belated concentration of manufacturing capital. The multi-divisional corporation finally became naturalized. But in Britain the giant firm did not usually mean the giant plant: integration was more organizational than technological, and signified no far-reaching overhaul of the equipment of British industry. The afterglow of military victory in World War Two had postponed any pressing sense of economic deficiency in the post-war epoch. Imperial powers above and beyond those of any European rival continued to be taken for granted, as a generally effective colonial *transformismo* evolved, and no major defeats of the kind that had driven the Dutch from Indonesia or the French from Indochina were suffered. It was not until the Anglo–French attack on Egypt in 1956 that the real relations of force between British and American imperialism were starkly displayed – when for the first time since the War the interests of the two collided directly, and the US halted the Suez expedition within days. Even so, continuing illusions of empire abroad and rising consumption at home were still sufficient to rule out any contemplation of British entry into the EEC shortly afterwards, in the name of a superior Commonwealth. But by the early sixties, the international decline of the UK economy was no longer maskable. In fifteen years West Germany, Japan and France had all overtaken it in national income and share of world trade. The weaknesses of British capital and of the British state in the new global order that had emerged during the long boom became brutally clear as a belated suit to join the Common Market was vetoed by France, and the project of an independent deterrent dwindled to the leasing of missile technology from America. The Macmillan years, clouded with decay and scandal, closed amid something like a public certificate of the general malaise of British capitalism.

7. Reprise

Such was the juncture at which *New Left Review* attempted to explore the historical reasons for the British crisis some two decades ago. The two principal themes of our analysis were the archaic nature of a ruling stratum, whose personnel and traditions stretched back to an agrarian and aristocratic past that had been unbroken for centuries by civil commotion or foreign defeat; and the defensive character of a labour movement intensely conscious of class but immured in acceptance of it. To the hegemonic predominance of the one – all too pervasive for British bourgeois society as a whole – we argued that there corresponded the corporate subordination of the other, reflected in its fundamental acceptance of that society.[74] This Gramscian polarity was given too cultural a turn, at any rate by myself. The crisis was also deduced too narrowly from the character of the hegemonic order alone. But the essential intuitions were not wrong. The crux of the problems confronting British capitalism lay in the knot that tied together the rulers of the country, the state which embodied their rule, and those they ruled over. The political dome of the dominant bloc had indeed been essentially landowning throughout most of the nineteenth century; beneath it, economically, came commerce rather than manufacturing. When agrarian property lost its weight it was not industry

74. Gramsci's use of the word 'corporate', of course, derived from Lenin and the Russian socialist tradition; it was quite unrelated to the official conception of 'corporatism' later theorized by Italian fascism, the source of the principal contemporary usage of that term, with its very different meaning – the one signifying a conscious subalternity, the other a spurious co-participation.

but finance which became the hegemonic form of capital, in a City socially and culturally in many ways closer to the wealth of estates than of factories. The arrival of modern corporations later reinforced rather than counterbalanced the outward bias of London as a world financial centre, by early orientation to production overseas. The empire which provided a congenial habitat for City and multinationals alike had traditionally been the principal positive care of the state. The combination of a Treasury determined to minimize government at home, and a Foreign Office of vice-regal horizons abroad, made this state eminently unsuitable as an instrument for redressing the decline of British capitalism. Its special skills lay elsewhere: in the mortification of political conflict or social revolt within civil society, through the venerable institutions of parliamentary sovereignty in a constitutional monarchy. In that, scarcely another European state could compete with its record.

If our portrait of the dominant bloc was the principal focus of Thompson's criticisms, it was our account of those who were dominated that aroused most objection from a younger generation of historians. The sore point here was our judgement of the labour movement. The burden of nearly all these critics was that we had failed to register the variations in the political hopes and horizons of the working class and its different institutions over a century and a half, attributing too homogeneous a subordination to it, and too static a hegemony to the exploiting classes over it.[75] A plea for finer conjunctural detail is always to be respected. But the history of a social class or a political movement cannot be dissolved into a sheer sequence of discontinuous conjunctures without losing its object altogether. The British labour movement never exhibited one unchanging essence; but nor did it display indefinite variation. Through every transformation and vicissitude, its history developed within a set of structural limits that placed strict bounds on its identity. The modern form of that binding has been Labourism, no mere theoretical phantasm but an all too tangible institutional and ideological reality, reproducing through multiple conflicts and oscillations across the years its peculiar, unchequered forms of subalternity. The measure of them came at the pinnacle of Labour power itself. For then – when the party represented sociologically the most numerous working class in Europe, and organizationally one of the least divided – it proved unable, not just to pose

75. This was a common theme of James Hinton, 'The Labour Aristocracy', NLR 34, July–August 1963; Keith Nield, 'A Symptomatic Dispute', *Social Research* 47/3, Autumn 1980; and Raphael Samuel and Gareth Stedman Jones, 'The Labour Party and Social Democracy', *History Workshop* 12, Autumn 1981.

any fundamental challenge to capitalism in the United Kingdom, as always in the past, but to constitute any incisive alternative stewardship of it either. The post-war Labour Government, commanding a huge parliamentary majority and a loyal trade-union movement, thought only of bettering the condition of the working class within a social order taken as given and an imperial heritage it strove to preserve, by reliance on American protection. Major change in the economic foundations of the country never occurred to it. Socialism had never been on the agenda of the Attlee administration. Its goals were social concessions from a capitalism whose strengths it accepted as beside contestation. What Labour had wholly failed to register were the surfacing weaknesses of British capitalism itself.

8. Losing Altitude

When the Labour Party returned to office in 1964, the ideological context had changed. Two decades later, the anaesthesia of military victory had finally worn off. For the first time since Chamberlain's campaign for Tariff Reform, political debate was once again dominated by the issue of national decline. The failing powers of the British economy were increasingly acknowledged, to general alarm. More and more frequently, the source of the English disease was traced to the unamended traditionalism of British society – not least by the new Labour leadership. Wilson's trademark in opposition had been rhetorical attacks on outdated inequality and amateur inefficiency, customary hierarchy and unmerited privilege, as fetters on national progress. Under him Labour now promised no major extension of social insurance or public ownership. The thrust of its programme was a novel one for the British workers' movement: in effect, a modernization rather than humanization of capitalism, stressing the need for science and technology as the condition of welfare, in a vocabulary of bourgeois rationality calculated to appeal to both expert and egalitarian impulses. Paradoxically the forensic radicalism of the Labour campaign was probably greater in 1964 than in 1945, comporting a more caustic and sweeping assault on Conservative rule than post-coalition pieties had allowed under Attlee. Among the ostensible targets of Wilson's criticisms were the dominance of finance over industry; the incompetence of hereditary directors and the unsuitability of existing civil servants; the inequalities of the educational system; the run-down of social services. More than a decade of rising levels of private consumption under the Conservatives, combined with the unpopularity of the models of nationalization imposed by Morrison, gave Labour a much narrower victory than in 1945. But in the mid sixties the Wilson administration succeeded in creating a reduced equivalent of the electoral bloc of the mid forties. The bulk of the working class, if no longer so committed to its community values as in the past, and a segment of the white-collar and professional middle classes, now moved less by a sense of social solidarity with those below than one of frustrated mobility and impatience with those above, gave Labour parliamentary power once again. The new regime presented itself as a force of resolute and realistic reform.

The limits of that realism were demonstrated immediately on Wilson's assumption of office. Labour's conception of national regeneration was all but exclusively domestic. A reformed civil administration would coordinate the energies of a rationalized industry, promoting higher levels of investment in equipment and research, and laying the foundations of a broad and modern educational system. Higher productivity and output would then permit more generous social provision. The programme said virtually nothing about the position of the UK in the post-war international order. Its only gesture to external modernization was a promise to abandon the country's nuclear deterrent as supernumerary. Labour's silence here spoke volumes. There had been no revision of the conventional definitions of the world role of British capitalism. The Commonwealth and the American Protectorate which guaranteed it remained mentally untouchable. The Sterling Area with the City at the centre of it, and the NATO–SEATO alliances with the functions of sub-imperial buffer that followed from them, continued to be regarded as intrinsic to the definition of Great Britain. No change from the legacy of the Attlee experience was envisaged, no lesson from its demise learnt.

The consequences did not wait. Within the very first month of Wilson's premiership, there was a run on the pound, triggered by the City's aversion to the prospect of higher taxation under Labour. Devaluation was the obvious, widely canvassed response – which could only improve the export prospects of national manufacturing. The Bank naturally opposed it, as the guardian of a high and stable exchange-rate. So too did the United States – which regarded sterling as an outwork of the dollar, and feared a cannon-effect on its own currency. Faced with this clear choice, Wilson opted to 'keep the pound riding high' – at the cost of a large American loan, and increased interest rates. Labour's rhetoric of renovation had been punctured at first contact with the traditional powers of the Bank and the US Treasury. After another year and a half, and a further election that gave

Labour an increased majority, the same scenario was repeated. The sterling crisis of the summer of 1966 forced a much more drastic squeeze of demand by the Wilson administration, now combined with a cut in public spending, to save the pound. That too proved vain. In 1967 yet another balance-of-payments crisis finally imposed the devaluation to stave off which industrial growth and investment had been pointlessly sacrificed.

The strategic bent of the administration, meanwhile, reproduced the drift of its financial policy. British nuclear submarines were preserved rather than scrapped, to keep a dependent deterrent in the Atlantic. Colonial wars were pursued in Borneo and Aden – settler peace in Rhodesia. The Labour government extended faithful diplomatic support to American intervention in Vietnam, regardless of worldwide protests against it, and maintained the highest level of military spending in Western Europe. This international course – unswerving adherence to official traditions held fast since the First World War – now formed a glaring contrast with that of America's other ally at Versailles. In the same years France expelled US bases from its territory, withdrew from NATO's military command, and disavowed the American war in Indochina. Britain under Conservative rule had been vetoed from entry into the European Community by de Gaulle as too subservient to the United States. Labour rule only accentuated the divergence between Europe's two principal imperial powers.

The external stance of the Wilson administration prepared – in good measure preordained – the fate of its internal programme. Labour had always designated the British State as its appointed instrument for achieving the modernization of British manufacturing, promising reforms of that State precisely to adapt it to this unwonted function. The two key innovations here were to be the displacement of the Treasury from its controlling position within the Executive, and the democratization of recruitment to the bureaucracy as a whole. In 1964 a new Department of Economic Affairs was set up to bypass Treasury obstruction of any economic *dirigisme*. Its task was to formulate a National Plan on an indicative basis, and to supervise the general rationalization of firms and sectors that was supposed to follow from it. The results were derisory. The Plan, lacking any binding force, was little more than public relations for the regime. The intended rationalizations took the form of state-sponsored mergers, creating larger conglomerates without higher productivity. Fiscal inducements to manufacturing investment were no more effective than these organizational recombinations. Growth did not accelerate: export shares did not increase. Intervention as feeble and superficial as this was an easy prey to the unreconstructed laissez-faire hostility of the Treasury. By 1967 the DEA was so discredited that its abolition was encompassed in short order, without a struggle, by a Labour Chancellor in the name of traditional orthodoxy.[76] The final years of the Wilson Government saw a classical deflationary policy of sound money and a payments surplus, pursued by a restored Treasury.

Reform of the civil service, a much broader objective, naturally got even less far – no more than a pallid Commission whose recommendations, modest enough, were shelved without a trace. The modernized educational system that was supposed to be the complement of a more *dirigiste* State was in its turn reduced to little more than an increase in the number of universities and colleges, without any significant shift of disciplines within them; and a general amalgamation of public sector schools in the name of equity, whose principal effect was to increase the size of the private sector above it – leaving unaltered the overall structures of British education, with their traditional exacerbation of class and indifference to science. Nor was any major extension of social security achieved under Wilson. These were the years in which a second wave of welfare reforms in Northern Europe – Swedish pension funds or West German unemployment insurance – was creating more advanced systems of provision than those established after the War. The English welfare state ceased to be an example to the world.

The complete failure of Labour's attempt to reconstruct industrial capital by deliberate state action, meanwhile, coincided with the unpremeditated emergence of a quite new basis for the hegemony of financial and commercial capital. The fall of the pound in 1967 meant the end of the Sterling Area as a coherent economic zone, a change long feared and resisted by a City grown accustomed to it since the thirties. But just before Wilson came to power, the US authorities had blocked foreign borrowers from the New York bond market. The result, from 1963 onwards, was the birth – little noticed at the time – of an offshore Eurodollar market. The London merchant banks moved quickly to capture the bulk of the enormous flows soon accumulating in this novel medium of international credit, which promised the City greater prosperity and strength than the Commonwealth of the past had ever afforded it. London as a world financial centre entered a new phase – of

76. The Department was formally wound up in the summer of 1969. The structural context of the failure of Labour *dirigisme* – obstructed not just by the Treasury as the principal bulwark of the state, but also by the weakness of the peak organizations of labour and industry, the TUC and CBI, as putative 'social partners' outside it – is sharply etched by Bob Jessop, 'The Transformation of the State in Post-War Britain', in Richard Scase, ed., *The State in Western Europe*, London 1980, pp. 39–41: a brilliant essay.

transformation and expansion – while Britain as a manufacturing nation slid into stagnation. By 1970 the size of the Eurobond market had multiplied nearly twenty times over. But in six years of Labour government, industrial production increased by only 15 per cent, less than under the Conservative regime before it.

Daunted by the City and thwarted in the State, the Wilson regime finally turned on the unions as the scapegoat for its failures – now treated as the major obstacle to the rationalization of the British economy. But its bid to control trade-union power with anti-strike legislation was no more successful than its attempt to sidetrack the Treasury, provoking rebellion in the ranks not just of the TUC but of the Labour Cabinet itself. Appropriately, the same Minister squelched both – Callaghan, first at the Exchequer and then at the Home Office. But the consequences of *In Place of Strife* were to be much more lasting than those of the defence of sterling or the demise of the National Plan. It was a Labour, not a Conservative government which pronounced official commination of the British trade-union movement as the principal, if not sole, cause of the decline of British industry – the dominant ideological theme of bourgeois politics for the next two decades. In fact, the strengthening of shopfloor bargaining-power during the post-war boom had worked its way through to greater industrial militancy, and a certain shift to the left in union leaderships, in the sixties. But although strike activity had increased, wages had not spurted with especial speed by international standards. The real difficulty for the overhaul of British capitalism was posed less by strike levels or wage pressures as such, than by the structural lock on production processes that a very traditionalist and decentralized union movement could enforce, in conditions where low economic growth gave little incentive to release it. The productivity gap between British industry and its competitors kept widening as manufacturing investment stagnated, and the rate of return on it declined. Informal labour recalcitrance was one of the dependent variables in the complex causation of this process:[77] perpetuated by sluggish rates of accumula-

77. Theo Nichols, *The British Worker Question*, London 1986, contains a trenchant critique of the fallacies of that conventional literature on industrial productivity in Britain which lays the blame for lagging national performance primarily on shopfloor resistance. Nichols argues that poor managerial education and coordination, combined with meagre workforce training, are in reality the two most plausible determinants of the low productivity of British industry in a comparative perspective: pp. 106–10, 161–3. Once these parameters are set, he suggests, then 'British workers give like for like, inefficient management fostering less than helpful workforces', although 'British trade-unionists have never been highly political nor, outside of some particular groups, highly militant': pp. 168, 218.

tion, and so lesser increases in popular income than elsewhere, and then perpetuating them by lesser yields on new fixed capital when it was forthcoming – in a framework determined by the overseas and entrepôt bias of the leading sectors of the economy as a whole. Demagogically extrapolated from this context and exaggerated in its scope, 'union power' became the whipping-boy of Wilsonite rhetoric, while the nullity of the administration's record became ever more apparent, and social unrest intensified in the country at large.

By the late sixties student radicalization, born of disgust with the regime's foreign and domestic record, threatened to throw up a new disaffected intelligentsia. Civil rights rebellion in Ulster put the unitary British State, never questioned by Labour, into crisis on its weakest flank. Racism spread in the moral vacuum left by the decay of Labourism in the big cities. But in the end the decisive undoing of the Wilson Government was its attack on the trade unions that had helped to bring it to power. The clamour of its own campaign against the organized strength of the working class in industry simply prepared the way for the victory of its opponents. In 1970 the Conservatives had no difficulty in pointing to the failure of Labour's measures to tame the unions, and in promising more drastic remedies for the root of Britain's troubles.

Political leadership within the dominant bloc had in the interim begun to shift from the traditional upper class of country connexions, temporarily discredited by national decline, towards a middle- and lower-middle-class stratum hitherto confined to non-commissioned ranks within the Tory Party: a change personified by Heath and publicized at Selsdon Park. The propagandist objectives of the new Conservatism were in many ways a right-wing version of the programme of the new Labourism six years previously – proclaiming the goal of a radical modernization of the British economy and society, in the interests of all classes. The means adopted to achieve this end were to be very different, however. The Heath Government consciously gave primacy to an alternative external policy. Conservative strategy for economic renewal now centred on British entry into the EEC – designed both to expose local manufacturing to stiffer foreign competition, and to provide larger markets for those companies that survived it. Diplomatic *rapprochement* with France, and an imperceptible distancing from the US, were accepted as the necessary price of the ticket to Brussels. Defence of a fixed exchange-rate was abandoned, and an all-out expansion of credit and money supply was uncorked to create a virtuous circle of high growth and high investment at home that would give British industry the necessary momentum for its European break-out. Both moves misfired. The Barber boom, instead of lifting investment in manufacturing, set off the greatest wave of speculation in stock and real estate in post-war English history. Without directive canalization by the state – abjured on principle by the regime – funds simply followed the natural slope of the economy into urban property and financial promotion. UK industry received scarcely any benefit. Fixed investment in manufacturing actually fell in real terms by 9 per cent in 1972–73, while investment in finance rose 42 per cent. As manufacturing profits grew a mere 6 per cent between 1970 and 1973, insurance, banking and finance profits jumped by 122 per cent.[78] Then, before the bubble burst of its own accord, the world recession was upon it – and the prospects for economic growth anyway collapsed. National decline now intersected with international depression, and a qualitatively new stage in the British crisis set in. In these circumstances, escaping into the European Community proved little less illusory than clinging to the Sterling Area had been, for the purpose of British export performance. The Common Market lost its dynamism just as Britain joined it, amidst generalized deflation and industrial retrenchment.

The consequences of the recession were, inevitably, especially acute in the UK, as insolvencies started to spread through the manufacturing sector. Internally, the Heath Government had preached the virtues of competition rather than planning, and the need for the state to withdraw rather than intervene in the economy. But once the world economic crisis broke, an administration which had set out as a champion of neo-liberalism and the bracing impact of unrestrained competition baulked at the political and social costs of allowing major bankruptcies to occur, and ended up intervening more actively in British industry than its predecessor. Its use of public authority, however, was essentially negative – rescue of selected companies rather than rationalization of major sectors. In one area alone was there a deliberate and concerted deployment of state power to alter existing arrangements across the board. The new Conservative regime was determined to break the autonomy of the unions by tough legislation on strike actions, enforceable through specially created courts. This was the issue that had contributed most to its election, and was the ideological centrepiece of its domestic programme. But in his bid to beat down the trade unions, Heath came to grief even more drastically than Wilson. A coercive Industrial Relations Act was passed through

78. Andrew Glyn and John Harrison, *The British Economic Disaster*, London 1980, p. 176.

Parliament, but rapidly proved to be unworkable when resistance to it on the docks threatened to escalate into a general strike. The decisive confrontations between the government and organized labour, however, erupted in the mines. In 1972, when the NUM struck for higher wages, its mass picketing shut down power supplies across the country. In a head-on collision with British unionism at its strongest, it was the Cabinet which went down to defeat. By the winter of the following year, the intensifying recession had driven the government to impose legislation to control wages directly – a policy it had always denounced as a bane of Labour rule. A second miners' strike challenged the statutory pay norm, with such overwhelming force that the Conservative government first imposed a three-day week on industry – nominally to conserve energy supplies, actually to rally support against the NUM – and then called elections on the issue of the threat to parliamentary sovereignty. Its ensuing defeat at the polls represented the most spectacular single victory of labour over capital since the beginnings of working-class organization in Britain. A bourgeois government had been brought down by the direct action of a strategic group of industrial workers – the only time in modern European history that an economic strike has precipitated the political collapse of a government.

The battles of 1972–74 marked a high tide of trade-union élan within the British working class. Yet its limits were soon apparent. A traditional corporate identity had for two years taken on a heroic pugnacity. But it had not transcended its customary self. The downfall of the Heath Government was not the deliberate object of the coal strike, which lacked any declared political goals. The industrial militancy of the miners was not reflected in any popular mobilization for Labour – which won the elections of 1974 by default, rather than any appeal of its own, on a lower vote than when it had lost in 1970. The sectors of the middle class that had previously swung to the Conservatives now switched to the Liberals, while nationalism gained ground in Scotland, and Protestantism cut loose as an independent force in Ulster. Wilson's mandate was weak and negative.

Formally, Labour was this time committed not only to economic intervention but to major social redistribution as well. In practice, the 'planning agreements' of the seventies proved even more notional and ephemeral than the National Plan of the sixties – tokens never implemented and quickly forgotten. The main brunt of government industrial policy became in effect a continuation of the direction taken by the previous regime. Membership of the EEC was renegotiated and ratified by referendum, and further bankrupt firms were bailed out by loans or nationalizations. No attempt at an overall *Strukturpolitik* was any longer made, even in gesture. Rather, the bulk of the government's energies, and claims for its performance, now went into the construction of an official pact with the unions. The Industrial Relations Act was repealed and new legislation passed somewhat improving on the status quo ante. The real substance of the 'Social Contract', however, was an exchange of welfare concessions – above all, increased pensions – for wage restraints. Its principal architect was the General Secretary of the TGWU, and for the TUC it represented a quite new initiative: for the first time direct participation in the formulation of a deal extending beyond conventional trade-union objectives. But this unfamiliar departure from the traditional economism of the British union movement only served to underline how modest its political horizons remained. At the crest of an industrial upsurge that had toppled a government, revealing a potential striking-power without equal in the West, the major union leaders showed no interest in planning powers, and complete indifference to the fate of the only interventionist in the Cabinet, the swiftly demoted Benn. They contented themselves with marginal increments in social insurance, and greater equity in the tightly controlled nominal pay rises that the official compact permitted. This was presented by the Labour Government as a triumph of social justice and anti-inflationary resolve.

The world economic crisis, meanwhile, had deepened. The Labour regime tried to stave off its impact by standard Keynesian expenditure for two years. At a time when every other major capitalist power was deflating sharply, and the productivity of British manufacturing was falling yet further behind that of its competitors, the result was a precipitous deterioration in the balance of payments. Once again, as in the past, Labour turned to foreign credits to salvage the situation – repeating in 1976 the scenario of 1966. This time, however, the IMF loan negotiated by the Callaghan Government was far more draconian in its terms, reflecting the lower state to which the UK economy had since fallen, and the harder monetarist doctrines that had become orthodox in international capitalism as a whole. In exchange for some nine billion dollars from Washington, social services were cut, nationally and locally, and unemployment was deliberately allowed to rise.[79] By mid 1977 it had topped one and a half million. Despite this complete reversal of the ostensible purpose of the Social Contract, the government continued to enforce, and even tighten, its wage controls.

79. For this episode, see David Coates's sombre obituary of the Wilson–Callaghan years, *Labour in Power*, London 1980, pp. 38–47.

After four years of voluntary restraint, trade-union patience broke in the winter of 1978, when the TUC rejected official pay norms and a flurry of private and public sector strikes followed. In the ideological climate created by the Labour administration itself, in which union docility was presented as the key to national revival, this recrudescence of industrial militancy could only mean electoral disaster for Labour. A rebellion by organized workers had in effect undone the third government in succession.

The *coup de grâce* was delivered by peripheral nationalism. Fearful of wholesale defection of its voters in Scotland, and dependent on nationalist abstention in Parliament, Labour had introduced a limited bill of devolution. This, its sole contribution to a reform of the British State throughout its existence, was wrung from it reluctantly, under external duress. But a parliamentary delegation which in two decades had never flinched from spending cuts, wage controls or colonial repression, now proved quite willing to jeopardize office for the integrity of the eighteenth-century United Kingdom. Advanced without conviction, devolution was abandoned without compunction by the Cabinet when its bill proved too much for the centralist zeal of many of its MPs, who torpedoed it by amendment – ensuring the fall of the government under nationalist retribution. Labour in the seventies rehearsed a shrunken repetition of its performance of the sixties. Without will to alter the financial–commercial complex that continued to thrive in the economy, or ability to change the structures of the state that presided over industrial decline, in the end it failed even in its attempt to coopt or erode the corporative resistance of the unions, singled out as the prime source of national sickness. It antagonized its own constituencies without winning over any adversaries and ended by undermining the very foundations of its own political fortunes, the commitments to welfare provision and full employment laid during the Second World War.

The Conservative leadership which took office in 1979 had been thoroughly recast, as certain central conventions of post-war English politics were discarded under Callaghan. A demoralized Labourism had released the forces of a radical Right that pioneered the general shift to Atlantic reaction in the eighties. The novelty of Thatcher's programme lay in its orchestration of targets. The new Conservative rhetoric linked ungovernable unions to an unproductive state that encouraged an incontinent culture. The middle term of this trio was the strategically critical one. Heath had originally been no less hostile to unions; but his leadership had proved fatally equivocal in its attitude to the state, eventually underwriting – even reinforcing – what it had initially rejected, the structures of post-war nationalization and welfare; just as it had lacked zeal in the face of the collapse of moral standards traceable to them. The central Thatcherite claim was that the British crisis was above all due to too much, rather than too little, interference by the state in economy and society; in particular to the creeping growth of public expenditure in social services and nationalized industries, and to the official protection and incorporation of union power into the machinery of government. The dynamic potential of native capitalism, in this diagnosis, had been crippled by a synthesis of meddling bureaucracy with extortionate militancy peculiar to Britain. The solution to the nation's ills was to restore the primacy of the market, which alone could make the country economically competitive once again, and to contract the state to its proper, neglected functions of police and defence.

This programme involved major changes on every significant front of government policy. On assuming power, the new Conservative regime intensified the deflation initiated by Labour, sharply tightening the money supply and imposing a reduction in public borrowing. This time the objective was not simply to correct a balance-of-payments deficit, but to squeeze every inflationary pressure – identified with a wage spiral and welfare profligacy – permanently out of the system. The result was a short-term slump of unprecedented severity in 1980–81, exceeding any deliberate calculation, and a long-term rise in unemployment that was consciously accepted as it remorselessly weakened the bargaining-power of labour. By 1982 the number of jobless had passed three million, the highest level among the major capitalist economies. In this climate it became possible to curtail union rights to organize and strike – something every previous government had failed to achieve – with the enactment, and later enforcement, of punitive Employment Acts. Trade-union membership dropped, and industrial stoppages plummeted. The one major union to mount a direct challenge to this course was the NUM. In 1984–85 it was isolated and crushed after the longest epic of collective resistance in the annals of British labour.

The key weapon in containing and destroying the third miners' strike was a national police operation, specially equipped and prepared to defeat the mass picketing that had won the first strike. Thatcher's programme involved not just a far more effective attack on union strength, but also a much bolder reorganization of the state than anything attempted to date. On the one hand, the coercive apparatuses of the police and the armed forces were carefully built up – with large pay increases, more sophisticated equipment and increasingly salient profiles. The colonial war with Argentina in 1982 provided a signal occasion for demonstrating the prowess of an Army steeled in Northern Ireland, and a Navy still capable of operations at the other end of the world. Military success, generating a nationalist euphoria that gave the Conservatives a second mandate in 1983, in reality depended on US logistic and intelligence support – the critical difference between the Falklands and Suez expeditions. The overall relationship between American and British imperialism held fast under Reagan and Thatcher. But it acquired a novel twist because of the peculiar ideological intimacy between the two governments – the first time such close domestic concord had existed – and the political seniority of the British regime, circumstances which gave London an unusual leverage. (Washington's interests in the South Atlantic were anyway much less important than in the Mediterranean, where it had no difficulty in forcing London to cooperate with its attack on Libya.) In the wider strategic theatre, the principal long-term project of the Thatcher Government was a massive jump in British nuclear striking power, to be similarly realized by the acquisition of Trident from the USA on favourable terms – weaponry that would put Britain ahead of France again in the European arms balance, and could be looked to for the winning of a third Conservative term of office.

At the same time the administrative centralism of the British State – by now the greatest in Western Europe – was further tightened. Treasury controls were imposed directly on local authority budgets, and metropolitan councils abolished altogether. Comprehensive though its security and executive programmes have been, however, these have represented a relatively orthodox set of moves for a regime of the hard Right. The major originality of Thatcher's remoulding of the state has lain on its other side – not so much the reinforcement of its repressive potential as the reduction of its socio-economic functions. Here it has shown an inventive capacity that has made it an international trendsetter. Public housing, once one of the two most popular planks of the Attlee administration, and always an electoral base of Labourism, now in widespread disrepair, was sold off to council tenants. Nationalized industries with any record or prospect of profitability – trucking, telecommunications, oil, gas, aviation – were floated on the stock exchange at low valuations, with preferential offers to employees. Within the reduced public sector, loss-making branches of heavy industry were contracted by drastic lay-offs of the workforce – steel, coal, auto. Where electoral reaction permitted, social services were pruned or leased, higher education cut and pensions partly commercialized. The drive behind such 'privatization' has been twofold. Its overt economic rationale has been to slim down a swollen and wasteful state, releasing the energies of an 'enterprise culture' from the dead hand of bureaucratic paternalization. At the same time its evident political intention is to create a popular clientele for the regime from a mass impropriation of public assets – a calculation lent a certain persuasive force by the social tone of Thatcherite ideology itself. Petty-bourgeois, like the Premier herself, the new Conservative rhetoric could now appeal more readily than the patrician style of traditional Toryism to upper layers of the working class not always that distant in residence and outlook from the lower middle class itself.

The last and in many ways most important development of the Thatcher period lay in its policy towards the external linkages of British to world capital. For the intimidation of labour and redeployment of the state were accompanied by the emancipation of finance from its remaining national constraints. In 1979 the regime abolished exchange controls – its first and most fundamental act on coming to power. The consequences were dramatic. The City had prospered through the whole recession, as the Eurodollar market grew through the very mechanism that had initially triggered the industrial downturn – the OPEC price rise, the bulk of whose earnings were subsequently deposited with London banks. The volume of the financial flows involved in the recycling of petrodollars through the City, much of it onwards in syndicated loans to the Third World, was so huge a magnet that it increasingly drew foreign – in the first instance, above all US – banks to London, as a major base of operations. Meanwhile the stock market was becoming ever more dominated by institutional investors – pension funds, insurance companies and unit trusts, which by the end of the decade held over half of UK bonds and equity. The complete liberalization of exchanges in 1979 unleashed a tidal movement into the purchase of overseas assets by these institutions, principally through portfolio investment. By the end of 1986 British holdings of net foreign assets had rocketed within a decade from £3 bn to £80 bn – an absolute figure only just below that of Japan after the great buying spree in the United States financed by Tokyo's huge export surplus, and larger than the total oil rents received by the UK from the North Sea. Britain is now once again the greatest international coupon-clipper per capita in the world.

At the same time the lifting of exchange controls triggered a quantum jump in foreign banking in London which, within a few years, had taken it over a historic threshold. By 1985 the City was a *plaque-tournant* for global funds amounting to over £1 trillion – or more than three times the gross domestic product of the UK.[80] The majority of these were now held not by British but by foreign banks, among whom the largest single group were no longer American but Japanese. Today not only are 70 per cent of all assets and liabilities in the UK monetary sector held in foreign currencies rather than sterling, but overseas firms, governments and individuals account for 75 per cent of deposits.[81] The deregulation of the Stock Exchange negotiated in 1983, the second long-term move by the government to assure London's competitive position, has since paved the way for an inrush of New York security houses or Swiss banks into the oldest citadel of the City. The gigantic nova of money capital now floating over London, in other words, has become denationalized in a quite new sense – no longer merely disconnected from the fortunes of domestic industry, as the City's commercial transactions always largely were in the past, but estranged from any original linkage with the national economy at all. This influx is, of course, enormously profitable to the core operations of the City as a complex of British capital.[82] In an epoch of vastly greater capitalization in New York and Tokyo, London still remains the most versatile and multi-purpose financial centre in the world – the largest foreign exchange dealer, international banker, and trade insurer of all.[83] The importance of the financial and commercial sectors within the UK economy, viewed statistically, has increased yet further, even as their articulation to it, viewed structurally, has become yet more attentuated. Under Thatcher, the City has boomed as never before: but never so much as an enclave rather than an engine of British capitalism as a whole.

Ultimately, of course, the historical objective of radical Conservatism was to achieve the revival of that capitalism – restoring it to the rank of

---

80. *Financial Statistics*, HMSO, December 1985 – a reckoning that does not include all interbank lending in London.

81. See Jerry Coakley and Laurence Harris, *The City of Capital*, Oxford 1983, pp. 120–24.

82. Financial and property concerns, in turn, have consistently been the most generous backers of Thatcher's Conservatism – providing about a third of all company contributions to it in the eighties; followed, suggestively enough, by food, drink and tobacco firms and construction enterprises: John Ross, *Thatcher and Friends, The Anatomy of the Tory Party*, London 1983, pp. 37–38.

83. For detailed figures on international banking and currency exchange in the City, see 'International Banking in London, 1975–1985', and 'The Market in Foreign Exchange in London', *Bank of England Quarterly Bulletin*, September 1986, pp. 366–82. Japanese banks commanded 31% of international liabilities by the end of of 1985, British banks 19% and American 16%. The volume of foreign exchange dealings in London is now over $100 billion a day, about 90% of it interbank transactions, and just under 80% conducted by foreign banks.

a fully competitive industrial power. Labour discipline, state retrenchment and financial decontrol were all means to this intended end. But the effects have not been commensurate with the aims. British manufacturing has failed to respond to this treatment, after so many others, too. The principal achievement of the regime has been to force labour productivity up, by widespread lay-offs and tighter invigilation of the production process – above all in the motor and steel industries, directly subject to government control. Bankruptcies among the least efficient firms in the private sector have raised average levels of per capita output nation-wide as well, at the cost of a fall in the total manufacturing workforce of 28 per cent under Thatcher – overwhelmingly concentrated in the North, Scotland, Wales and Ulster. The overall rate of growth of labour productivity in the eighties has increased by about a third over performance in the sixties and seventies. But such improvement has been slight compared with the advances registered in the same period by West Germany and Japan, which from their much higher bases have left British manufacturing yet further behind.[84] After the slump of 1980–81, industrial profits have recovered significantly in Britain from their decline in the previous decade. Yet they too remain far lower than in Japan, the USA, West Germany, Italy or France, with a rate of return in British manufacturing of about 8 per cent, compared with an average of nearly 18 per cent in the other major industrial economies.[85] Even after the worst of the trough had passed, the index of manufacturing production only just exceeded its 1980 level six years later. Rationalization of labour was not accompanied by any major renovation of plant. Investment in British industry actually fell by two-fifths between 1979 and 1983. By then the volume of overseas investment was double that at home.[86] Moreover, despite 15 per cent unemployment, a 20 per cent drop in trade-union membership, and the virtual disappearance of strikes, wage drift had re-emerged. By 1985 Britain's increase in unit labour costs was higher than that of any of its leading competitors[87] – suggesting that the

---

84. 'With the exception of agriculture and energy industries, the UK's productivity growth has been worse over the decade than other countries in all industries', gloomily notes the NEDC's *British Industrial Performance. A Comparative Survey over Recent Years*, London 1985.

85. See OECD, *Economic Outlook* 40, December 1986, p. 49.

86. Colin Leys, 'Thatcherism and British Manufacturing: A Question of Hegemony', NLR 151, May–June 1985, pp. 12, 11.

87. OECD, *Economic Outlook*, December 1986: 'Real wages have been growing at a rate of 3 to 3½ per cent, much faster than labour productivity. . . . The continuing high wage growth projected for the United Kingdom falls outside the OECD mainstream to an increasing extent': pp. 93, 47.

subterranean balance of forces in much of British industry had shifted less than the regime claimed, and certainly not enough to inspire the requisite animal spirits in capital. The bottom line of the Thatcher years is unequivocal. UK manufacturing firms have failed to regain any ground internationally. Their position has in fact steadily worsened, as import penetration has reduced their share of one home market after another, without any corresponding gain in exports. In the twenty years between 1964 and 1984 the UK's share of manufactured exports in the advanced industrial world fell by half – while since the early seventies, the volume of manufactured imports has nearly trebled.[88] In 1983 Britain became for the first time in its history a net importer of industrial goods.

The consequence has been a growing visible trade deficit, covered by oil surpluses. North Sea revenues have throughout been the background condition of the whole Thatcherite experience. The regime came to power in the year that the UK became a net exporter of petroleum – and just at the moment when the second OPEC rise doubled the price of oil. Without this windfall, the political economy of Thatcherism would have been unsustainable. Balance-of-payments crises would rapidly have overwhelmed it, as Britain's competitive capacity in manufactures slipped further behind, and far more savage cuts in social spending would have been unavoidable – undermining both the international standing and domestic support of the regime. In the event the sum of unemployment benefit alone has equalled the oil rent, and could scarcely have been paid – by this government – without it. The electoral formula of Thatcherism has always depended on a fortuitous offshore income, just as its economic record has rested on a wasting asset, never converted into future productive potential. The verdict is inescapable. After seven years, the regime that has made the most determined effort since the war to transform the co-ordinates of Britain's decline has ended up reinforcing the central drift of it.

9. Conclusion

Twenty years later, then, how have the NLR theses on Britain fared? The historical depth of the crisis that we sought to sound in the early

88. House of Lords, *Report from the Select Committee on Overseas Trade*, vol. 1, July 1985, pp. 21, 9. Meanwhile the City's overseas earnings have been increasing over twice as fast as exports since 1980.

sixties has been confirmed beyond doubt, even expectation. At the time its existence was ignored by Thompson and contested by others. Today a similar insouciance would be impossible. By every available index, the position of the UK in the capitalist world has subsided ever further across two relentlessly lowering decades. By the mid seventies a general malfunctioning of advanced capitalism was superimposed on the particular decrepitude of Britain within it, drastically aggravating most local symptoms. Paradoxically this coalescence of two crises – one national, the other international – has been of immediate political benefit to the new Conservatism, relieving it of much of the onus of the British malady itself, now half concealed behind the global breakdown of the Keynesian order. The world recession has operated as a partial decoy, in this sense, for a local administration that has accelerated rather than checked an inherited decline. It has rendered politically palatable measures that were bound to prove economically futile, for a national recovery.

The unifying principle of Thatcherite economics, as a project for halting the country's slide, has been the restoration of the market. But as a physic for the British illness, this was never likely to work. The starting-point for the decline of British capitalism lay in its initial conditions. As the historical first-comer, British industrialization arrived without deliberate design, and triumphed without comparable competitors.[89] British manufacturing acquired its early shape unawares, from modest immediate constituents; just as it won world hegemony with no strategic plan, but simply from the spontaneous force of its own chronological lead – within the framework of an English commercial imperialism that preceded it. The easy dominance that British industry achieved in the first half of the nineteenth century laid down certain durable lines of development. The first country to mechanize textiles and build railways, Britain generated 'development blocs' of interrelated capital investment around them,[90] embodied in

---

89. It is Colin Leys who has argued the overriding importance of this second point most forcefully. 'One thing is clear: speaking generally, British *capitalist* manufacturers never did compete successfully against other capitalist manufacturers. What they did was to overwhelm *pre-capitalist* production everywhere; and it was the comparative ease of this victory, rather than the commitment of capital to particular sectors, such as textiles or railways, or to particular forms of business organization characteristic of early capitalism, that led to later problems': *Politics in Britain*, London 1983, p. 38, a book which (belying its title) represents the best single synthesis on the British crisis and its contemporary consequences that now exists.

90. A term coined in the early forties by the Swedish economist Erik Dahmén – *utvecklingsblock*. For Dahmén's initial use of the notion, see his *Entrepreneurial Activity*

physical technologies and spatial regions which then took on a massive historical inertia. Its enterprises started out small in size, and provincial in location; and the family firm persisted as a typical ownership pattern long afterwards. Its labour force achieved forms of collective organization well before any other, reflecting the decentralized company landscape and embedded in the early bloc of technologies. Once set, these structures became progressively greater handicaps in competition with later industrial economies – which started with newer fixed capital, embodied in more modern technology, larger entrepreneurial units, and less unionized workforces. Characteristic of these followers was an element of conscious digression from the market, inherent in their situation as they confronted an established leader that had always relied on it – the emergence of tariffs at the level of the state and cartels at the level of the firm, in Germany, the USA or France.

For the logic of the market, left to itself, necessarily tends to be cumulative rather than corrective. Its dynamic is the play of comparative advantage and disadvantage from existing or entering endowments, as these are calculated by individual entrepreneurial units. It was precisely such a play that fixed the path of subsequent Victorian involution itself. The sum of perfectly rational choices for particular capitals – to persist in traditional industrial sectors in which investment had already been sunk, to move into those overseas markets where competition was least, to avoid extensive reorganization of labour processes at home, or simply to shift from profit-making altogether into rent or interest – all together determined a creeping loss of competitive capacity for British capitalism as a whole, confronted with Germany or the USA.[91] The combined and uneven development of capital that is a product of the world market, in other words, is not amenable to correction by it. The experience of English neo-liberalism in the 1980s has in this respect merely repeated the ancestral lessons of the 1880s. The tougher labour regime brought by Thatcher's stabilization programme was no match for those in the repressive semi-industrialized states of the Third World, bringing little benefit to Britain's manufacturers in exchange for the demand costs incurred by

---

and the Development of Swedish Industry 1919–1939, Homewood (Illinois) 1970, pp. 424–7. Blocs of development, as associated chains of fixed investment, could then become blocks to development, as so many interconnected fetters on movement into later technologies or industries.

91. The classical description of this logic remains Eric Hobsbawm's *Industry and Empire*, London 1969, pp. 187–192.

it; while the greater freedoms of capital have simply accelerated what Tom Nairn has called the habitual 'eversion' of British financial flows abroad.[92] Deregulation – of labour and capital markets – could only mean still more deindustrialization, in pre-established conditions. The laws of comparative advantage have continued to work themselves out, by their own momentum. The rectification of disadvantages requires another kind of social logic. For it to occur, a centralizing force capable of regulating and counteracting the spontaneous molecular movements of the market must exist.

Since the Second World War there have been three major types of such a regulative intelligence in advanced capitalism, with a fourth sub-variant. In France post-war economic reconstruction was directed by a highly trained and cohesive technocracy, closely connected to private business, but with its own independent base in the public administration of the Fourth and Fifth Republics. This stratum of *grands commis* was responsible for the modernizing strategy of an interventionist state, whose planning mechanisms mobilized investment – through subsidized credits – for the deliberate and long-term project of overcoming the historic backwardness of French capitalism. The result was the creation of an industrial park of advanced, if selective, technologies that allowed France to overtake the UK in national product by the mid sixties, and to give it today a 50 per cent higher per capita income. In West Germany, on the other hand, there was no bourgeois state adapted to a similar role after Allied occupation and federalization. There it was the banking system that performed comparable functions for the economy as a whole. Germany had always been the classical land of the investment bank, from the Wilhelmine epoch onwards – that is, of a finance capital accustomed to direct monitoring and control of the performance of industrial concerns dependent on its loans. After the Second World War this national tradition took on renewed importance, as the three big private banks came to own over a third of the equity of the country's major corporations, with commensurate representation on company boards and power over share prices,[93] while at the same time rapidly expanding their retail functions. The resultant 'universal banks' have acted – in concert with the Bundesbank – as the coordinators of the West German 'miracle', and overseers of the export supremacy of Federal manufactures from the sixties onwards. The even

92. *The Break-Up of Britain*, London 1977, pp. 382–8.

93. John Zysman, *Governments, Markets and Growth, Financial Systems and the Politics of Industrial Change*, Ithaca 1983, p. 264.

more spectacular growth of Japanese capitalism, after yet greater physical devastation and defeat, has for its part been based on a combination of the French and German patterns. For in Japan a purposefully interventionist state, with a masterful bureaucracy, has worked in tandem with the cluster of powerful banks that constitute the strategic core of the *keiretsu*, the great Japanese multi-industrial groupings, to lend a uniquely centralist cast to the national economy. High rates of corporate investment, for long-range returns, are orchestrated by abundant low-cost credit from these banks, covered in their turn by the Bank of Japan. Through this dual system, public planning and private accounting can interlock effectively across the commanding heights of industry, giving Japan its unrivalled capacity for rapid and flexible reconversions in response to changing conditions of international competition in different product lines.

These cases of a supra-market logic have each in their own way exemplified the two typical agencies distinguished by Gerschenkron in his account of the motor forces of late-comer industrialization in nineteenth-century Europe – first industrial banks, then the state.[94] They can be regarded as twentieth-century versions of the same imperative – the need for a qualitatively superior quota of central orchestration if economic handicaps are to be reversed rather than aggregated, on the world market.[95] The contemporary epoch has also seen, however, a third model of this kind of agency, of more recent formation. In Sweden or Austria – small countries occupying marginal, and potentially precarious, niches in the world economy – labour has played an institutional role comparable to that of bureaucracy or banking elsewhere. There, stable social-democratic hegemony in the political order, based on mass trade-union and party organization, has been translated into sustained economic steerage towards competitive industrial branches, capable of assuring long-term employment in favourable social conditions. The key to this variant is a highly unified

94. Alexander Gerschenkron, *Economic Backwardness in Historical Perspective*, Cambridge (Massachusetts) 1962, pp. 11–22, 45–9, 353–7.

95. The diametrically opposite argument is expounded in Mancur Olson's neo-liberal study of *The Rise and Decline of Nations*, New Haven 1982, whose central theme is that economic decline is due to ever-increasing encroachments on the market from organized 'special interests' intent on violating its competitive laws, whose untrammelled operation alone can assure national dynamism. Trade unions, trusts and the state figure prominently among such interlopers. Apart from its empirical naiveté (Japan is actually treated as an exemplar of his free market principles), Olson's theory cancels itself logically, for his only remedy against decline induced *par excellence* by too much state intervention is unthinkably more of it – nothing less than the complete liquidation of all special interests by the state: p. 284.

and disciplined labour movement, capable not only of winning repeated electoral victories but also of centralizing wage-bargaining on a national scale; willing not only to respect the rules of capital accumulation but actively to enforce and promote them, in exchange for the benefits of economic growth and social security. Swedish labour market policy and Austrian concertation, each deliberately geared to export performance, have been the expression of working classes at once self-confident and self-limiting, habituated equally to the occupancy of offices of state and to the permanency of bourgeois society outside them.

The singularity of Britain has been to lack any of these three possible correctors, once the process of decline became manifest. Not that their equivalents in the UK have been weak, or negligible. On the contrary, it is an irony that they have all of them been exceptionally strong in their own terms. But in each case, it was the wrong kind of strength – one which disabled rather than fitted them for a historical rectification of the plight of British capitalism. The UK state has long been uniquely formidable as a constitutional structure for securing the active consent of the population to the political order; it is now equipped with the most experienced and professional apparatus for the exercise of coercion in any domestic emergency as well. No other major Western society of this century has been so stable and secure, civically and ideologically, as the one over which Westminster and Whitehall preside. But the British State, constructed to contain social conflict at home and police an empire abroad, has proved impotent to redress economic decline. The nightwatchman acquired traits of the welfare officer, but never of the engineer. Sustained and structural intervention in the economy was the one task for which its organic liberalism was entirely ill suited. Similarly, Britain has always possessed the most powerful financial sector of any imperialist economy in this century, or the last. Its bankers and brokers have amassed outsized fortune and influence within the constellation of English capital as a whole. From the epoch of the arrival of modern industry to that of the onset of its departure, the weight of the City in national development has not had a proportionate equivalent in any other country. Yet precisely the success of the peculiar British form of financial and mercantile capital on a world stage has prevented it from acting as the central nervous system of corporate manufacturing at home. The profits of global intermediation have so eclipsed those of industrial supervision that the actual effect of City institutions has been the very opposite of that of the classical investment banks – not coordinating and reconstructive, but centrifugal and unbalancing.

Finally, the labour movement too has its own claims to some international precedence. Working-class organization in the sphere of production is not only the oldest in the world, but also still among the least tamed or tractable. There have been labour movements which have achieved more impressive levels of unionization and superior electoral records – above all in Scandinavia or Austria. There have been others which have demonstrated greater revolutionary ambition and political insurgency – above all in the Latin countries. But the British labour movement has been marked by a combination of traits that set it apart from either – a pervasive and deep-rooted union implantation, unlike its Mediterranean counterparts, with a traditional lack of central authority and obdurate resistance to rationalization of the factors of production, unlike its Nordic equivalents. It was this configuration which blocked any prospect of a Swedish or Austrian path in the post-war UK. The alloy of class ambition and accommodation that characterized the successful reformism of Central and Northern Europe was missing – indeed, inverted in the specifically British mixture of demission and recalcitrance. Hence the complete failure of social democracy in Britain to acquit any of the tasks of bourgeois modernization whose urgency it eventually came to proclaim. Trade-union powers were not sublimated into a successful tripartism in the service of reindustrialization, but harassed in vain attempts to break the springs of shopfloor solidarities. The result was that just as Britain possessed a state inured to colonial military intervention yet incapable of consistent economic intervention at home, and a world capital of finance without true finance capital, so it had a corporate working class that never generated an operative corporatism. In each case, on the contrary, the particular strength of the forces in presence was not merely displaced but actually counterproductive for the recovery of the first industrial nation. The imperial traditions of the state led to the subcontracted rearmament and overseas commitments that dissipated a post-war export lead; the global transactions of the City diverted potential investments abroad; the localized unruliness of labour discouraged a general reconversion of production processes. The *fainéant* industrial bourgeois of modern British history found no understudies for their role. The other actors compounded rather than compensated for their abdication from the scene.

The predicament of British capitalism, confronted with deepening decline and short of any credible corrective against it, can be seen in a yet clearer relief by one further comparison. Its patron is today before a not dissimilar situation. The United States has been the other great loser in the race for higher-than-average productivity, during the boom and into the slump. Its rates of increase of output per labourer have been persistently lower than those of any other country since the mid sixties, save the UK itself. The basic historical reason for that slowdown must be sought in the American triumph in the Second World War itself, which made the USA the world's premier power. The colossal growth of the US war economy, and the post-war prosperity that succeeded it, which laid down the grid of the major part of the country's stock of fixed capital, created a set of development blocs that would ultimately prove as fateful for subsequent accumulation as the mid-Victorian proved to be for English capitalism; while at the same time, world imperial commitments further narrowed the domestic path of growth, by their diversion of research and investment into military technologies.[96] America's defeated rivals, by contrast, started their cycles of post-war accumulation a decisive period later, after far-reaching dislocation and destruction of their pre-war or wartime industrial landscapes; nor were they burdened with the same military wastage. Once overall US dominance began to falter, as the American share of world manufacturing trade dropped steadily under the impact of their competition, Washington was faced with much the same historical issues as London. For American capitalism also lacks any of the proven mechanisms for checking or reversing the laws of uneven development, once the play of comparative advantages turns against it. The Federal State is still less equipped, by tradition or vocation, for purposive reindustrialization than its unitary British opposite. The banking system, technically debarred since the Depression from fusing investment with clearing functions or retailing across state lines, is poorly positioned for central steerage roles, which it effectively lost before the First World War. The labour movement is politically vestigial. In these circumstances, coherent remedies or reactions to relative economic decline are likely to prove very difficult. The great difference between the two Anglo-Saxon cases, of course, is not just their timing but the still towering force of large industrial capital in the USA, to which Britain has never possessed any equivalent. Its logic, however, is that of the world market rather than the national economy. For all the local advantages of their sun-belt internal frontier, the reality is that the

96. See Robert Brenner's essay, 'US Decline in the International Crisis', forthcoming in *New Left Review* 1992 – both a formidable specific analysis of the American case, contrasted principally with its main competitor Japan, and the most compelling general theoretical explanation of differential capitalist development to have been produced by any contemporary Marxist. The few remarks on the subject above have their basis in this fundamental contribution.

largest and most advanced manufacturing corporations of the United States are even more thoroughly multinational than those of the UK in their location and direction. Their anchorage in domestic supply or demand is progressively loosening. An ever greater extra-territoriality lies ahead of them.

Britain, then, not only witnesses the probable early beginnings in America of something like a vaster repetition of the same historical process it has undergone, in the absence of the same gyroscopes it has lacked, but also perhaps the signs of its ultimate generalization throughout the advanced capitalist world. For the radical internationalization of the forces of production – not to speak of circulation – that defines the spearhead forms of capital in the final years of the twentieth century promises to render all national correctors, whatever their efficacy to date, increasingly tenuous in the future. In that sense, no bourgeois society – not even the last great classically national economy, Japan – will be immune from the unpredictable tides and tempests of an uneven development whose elements are acquiring a well-nigh metereological velocity around the world, across all frontiers. The British crisis has no solution in sight; and perhaps the time in which one was possible, as a national recovery, has passed. At the zenith of English capitalism, Marx declared that his portrait of it in *Capital* held a mirror of the future to the rest of the world. Now, towards its nadir, the superscription may read once again: *De te fabula narratur.*

1987

5

A Culture in Contraflow

Few subjects can be so elusive as a national culture. The term lends itself to any number of meanings, each presenting its own difficulties of definition or application. Towards the end of the sixties, I tried to explore what seemed one significant structure to fall under such a heading in Britain – the dominant pattern of social thought, as displayed in a range of intellectual disciplines.[1] The product of this attempt had many failings. Written at a time of rebellion, in a spirit of *outrance*, it mounted a peremptory broadside on its chosen target. The price of this general excoriation was paid in a variety of local simplifications or misjudgements. Overstatement in critique was also accompanied by overconfidence of cure – a theoretical triumphalism that was no service to the radical alternatives advocated. These shortcomings aside, however, there was also a broader problem of method. For the procedure of the essay was open to two opposite, yet in some ways equally cogent, objections. From one standpoint, how could such a wide diversity of learned pursuits – roughly, the different humanities and social sciences – be responsibly brought into a single focus? From another, why give such attention anyway to a set of narrow academic specialisms, rather than to major popular manifestations of the national culture? The moment of 1968 explains why it was possible to be at once so selective and so sweeping. The choice of ground was a natural expression of campus ferment; as was the *coup de main* that could scoop its landmarks together into a systematically interrelated set of obstructions.

The exemplary antidote to any too intellectualist approach to our national culture – a work that probes the first as much as the second of

1. 'Components of the National Culture', *New Left Review* 50, July–August 1968. See Chapter 2 above.

these terms – is now to be found in Tom Nairn's tremendous study of the place of the British monarchy in official and popular sensibility.[2] No more compelling portrait of the construction of a certain profane *Volksgeist* has ever been written. But as this enquiry into an English Ideology itself makes clear, an effective hegemony is exercised in a variety of modes (whose relationship is often one of compensation rather than congruence), and at many different levels. Hence even a crude sketch of its arcaner reaches could serve a common end. Today, as it happens, there is good reason to look again at the intellectual region scanned twenty years ago, from something like the same vantage-point. For a large change has come over it. Then, the academic institutions of the country were the objects of a student revolt, from below. Now they are the targets of government hostility and intimidation, from above – a campaign of harassment described (in private) by a Ministerial spokesman with brutal candour as 'a *Kulturkampf* against British universities'. Once pilloried from the Left, the world of higher education has become a bugbear of the Right. What has happened in the intervening decades to bring about this change of fronts?

1. Political Changes

The predominant outlook of the English intelligentsia in the post-war settlement, once the Cold War set in, was parochial and quietist: adhering to the established political consensus without exercising itself greatly to construct or defend it. 'Cultivated but distrustful of ideas, socially responsible but suspicious of politics', Francis Mulhern has noted, its members were 'decidedly Anglican in temper: aware of higher things but careful not to become tedious on that account, and not really in much doubt of the basic good sense of the nation and those who governed it.'[3] Such peaceable conformism lasted down to the first Wilson years, supplying much of the sere backcloth against which campus revolt finally exploded in the late sixties. This was the cultural formation on which rebellious sights were trained in the movement of 1968.

The active unrest of those years was suppressed, or subsided, fairly quickly. But it altered the intellectual climate in the country durably.

2. *The Enchanted Glass*, London 1988; which points out, with justice, how large are the dimensions missing from the analysis I attempted: pp. 274–75.

3. 'Introduction: Preliminaries and Two Contrasts', to Régis Debray, *Teachers, Writers, Celebrities – The Intellectuals of Modern France*, London 1981, p. xix.

For the first time there emerged in Britain a stratum of radicalized graduates of a certain numerical mass – one which did not peter out, but was reinforced under the impact of the industrial battles of the early seventies. This provided the ambience in which a militant culture well to the left of the previous spectrum could take wider shape. The strength of the new area derived not merely from those marked by the break itself, but even more from the accumulation of ideas and forces which the space it created henceforward made possible. A superimposition of generations now combined to create a public sphere unlike any other since the Second World War – one whose dominant temper was pervasively, if never rigidly or exclusively, Marxist; and whose influence stretched from slowly increasing positions in colleges and universities and an intermittent presence in the national media, through a numerous undergrowth of its own periodicals and associations, across to allied strands in the performing arts and metropolitan counter-culture. The growth in size and significance of this sphere reflected in part the transformation of higher education itself. A student population of about 100,000 in 1960 had doubled to 200,000 by 1967–68, and had nearly trebled again by 1988, to some 580,000 – half of them by now in polytechnics. This sociological expansion of the basis for a British intelligentsia coincided with institutional changes that gave more outlets for radical intervention: among them the advent of the Open University, and the relocation of the *Guardian*; the rise of listings journalism, and the success of Channel Four. But the real foundation of the new sector lay in the interplay between three or four generations of socialist intellectuals, in such conditions.

The most important of these was, of course, the remarkable levy of the late thirties – nearly all active when young in the Communist Party, and most of them members of its Historians' Group after the War. Christopher Hill, Eric Hobsbawm, Edward Thompson, John Saville, Victor Kiernan, Gwyn Williams, Rodney Hilton, Raymond Williams were each leading figures in their own field by the mid sixties. Their collective influence, however, acquired a different weight over the next two decades – one due not simply to their intellectual gifts, outstandingly endowed though this generation was, but also to the blend of political steadfastness and moral independence that made them distinctive among their European counterparts. The productivity of this cohort continued unabated, yielding such major new *œuvres* in the eighties as that of Geoffrey de Ste Croix. It was followed by those whose formative experience lay in the late fifties – another period of established torpor and burgeoning protest against it. The New Left was the home of most of this generation, which lacked the organizational tradition of its predecessors, but was linked to the principal mass movement of the time, the Campaign for Nuclear Disarmament. When CND peaked, much of it suffered dispersal and withdrawal. But after the upheaval of the late sixties, it recovered a strong presence in the subsequent political climate. The careers of Stuart Hall or Raphael Samuel have been emblematic in this regard; somewhat apart in origin and evolution, the work of Tom Nairn rejoined company with them here. The linkage provided by this intermediate cluster of socialists, in their different ways, was vital for the consolidation of a mutually communicating Left.

The turmoil of the late sixties and early seventies threw up in turn its own political generation, whose characteristic form of expression became the critical journal, generally produced on the edges of the academy and against it. The formidable success of *Past and Present*, created by the Communist historians in the early fifties, did not serve as a model for these reviews, whose stance was more oppositional. Their number multiplied steadily over the decade, till they eventually covered virtually the whole range of social disciplines: philosophy, history, economics, sociology, anthropology, literature, among others.[4] Small and specialized, they coexisted with a buoyant press of counter-cultural leisure born from the same moment, enjoying wide readership in the capital. Expressive of this generation, whose rise in departments and media institutions was fairly rapid, has been the vivid career of its most fertile writer, Terry Eagleton. Finally, overlapping from the late seventies onwards, there emerged feminism – which, unlike its counterpart in the USA, was always predominantly a movement of the Left in Britain. In the neo-conservative eighties, its persistent dynamic helped to ensure that a radical public sphere did not lose ground even in a time of deepening political reaction.

For the arrival of the Thatcher regime, in effect, did not undo these cultural gains. Put to the test, the critical zone not only resisted but grew. Although the Conservative ascendancy soon transmitted a whole series of tensions through the Left, as Labour cracked and subsided, these stimulated rather than depressed theoretical debate and exploration. The liveliest vehicle of response to the new order became the reconverted *Marxism Today*, the mascot of the period, which owed

4. Among these journals, and their dates of inception, were: *Screen* (1969), *Radical Philosophy* (1972), *Economy and Society* (1972), *Critique* (1973), *Oxford Literary Review* (1974), *Critique of Anthropology* (1974), *History Workshop* (1976), *Social History* (1976), *Capital and Class* (1977), *Cambridge Journal of Economics* (1977), *Feminist Review* (1979), *Theory, Culture and Society* (1982).

much of its success precisely to its particular generational synergy – symbolized by its four keynote thinkers: Eric Hobsbawm, Stuart Hall, Martin Jacques and Beatrix Campbell. The controversies set off by the analyses and proposals of such writers as these, and the various alternatives or rejoinders to them, typically involving the same mixture of generations – say Raymond Williams, Raphael Samuel, Anthony Barnett or Hilary Wainwright – were often intense enough. But whatever the strains imposed by political adversity in these years, with its train of muffled frictions or misfired arguments, basic solidarity on the intellectual Left was rarely breached; and out of the trial emerged the liveliest republic of letters in European socialism. What other country in the 1980s generated a polemical library to rival *Iron Britannia*, *Zero Option*, *Towards 2000*, *Wigan Pier Revisited*, *For a Pluralist Socialism*, *The Enchanted Glass*, *The Hard Road to Renewal*, *Politics for a Rational Left*, *Theatres of Memory*? Much, although not all, of this literature was produced for an audience of the committed Left. But it was a characteristic of the new situation that its major voices were heard more widely. The two commanding cases were Edward Thompson's campaign for European nuclear disarmament and Eric Hobsbawm's call for a reconstruction of the British labour movement: each sustained appeals, from very broad platforms, of national resonance.

The appearance of a radical band – para, plain or post Marxist – at one end of the intellectual spectrum was in due course matched by the emergence of an ultra sector at the other. Here the decisive experience was the traumatic defeat of the Heath Government by the miners' strikes. From the mid seventies onwards a hard and effective Right broke away from the conventional post-war wisdoms, creating its own network of influence, whose strengths bore no symmetry to those of the Left.[5] The original core of this formation lay in a cluster of high-voltage policy institutes, well funded by business and devoted to uncompromising market principles: the Adam Smith Institute, the Centre for Policy Studies, Aims for Industry. It then acquired a spirited corps of younger publicists, many trained on the *Telegraph*, flanked by a somewhat older group of converted ornaments of the previous consensus. The skills of this amalgam made the *Spectator* the most polished weekly of the decade, its circulation overtaking that of a floundering *New Statesman*, for most of this period a casualty of the

5. See Maurice Cowling, 'The Origins of the New Right', *Encounter*, November 1989.

demise of Fabianism. On its farther side, a more abstruse coterie of High Tory theorists extolled the organic virtues of church or state, rather than the atomic principles of consumer sovereignty and the market, in the *Salisbury Review*. Limited in size, the new Right made up in leverage. Variously locked into the backlands of company finance, the counsels of the Conservative leadership, and the service of the press tycoons – the worlds of Michael Ivens and Digby Anderson, Ferdinand Mount or Hugh Thomas, John Vincent and Roger Scruton – its contribution to the ideological momentum of the Thatcher regime was considerable.

But the political prominence of this sector was never proportionate to its more strictly intellectual impact. Not large in numbers, it depended for much of its sound on the amplifiers to which it was wired. For a brief moment, in the early eighties, it looked as if it might capture the traditional gazette of mainstream intellectual life, when the *Times Literary Supplement* swerved rightward with a series of tirades against the evils of Marxism and its exponents – historical, political or philosophical. But this prospect soon faded, temporary editorial whim being no substitute for real collective dispositions. The new Right had always been relatively weak in the academy, and lacked the cadres to impose its vision at large. The great bulk of the British intellectual establishment held fast to its moderate liberal verities, indifferent or hostile to creeds of either Left or Right. The deep structures of its inherited outlook remained largely unshaken through all the zig-zags of British politics in these years. But whereas in the first half of the period these had appeared to be under threat from student power and trade-union militancy, arousing a general reactionary alarm, in the second half it was a vindictive government squeezing budgets and slicing departments which put them under severe pressure. The result was an unmistakable radicalization of Centre opinion, within its traditional parameters. By the time of Thatcher's third electoral victory, academic dislike of the regime was so widespread that the level of Conservative support had fallen to less than a fifth of the lecturing body, and despondency at the state of higher education was so acute that nearly two-thirds had contemplated quitting it.[6] The oppositional sympathies of this stratum, overwhelmingly with the Alliance a few years earlier, were by then equally divided between it and Labour, as the latter moved towards normalcy again. Viewed over two decades, the

6. See the MORI poll in the *The Times Higher Educational Supplement* of 5 June 1987.

principal change was that the major contingent of British intellectuals now felt not so much, perhaps, disaffected as disestablished. A conventional culture of the Centre had been dislodged from its familiar habitat. The most significant sign of this shift was probably less the decline in Conservative affiliation than a weakening of automatic allegiance to constitutional tradition. The rise of the Alliance, in most other ways distilling the received wisdom of the past, in this respect marked a break with it. Once electoral reform was put on the agenda, some at least of the structures of the British State were for the first time since the War exposed to question.

A good barometer of these alterations was the periodical founded within a few weeks of Thatcher's arrival in power in 1979, the *London Review of Books*. Its initial editorial stance reflected the typical concerns and fears of the median intelligentsia after its buffeting between the Campus Revolt and the Winter of Discontent, reasserting the traditional priorities of literature and democracy, against such dangers to them as the 'shameful politicising and destruction of the literary content of the *New Statesman*' and deceitful 'hostility to parliamentary government' disguised in the name of democratizing the Labour Party.[7] The creation of the SDP a year later, and its early success, were welcomed by the paper, whose pages regularly hosted its leading figures. But by 1985, while still warning of the 'violence and conspiracy' countenanced by sections of the Left, and approving the defeat of the miners' strike, the LRB had cooled towards the new party – in whose leader it had no confidence and whose doctrine of the social market economy it found vacuous.[8] Thereafter it increasingly concentrated its fire on the Right, in what became over time a savage opposition to Thatcher's rule, generating some of the most ferocious and iconoclastic writing of the decade. For these grenade attacks on the regime, the journal now often drew on both mainstream and Marxist writers of the Left: Paul Foot and Victor Kiernan alongside R.W. Johnson and Tam Dalyell.

The period 1968–1988 thus saw a set of gradual changes in the historic physiognomy of the British intelligentsia. An original Marxist culture of the Left gained ground, against a background of campus unrest and industrial militancy; a combative culture of the Right, interbreeding Chicago and Hatton, emerged to inform a government

7. Karl Miller, LRB, 25 October 1979; 'Preface', in M. Mason, ed., *London Review of Books, Anthology One*, London 1981, p. ix.

8. Karl Miller, 'Introduction', Nicholas Spice, ed., *London Reviews*, London 1985, pp. 5–6.

determined to wipe the slate clean of them; and the traditional culture of the Centre, still far the most extensive in influence, was ruffled into an unaccustomed *fronde* by the outcome. The net balance of these shifts was a movement running contrary to the course taken by the state: the political and intellectual worlds went in opposite directions. That happened during the eighties in France too. But there the long-delayed arrival of social-democratic government coincided with the newly minted dominance of a local neo-conservative ideology. Here a regime of the radical Right part confronted, part created an overall cultural drift to the left. Prompted by social resentment and doctrinal animus, its attempt at a *Gleichschaltung* of the academy tended to raise up the very adversaries it sought to stamp out, even as its drive to impose the values of the counting-house and constabulary on society swept forward elsewhere. While an authoritarian populism was redrawing the electoral contours of the country to the advantage of capital, in this domain the hegemonic legacy weakened.

2. Boundary Changes

A second, perhaps deeper, transformation occurred in these years. Twenty years ago it was possible to take the nation – actually, the meta-national state making up the United Kingdom – as an unproblematic unit for cultural enquiry. There was a general and a specific reason for that. The economies of the West were still relatively self-contained entities across the major branches of industrial production, nowhere more so than in the publishing and broadcasting sectors; while their educational systems had few points of interchange. Particular intellectual patterns do not, however, depend only on such institutional infrastructures. They are formed by political history and social tradition. Within the set of major Western societies, Britain in the immediate post-war decades possessed a peculiarly stable and insulated culture. Alone of them it had never known either social upheaval, foreign occupation or mass immigration – the three great solvents of fixed collective identity in the twentieth century; while unlike the few smaller European countries which had also escaped these, it had been the world's premier empire for two centuries, with all the confidence of superiority imparted by global power. These were circumstances which made British intellectual life exceptionally well defined. Even the admixture of conservative refugees who achieved post-war salience essentially confirmed rather than contested its standing dispositions. The national stamp of the prevailing outlook was one of its own proudest themes. In these conditions the frontiers of the spirit were indeed largely one with the borders of the state.

The ferment of 1968 thus represented not only a political break; in consciously forming part of an international chain of revolts, it marked a geo-cultural one too – of no less moment. This was the first time since the War that a significant movement within British society was directly synchronized to counterparts outside the country. The role of television in making the connexions possible was much commented upon at the time. The next two decades were to see a vast amplification of the material changes these events portended. Internationalization of the forces of production accelerated rapidly throughout the capitalist world, bypassing and diminishing the nation-state. Global corporations, outsourcing their manufacturing sites, were followed by offshore credit systems and interpenetrating financial markets. Travel became a huge industry in its own right, tourism intercontinental. Similar developments in due course found spectacular expression in the fields of publishing and broadcasting themselves, with the media empires of Bertelsmann, Murdoch, Elsevier, Berlusconi, Maxwell or Hachette. In this epoch, no culture could remain national in the pristiner senses of the past.

These processes affected the whole OECD zone. Arguably, however, Britain underwent the greatest transformation in this respect. Only recently the most self-contained of the larger NATO cultures, it was now to become in some ways the least closed to the surrounding world. The terms of this change were basically set by its peculiar crossroads position: geographically part of Europe and linguistically tied to America. By the late 1980s, there was probably no other country where influences from both sides of the Atlantic intermingled so freely. This inrush was not simply a matter of natural–historical location, and its two currents were not equivalent in character. Political shifts, indicated above, were necessary to convert a combination of general economic forces and particular geo-cultural emplacement into specific intellectual results. The emergence of a substantial culture of the Left after 1968 was the key which principally unlocked the gates to Europe. A wide absorption of the corpus of continental Marxism was the main initial consequence: a decade later, it was easier for a student to gain exposure to its full range in England than in France or Germany, where translations were fewer. Structuralism, less affiliated in origin, was received in an overlapping intellectual milieu through the seventies. Hermeneutics and post-structuralism followed in the eighties, entering through more diffuse channels, but by and large still issuing into a public sphere whose sympathies were with socialism and now feminism. Publishing houses of the Left, NLB in the first phase and Polity in the second, were the most concentrated transmission points for this process of assimilation. But in its later stages it extended into the area of the liberal centre, as membership of the European Community became normalized. A period which began with Althusser and Gramsci, Adorno or Lacan pioneered by journals like NLR, ended with Habermas and Bourdieu starring in a chastened TLS, and Derrida or Foucault admired by an LRB recanting its suspicion of deconstruction.

If the European influx was in the main a deliberate work of left and centre–left impulses in Britain, the American osmosis was by contrast partly an unintended consequence of the rise of the Right, although it was always a more mixed and multifaceted process. Common language and legal customs had traditionally bound the two countries together, although in many fields the US had often enjoyed a more diverse intellectual life because of its composite immigrant background. In the fifties, Washington's imperial interest in securing London as a junior partner and staging-post led its espionage service to create *Encounter* as a conduit for the Cold War ideology of the time in the UK. Effective enough in this political role, until its cover was blown by CIA boasts in the mid sixties, the journal was more limited as a vehicle for familiarization with American culture; its format was actually more oriented to Europe, as the endangered front-line of the Cold War, than to the safe rearguard of the US. More generally, Anglo–American intellectual relations still remained uneven, often distant. In the seventies, this changed. For the first time, central social disciplines became dominated by US developments. Outstanding cases in point were analytical philosophy, political theory and neo-classical economics, in each of which there was a certain traditional basis for Anglo-Saxon congruence. Although the new English Right could and did appropriate trends within these for its own purposes, naturalizing Friedman, Nozick or Buchanan, this was not the general pattern. The culture of the Centre filtered the distribution of influences, in which Rawls, Arrow or Chomsky loomed larger. In other areas American reception of European ideas predated or exceeded British, US adaptations then becoming a significant local reference in their own right, as in the Yale school of literary criticism; or formed distinctive hybrids like an existentialized neo-pragmatism. Overall, the American intelligentsia had followed a trajectory not unlike that of the British in these years – a radical breakthrough after the late sixties, a neo-conservative counter-thrust from the late seventies, with a continuing centre–liberal majority throughout. The two principal differences were the far weaker Marxist strain on the left – McCarthyism having ensured that there was no equivalent of the British Communist historians; and the more externally coloured alterations of mood in the liberal mainstream, troubled by visions of Soviet gain or US loss abroad rather than fears of trade-union militancy at home, before turning against Reagan's domestic programme in much the same way as its British counterpart did against Thatcher's. There was little potential here for comprehensive reinforcement of the radical Right in England, anyway scarcely warmed by the Presidential deficits.

In itself, of course, the general growth of the transatlantic presence within British intellectual life reflected the changing material balance between the two societies. The far greater resources and responsibilities of the hegemonic power were in due course bound to have their cultural effects. The rise of the *New York Review of Books*, from its beginnings in 1967, to become the peak literary–political periodical in the English-speaking world, with a circulation some four times those of its UK counterparts combined, was the most visible sign of the new correlation of forces. Drawing from the outset extensively on British contributors, to the point of incurring occasional reserve at home, the Manhattan fortnightly eventually achieved such international dominance that it seeded its opposite number in Bloomsbury. Given their approximate similarity of stance, the difference between the two publications said much about their respective contexts. Where its London offshoot exhibited a quirky individuality of temper, relatively indifferent to celebrity or news-value, combining independence of mind and a certain levity of interest,[9] the much wealthier New York original was more corporate and predictable in style, attached to conventional eminences, but also possessed of another political weight and sense of global priorities, as the intellectual look-out of a superpower.

This alteration in the periodical world, and its economic background, was a harbinger of wider energy transfers in the academic world. From the later sixties onwards, there had been a certain number of migrations from English to American departments. But these remained relatively isolated cases for another decade. It was not until the Conservative regime unleashed its campaign of attrition and compression against the institutions of higher education that a major exit to the United States occurred, in the eighties. By then the differentials in

9. October 1987 provided a nice illustration of the contrast: the cover of the NYRB was dominated by the crash of the world's stock markets, the LRB's devoted to the fall of trees in the English storm.

rewards and resources between the two university systems had increased enormously. In a federal state the Reagan administration, anyway more conscious of Japanese rivalry, had neither the same power, nor quite the same inclination, to wage a *Kulturkampf*; competitive pressures in boom conditions rather worked in the opposite direction, at certain levels creating something like an academic bull market. The economic contrast was also one of psychological climate, faculty morale often reflecting available matériel. The result of these push and pull forces was a well-publicized exodus from British universities. Although often exaggerated in extent, by the end of the eighties selective departures had affected virtually all social disciplines, and different generations within them, from the retired to the rising. Prominent instances included Ricks, Kermode, MacCabe, MacIntyre, Wollheim, Miliband, Ryan, Mann, Clark, Ryckwert, Brewer, Hobsbawm, Schama, Sen. This was not an emigration in the traditional sense. Many of those who now worked in the US either continued to reside partly in the UK or would return there; nearly all still comprised part of the British intellectual scene, even where assimilation into the American had gone furthest. What the new phenomenon really represented was the increasing erosion of boundaries between the two. The overall process was, of course, rather like the respective visa requirements between the two countries, less than symmetrical in effect – given their discrepancy in size. In the standard hyphenation, it necessarily modified Anglo more than American culture.

The sum of these developments, coming from different horizons and having different effects, amounted to a notable mutation. Englishry in its worst, caricatural forms declined. The ferruginous philistinism and parochialism of long national tradition were discomposed. The monotone political conformities of the ordinary intelligentsia broke up. British culture became looser and more hybrid. What were the consequences, in the principal areas touched on twenty years ago?

Any survey of these can only be selective and uneven, for obvious reasons of competence. The rough outline attempted below reflects not only these limitations. Others follow from the order of approach originally adopted, to which it seems best to remain accountable. The result is bound to be a partial view, liable to many an imbalance and omission. In a first group of disciplines – sociology, anthropology, cultural studies, art history – emphasis falls on individual thinkers, at the expense of a more general report. In a second group – philosophy, political theory, economics, history – attention goes rather to collective trends, with slighter focus on particular figures. Each procedure has its disadvantages: either treatment that is superficial or choice that is arbitrary. If there is a rationale for the difference of approach here, it may be that the newer fields are also less populous, allowing individual bodies of work to achieve a kind of salience that is rarer in older disciplines, with longer traditions. At all events, the interest in looking at them here will be the same: to consider the political currents and intellectual energies each has displayed. These two are, of course, by no means identical. A culture may lean to the left without being lively, just as it can innovate without being radical. How have recent British patterns looked in either regard?

3. Sociology

The sketch attempted in 1968 started with a general observation about the lay-out of the whole zone lying between the arts and the natural sciences. Its argument was that Britain had been peculiar among the leading European countries in never having produced either a national Marxism or a classical sociology. These two lacunae were seen as linked. Both historical materialism and the continental sociology which followed it were taken as paradigmatic attempts to grasp the nature of social totalities as a whole – the first a product of the rise of revolutionary labour movements, challenging the order of capital as such; the second an alternative articulated in reaction to them, within the bourgeois civilization of the time. Britain, however, lacking – unlike *fin-de-siècle* Germany, France or Italy – the spur of an insurgent socialism, missed the moment of a Weber, Durkheim or Pareto; and never knew the Marxist reprise of a Lukács, Sartre or Gramsci. Its dominant bloc had no interest in, or need for, any social theory liable to look too analytically at the social formation it governed as a natural kingdom. Piecemeal empirical research, serving practical adjustment or partial reform, was all that was required. Hence the curiosity that, as late as the epoch after the Second World War, sociology had still not gained any general acceptance as a subject in English universities – setting Britain apart from any other major Western country.

This account had various flaws. It relied much too heavily on Parsons's classical reconstruction of the European sociological tradition in *The Structure of Social Action* – a magisterial, but also in many ways misleading work – in dispatching the career of Spencer: a British sociologist of the largest ambitions, even if his major audience was significantly in the USA rather than the UK. Around Spencer, too, there was an underbrush of home-grown enthusiasts for practical brands of

Victorian ratiocination.[10] The earlier English record had thus not been so blank. At the same time the figures of the later European sociologists were also summarily foreshortened, by a too easily constructed contrast with Marx typical of the time. Nevertheless the main judgement was sound enough, and was to be confirmed by the much better founded and more nuanced comparative history of social theory that appeared in the next years, Geoffrey Hawthorn's *Enlightenment and Despair*: 'Sociology was virtually absent in England as an intellectually and academically distinctive pursuit', through the first half of the century, in 'the absence both of any threat of revolution from the left and of any concerted resistance from the right'.[11]

From the early fifties, however, a generation of sociologists formed at the LSE started to emerge, all – as their chronicler puts it – 'provincial in social origin, provincial in their political preoccupation, and provincial in their early jobs'.[12] These helped to provide the personnel for the belated institutionalization of the subject in the sixties, when some thirty new university departments were created. Behind them stood their one original senior, T.H. Marshall, theorist of the welfare state: in front, large unexplored tracts of the English class system, to whose empirical study they mostly addressed themselves. A.H. Halsey, drawing their collective self-portrait, admonishes underestimates of their radicalism – 'a socialism which had no need for Marxism and no time for communism'. But the terms in which he does so illustrate the charge he seeks to refute: for, he goes on, having learnt the lesson of 'My Country – Right or Left', these were above all intellectuals who knew 'Britain as a decent society' amidst fruitful converse with Whitehall and Westminster.[13] Such was the placid self-satisfaction of the period.

It was this scene which saw the most pronounced change of any discipline in the next twenty years. The original argument, made in 1968, associated the fates of Marxism and sociology – Britain, lacking a national version of the one, had failed to generate a classical achievement in the other. This linkage now found what looked like an *a contrario* vindication. The seventies, as we have seen, did witness the consolidation of a quite powerful Marxist culture in Britain for the first

10. See Lawrence Goldman, 'A Peculiarity of the English? The Social Science Association and the Absence of Sociology in Nineteenth-Century Britain', *Past and Present* 114, February 1987, pp. 133–171.

11. *Enlightenment and Despair – A History of Social Theory*, Cambridge 1987, p. 170.

12. A.H. Halsey, 'Provincials and Professionals: the British Post-War Sociologists', *Annales Européennes de Sociologie*, no. 1, 1982, p. 152.

13. Ibid., pp. 161–62.

time, centred on a considerable and distinctive corps of historians, one that largely defied the general tide of European opinion. As if in response, there then emerged – as it were on schedule – an outstanding indigenous sociology. Some of the roots of this development went back to the traditional concerns of the fifties and sixties, the patient enquiries into local class lauded by Halsey. But its most remarkable feature represented a striking departure from that past. For what now principally set British sociology apart from its neighbours was the appearance of a series of large-scale theories of history, comparable in scope to that adumbrated by Marx, and conceived to outmatch it. Four major ventures, each with its own leitmotifs, led the field.

Closest in intellectual origins to the legacy of Marxism, the work of Anthony Giddens has also involved the most direct critique of it. Giddens started his career with a forceful reconstruction of what he argued was the classical baseline of modern social theory: the nature of capitalism as construed in the contrasting thought of Marx, Durkheim and Weber. This inaugural gesture, repeating that of Parsons, consigned it to retirement. *Capitalism and Social Theory* tacitly but conclusively rewrote *The Structure of Social Action* by taking as an organizing framework not the generic problem of order, but the specific arrival of capitalism; eliminating Pareto for Marx as a central figure; and bringing a much finer scholarship to bear, in particular, on Durkheim. Where Parsons ended his book by lamenting Weber's misplaced interest in comparative historical enquiry, as a lowly diversion from the royal road of general action theory, Giddens concluded his by insisting on the need for fresh analysis of the variety of advanced societies in the contemporary world. This task he undertook in his next work, a level-headed and lucid theory of social class that reaffirmed its central importance to the overall structure of capitalist society, with nuanced accounts of upper, new-middle and working classes alike; while at the same time maintaining the relatively lesser significance of class – but not thereby of domination – for the character of communist societies. In either category, Giddens stressed the need for differential analyses of specific countries – rather than indolently taking the (largely atypical) USA as paradigmatic of the former, or the (no longer standardizing) USSR as the model of the latter. Often treated at the time as a neo-Weberian, Giddens could reply with reason that *The Class Structure of Advanced Societies* owed 'considerably more to Marx than to Weber'.[14] One could add, not only in conception but in sympathy.

---

14. *The Class Structure of Advanced Societies*, Second Edition, London 1980, p. 296.

Behind the book lay a steady, quietly indicated inclination to the left – quite free from Cold War reflexes, but equally persuaded that the labour movement retained a revolutionary impulse only so long as capitalism still confronted survivals of feudalism.

The later seventies saw a change of focus in Giddens's interests. He had started by criticizing Parsons for displacing sociological attention away from the concrete questions of capital and class that exercised Marx, Durkheim and Weber, and then offered the called-for corrective by reworking their agenda through to the present. He now seems to have felt that the time had come to double back and confront Parsons's original swerve away into a highly generalized action theory, on its own terrain. Arguing that the ostensible 'voluntarism' of the 'action frame of reference' in *The Social System* concealed a surreptitious behaviourism, in which socially effective agency was reduced to a set of need dispositions and role expectations, co-ordinated by internalized values, Giddens turned for remedy to the resources of two opposite traditions: a phenomenology derived from Husserl and Heidegger, and a structuralism descending from Saussure to its posted reversal in Derrida.[15] What Giddens was looking for in these lines of thought was a less determinist notion of social constraint and a more witting conception of human action than Parsons had afforded. The result was a 'theory of structuration', designed to steer between any still undue objectivism and any too aerated subjectivism.

Social structures were henceforward envisaged as virtual sets of rules and resources, at once enabling and constraining human actions. As such, they form both the medium and the outcome of the practices composing a social system – whose agents, for their part, always possess a working knowledge of its institutions that is integral to their operation. Society at large is in this sense 'constituted' by actors reflexively monitoring their own conduct as they reproduce or transform the rules and resources available to them. The intention of Giddens's theory is to strike a just balance between structure and agency in social explanation. But both intellectual and practical impulses tilt his account towards the latter. His original theoretical motive was a rejection of what he saw as Parsons's crypto-determinism; while a political commitment to libertarian socialism, increasingly explicit in his writing, spelt a natural aversion to 'derogation of

15. See especially *New Rules of Sociological Method*, London 1976, pp. 23–70; and *Central Problems in Social Theory*, London 1979, pp. 9–48.

the lay actor' – the insistent charge Giddens laid at the door of structuralism. The result, however, was to understate considerably the typical pressure of social determinations. Structural relations are not simply rules and resources for actors to employ: they are also forces that shape the nature and aims of actions themselves. Giddens is not unaware of this. Elsewhere he stresses the 'unacknowledged conditions and unanticipated consequences' of human agency – a better formula but one which necessarily weakens the status he claims for the 'knowledgeable actor' – bespeaking all that is not known, and undergone. In the domain of power too, the same bias for the subject reappears, in what is perhaps Giddens's most striking thesis – 'the dialectic of control' he suggests is built into the nature of agency as such. 'However subordinate an actor may be in a social relationship, the very fact of involvement in that relationship gives him or her a certain amount of power over the other', such that 'the weak always have some capabilities of turning resources back against the strong'.[16] If the moral–political appeal of this argument is evident, its empirical validity is less so. Perhaps significantly, Giddens's 'type case' is the labour contract in early capitalism – initially strengthening the power of employers over workers, subsequently prompting collective organization against them. It would be more difficult to view the extermination camp in the same light. No universal come-back is granted to every victim of oppression. The realities of the dialectic to which Giddens points are always historically variable, and can be truncated altogether. Parsons, declaring his theory of action to be voluntarist, made of it in effect a determinism; Giddens, intending his theory of action to be recursive, renders it close to a voluntarism.

After advancing a social ontology, Giddens moved on to the record of actual history. His way of doing so was to produce *A Contemporary Critique of Historical Materialism* – that is, of Marx's general account of human progress, rather than his particular analysis of capitalism – of a new kind: one not merely concerned to identify its errors or contradictions, as in a vast existing literature, but for the first time to present a worked-out alternative covering the same ground. The result was to be a trilogy, of which the first two, overlapping volumes have so far appeared. In Giddens's counter-construction, history is not a more or less continuous record of class struggles, but reveals a profoundly discontinuous

16. *Central Problems in Social Theory*, pp. 69–73, 6, 145–150; *A Contemporary Critique of Historical Materialism*, London 1981, p. 63.

structure – the advent of capitalism marking a qualitative break with all forms of civilization that had gone before it. Before, political domination in a broad sense – control of 'authoritative resources' – was always more significant than economic domination or control of 'allocative resources', and typically provided its foundation: class power largely deriving from state power, rather than vice versa. Societies of this kind – agrarian empires, city-states, feudal realms – were indeed class-divided, but struggle between the classes was no more than sporadic. Later, a 'class society' proper emerged in which such conflicts became endemic, as for the first time the economic and political domains were insulated and control of allocative resources became the primary basis of the power of the dominant class (although state administration also penetrated society more thoroughly than ever previously). The real periodization of history is thus not serial, but dichotomous. As such, it reveals no evolutionary pattern of the kind discerned by Marx. Humanity is defined not so much by labour as by meaning, and the forces of production contain no immanent dynamic prior to the arrival of capitalism – the technology of war developing more rapidly than that of agriculture. Where an upward curve can be registered is in a general widening of 'time–space distanciation', or the increasing societal capacity to gather, transport and store resources – whether authoritative (taxes, troops, censuses) or allocative (tools, foodstuffs, manufactures).

These proposals, as critics have pointed out, are less at variance with the traditional emphases of historical materialism than Giddens contends. The contrast between the dominance of extra-economic and economic modes of surplus extraction forms, after all, the central theme of Marx's own distinction between pre-capitalist and capitalist social formations; indeed, there is a striking coincidence between the thrust of Giddens's dichotomy and the views of a Marxist like Ellen Meiksins Wood.[17] A gross divide of the kind such accounts dwell upon is not, of course, incompatible with a finer periodization of historical forms – a major concern for the Marxist tradition in its own right. Rejection of any cumulative trend for the forces of production to develop across time does, by contrast, directly contradict a central premise of historical materialism. But here the weight of evidence is clearly on its side: a moderately formulated evolutionism has no difficulty in defending its plausibility, as Erik Olin Wright has

---

17. Compare, for example, *A Contemporary Critique of Historical Materialism*, pp. 210 ff., with Ellen Meiksins Wood, 'The Separation of the Economic and the Political in Capitalism', NLR 127, May–June 1981, pp. 83–86 ff.

shown.[18] In fact Giddens himself, while overtly repudiating all evolutionary theories of history, tacitly reinstates one. Simply, directionality lies in the stretching of time and space rather than in increasing the productivity of labour.

The difference between the two is, of course, that whereas the latter is an economic dynamic, the progress of the former mingles political and economic elements – advance in the resources of authority and allocation alike. If Giddens differs less from Marxist traditions than might appear in his periodization of human development, and attribution of a trend-line to it, his view of its causality does separate him sharply from them. Within the gamut of his key resources, the proportions are in principle indeterminate. 'All social life is contingent, all social change is conjunctural.'[19] There is no predominant or persistent hierarchy of causes. Giddens presses this claim most directly in his second volume, where he argues that capitalism, industrialism and the nation-state – treated as a unity generated by the first term, in historical materialism – represent three separate 'organizational clusters', whose original association in Europe was fortuitous: indeed could have been cancelled but for the accident of the First World War.[20] While Giddens's rejection of reductive explanations of the nation-state – and the new administrative and ideological powers it could mobilize – in terms of the sheer functional needs of capitalism is well founded, his appeals to chance disable the possibility of better ones. His own account makes little attempt to trace out a more complex and precise causality of the connexion between his three clusters; rather than an explanatory analysis it rests on a descriptive juxtaposition of them, whose warrant is the waiver given all requirements of deeper necessity.

From his theoretical corrections of historical materialism, Giddens draws political conclusions. From the outset, he consistently stated his aim to be a critique of Marxism from the Left, 'outflanking' it with a more radical scrutiny of the problems and prospects of human emancipation.[21] The corollary of his dissociation of capital, industry and nation-state is thus a political agenda that seeks not to dismiss the

18. See his fine essay 'Giddens's Critique of Marxism', NLR 138, March–April 1983, pp. 24–34.

19. *The Constitution of Society*, London 1984, p. 245.

20. 'If the course of events in the Great War, including the participation of the USA in the hostilities and the peace settlement, had not taken the shape they did, the nation-state in its current form might not have become the dominant political entity in the world system': *The Nation-State and Violence*, London 1985, pp. 234–35.

21. *Sociology – A Brief but Critical Introduction*, London 1982, p. 169; *Profiles and Critiques in Social Theory*, London 1982, p. 227.

exploitation of labour, but to avoid assimilating, or subordinating, the dangers of ecological destruction and of military violence – or civil invigilation – to it. Among these, Giddens gives greatest attention to the threat of nuclear war. In its shadow we live in a world 'at a vast distance from the future anticipated by Marx, with few obviously available paths of moving towards it', where in any case the multiformity of jeopardy and injustice means that socialism can itself no longer be 'the sole model of the "good society"'.[22] In consequence, a viable critical theory today will inevitably be post-Marxist. In common with most exponents of the term, Giddens stresses the absence of any privileged agents of liberation (or pacification), and the disparate character of the existing forces struggling towards them. But untypically, he is sceptical of the view, to be found in Habermas or Gorz, that 'the "newer" forms of social movement are increasingly replacing the labour movement as frameworks of struggle'.[23] Giddens has never believed in a revolutionary vocation of the working class, once capitalism had reached maturity; but he also seldom doubted the relative political efficacy of the labour movement in its subsequent forms. If Marx was wrong in the nature of the world-historical role he ascribed to the proletariat, he was nevertheless right in predicting that it would play one. No such forecast can be made, with any confidence, of the peace movements today. 'In terms of historical agencies of change, there is no parallel in the sphere of weaponry to the proletariat in the area of industrial labour. No plausible "dialectical counterpart" to the progressive accumulation of military power seems to exist.' Hence the need, felt by others besides Giddens, to summon a 'renewal of utopianism, mixed with the firmest forms of realism'.[24] Politically, few socialists would dissent. But in terms of Giddens's theory as a whole, it is as if here the dialectic of control threatens to become suspended, or peter out. The outlook for the subject has changed. Where Giddens's ontology evinces an unreasonable optimism of the agent, his history moves towards an unseasonable pessimism.

Parallel or overlapping in many respects, Michael Mann's work has issued into a different kind of achievement. After beginning as an empirical sociologist of class in the regular British mould, with a monograph on the effects of factory relocation on labour-force atti-

---

22. *The Nation-State and Violence*, pp. 3, 337.
23. *Social Theory and Modern Sociology*, London 1987, pp. 50, 225–252, 275–296.
24. *The Nation-State and Violence*, p. 326.

tudes, Mann published a seminal essay on the 'Social Cohesion of Liberal Democracy', attacking the prevalent view that value-consensus was the cement of political order in Western capitalism. Anticipating by a decade subsequent critiques of 'the dominant ideology thesis', Mann argued that normative patterns in US or British society were in fact heterogeneous and inconsistent, amounting to no governing belief system that would ensure the stability of the state: the subordinate classes accepted the status quo for pragmatic reasons, in the absence of visible alternatives, rather than out of any inward conviction of its rightness.[25] The critical thrust of this thesis was aimed both at Parsonian apologias for capitalist democracy, and Western Marxist exposures of it.

Consciousness and Action among the Western Working Class had the same two-edged force, cutting against the claims of end-of-ideology and Marxist theories of labour alike. At a time of generic rhetorical declamations on either side, Mann pointed out the range of potential varieties of working-class consciousness, and the need to distinguish between simple awareness of class identity, elemental sense of class opposition, developed conceptions of a class-determined social totality, and revolutionary conviction of overall class alternatives to the existing order. The predominant pattern in the contemporary Western world combined only the first two elements, with the result that industrial and political action were rarely integrated by the labour movement. Within the typical forms of industrial action itself, struggles over pay were usually separated from struggles over control, and the former nearly always prevailed over the latter; for an aggressive economism can extract higher wages from employers without loss to them if productivity is growing, while disputes over control tend by their nature to be zero-sum conflicts in which workers can gain only if management loses – hence the far tougher stance of capital in this area, and the much more defensive posture of labour, for the most part concerned only with job regulation. If technical and scientific workers reveal more sense of totality and alternative – hence greater interest in issues of control – than the traditional working class, they also – by reason of their relatively privileged position – possess less sense of collective identity and opposition.

Mann's conclusion was therefore that there existed 'a fatal contradiction within the working-class movement. Those who are most alienated and most desperate are those who are least confident of their

25. *American Sociological Review* 35, 1970, pp. 423–439.

ability to change the situation. Those who are most confident in their own power and clearest in their intentions feel least embattled and disposed towards desperate remedies.'[26] Historically, this had not precluded the emergence of genuinely revolutionary labour movements. But these arose where the ruling order was not yet a fully modern capitalist hegemony, and uprooted migrants from an archaic rural society encountered large-scale industry, in contexts where there were strong pre-capitalist traditions of violent political conflict. Marx was right to identify the central contradiction of capitalism as the conflict between the interests of capital and of labour, and to assert the inherent tendency of the working class towards its own collective identity and organization. But the long-term outcome of these processes was by no means the proletarian revolution he had predicted. 'The working class does not carry within itself a new form of social order.'[27]

The similarities between the positions of Giddens and Mann at this date were obvious, and acknowledged. Mann was less concerned with theoretical definitions of class structure, and more interested in the practical upshots of class action. Politically there was probably little separating the two, though Mann's socialism seems to have taken a more institutional and programmatic direction. Active on the Left of the Labour Party in the late seventies, by the mid eighties he was offering a detailed social analysis of the British electorate to the party, as an empirical basis for identifying those constituencies that could be won to it – perhaps the most informed and concrete map of its kind to be produced in the Labour debates of that time.[28] The ideology capable of uniting the party and conquering a majority, Mann argued, would be a contemporary version of the idea of social citizenship once theorized by Marshall.

During the 1970s, Mann's major interests had meanwhile moved – like those of Giddens – away from the problematic of class. But where Giddens shifted towards the area of ontology, Mann plunged directly into history, and in far greater depth and detail than his colleague was subsequently to do. The outcome was the grandiose project of *The Sources of Social Power*, the first volume of which is the most commanding single work of the new British sociology, and a landmark in

---

26. *Consciousness and Action among the Western Working Class*, London 1973, p. 70.

27. Ibid., p. 71.

28. *Socialism Can Survive – Social Change and the Labour Party*, Fabian Pamphlet No. 502, London 1985.

the discipline *tout court*. Following Parsons, Mann distinguishes at the outset between two types of power: 'distributive', or control by some agents over others, and 'collective', or mutual enlargement of capabilities; but refines them into the 'extensive' and 'intensive', 'authoritative' and 'diffused' forms of each – corresponding roughly to their geographical reach or vertical efficiency, extent or lack of premeditation, respectively. At the same time, following Weber, he postulates three general sources of such power – economic, ideological and military – no one of which possesses any overall causal primacy in history, their order of relative significance varying greatly by epoch and region; but adds territorial administration as a fourth 'political' source of power, separate from armed coercion. These diverse sources of power, in turn, are not tidily stacked within societies that encase them. For 'societies' themselves are neither unitary nor bounded totalities but heterogeneous, overlapping networks of social interaction, without fixed edges – which, precisely for that reason, characteristically tend to permit the emergence of 'interstitial surprises' capable of eventually challenging or bypassing the dominant institutional forms of power.

With these navigating instruments, Mann undertakes a Magellan-like voyage through the history of humanity from the Neolithic Age to the Enlightenment. The result is a vast narrative of power, of great deftness and assurance, marrying theoretical subtlety and empirical grasp. Mann's complex typology of the modes and sources of power does not remain a mere formal taxonomy. It is put to work, with arresting effect, through his study of the 'exact infrastructures' of each medium of power in successive epochs: military logistics, cultural literacy, bureaucratic recruitment, juridical machinery, monetary flow, fiscal catchment. The unremitting attention given to these practical preconditions for the activation of formal claims to power is what gives Mann's account, for all his own disavowals, its peculiarly materialist cast.

Yet the disavowals are also germane. Historical in its conception and materialist in its application, Mann's work is at the same time a rejection of historical materialism – or a reminder that there may be more than one of them. Denial of any generalizable causal hierarchy in the record of the past is a central tenet of *The Sources of Social Power*, as it was for Weber. Mann, however, sets out to specify the permutations in the dominant source of power across several millennia, a diachronic reconstruction Weber never attempted. On the other hand, Weber's sociology explored large synchronic comparisons between civilizations, which Mann renounces. The result is to narrow his history, original in its conceptual framework, to a conventional spatial zone: essentially the familiar story of Occidental civilization, from its origins in the Near East and Mediterranean to its apotheosis in the North Atlantic. Mann wishes, like so many others, to explain the reasons for the ultimate triumph of Western Europe over the rest of the world – what set it apart from and then above all rivals, on the plane of power. But true difference can only be established by contrast. Avoiding all comparative analysis of Chinese or Arabo–Turkic civilizations, among others, Mann would seem to deprive himself of any basis for a causal explanation of Western specificity. In fact, however, an originating comparison quietly straddles the narrative, and covertly dictates its outcome. Its medium is religion. After a masterly analysis of the spread of Christianity in the Roman world, Mann appends a digression on Confucianism, Islam and Hinduism as alternative doctrines of salvation. Here the *differentia specifica* of the faith of the West is insinuated between the lines. The dynamism of these 'transcendent ideologies' depended on their degree of egalitarian universalism, everywhere in contradiction with the authoritarian – clerical or secular – institutions embodying or diffusing them. By this standard, Confucianism was at once too elite and too ethnic a creed – Chinese identity being unproblematic; Hinduism was too blatantly hierarchical in its proliferations of caste and fixations with purity; while Islam was too compromised with tribalism, as well as too rudimentary in doctrine. All of these religions provided a 'normative pacification' vital to the zones where they prevailed, but the Christian faith achieved a higher order of it by a combination of greater social universality and spiritual complexity. As a track-layer of civilizational development, 'Christianity proved so far superior to the others that all had to adapt to its encroachments' in the end.[29] For while economic, political and military networks of power all played contributory parts in the later genesis of the 'European miracle', it was the ideological network of Christendom that alone was essential to it.

The decisive determinant of the largest watershed in world history – the advent of European commercial and industrial supremacy – is thus located in the mediaeval Church. This may look like a down-dated version of Weber's claims for the Protestant ethic. But it is in fact much closer to Durkheim's view of religion – the central achievement attributed to Catholic Christianity being its creation of a common identity across the continent, through its missionary and pastoral work from the Dark Ages onwards. Social cohesion, not individual vocation, is the

29. *The Sources of Social Power*, vol. 1, London 1986, pp. 341–371.

leitmotif of Mann's explanation. The empirical weaknesses of this construction have been pointed out recently.[30] They may derive, however, from a theoretical predisposition. Mann starts by defining his focus as 'social power': that is, if distributive, 'mastery over other people', and if collective, dominance 'over third parties or nature'.[31] Relations with nature thus comprise only, so to speak, a quarter of his initial agenda. One result is to tilt his account of religion sharply away from its resolution of human tensions with the natural order, towards its function as a mortar of the social order. Theology is, so to speak, over-socialized. Another consequence is that Mann's attention to the economic processes that are usually taken to be the centrepiece of the unique metamorphosis of Europe becomes relatively marginal. For production is always necessarily, in the first instance, a transformation of nature. In the pre-modern world ideology and economy alike are irreducibly connected to the physical universe – as practical and imaginary mediations to nature. By contrast Mann's other two sources of power, the military and the political, are purely intra-social in their operation, and it is no accident that it is towards them that the weight of his account shifts once the Christian faith has laid the groundwork for European ascendancy.

The development from 'co-ordinating' mediaeval princedoms to 'organic' national states forms the real climax of Mann's story. Essentially, what he shows is the way in which the exigencies of war were the forcing-house of taxation and administration – the requirements of external military power nursing the conditions of internal political power. Yet for Mann, the state as such is defined by its monopoly of the latter rather than the former – since military violence, like economic wealth or ideological authority, has historically been a capacity of many groups within civil society, as well as the state. It is only 'centralized territorial regulation' that has been an exclusive attribute of the state; and it is this political power proper that is the foundation of its autonomy from civil society. Mann's bid to break with the trichotomy common to the Marxist and the Weberian tradition thus has a strong conclusive purpose. But it issues in a – perhaps provisional – double paradox. For the source of power that confers autonomy on the state itself enjoys least autonomy of all: political regulation is scarcely conceivable without the resources of armed coercion, fiscal revenue and ideal legitimation. At the same time, the development of

30. Chris Wickham, 'Historical Materialism, Historical Sociology', NLR 171, September–October 1988, pp. 63–80 – the best critical assessment of Mann's work to date.
31. *The Sources of Social Power*, p. 6.

centralized territorial administration culminates in 'organic' national states that not only penetrate civil life deeply at all levels for the first time, but also demarcate it with frontiers of a quite new institutional efficacy – thereby tending to create something very like those 'bounded totalities' Mann's theory set out to deny. Rather than states arising from societies, one might say, societies – hitherto declared notional – risk appearing the offspring of states. Problems such as these are left for the sequels.

The intellectual background of the third outstanding construction of this period was rather different. The career of W.G. Runciman started earlier, well before the commotion of the late sixties; something of the characteristic tone of the fifties, a certain self-conscious formality of manner, attaching to all his later writing. His first short book, *Social Science and Political Theory*, took the Anglo-Saxon political philosophy of the time as an accepted starting-point, but sought to impress on it the need to be informed by unfamiliar traditions of European sociology. Among these, pride of place was given to Weber. Class was indeed the most important social basis of political conflict in industrialized societies, but it was to be viewed as Weber and not Marx had understood it.[32] Democracy was best theorized by Schumpeter, and the British version of it – whatever objections might be made to our electoral system – was a model of stability and strong government. The one weakness of Weber was his belief that all values were relative to the social scientist – a fallacy corrected by H.L.A. Hart, who had demonstrated the universality of the 'minimum content of natural law', so providing a sound common basis for political philosophy. Subsequent essays, collected under the significant rubric of *Sociology in its Place*, confirmed much of this initial set at the subject. Weber's triad of class, status and party was upheld so firmly that its lack of universal acceptance could be treated as an intellectual puzzle; just as his account of religion was preferred to that of Durkheim, and his typology of legitimacy was vindicated through contemporary African example. This strong Weberian commitment was nevertheless not undiluted. The force of the title essay was to cut the pretensions of sociology down to the standard bedrock of current Anglo-Saxon positivism – behavioural psychology. Sociologists, Runciman declared flatly, 'will never develop an autonomous "sociological" theory' that could be a substi-

32. *Social Science and Political Theory*, Cambridge 1963, p. 4.

tute for such a 'psycho-ethology'[33] – a reductionist credo testifying to the persistence of the psychologistic strain in the intellectual orthodoxy of the time.

On the other hand, Runciman had meanwhile published an influential study, *Relative Deprivation and Social Justice*, designed to execute his more fruitful programme of bringing together sociology and political philosophy. Runciman borrowed the notion of 'relative deprivation' to explain the discrepancies between objective social inequalities in Britain and subjective perceptions of them. But the real innovation of the study lay in its extended deployment of Weber's three types of stratification as distinct dimensions of inequality in British society, tracked historically from the end of the First World War to the early sixties, and its carefully periodized enquiry into the reaction of the working class to them. Runciman's findings were that British workers had shown decreasing resentment of class inequality after the Depression, although actual income had not been commensurately redistributed; on the other hand, increasing resentment of status inequality since the Second World War, although actual differences of esteem had diminished; and declining political militancy since the Attlee Government, despite the absence of any basic change in the pattern of power. All these conclusions remain persuasive. Unnoticed in the arrival at them, however, was an anomaly running through Runciman's whole procedure. Class was taken as merely one of Weber's three dimensions of inequality, on a par with status and party, in the social consciousness of agents; but it was simultaneously taken as the basic ground of the social being of those agents – the 'British working class' appearing unproblematically throughout as the objective vector of those variations in subjectively experienced 'deprivation' Runciman was concerned to trace. One might say this was to have a Marxist cake and make a Weberian meal out of it.

The second part of the book shifted gear to sketch the normative outline of a society more equal than that of contemporary Britain. Here Runciman drew on Rawls's early work. This was historically the first use of the contractarian model later developed in *A Theory of Justice*, and its great interest – apart from its date – is the 'fairly radical' consequences, in his own words, which Runciman derived from it: much greater industrial democracy than mainstream British trade-unionism demanded; stiff progressive taxation to ensure egalitarian provision for needs; and a common system of education for all

33. *Sociology in its Place*, Cambridge 1970, pp. 41–42.

children.[34] A just society would resemble the USA in democracy of manners, but with the 'missing ingredient' of socialism – understood not as social ownership of the means of production (possibly, but not necessarily, preferable to private control of them), but as acceptance of the criterion of social need. Perhaps more strikingly, Runciman directly confronted a central question avoided by Rawls, the problem of the transition to any just social organization. Since the achievement of social justice could never be swift or painless, Runciman observed, 'there may always be good reasons why social justice should not be done, even where it can be shown that inequalities are unjust.' Consequently, in his own society, 'if the evidence has shown that the British are a people little given either to envy or to radicalism, this is not something which calls at once or without question for remedy.'[35]

This Laodicean note was to become more rather than less pronounced as significant social sectors started to behave in unBritish fashion soon after the publication of Runciman's book. A decade later he set out his political positions in a pamphlet for the Tawney Society, linked to the newly formed SDP. *Where is the Right of the Left?* argued that the state should seek to spread private ownership of companies rather than extend the public sector, and that managerial hierarchy within them ought to be free from government or union interference. But taxation should be progressive, educational opportunity increased, monopoly restrained, and employees consulted. Such a package, Runciman explained, dispensed with the terms 'capitalism' and 'socialism', for it was 'compatible with a society that could quite well be labelled as a version of both or either'.[36] Ideological amenability of this kind is usually less than it appears, and Runciman was rather blunter elsewhere: 'The truth is that it is no longer possible to formulate a "radical alternative" which can coherently reconcile the traditional set of socialist but still democratic objectives.'[37] While Runciman continued to reject the notion of a Centre politics, the shift along the spectrum within the Left is clear enough.

Runciman's major sociological enterprise, *A Treatise on Social Theory* in three volumes, started to appear in the early eighties. In conception, this was the most original of all the large projects undertaken in this period. The methodology of the social sciences occupies the first volume; a substantive theory of social evolution is presented in

34. *Relative Deprivation and Social Justice*, London 1966, pp. 258–272.
35. Ibid., pp. 294–95.
36. *Where is the Right of the Left?*, London 1983, p. 12.
37. 'On the State of the Left', *London Review of Books*, 17 December 1982.

the second; the history of twentieth-century Britain will form a case-study calculated to illustrate method and substance alike in the third. Runciman's epistemology formally aims at 'steering a safely manage-able course between the Scylla of positivistic empiricism and the Charybdis of phenomenological hermeneutics'[38] – a goal that looks deceptively close to formulations of Giddens. Runciman's stance is in fact absolutely distinctive. The first volume of the *Treatise* unites four claims, each bold enough in its own right, in a provocative synthesis of opposites. The understanding of any society comprises, for Runciman: theory-neutral reportage of the empirical facts of the social order; theoretical explanation of its governing structures, common in kind to the natural sciences; and authentic description of its lived textures. Such understanding, if properly conducted, moreover always involves an evaluation specific to the social sciences, informed by the principle of an impartial benevolence. Scarcely one of these contentions is free from scandal, in many circles – the notion of an unprejudiced inventory of data, without conceptual pre-emption, being widely deemed the positivist illusion *par excellence*, and any assimilation of the social to the natural sciences *a fortiori* anathema. Even opinion more inclined to accept these tenets might well draw back from the further assertion that there exists a universal moral ground at once inherent in and manda-tory for any social science, which can be expressed in terms derived from Bentham. The confidence of these claims could be taken for an arrant scientism. The other ingredient of Runciman's programme, however, calls for an imaginative recapture of subjective experience normally associated with poetry or fiction: his own exemplars, indeed, including Flaubert and Angela Carter. Under the mild guise of 'descrip-tion', in other words, there lies a prodigious hermeneutic ambition. Nor is this mode of social understanding any mere extra, or intellectual luxury. On the contrary, it marks what is specific to the enterprise of sociology itself: 'The distinctive problems of the social sciences are problems of description and not of explanation.'[39]

Each element of the complete prescription is set out with great cogency. There has been no better recent statement of the unity of scientific method in the task of explanation; and few more vivid accounts of the literary requirements for the task of recreation. But can these two be so readily reconciled? Setting aside the – daunting – practical demands their combination would put on most adepts of the

---

38. *A Treatise on Social Theory*, vol. 1, *The Methodology of Social Theory*, Cambridge 1983, p. 144.
39. Ibid., p. 41.

social sciences, there is a theoretical dislocation between them. For while reportage and explanation, Runciman remarks, inevitably answer to a correspondence theory of truth, he argues that description is subject to a coherence conception. A strict rationalism of structural analysis is thus joined to something like a broad relativism of experiential retrieval. The polarization seems undue: all descriptions, in Runciman's sense, being subject to judgements of accuracy as well as authenticity. On the other hand, if Runciman overstates the veridical difference between explanation and description, he understates – to put it mildly – the difficulty of lodging consensual evaluation in the act of reportage (or explanation) itself. The notion that all social scientists, of whatever school, 'share some sort of tacit, if unspecific, commitment to the value of benevolence',[40] has forgotten the statisticians of the SS. Where Weber once saw the social sciences haunted by the warring deities of a new polytheism, in incurable conflict with each other, Runciman appears to project a placid division of labour between them.

The second volume of the *Treatise* aims, in its turn, to surpass *Economy and Society* in two fundamental respects, by proposing a more orderly and systematic taxonomy of the historical range of societies than Weber's uncompleted *chef d'œuvre* was able to do, and by demonstrating a directionality to them more compelling than his epos of rationalization. Runciman's classification of social forms is founded on the Weberian triad that runs through all his work, here lent a vocabulary deliberately adapted from Marx. Power comes in three, and only three, forms – economic, ideological and coercive – which compose separate modes of production, persuasion and coercion. Although always interwoven, these may vary independently of each other: no fixed interrelation or causal hierarchy exists between them. Each mode has its gamut of distinct historical variants – here reckoned as eight of economic power, eight of ideological, seven of coercive. It is the specific combination of these that constitutes any given society, defined as a particular 'mode of distribution of power'. From this Linnaean-style grid, Runciman develops a typology of the actual societal forms exhibited by the historical record. The sweep of the resultant survey is magisterially comparative, embracing not only the East Asian, Islamic or Indo–American experiences set aside by Mann, but a rich spectrum of African and Pacific communities as well.[41] The

40. Ibid., p. 304.

41. Earlier case-studies of Classical Greece, Republican Rome, Anglo-Saxon England, the French Revolution and Polish Communism are now collected in *Confessions of a Reluctant Theorist*, London 1989, pp. 53–189.

resultant taxonomy is without question better organized and more fully informed than Weber's. But its fulcrum exacts a perceptible cost. For the distribution of power is never simply coextensive with the contours of society. Runciman's focus on it alone is still more single-minded than Mann's, and with some nuances it yields the same kind of effects. In this treatment ideological life is reduced to the work of securing, not socialization, but deference – its every other dimension set aside. Economic life, despite ostensible reference to modes of production, is equated with mechanisms of exchange and exploitation alone, as in those versions of Marxism that subsume or dissolve forces of production entirely into relations of production.

One consequence is that Runciman's typology itself lacks any dynamic, of the sort assigned to such forces in a more classical historical materialism. His inventory of some fourteen basic patterns of power is nevertheless aligned in a temporal series from hunter-gatherer to industrial societies. But this economic chronology, figuring a long-run growth of 'resources',[42] remains extrinsic to the political typology of 'power' – a shadow reference lying unarticulated behind it, rather than a directive principle of it. The function of a narrative, disavowed in traditional forms, devolves onto a general theory of social evolution. Each dimension of power, Runciman argues, is sustained by specific practices, carried by particular groups. It is the competition between rival practices, in which the criterion of success is the exercise of power itself, that acts as the equivalent of natural selection, generating the morphology of social forms. In this process, no less objective and unintended than its biological counterpart, the origins of practices themselves can be treated as random inputs, like genetic mutations, for the explanation of evolutionary shifts. Not innovation, but selection, is what matters for the course of history. Runciman brings this Darwinian model of social change to bear on an extended set of test cases: the emergence of feudalism in Western Europe, Poland, Japan, Iran, the late Ottoman Empire, Latin America; of absolutism in China, Japan, France, Prussia, Russia, the Roman Empire; of a liberal industrialism in England, authoritarian in Japan and Argentina, socialist in Russia. The directionality of these transformations is, as in Spencer, towards increasing complexity; but the subtlety with which they are explored is of another order. Curiously, however, the central mechanism of social selection is by comparison somewhat underspecified: competition is

42. *A Treatise on Social Theory*, vol. 2, *Substantive Social Theory*, Cambridge 1989, pp. 39, 76–77.

more invoked as a principle than traced through as a process, the alternative practices actually outrivalled often remaining elusive. At the same time, the sources of variation in human history – that which throws up new material for the process of selection itself – are not easily compared with the mutations of biological evolution. For there is no radical difference in nature between the innovation and adoption of practices, as social processes: conscious intentionality is the common medium of each, calling for the same kind of theoretical explanations. Beginnings cannot be divorced from endings, as if they belonged to another order accidental to this one. Through the customary web of unlooked-for consequences, human agency unites them. Runciman exactly reverses Weber's option, who declared that it was the origins of the Protestant ethic that interested him, not the reasons why it was selected by the spirit of capitalism.[43] A fully historical sociology, however, will pursue both sorts of question, and the vocabulary of its answers can only be one. It will be intriguing to see how far the division between the random and the regular, inscribed here in a general theory of social evolution, can be maintained in the closer account of modern British development to follow it.

Set somewhat apart from these serialists and system-builders, there is finally the singular *œuvre* of Ernest Gellner. Senior in generation and Central European in background, Gellner has also always been a philosopher and anthropologist as much as – indeed before – a sociologist. His multifarious writings, a rutilant harlequinade of ideas, cover a wider span of topics than that of any contemporary: the epistemology of Wittgenstein, Quine or Popper; the foibles of ethno-methodology, and the merits of functionalism; the social mould of the Muslim world, and the cultural sway of Freudian psychoanalysis; the rise of nationalism, and the nature of science; Weber's disenchantment and Arendt's totalitarianism; relativism, expressivism, structuralism; Hume and Nietzsche; revolution and liberalization.[44] Gellner's position within the national culture, less that of an academic authority than of an Enlightenment intellectual, is a reminder of something that has changed since the time of *Words and Things*. The dominance of a

43. Compare *A Treatise on Social Theory*, vol. 2, p. xxv with *The Protestant Ethic and the Spirit of Capitalism*, London 1930, p. 55.

44. See, in the past decade, *Spectacles and Predicaments* (1980); *Muslim Society* (1981); *Nations and Nationalism* (1983); *Relativism in the Social Sciences* (1985); *The Psychoanalytic Movement* (1985); *Culture, Identity and Politics* (1987).

White emigration has passed away. Not that there were fewer such arrivals in the Anglo-Saxon world in the past twenty years – on the contrary, police repression and persecution in the East ensured a greater flow than before the War. But now, in a suggestive reversal of the pattern of the thirties, the majority settled in the United States (or France), rather than the United Kingdom. The archetypal figure of the new wave, who might have filled the role of disillusioned sage in Britain, was the Pole Leszek Kolakowski; but he seems to have found Oxford insufficiently bracing, preferring the more congenial environment of Chicago.

Gellner's politics have none of the connexions with the Left that mark the work of Giddens, Mann or Runciman, but they are free from any zealotry of the Right as well. They might be described as that rare thing, a genuine independent liberalism. Class and capitalism ('an overrated concept') were never central preoccupations, as they were for the younger generation of British sociologists. On the other hand, the ideology of the free market was always caustically viewed as a screen for political distribution of life chances. Given this very different outlook, it is all the more striking that Gellner too developed much of his historical sociology through a confrontation with Marxism. In his case, however, it was Eastern rather than Western Marxism that provided the critical foil. No country in Central Europe had a more tragic fate under Communist rule than his native Czechoslovakia, an experience about which Gellner has written well.[45] But this never prevented, may even have partly prompted, a sympathetic interest in the intellectual life of the USSR, which eventually produced *State and Society in Soviet Thought.*

Two themes emerge from this critical survey of the better Soviet Marxism that found expression in the depths of the Brezhnev period. The first is respect for its typical concern with large issues, about which too many Western thinkers had become, as he puts it, blasé. 'The crucial fact about humanity is that a species, which a few millennia ago consisted of small, powerless and ignorant bands, is now unbelievably numerous, powerful and knowledgeable. This is *the* rags-to-riches story which, above all others, needs to be understood.'[46] In Gellner's view the more intelligent Soviet thinkers rarely lost sight of this central question, and in trying to answer it developed evolutionary typologies at least as fertile as conventional functionalist paradigms on the other

45. See *Spectacles and Predicaments*, Cambridge 1980, pp. 341–49; *Culture, Identity and Politics*, Cambridge 1987, pp. 123–33.
46. *State and Society in Soviet Thought*, Oxford 1988, p. 116.

side of the Iron Curtain, with a robust spirit in refreshing contrast to the evasive and etiolated styles of Western Marxism. On the other hand, Gellner points to recurrent weaknesses of much of this theoretical work: above all, in his opinion, a reluctance to admit that coercion is often historically more decisive than production in shaping societies, and does not arise from it. In 'Asiatic' empires, states led to the creation of classes rather than vice versa. In nomadic societies, lack of major internal stratification was no obstacle to practices of predation spiralling into state construction, and then lapsing back to clan level, without any change in the economic base. Communist societies themselves display, supremely, the elevation of political coercion over economic possession as a structural principle. Gellner's insistence on the role of force in determining particular social outcomes coexists with an equal emphasis on the impact of technology in marking general historical watersheds. Against the fivefold schema still prevalent in Soviet Marxism – primitive society, slave society, feudalism, capitalism and socialism – he upheld a simpler three-way classification into foraging, agrarian and industrial societies, contending that this is actually the more materialist, in so far as it turns on fundamental techniques of securing a livelihood rather than more superficial vicissitudes of social organization. Marxist interpretations of history are thus, as it were, trumped at both ends – convicted at once of giving too much and too little importance to material production.

These themes reappear in the wide-angled synthesis that brings together Gellner's own vision of past and present, *Plough, Sword and Book*. Subtitled simply 'The Structure of Human History', this distils his distinctive sociology of development, hitherto strewn across a profusion of topics, into a single master-story of the species. By contrast with Mann, Gellner disavows any inductive ambition. His account, although empirically well-informed, does not proceed evidentially but deductively, seeking out the logic of world history, rather than reconstructing the details of its episodes. Unlike Runciman, on the other hand, he rejects any analogy with biological evolution, on the grounds that historical innovations are transmitted by culture, which therefore perpetuates acquired characteristics in a way that natural selection forbids. The enumeration of the main phases of human development is actually much the same in the two; but what is a background sketch for the one becomes the foreground drama of the other. If Runciman's typology remains unintegrated with his periodization, however, Gellner's periodization dispenses with any typology. Each of his three great stages of development – Foragia, Agraria and Industria – permits a 'bewildering variety' of societal forms, undetermined by their respective bases of production. The technical level of economic life only sets problems for social organization: it supplies no solutions. Specific social structures are always shaped by a triad of forces – production, coercion and cognition – whose relative importance varies significantly throughout history.

This standpoint looks very close to that of the *Treatise on Social Theory*. But there is one critical difference. Gellner speaks of cognition, not persuasion. Nor does he treat such cognition as *ipso facto* a modality of power. The realm of ideas and meanings, reduced to ideological domination or cohesion by Runciman and Mann, is here granted something more like its real space, between nature and society as well as within society. Yet this gain is not unqualified. For Gellner's account exhibits a deep and pervasive ambiguity about the nature of 'cognition' itself. Taken at face value, the term seems just to connote knowledge – above all, perhaps, of the physical universe. In modern conditions, Gellner indeed formally distinguishes it from 'culture', which he defines as 'conceptualization minus cognition'.[47] Culture in this sense, as custom and credence rather than knowledge, receives a cool billing in his writing as a whole: exaggeration of its importance in shaping society and history is repeatedly attacked, as an idealist illusion.[48] In other words, where for his juniors it is overwhelmingly ideology, for him – so it would appear – it is essentially knowledge that is historically salient, as one of the three great causal forces of social development. In practice, Gellner does not maintain a consistent distinction between the two, and normally uses cognition as a virtual synonym for culture in its inclusive sense, embracing ritual, belief or value as well as knowledge. The bias of the underlying conception, however, has a very strong and ironic consequence for the realization of his theoretical programme. For paradoxically, once cognition is presumptively separated from culture, it can be tacitly promoted to the very role Gellner refuses the latter. In *Plough, Sword and Book*, the transformation of knowledge becomes to all intents and purposes the prime mover of historical change. Dismissing all culturalism, Gellner advances instead a cognitivism: Hegel gives way to Comte.

The structure of human history, in this account, is marked by two great watersheds, the transition from hunting-and-gathering to agriculture, and from agriculture to industry – the Neolithic and the Industrial Revolutions. The first of these, Gellner contends, must have occurred

47. *Plough, Sword and Book*, London 1988, p. 206.

48. See inter alia *Plough, Sword and Book*, p. 274; *Relativism in the Social Sciences*, p. 179; *Spectacles and Predicaments*, pp. 54–56, 98–99.

when certain foraging bands hit on the notion of delayed returns, sowing today in order to reap tomorrow. It was thus an intellectual shift in preference horizon that originally allowed sedentary agrarian societies to emerge. Once these became consolidated, they were usually dominated by military–clerical elites specializing in coercion and cognition. But since coercive strata were typically fragmented, in conditions of precarious central control and endemic potential division between them, ideological legitimacy became critical to their rivalries, and this was in the keeping of the cognitive guardians – the clerisy arbitrating the fortunes of the military. In this long interval, the great stretch of Agraria lying between foraging and manufacturing societies, a basic change came over cognition itself. Originally tribal humanity employed a multi-stranded language, in which referential and ceremonial dimensions were essentially fused: sophisticated awareness of the physical environment inextricably mixed with superstitious investment of it, practical adjustment and magical belief joining in *la pensée sauvage*. With agricultural civilizations, however, came world religions. Based on written texts, these by contrast developed a single-stranded but non-referential language – a doctrine of the divine order beyond the tangible world whose purest version was Platonism. For Gellner this change marks a momentous advance, 'the first unification' of cognition. For although it embodied less information about the real world than its predecessor, it generated the ideal of a logically related, orderly corpus of concepts that could in a subsequent epoch 'flip over' into the single-purpose referential language of modern science,[49] capable of dispensing with the deity and rationally explaining the processes of nature.

In this schema, however, the slippage between knowledge and credence in the meaning of 'cognition' leads to an evident contradiction in the narrative logic itself. For Gellner treats the culture of the agrarian civilizations as if they did not also encompass major empirical advances in understanding and transforming nature, involving a notably higher – not lower – degree of referentiality than anything to be found in the foraging bands before them. In this confusion, sight is lost of the initiating argument of delayed returns itself. On the other hand, when Gellner's account moves to the transition beyond agricultural societies, the emphasis reverts to cognition as actual knowledge again. The advent of Industria is interpreted in quasi-Weberian style as the triumph of a new rationality. In Gellner's more tightly focused version,

49. *Plough, Sword and Book*, pp. 79 ff.

it was growth of cognition which alone made possible growth of productivity in market economies. The original impulse came from the European Reformation, which promoted an instrumental and egalitarian inflexion of the local cosmology, that sanctioned the pursuit of wealth while actually aiming at a puritan theocracy. It was then the failure of rule by the saints, in the Commonwealth epoch, that cleared the way for the unprecedented emancipation of cognitive enquiry that began with Descartes and culminated with Hume and Kant in the European Enlightenment. This intellectual revolution prepared a technological transformation for which the requisite economic motivations now existed. But for the Industrial Revolution to occur, a 'miraculous political and ideological balance of power' had to prevail in England, so that the traditional forces of the sword and the book did not block the path of the machine. Gellner lists some fifteen separate candidates for an explanation of this miracle, only to conclude – as the term itself implies – that it is well-nigh beyond rational reconstruction, an unfathomable 'series of accidents'.[50] The real work of explanation is thus carried by cognition, now understood in more exacting philosophical mode: not by production, which is released by such knowledge, nor by coercion or ideology, which simply perform the service of not getting in the way. Once a sharp critic of current culturalist doctrines of the primacy of the conceptual in the social, judged a facile idealism, Gellner here risks landing in a rarefied one: the *Discourse on Method*, rather than Methodism, as turnkey to modern manufacture.

Gellner's enterprise ends with a series of tantalizing reflections on the present. In these, the tensions in his treatment of cognition as a historical force finally surface, as they come to form a substantive issue for his argument in their own right. Outside the West, in the Communist or Third World, the politics of coercion still may rule the roost – in some areas dominating the realm of production to an even greater degree than during Agraria. In the capitalist democracies, on the other hand, the acquisition of wealth has long been possible without the exercise of power; in the future, for the first time in history, power could perhaps become attainable without wealth. But here cognition and culture enter into direct conflict, as the successes of science fail to provide meaning or value for social or personal life, which inherently demand complex satisfactions of a kind its isolated goals can never yield. The result is typically the coexistence of a rationalized production with a lax, irrationalist culture of consumption and superstition –

50. Ibid., pp. 132, 199.

a 'rubber cage' of factitious re-enchantment seemingly compatible with any amount of bureaucratic administration or industrial progress, confounding Weber's expectations. These are conditions in which the feverish pursuit of material goods still obtains. Yet material needs are by their nature relatively limited, and as poverty is absorbed could soon be saturated. At that point the symbolic substitutions of consumption itself might become exhausted, leaving the necessities of production and the requirements of meaning entirely dissociated from each other. Cognition, knowing no such contradiction, would by contrast advance with undiminished, even accelerating momentum. In these circumstances, the future would be dominated by a question without precedent. What social forms might arise when the pervasive compulsions of work and force have lapsed, leaving knowledge alone face to face with itself? If cognition should extend to the capacity to mould – genetically or psychically – human nature itself? On this note of utopian trouble, *Plough, Sword and Book* effectively concludes. The import of its final term not only precedes and supervises, but outlasts the others.

Looking back, it seems doubtful if any country has produced an equivalent cluster of large-scaled theories of history in such a short span of time: as if British culture, so long a laggard or absentee in the field, now made up for it with a vengeance. Certain commonalities are evident in the results. Whether starting from problems of class in the West, or stimulated by discussions of state and society in the East, all of these bodies of work emerged in dialectical tension with Marxism – in different ways illustrating Gellner's observation that 'Marxism is the major sociological theory to have emerged in the nineteenth century. Its standing is confirmed by the fact that such a large proportion of non-Marxist thinkers continue to define their positions by reference to it', since 'as people must needs think against some kind of grid, even (or perhaps especially) those who do not accept the Marxist theory of history tend to lean upon its ideas when they wish to say what they do positively believe.'[51] But this relationship should not be exaggerated, or isolated. In each of the four cases, there have been major intellectual influences coming from outside the discipline of sociology, having nothing to do with historical materialism: existential and post-structuralist philosophy for Giddens, diffusionist archaeology and logistics for Mann, neo-contractarian political theory and evolutionary biology

51. *State and Society in Soviet Thought*, p. 176.

for Runciman, functionalist ethnology and empiricist epistemology for Gellner. These have their bearing on the specific preoccupations that distinguish them – the respective themes of the lay actor, of material infrastructures, of practical competition, of cognitive development. But these constructions also share a general architecture that derives its design from the confrontation with Marxism. Their central claim about the structure of human history is twofold. Firstly, there is no primacy of economic causation to it: military–political and ideological–cultural determinations are of equivalent significance. None of these three has any universal privilege: different societies and different epochs exhibit different dominants, which have to be established case by case. Secondly, this permutation in rank of importance obeys no pattern: the procession of variant institutional hierarchies that makes up the record of human development is contingent – not a chapter, but an encyclopaedia of accidents. In their negative sense contentions like these have, of course, long formed part of the critique of historical materialism in the West. What is new here is their positive instrumentation into a full-scale *alternative* to historical materialism, worked through with commensurate reach and detail. In the years in which they became the bugbear of advanced opinion on the Continent, totalizations – of heroic magnitude – finally acquired *droit de cité* in Britain.

During the long period when British sociology remained a cramped and arid affair, British anthropology – so I had argued – flourished as a discipline. Principles of totality shunned at home could be projected abroad, into the investigation of tribal societies caught in the net of colonial rule, generating a remarkable tradition of empirical fieldwork and – mainly functionalist – social theory. What has happened in this zone in the past twenty years? The principal development has lain in the work of one thinker, whose character breaks the conventional bounds between anthropology and sociology – a division it expressly rejects – to form what is effectively a fifth great body of historical sociology. More empirical and topical in composition, comprising a brilliant necklace of particular studies, it is also more original in its research. There is one further difference that sets it apart. Here, historical materialism has been not the foil but the form of the direction taken by the work. Jack Goody was a member of the Marxist generation formed in the late thirties, a contemporary of Eric Hobsbawm and Raymond Williams in the Communist milieu at Cambridge. Trained in English literature, he did his anthropological fieldwork in Northern Ghana, at the time of the independence struggle, where – in contrast to the typical predecessor, linked to the district officer – he became a local member of the CPP.[52] After a set of distinguished monographs, he started to produce from 1968 onwards a series of far-reaching general studies, across a broad swathe of topics – many of them well outside the conventional purview of the anthropologist. The predominant British tradition of anthropology was particularist, and functionalist: focused essentially on single societies, and their synchronic integration. Breaking with this still active legacy, Goody's work took a deliberately 'macro-evolutionary' tack, systematically committed to historical problems of 'comparison and long-term change'.[53] But by the same token it also came to embody a powerful critique of the opposite French tradition, which was structuralist and universalist. No one has taken issue with Lévi-Strauss more effectively. Critical of any over-valuation of problems of meaning at the expense of those of explanation, Goody has also pointedly rejected the French anthropologist's oscillation between a 'diffuse relativism and sentimental egalitarianism' that stresses the fundamental identity of the operations of the human mind, and a crude 'bimodalism' that constructs a contrast between 'neolithic' and 'modern' forms of science as the fundamental dichotomy of human history.[54] Rejection of all 'Great Divide' theories of social development, a consistent feature of Goody's writing, naturally affects versions such as that of Gellner (his successor at Cambridge) too.

Goody's relationship to Marxism has, at the same time, always been a subtle and critical one. His work extends well beyond its classical range of interests, and recasts many of its customary emphases in doing so. Determination of social life in the last instance by forms of economic livelihood has remained his point of departure. But the destination of his research has been modes of reproduction, destruction and communication as much as of production itself. Family, warfare and writing are among its leading themes. Military–political and cultural–ideological processes have as much focus as in the sociology of power; but the domestic–demographic regimes it neglects are included as well. A more wide-ranging curiosity about the 'ideal' dimensions of history than has been general in Marxism is controlled by a firmer attention to its 'material' – physical or technical – conditions. The short

52. See *Production and Reproduction*, Cambridge 1976, p. ix.
53. Ibid., p. i.
54. *The Domestication of the Savage Mind*, Cambridge 1977, pp. 2–8; J. Goody and I. Watt, 'The Consequences of Literacy', in J. Goody, ed., *Literacy in Traditional Societies*, Cambridge 1968, p. 67.

book Goody published in 1971, *Technology, Tradition and the State in Africa,* in some ways the pivot of his *œuvre,* is a signal example. Its starting-point is a critique of Eurocentric ascriptions of feudalism to sub-Saharan Africa – not least Marxist ones. In reality, Goody argued, feudalism never took root there because the ecological, demographic and technical conditions for it were absent. By comparison with most of Eurasia, land was abundant, but soil poor and population scarce. The Bronze Age invention of the plough never spread south of the Sahara, nor the wheel: hence there was no animal traction, wind or water-power, nor irrigation. Since people rather than land were in short supply, chiefly powers were more directly exercised over the former – dependent labour taking the form of slavery rather than serfdom, in a milieu where rights over the soil were less individualized than in most of Europe. The only area of exception was Ethiopia, which significantly knew both plough and serf-based landlordism. Horses, for their part, never penetrated south of the Sudd marshes in the Sudan, their path blocked by tsetse fly and forest – preventing major investment in warfare, among acephalous societies whose weapons were the bow and arrow. Where they did arrive, in the circum-Saharan belt, cavalry generated the 'mass dynasties' of the savannah, while the later importation of guns produced the centralized forest autocracies of the West African coast. Contrasting political orders were thus founded on differences in the means of destruction, rather than of production.

These findings on agriculture and war subsequently flowed into a much broader comparative enquiry. Most macro-historical investigation has traditionally worked through contrasts between European and Asian experience. Goody's vantage-point in Africa allowed him to 'triangulate' this venerable dualism, yielding novel results that often shifted the axis of contrast to one between Eurasia as a single zone, and Sub-Saharia. In *Production and Reproduction* (1977), he developed a striking typology of inheritance and dowry systems as determinants of conjugal forms, that essentially picked out two configurations. In Africa, only men could inherit and there were no dowries; hence genuine polygyny was widespread, and there was little or no practice of concubinage. In Europe and Asia, on the other hand, there was 'divergent devolution': both sexes could inherit or receive property, so the trend was always towards monogamy, with concubinage mainly as an heir-producing insurance. Lateral inheritance (priority of brothers over sons) was common in Africa, vertical all but universal in Europe. This bifurcation of inheritance and therefore marriage patterns, Goody suggested, was itself determined by the economic and sociopolitical constellation of each zone: plough agriculture, pronounced class division, more complex states in Eurasia, as opposed to hoe agriculture, more fluid social differentiation and less developed political authority in Sub-Saharia. Culturally, he terms this a difference between 'hierarchical' and 'hieratic' societies – that is, those where stratification of classes, castes or estates gives rise to separate sub-cultures for each, and those where such cultural laddering is minimal, even where state and social inequality subsist. In Africa, traditional custom actually promoted marriage between status groups, and rulers preferred commoner wives; whereas Eurasian societies typically banned such unions, the general rule being that 'like had to marry like'.

In *Cooking, Cuisine and Class* (1981), Goody explored a further significant dimension of this contrast. The general argument of the book is a riposte to Lévi-Strauss's formalization of culinary systems as binary codes translating the unconscious structure of societies into so many recipes. Criticizing the abstraction of this procedure from the realities of either biology or history, as well as its preoccupation with meaning dissociated from cause, Goody proposed instead a comparative social explanation of major variations in the preparation of food across the world, in terms of the patterns of local economic production and social differentiation. The emergence of 'cuisine' proper – the separation of high and low, central and regional, cooking – is traced to the emergence of class distance and court cultures in Eurasia. In precolonial Africa, the only society where something like it appeared was Amhara. Elsewhere, there was a uniform demotic cooking, with a relatively limited range of ingredients: low-status wives in high-status households stabilizing the general norm. The European and North American industrialization of food in the nineteenth century transformed all these conditions, creating new mixed diets everywhere, in Northern Ghana as much as Northern England, closing consumption gaps in the more advanced countries and opening them in the more peripheral. The symbolism of gastronomy is not discounted; but it is not to be over-interpreted either, in 'uncheckable speculation'.[55] The persistence of specific dishes in a given culture may often reflect their lack of importance for society as a whole, rather than their expression of it – simply providing existential continuity in epochs of great change. Food is above all humanity's primary means of subsistence, rather than of self-expression: it calls quite particularly for a materialist analysis of the whole cycle of its production, preparation and consumption.

Goody's research next moved from broad contrasts between Africa

55. *Cooking, Cuisine and Class*, Cambridge 1981, p. 32.

and Eurasia, to one major divergence within the Eurasian zone itself. From Late Antiquity onwards, the Northern and Southern shores of the Mediterranean exhibited quite different matrimonial patterns. 'Close' marriages, especially between first cousins, characterized the Arab South, whereas they were forbidden in the Christian North, a contrast between endogamous and exogamous systems that had not existed in Classical times. Neither Roman, nor for that matter biblical, law had proscribed close marriages, just as they had also allowed concubinage, divorce and adoption. Why then, starting at the end of the fourth century and culminating in the eleventh century, did the Catholic Church not only ban marriage between cousins, but steadily multiply the 'prohibited degrees' of consanguinity for conjugal partners? The conventional answer had been that it was the new Christian sexual morality which sought to stamp out close marriages as tainted with incest, and concubinage and divorce as threats to fidelity. Pointing out that adoption, without any such carnal dimension, was also forbidden, Goody argued that the real drive behind the Church's proscriptions was not so much ethical as economic. What all the practices that fell under its veto shared was their role as 'strategies of heirship', designed to keep property within the family. Blockage of these devices increased the chances of individuals dying heirless, and so of them making bequests of their property to the Church – which, for its part, conversely enforced celibacy on its priests, to guard against private appropriation of clerical wealth. The result was an accumulation of church lands, which came to account for about a third of the cultivated area of France by the Merovingian period. Yet if the dynamic of this process was essentially economic, it had major affective consequences: by emphasizing in its own interests mutual consent in marriage, at the expense of the secular code of parental permission, the Church unintentionally fostered ideals of conjugal equality and sympathy that became part of the cultural heritage of modern Europe.

Goody's contributions to the comparative sociology of environment and warfare, class and gastronomy, family and property, represent a unique cluster in their own right. But the most influential of all the strands in his work has certainly been his exploration of the impact of writing in the history of human development. His background in English studies was clearly of importance for this line of enquiry – his first essay on the subject was co-authored with Ian Watt. The texts in *Literacy in Traditional Societies* (1968) take the spread of the principles of the Semitic syllabary in the second millennium BC as 'the supreme example of cultural diffusion' – all known alphabets through Eurasia and Africa deriving from it – but insist that the cultural effects of this technical breakthrough were determined by the social context in which it became available. Writing, whether alphabetic or ideographic, permitted no more than a very restricted literacy where religious tradition (India) or political exclusion (China) controlled its usage. Only in Greece did a truly extended literate culture emerge, among the citizenry of the *polis*; and, however much Socrates or Plato might attack writing, it was this which permitted the unique Greek achievements in epistemology and taxonomy.

When he came to treat the subject at full tilt a decade later, Goody was critical of what he evidently felt was a conventional element in this last emphasis. In form, *The Domestication of the Savage Mind* (1977) is a sustained critique of Lévi-Strauss's dichotomy between a 'science of the concrete' concerned to classify the 'sensible' world, characteristic of the savage mind, and a 'science of the abstract' designed to explain an 'intelligible' world, peculiar to the modern mind: a search for order dominating the one, the pursuit of security the other. For Goody, by contrast, pragmatic needs and categoric classifications are not alternatives but complements, at every stage of social development. It is the quest for material security that normally dominates actors, for inescapable reasons, but there is never a time when this can be satisfied without an intellectual order. The anthropologist from an English university and the adolescent from a Ghanaian tribe do not approach 'the physical world from opposite ends' – 'the boy brought up as a *bricoleur* becomes an engineer. He has his difficulties, but they do not lie at the level of an overall opposition between wild and domesticated minds.'[56] Lévi-Strauss's bi-modalism, built around a stark division of human intelligence into neolithic and modern forms, is empirically incompatible with the record of crucial social inventions, many of which predated neolithic times (speech, tools, cooking, weaponry), while others lay between them and modern times (metallurgy, wheel, writing). But it is also, Goody argued, theoretically vacant, since it merely advances a contrast without accounting for it. His own strategy would be to relate ascertainable differences in mentality to historical changes in modes of communication, above all the introduction of various forms of writing.

The central transformation brought by the invention of writing was the ability to preserve speech over time and space, so that intellectual life was no longer constrained by problems of memory storage, but could develop cumulatively across the process of transcription. Pre-

56. *The Domestication of the Savage Mind*, pp. 8–9.

literate societies, contrary to conventional belief, could produce sceptics – by no means unknown in the simplest tribal communities; but sceptic*ism* as a critical tradition could only emerge once there existed the means to preserve and transmit sceptical thoughts. Without literacy, no philosophy. The gains of writing, however, long predated the Semitic syllabary or Greek alphabet. Cuneiform inscriptions, overwhelmingly administrative and economic in character, pioneered the vital device of the list – inventorial, chronological or lexical. These acted as powerful stimuli to the growth of observational sciences, the activity of early historians (of Lévi-Strauss's dictum that there is no history without dates, Goody remarks that it would truer to say: without archives), and the rationalization of language itself. Above all, the possibility of 'backward scanning' permitted the cumulative development of arts and sciences. None of these developments was independent of social structure, but the general historical importance of such innovations can be seen from the fact that scientific advances regularly followed major changes in the means of communication, whether with the discovery of writing in Mesopotamia, the alphabet in Greece, or printing in Western Europe.

Goody's most recent work, *The Logic of Writing and the Organization of Society* (1986), enlarges his focus into a survey of the consequences of early literacy for the principal institutional complexes of society – taking among his main fields of contrast the Ancient Near East and West Africa. The advent of writing everywhere generated its own specialists, scribes whose skills powerfully promoted the structural differentiation of each of the major organizational orders. Religion acquired priesthoods, supported by temples and monasteries – where the pre-literate languages of Africa lack even any concept of it, as a phenomenon distinct from social life at large. Universal creeds, typically though not invariably oriented towards conversion, could then emerge because of the decontextualization of belief through sacred texts. States acquired bureaucracies, capable of storing information, relaying instructions, computing taxation, conducting diplomatic negotiations – the 'tyranny of distance' yielding to 'tyranny over big distances'. Property and trade acquired the instruments of alienation and credit, the devices of book-keeping and banking. Law acquired new authority and regularity, the inscription of edicts and the record of courts replacing informal custom and sanction. All of these changes brought with them greater social inequality. But although the immediate impact of writing was typically accompanied by an increase in stratification, its long-term dynamic proved – very gradually – egalitarian, as literacy spread and dissent became cumulable. Two lessons stand out in any study of this whole process. Conventional stage theories of history, most of them Eurocentric in bias, typically impose artificial demarcations on the societal forms of the past – as if they were homogeneous units whose transformation could only occur through inner contradiction and scission. But in reality, empirical societies are nearly always a mixture of forms, and change in them is more usually the result of an expansion of one of them at the expense of others, so that historical development proceeds not by stages but by overlaps. In these, the technologies of the intellect – as distinct from the epiphanies of cognition – play a central role, determining 'what we can do with our minds, and what our minds can do with us'.[57] To acknowledge this role, Goody concludes, is necessarily to shift some of the weight Marxists have traditionally put on the means and relations of production to the means and relations of communication.

4. Aesthetics

The movement from modes of production to those of communication that marks the historical anthropology of Jack Goody was, of course, also one of the central themes of the work of Raymond Williams. The parallels in the development of an original cultural materialism in the two bodies of writing are not a mere coincidence. For both thinkers started out under the joint influence of Leavis and the Marxism of the anti-fascist moment. Politically, it was perhaps the tension in this background which kept them from rejoining the ranks of British communism after the war. Intellectually, it seems likely that it provided much of the impulse behind the eventual syntheses at which each arrived – whose affinities can be seen in their collaboration in a collective project on human communication.[58] Logically enough, literary criticism had been the other refuge of the idea of a social totality within English culture, at a time when it was virtually everywhere else repressed. Already by 1968 it was clear that this was the area from which a socialist theory able to measure itself against the overall forms of life in capitalist Britain had emerged, with *The Long Revolution*. The next twenty years saw Raymond Williams become, not only the most distinctive political thinker of the British Left, but the central figure in literary studies in the country at large. There is a paradox in

57. Ibid., p. 160.
58. Raymond Williams, ed., *Contact: Human Communication and its History*, London 1981, pp. 7–20, 105–126.

any such description, because the whole force of Williams's work in this period was eventually to undo the very notion of 'literature' as a separate kind of writing. Literary criticism itself, in the traditional sense, formed in many ways the smallest part of his output: of his books after *Drama from Ibsen to Brecht* (1968), only *The English Novel from Dickens to Lawrence* (1970) really fits the term, though particular essays approximate it.

The work of the 'break', with all current critical forms, was *The Country and the City* (1973), which remains Williams's masterpiece: a study of the changing representations of rural and urban life in English writing since the Jacobean period, and of the social transformations they refracted or hid, which is also an unforgettable critique of agrarian nostalgia and industrial hubris alike. There followed a pioneering study of the interplay between technology and cultural form in television, drawn in good part from American experience, and the first critical exercise of historical semantics in English, a field largely unexplored outside Germany.[59] *Marxism and Literature* (1977), in more ways than one marking a significant radicalization, sketched out a systematic theoretical agenda for future work intended to subvert the orthodoxies of both the traditions from which Williams had begun. Rejecting the distinction between base and superstructure – not on the usual grounds that the ideal sphere of the latter was indefensibly reduced to its material supports, but rather because if anything the former was wrongly narrowed and abstracted by the exclusion from it of the forces of cultural production – Williams taxed Marxism with too little rather than too much materialism. But in the same movement he also repudiated the distinction between a separate category of literary texts and other practices of writing – the very notion of a canon, central to Leavisite criticism – for captious selection and unselfconscious elitism. In its stead he argued for a democracy of signifying practices, each calling for its own appropriate responses, in a process dissolving aesthetic judgements into a tracing out of the conditions of production of any given piece of writing, and then of its reception by the current reader. Such deliberate, unfussed historical levelling recalls Gramsci, and it is perhaps no accident that Williams should here have taken over his notion of hegemony. But he gave it a characteristic twist, by emphasizing the continual processes of adjustment needed to secure any political or cultural hegemony above, and its perpetual failure – as

59. *Television – Technology and Cultural Form*, London 1974; *Keywords*, London 1976.

an inherently selective definition of reality – to exhaust the meanings of popular experience below. These themes, providing the programme of such later collections as *Writing and Society* (1984), and finding fresh development in *Culture* (1985), effectively set many of the terms of the cross-disciplinary growth of 'cultural studies' – abjuring 'literary criticism' – in these years, of which the work of the Birmingham Centre became the most influential example. Although Williams was not the only source of this shift, he was the outstanding individual one; the extent of his impact visible in the general direction of the change. For the rest, the magnitude of his legacy – from the fictional to the political – exceeds the bounds of any sectoral survey such as this.

In a clear if complicated sense, Terry Eagleton has been the principal successor in the professional field they both occupied. From Williams's 'Second Generation', his intellectual background was very different: left-Catholic and existentialist at the outset, the student upheavals of the sixties brought him to Marxism, and a strong appropriation of Louis Althusser. After sharp studies of Waugh and Greene in *Exiles and Emigrés* (1970), he published a vigorous attack on every prevailing form of liberal humanism in English literary studies in *Criticism and Ideology* (1975). Inspired by the structuralist ferment within French Marxism of the time, this polemic took among its prime targets *Scrutiny* and the work of Williams himself, treated as recalcitrantly petty-bourgeois and attractively socialist variants of the pursuit of humane literary values – where what was really needed was scientific investigation of the several ideologies at work in any given text. This swashbuckling objectivism dissolved through the encounter with Walter Benjamin which was the occasion of Eagleton's next work. An effervescent cocktail of different forms, *Walter Benjamin, or Towards a Revolutionary Criticism* offered a set of variations on its subject's philosophy of history, theory of baroque drama, ideas of artistic aura and reproduction, and last but not least revolutionary politics, in which a distinctive strain of *plumpes Denken* was crossed with the first signs of post-structuralism.

In the previous ten years, the once-sheltered world of English literary criticism had been lapped by successive waves of theory from Russia, Bohemia, Germany, France, the United States. The result was considerable disorientation among new entrants to the discipline. With *Literary Theory* (1982), Eagleton took the opportunity to chart this unfamiliar scene. Beginning with the heritage of Arnold, Eliot and Leavis, it looked pithily and entertainingly at the New Criticism and Northrop Frye, Husserl and Heidegger, Lévi-Strauss and Barthes, Bakhtin and Derrida, Bloom and Kristeva, among others. Calculated to dispel any neophyte dizziness amidst this carousel of schools, by plain-spoken exposition, Eagleton's survey also had decided messages of its own. With small time for the nostalgias of New Criticism, the essentialism of phenomenology, or the technocracy of Frye, it struck a more lenient note with Prague structuralism, and a noticeably warmer one – with due qualifications – about post-structuralist and psychoanalytic trends, at any rate as exhibited by Derrida and Kristeva, viewed as welcome relays to feminist concerns. The overall argument of the book, however, converged with that of Williams. Literature as such was an illusion: it was that segment of writing socially valued at any given time – such valuations being always imbued with the dominant relations of ideology and power. Literary criticism, or theory, was therefore no more than a branch of such ideologies, without unity or identity, to be buried unceremoniously.[60] What is required instead is a cultural theory equivalent to the older science of rhetoric – that is, a typology of the different forms and functions of signifying practices at large. Liberated from any canonical incubus, such a rhetoric could then freely mine every available methodological resource for particular ends, in the general service of a socialism giving substance to the liberal ideals of human betterment.

This obsequy for literary criticism left one ambiguity unresolved. Was it just literature that had been laid to rest, or the critical attitude as well? Williams had repudiated the very term criticism, as too contaminated by invidious judgement. But the strict logic of this position undermines the very politics it is designed to advance: for if texts are not to be criticized, on what grounds can societies? Eagleton's solution was to retain the term, but reposition it – shifting it from the terrain of the aesthetic to the experiential and symbolic. *The Function of Criticism* (1984) pursued this strategy by reconstructing the actual history of the idea and the practice of criticism, from the Enlightenment onwards. Born in Europe of the struggle against Absolutism, criticism flowered in England after the battle was won, as a meliorating consolidation of the class compromise achieved at the Glorious Revolution. Addison and Steele wrote as counsellors to a polite public in matters not just of books or plays, but manners and morals, as critics of everyday life as much as of the higher arts. That capacious, unforced sense of the continuity of social living, together with the ambition to educate and improve it, rested on the unity of what Habermas classically depicted as the new bourgeois world of the time – the eighteenth-

60. *Literary Theory*, pp. 10–16, 201–204.

century public sphere of newspapers and coffee-houses, clubs and circulating libraries.

By the early nineteenth century, this consensus had broken down, under the opposite pressures of commercial publishing and popular politics, producing a vehemently factional journal culture on the one hand, and the lonely voice of the Romantic poet or moral sage on the other. The growth of working-class readership saw a further disintegration of the public sphere, into a received polarity between the educated elite and semi-literate masses. The meaning of criticism now became redefined. For Arnold it was the uplift of great works of literature alone that could redeem the lower orders. This conception of literary value passed down to Leavis, who attempted to reconcile Augustan and Romantic stances by emphasizing both the sociability of literature and the arduousness of understanding it – in opposition to either academic isolation, or amateur appreciation, of its abiding tradition. In fact, *Scrutiny* merely became one more embattled minority. Its failure paved the way for ever more technical conceptions of criticism as a professional discipline, without civilizing pretensions. Their sway was in due course overthrown by the vocally anti-objectivist 'literary theory' of the most recent period. Yet this too is only another avatar of the shrinkage of the critical project itself. Latter-day criticism, Eagleton concluded, serves no wider interest than itself. Williams's greatness was to escape its horizons, in a radical and unclassifiable *œuvre*. But this work was in effect addressed to a counter-public that was missing – a politically organized, class readership, such as had once existed in Weimar Germany or Britain in the thirties. In the eighties, under the stifling weight of the mass media, feminism has come nearest to creating such an alternative public sphere. Although quite distinct in character from the rationalist model of the Enlightenment, it is this cultural space which points best to what ought to be the aim of contemporary criticism – to recover the original unity of its practice. Today, that means reconnecting the symbolic processes and shapings of subjectivity in social life to the unfinished political struggle for equality and emancipation.

Eagleton's re-functioning of criticism is thus very close to Williams's displacement of it. But it is not identical. There have been two directions from which literary value has come under pressure in the recent period: one a movement towards the social, or the democracy of significations, the other a shift towards the metaphysical, or the instability of significations. These might be called the Low Road and the High Road to the dissolution of the aesthetic. Williams unambiguously took the first route. Eagleton's sorties, by contrast, have proceeded along both lines – combining demotic and deconstructionist motifs. There can be little doubt of the audience won for the case against literature made by these two foremost theorists of the Left in English studies. But such post-critical success has inevitably also had its pyrrhic side. For aesthetic value is not to be dispatched so easily – the wish to finish with it recalling Dobrolyubov, or Bazarov, more than Marx or Morris. Railing at canons is not the same as replacing them, which they have resisted. Evacuation of the terrain of literary evaluation in the traditional sense necessarily leaves its conventional practitioners in place. In England, this has meant the undiminished salience of such old-world figures as John Bayley, don *à tout faire*, Christopher Ricks or John Carey, professional *précieux* or stage-boor – if only because each represents an unignorable body of evaluation, treating of Hardy or Milton, Donne or Keats. In the wider world, the critics of the Yale School – de Man, Hartmann, Bloom – exercise much greater influence than these local notables,[61] because they were able to combine substantial specific revaluations with more intoxicating philosophical ambitions: new visions of Rousseau, Wordsworth or Shelley alongside high doctrines of allegory, unreadability, gnosis. Eagleton, a skilful deflator of such reputations on either side of the Atlantic, has himself written well on Richardson or Shakespeare. But the centre of gravity of 'cultural theory' in Britain does not lie in this kind of work.

That theory also has its own partiality. Although it formally aims to address all signifying practices and symbolic processes in a single egalitarian spirit, its bias is overwhelmingly verbal. Indeed, there is a sense in which this is a necessary condition of its plausibility. For writing is continuous with speaking as a generalized everyday practice, in modern literate societies. There is no such ready prolongation from spontaneous *Lebenswelt* to skilled performance in the field of visual – let alone aural – signification. The arts of painting or music, as of course architecture, remain specialized and discontinuous from any common daily capacities. It is probably no accident that they are consistently neglected in this approach to culture. The visual deficit in traditional British education has been largely reproduced in the left insurgency against it. Film itself, like rock, has proved more assimilable to the radical paradigm here, as itself part verbal in form. But it is

61. The liveliest survey of the current theoretical scene, Imre Salusinszky's collection of interviews *Criticism in Society*, London 1987, includes only one English critic, Frank Kermode.

striking that in the end the major attempts at a totalization of contemporary 'symbolic processes and forms of subjectivity' should have started out from architecture and painting, in the constructions of postmodernism by Fredric Jameson and his interlocutors (among them, in the event, Terry Eagleton).[62]

Developments in the study of the visual arts provide an instructive comparison with these shifts in the literary field. Here there was little recent tradition of either wider intellectual ambitions, or significant radical influence, in the mainstream of the discipline. In the post-war period, art history in Britain came to be dominated for the most part by a rather narrow version of the Warburg tradition of high iconography – without any of the prodigious variety and invention of Panofsky – and the concern with formalized schemata of perception that was Gombrich's major extension beyond it. Attempts at more materialist enquiries never crossed a certain threshold of repute, whether from academic outsiders like Antal or Hauser or public sharpshooters like John Berger. From the early seventies onwards, however, the change was startling. Three contributions to this transformation stand out.

One way of describing the work of T.J. Clark would be to say that with it a modern Marxism became for the first time central to the discipline. But this would also be less than appropriate, because of the suspicion each of these terms falls under – for different reasons – in the exceptional writing in question. Clark's first pair of books, *The Absolute Bourgeois* and *Image of the People* (1973), studies in French painting under the Second Republic, took their distance from Gombrich's legacy at the outset. A pictorial tradition, Clark pointed out, is always more than just a set of enabling visual schemes: it involves a repertoire of beliefs as well – a combination which normally renders invisible as much as it makes visible to the artist. To understand the foundations of the particular subject and style of a painter, it is necessary to look through the general constraints of the tradition to the specific situation and complex experience of the artist. Here, however, the 'social history of art' as customarily practised (by Hauser or others) was the reverse of a guide: a positive obstacle, in its assumption that works of art passively 'reflect' classes or ideologies, which can then be taken as the relevant 'background' generating them. In reality artists actively 'convert' rather than express the social or aesthetic relations

62. 'Capitalism, Modernism and Postmodernism', in *Against the Grain*, London 1986, pp. 131–148.

they encounter, into works that do not yield general 'analogies' between their forms and a wider history, but reveal variable detailed linkages.[63] A sense of detail was, of course, one of Aby Warburg's most famous directives. Clark owes his more to Walter Benjamin, whose writings on Baudelaire and Haussmann lie behind his reconstructions of the upheaval of 1848 (including the part of the poet himself), and of the remodelling of Paris under the Second Empire. There is the same flair for the unexpected, diagonal threads between the minutiae of trades, locales, persons, events, opinions, politics, within the tangled web of class: literary texts, commercial entertainments, legal processes, electoral statistics brought into constellation with the canvasses themselves. The firmer organization of this Arcades-like mosaic, however, is in part due to themes derived from a quite different kind of Marxism – the theories of ideology (a topic in which Benjamin was not much interested) developed by Althusser and Macherey. Most important of all, in some ways, has been Clark's deployment of concepts that descend from the arsenal of Situationism – the most original of the iconoclasms of 1968. If there is any primary allegiance traceable in his writing, it would perhaps be to the ideas of Guy Debord on the spectacle.

The object of Clark's early work was the possibility of political art in the nineteenth century, taking the conjuncture of 1848–52 as a privileged moment for the exploration of what revolutionary painting or writing might have meant. Unlike those of 1830, the barricades of 1848 produced no potent imagery. Of the artists who left indelible representations of the time, Millet helped to put down the June days, Daumier remained silent during the massacres, Delacroix denounced Republican government – only Baudelaire fought with the insurgents, from an outlook far from socialism if close to Blanqui. All these came at politics 'sideways', in responses that were private, quirky, even sullen – anything but the spirit of David half a century earlier. The one painter who wrested a truly public art – revolutionary in form and in matter – out of his private experience was Courbet, inactive in Paris during 1848, but great, ironic pictorialist of rural class relations in his native Doubs, as the backwash of radical politics stirred the French countryside in 1849. Courbet's achievement was to appropriate the traditions of high art to renew popular art, and project for a flickering moment its hegemony over the dominant culture. Everything in nineteenth-century painting – the easel tradition, the art market, the cult of the individual – weighed

63. *Image of the People*, London 1973, pp. 10–11.

against such a political break, and it was soon stifled. After Courbet, there was no effective subversive art again till the epoch of Lissitsky and Tzara.

In his sequel, *The Painting of Modern Life*, Clark looks at what developed instead – the commercialization of leisure. Under the Second Empire, Paris was brusquely remodelled by Haussmann, creating new kinds of urban space and entertainment, while round it a belt of suburbia extended into the countryside, the setting for other forms of weekend recreation. It was these scenes of capital's colonization of everyday life – no longer just of production, but now of distraction – that formed the moral landscape of Impressionism. It was the expanding population of white-collar employees, the new petty bourgeoisie of shops and offices burgeoning in the big city, that especially lived them out. The apparent social indeterminacy of this stratum – its defiance of any rigid classification – provided an essential support to the mythology of modernity that came to define the self-conceptions of advanced art. For this ideology, which has persisted down to the present, the modern is the marginal, the mixed, the equivocal – that which eludes any order; and in this the *couches nouvelles* were like a diffuse alter ego of the avant-garde, offering its natural avenue into contemporary life. What such tropes of modernism, in their emphasis on anomie rather than division, characteristically excluded from their line of sight was class. Here the alchemy of the spectacle was already at work, in those *café-concerts* where a petty-bourgeois audience patronized popular singers in sham-plebeian identification with those below, and would-be connoisseur aspiration to those above – attracting the complaisant brush of Degas or Toulouse. This was, in effect, the founding moment of 'popular culture' in the sense we know it today – the very reverse of the hope nourished by Courbet: an unending expropriation of the imaginative forms of working-class experience, rendered into innocuous simulacra of themselves, for the reanimation of a middle-class sensorium. In this process the very notion of the 'popular' operates to suppress the 'collective' – even if that substitution can never be absolutely secured, since the masters of the means of symbolic production 'cannot control the detail of performance, and cannot afford to exorcise the ghost of totality once and for all from the popular machine.'[64] Impressionism generally affected a sardonic distance from the spectacular, but in truth such mildly playful superiority connived at it. Manet and Seurat were exceptions: their grandest compositions

64. *The Painting of Modern Life*, London 1985, p. 236.

reticent in gaze, undeceived by the cult of the marginal, respectful of the unassuming dignity as well as comedy of leisure. The radical and democratic potential of depictions of modernity like these, on which Mallarmé even pinned political hopes, came to nothing as commercial dealing eventually made Impressionism a cynosure of high society. Such capture was inscribed in much of its conventionality from the start; but 'subservience to the half-truths of the moment', even 'dogged servility', was never – Clark notes – incompatible with artistic intensity, the value of paintings always lying primarily in their visual order rather than their ideological materials, for all the importance of the latter.[65]

Interest in the tension between the two has by no means been confined to Clark. Indebted to him, but interweaving the pictorial and the literary even more centrally, John Barrell's *Dark Side of the Landscape* (1980) looked at the ways in which rural poverty was figured in the English pastoral art of the eighteenth and early nineteenth centuries, using the poetry of Gay, Crabbe, Goldsmith or Gray as a control for a series of sharp and unforeseen readings of the social conflicts beneath the surface of the paintings of Gainsborough, Morland and Constable – at variance with critics of the left (Berger, Williams) as much as the centre or right (Brookner, Vaizey). David Solkin's *Richard Wilson – the Landscape of Reaction* (1982) scrutinized the relations between the artist's commitment to classicism and his viewers and buyers among the conservative lesser gentry, in singularly unwavering mood. But changes in art history have not lain simply in the growth of concern with the complex relationships between visual representations and social class. Another body of work of the greatest distinction has been materialist in a different kind of way – no less historical, but on the whole seeking 'lateral' connexions between painting or sculpture and other specific practices or institutions, rather than 'longitudinal' links through the social structure. Michael Baxandall first put his distinctive impress on the field with *Painting and Experience in Fifteenth-Century Italy* (1972). *Quattrocento* art was here studied through two prisms: the commercial conditions of a bespoke trade, in which painters worked to detailed contracts drawn up by their clients, and the period eye with which such Renaissance patrons viewed paintings, a 'cognitive style' derived from other kinds of germane experience that brought its own set of expectations to the interpretation of pictures. Emphasis on the importance of money in the history of art, familiar enough in itself, was here linked to a new

65. Ibid., p. 78.

enquiry into the visual skills of the customers who expended it – derived from such variegated activities as religious exercises, formulaic codifications of gesture, lay dancing, volumetric barrel-calculations, currency exchanges, which yielded specific pictorial values: a 'danced' kind of painting in Botticelli, 'gauged' in Piero, 'preached' in Fra Angelico. Such horizontal affinities reveal paintings as genuine social documents, Baxandall argued, but in a way that has little to do with crude illustrations of class.[66]

If class in Urbino or Florence received only a glance, it came into full focus in Augsburg or Ulm, when Baxandall came to his study of *The Limewood Sculptors of Renaissance Germany* (1980). This great work enlarged his scope in a number of significant ways. The economic conditions and social hierarchies of South German towns in the half century before the Reformation were set out with meticulous care, at the head of the book; but so too were the religious tensions on the eve of the upheaval which ultimately helped to bring this art to an end; the detailed mechanisms of the market for retables, amidst tenacious guild controls; and last but not least, the physical qualities of limewood itself, as a carving medium. These were then put into play with an unexpected array of practices that, Baxandall suggests, bore on the local cognitive style: among them chiromancy, calligraphy, and mastersong, which contributed to the forms of the Florid Style in German sculpture. All such collective circumstances, however, furnished only the gamut of possibilities available to the individual artists of the time; and it is with the choice of carved images they realized out of them that the study concludes.

In his most recent work, *Patterns of Intention* (1985), Baxandall has moved to define – and also to extend – the principles of the kind of criticism he has been developing, in a quietly elegant theoretical programme for the history of art. Taking a case of engineering design, the construction of the Forth Bridge, as preliminary illustration, he argues that the right way to look at works of art is as solutions to problems in situations. The task of an 'inferential criticism' is to reconstruct the historical relationships between these three terms in a 'triangle of re-enactment', whose sides will be formed by: the charge and brief set the artist (problem); the cultural resources for tackling these (situation); the artist's own selection of options as they crystallize in the work itself (solution). Such a procedure puts active intentionality

66. *Painting and Experience in Fifteenth-Century Italy*, London 1972, p. 152: understood here is a polemical reference to Antal's work on Florentine styles.

at the centre of its concerns: Baxandall polemicizes – in terms very similar to Clark's attack on 'expression' – against the whole idea of 'influence' with its 'incongruous astral background' as a passive travesty of the actual response of one artist to another.[67] But it must proceed by inference in so far as the only final evidence of the artist's intention is the actual work itself. Baxandall then sets his programme to work with three pointedly disparate examples: Picasso's *Portrait of Kahnweiler*, Chardin's *Lady Taking Tea*, and Piero's *Baptism*. In each a strikingly different cluster of resources is given salience, and a subtle quarrel made with customary interpretations. For Picasso, the importance of Apollinaire as avant-garde crier for 'that wretched term cubism'[68] is not set unduly high – but wider quasi-market relations of *troc*, in which a painter's output might be exchanged for historical reputation as much as for income or popularity, loom large. In the case of Chardin, on the other hand, Locke's philosophy of sensation, as mediated by French optical scientists, could inform his handling of perception (as Einstein's theory of relativity could not, *pace* Berger, Cubism). Piero would have been acutely aware of the mathematical problems of *commensurazione*; there is no need (*pace*, say, Ginzburg) to alembicate a High Iconography to understand his *Baptism*, whose formal design was essentially controlled by the need to accommodate his monumental figure style to the unusual format of a large-scale vertical panel. The variability in the constituents of such criticism is a function of their relative yield in each case: political ideology or economic position would feature more prominently in other instances, although always needing – like other aspects of a painter's social being – to be treated with tact. For if the purpose of criticism is to sharpen our 'legitimate satisfactions' in works of art, its enquiries must be plausible and pertinent to that end – responsible to criteria of historical truth and aesthetic coherence. Baxandall, in words involuntarily echoing across a disciplinary divide, declares his preference for the pursuit of causal explanation rather than hermeneutic meaning, as the most rational and sociable service to a common visual experience: 'it is an important and attractive irony that here history should be the more scientific, in a sense, the more it tends to criticism.'[69] There is a difficulty in this scheme of things. By effectively equating 'intention' with outcome, on the grounds that the mind of the artist is unknowable, Baxandall

67. *Patterns of Intention – On the Historical Explanation of Pictures*, London 1985, pp. 58–60.
68. Ibid., p. 52: for a – typically tacit – disavowal of Berger's account of Cubism, see p. 76.
69. Ibid., p. 136.

productively detours standard issues of signification. But the price is a terminological act of force that virtually endows the painting itself with purposive agency – an object more intent than the subject which intended it. The risk of such pragmatics is a – perhaps unobjectionable, or well-intentioned – fetishism. The title of *Patterns of Intention* is its least successful promise, amidst so many fulfilled. A final irony of this theory of the visual arts, instructive for current doctrines of literature, is that it should stress its commitment to a pictorial criticism as something, above all, 'conversable and democratic'.

For all the force of the counter-examples represented, in their different ways, by Clark and Baxandall, no reconstruction of the field at large was likely to be able simply to bypass the intellectual hegemony of Gombrich, whose post-war position within it probably had no counterpart in any other English discipline. It fell to Norman Bryson, towards the end of this period, to develop the most effective critique of the perceptualism of *Art and Illusion* – the modelling of painting on isolate visual cognition, as filtered by an inherited scheme and corrected by an incremental brush. Against this whole conception, *Vision and Painting* stressed the nature of art as a set of intersubjective signs, anchored in specific social formations, whose analysis must always combine the resources of stylistics and iconology. Remarking on the lateness with which art history encountered recent theoretical history, Bryson's work mobilizes post-structuralist along with structuralist motifs in its pursuit of the production of pictorial meaning. But it also seeks to capture the immanence of power within the image: the social inscription of painting. Here, however, an account that sets out to surpass the intuitions of Barthes or Bakhtin, held insufficiently radical, runs aground – in more senses than one, comes to rest – on those of Foucault. A brilliant meditation on the political limits of the hortatory image – *Marat*, *Guernica* – concludes by dismissing all idea of prescription from art, as redundant to a practice that always already juts into the social, and by discounting all real capacity for disruption, as incompatible with the self-enforcing contract of signification itself. Since 'no one can depart from the consensual formations – the discourses – of the signifier without, at the level of information, risking a fade-out into non-intelligibility', censorship of the canvas is inherently unnecessary: 'painting and viewing are ultimately self-regulating activities, and do not require such anxious monitoring and exhortation: this is a *serene* system.'[70] A politics of the sign, once rendered all-pervasive,

70. *Vision and Painting*, London 1983, pp. 160–62.

fatally veers towards a poetics of resignation. In this vision, only the labour of the painterly body, generating an imagery that characteristically excludes it, is left as illogical hope of subversion or intrusion.

In Bryson's sequel, *Tradition and Desire*, the intimations of value remain somatic, but now sublimated to a Lacanian register. In a series of virtuoso readings of David, Ingres and Delacroix, it is no longer the work of musculature but the dialectics of death and desire that escapes regulation, affording the chance for the oppressive weight of an all-too-cumulative pictorial tradition to be turned by the artist, in the act of innovation. The seductive ingenuity of many a local reflection here nevertheless issues into the same general paradox, resistance or revolt against tradition proving in the end no more than inflections in the repertory of its self-sealing power.[71] In this Foucauldian trope, predictably, what Bryson once described as the 'hard logistics' of social demand or appropriation effectively disappear – the materialist instances of the enquiry dwindling to perfunctory background allusion in what comes near to a conventionally internalist study of the procession of the canon. Perhaps, among the new generation of art historians, Bryson could write the most penetrating critique of Gombrich because in the end he remains closest to him.

Behind these displacements and transformations of two adjacent fields of criticism lay – perhaps increasingly uncontainable – pressures concerned with the category of the aesthetic itself, at stake in all of them. Eagleton's recent *magnum opus* is a bid to master, or deflect, these. *The Ideology of the Aesthetic* explores, criticizes, traverses a vast philosophical circuit, from the moment of Baumgarten to that of Baudrillard, in irregular orbit around the path of European reflections on art since the Enlightenment. The splendour of this enterprise comes not only from the wit of each particular portrait in Eagleton's gallery, but more generally from the amplification of vision that his distinctive attack on the topic brings. In effect, the aesthetic becomes preamble or password to the operations of the political, in the progress of bourgeois civilization from the dawn of the middle class to the noon of its postmodernity, where the sun now seems to many all but biblically to stand still. In this history, its appeal functions primarily as compensation or collusion. But its promise remains rooted in the corporeal realm of the senses that originally gave rise to the term – the body physical featuring as tacit valency against the body political. In between these two,

71. *Tradition and Desire*, Cambridge 1984, pp. 212–14.

Eagleton moves without constraint or intermission from the appetitive to the affective, from the imaginary to the mannerly, from the sentimental to the habitual, from the sensual to the spiritual, as so many variously pertinent registers of the aesthetic, in different times or thinkers. The largeness and ease of this traffic is one of the pleasures of the book. But it has its cost, lodged in the *parti pris* of the title. Is the aesthetic – only – ideology? What the expansion of the category effects is, of course, the effacement of art within it. Animating it is a profound protest, drawn from the whole Marxist tradition, against the lures of any rarefaction of beauty. But that tradition has also often been characterized by a confusion between the technical specialization and the social separation of art. The former, a historically irreversible moment of the division of labour, would outlive any passing away of capital itself. One might say that while a rhetoric of the body, as undifferentiated site of experience, does generate an ideology of the aesthetic, it is the discrimination of skills that founds its reality. In the great roll call of German names that peoples Eagleton's account, the sobering voice of Max Weber is missing.

5. Philosophy

Sociology, which gained a reputation for radicalism in the late sixties, was predictably a target of official dislike by the early eighties – an aversion given literal-minded expression by Ministerial insistence that the Social Science Research Council must change its name if it was to continue to receive (reduced) public funds. But it was actually philosophy which, more surprisingly, provoked perhaps the baldest confrontation between the Thatcher regime and the world of higher learning, towards the end of the decade – when the editor of *Mind* mounted such a withering attack on government treatment of the discipline as to sting the Minister for Higher Education into a furious reply, followed by a virulent further outburst over the coffin of England's most famous post-war philosopher.[72] Little of this could have been expected from the starting-points of the mid sixties. English philosophy had then been

72. See the exchange between Simon Blackburn, editor of *Mind*, and Robert Jackson, Minister for Higher Education, in the *Times Literary Supplement*, 30 December 1988–5 January 1990 – addresses originally entitled 'Philosophy and British Universities', and 'Philosophy and Higher Education'; and Jackson's letter to *The Independent* on the death of A.J. Ayer, of 30 June 1990.

the most uncontentious of disciplines, as the doctrines of the later Wittgenstein had settled down into the routines of ordinary-language analysis propagated from Oxford: proudly formalist, provincial and ahistorical, with little or no connexion to surrounding branches of thought.

Twenty years later, little was left of this. Substantive enquiries had multiplied; international influences had become general; intellectual memory more widespread; inter-disciplinary linkages fairly numerous. British philosophy remained analytical, and its commonest concerns continued to lie within what was once the traditional ambit of epistemology. But this itself underwent major changes. After the passing of Austin and Ryle, the Oxford cult of ordinary language faded. With the gradual widening of parochial horizons, the authority of Wittgenstein became relativized: Carnap was rediscovered, Quine more seriously assimilated, and – in particular – Frege acquired new centrality. In these conditions, the balance of influence within the field shifted across the Atlantic. The leading edge of an English-speaking analytic philosophy, now more unified than ever before, became predominantly American, in the writing of Davidson, Sellars, Kripke, Nagel, Putnam, Dennett, Searle and others. In England, the outstanding figure has been Michael Dummett. It is essentially his reception of Frege that has distinguished local discussion. Dummett's best-known thesis is that Frege revolutionized philosophy by overthrowing the long Cartesian tradition that accorded priority to the theory of knowledge, in favour of a theory of meaning: thereafter, definitively, semantics rather than epistemology would become its foundational pursuit. 'Only with Frege was the proper object of philosophy established.'[73] But the force of Dummett's account of Frege rests less on this claim, which he readily admits might be thought over-pitched, than on its argument for the superiority of Frege's outlook over that of Wittgenstein, in two central respects. Whereas Wittgenstein had imagined an indefinite multiplicity of language-games, incommensurable with each other, so paving the way for the particularist doctrine that the signification of sentences could only lie in their heterogeneous usages, Frege understood that language is by its nature a *system*, competence in which presupposes a tacit grasp of certain general principles that are never reducible to a mere tally of local utterances. At the same time Frege's philosophy, for all its emphasis on meaning, was not only systematic but critical. For it retained a stringent concern with truth, where the laxity of Wittgen-

73. *Truth and Other Enigmas*, London 1978, p. 458.

stein's eventual pragmatics – his notion that all language-games can find their warrant in culturally variable 'forms of life', as apprehended by Spengler[74] – was inevitably to afford a franchise for intellectual relativism. Initially close to Wittgenstein's legacy, Dummett came through his prolonged work on Frege to a reaffirmation of the central importance of the assertoric dimension of language – the specificity and necessity of its claims to accurate report of the world – as against the performative functions so favoured by Austin, for whom there could be no critique of current usages. Wittgenstein's basic programme thus had to be rejected: 'philosophy cannot be content to leave everything as it is', for 'linguistic practice is not immune to, and may well stand in need of, revision'.[75] Upholding by contrast the traditional conception of philosophy as a 'sector in the quest for truth',[76] Dummett in effect reinstates epistemology within the framework of semantics.

Dummett's technical work in the philosophy of meaning has been combined with a *tour de force* in the history of cards, and a critical theory of votes: cultural and institutional interests not entirely unconnected with certain of his professional themes.[77] It has also been accompanied – in his own account dogged – by political concerns of an

74. For Wittgenstein's debt to the author of *The Decline of the West*, the best commentary is Stephen Hilmy, *The Later Wittgenstein*, Oxford 1987, pp. 83–86, 260–63. The collection of texts in *Culture and Value*, Oxford 1980, contains many insights into Wittgenstein's general outlook on the world. See, for example, his welcome for the atomic bomb, or his eminently contemporary reflection: 'I believe that bad housekeeping in the state fosters bad housekeeping in families. A workman who is constantly ready to go on strike will not bring up his children to respect order either': pp. 49e, 63e.

75. 'Reply to Crispin Wright', in Barry Taylor, ed., *Michael Dummett – Contributions to Philosophy*, Dordrecht 1987, p. 234. Dummett's view of Wittgenstein continues to bear traces of his early loyalty, as can be seen from his somewhat tortured later explanations of his attack on Gellner, and the pardonably desperate claim that it is best 'to approach Wittgenstein's later work bearing in mind different possible interpretations, without always trying to decide which is the intended one; frequently, his ideas will be found fruitful and stimulating under all possible interpretations of them' (*sic*): *Truth and Other Enigmas*, pp. xi–xiv, 451.

76. *Truth and Other Enigmas*, p. 456.

77. *The Game of Tarot* (with the assistance of Sylvia Mann), London 1980, an august celebration of the intricacy and diversity of the game as it spread across Europe from its origins in *trecento* Italy, could be read as a kind of homage to Wittgenstein's favourite metaphor; but Dummett parts company with him on just the epistemic point that Wittgenstein would have 'excessively purged' – as he notes, received occult interpretations of Tarot are not seamless parts of playing the game, as a form of life, but parasitic errors about it, harmful to those who believe in them. *Voting Procedures*, Oxford 1984, brings systematic mathematical theory sharply to bear on electoral arrangements, as a condition of arriving at the truth about them, finding those in England scandalous in their lack of protection for minorities, and proposing a simpler and more equitable alternative to the single transferable vote – the quota preference score.

intensity which, even more than his commitment to system, set his writing apart from the school that preceded him. A Catholic of strong moral conviction, he threw himself into work against the growth of racism in the late sixties, regarding it as the most important and disastrous development in Britain since the War. For 'racism is quite exceptional among social evils in requiring no calculation whatever of cause and effect to see what its elimination involves. Of almost any other injustice, it is possible to put up some argument that it must be tolerated because, if we try to remove it, worse will befall; but racism has no compensating advantages, but merely allows the exploitation of one group by another.'[78] It was not until the Commonwealth Immigrants Bill passed by the Wilson Government in 1968 had brought a 'tragic termination' to initial attempts to stop the development of the UK into a racist society, with all its consequences for future suffering, that Dummett – registering a 'decisive defeat' – reverted to his work on Frege.[79] A decade later, he was still outspokenly attacking Christian glosses on the new Conservatism that covered over not only the evils of institutionalized racism, but also the indignities of industrial drudgery, the enormities of nuclear deterrence. The sense of Dummett's public interventions over these years is contained in a characteristic confession: 'I expect there are many people who long, as I do, for a political programme of a radically new kind, not just an uneasy compromise between capitalism and socialism, but one that would sweep away the injustices and inhumanities of capitalism as effectively as would socialism, but would provide a rather more effective safeguard against State tyranny than does existing parliamentary democracy.'[80]

The substantive turn, evident within epistemology, has been even more marked in what once would have fallen into the domain of ontology. The change here could be described as that from the moment of Strawson to that of Parfit – from the studiously 'descriptive' metaphysics of *Individuals* or *The Bounds of Sense* to the actively prescriptive agenda of *Reasons and Persons*. Where the former limited itself to formal properties of our existing conceptual scheme of the world, disavowing any possibility or intention of 'dreaming up alternative

78. *Catholicism and the World Order*, London 1979, pp. 27–28.
79. *Frege – Philosophy of Language*, second edition, London 1981, pp. x–xi.
80. *Catholicism and the World Order*, pp. 31–32.

structures',[81] the latter takes as its object our sense of natural identity and seeks to demonstrate – to practical effect – that we are typically in error about it: 'philosophers should not only interpret our beliefs; when they are false, they should *change* them.'[82] The changes proposed by Parfit, the most original thinker of the younger generation, are stiff medicine: nothing less than the dissolution of traditional ideas of the person into a succession of contingently associated states, with no more necessary unity or continuity than nations or parties – something closer to the divisible segments of the amoeba or the mutable referents of the SFIO, than to the integrity of the person as normally understood.[83] The dismantling of identity is a familiar theme in contemporary continental philosophy. The startling feature of *Reasons and Persons* is that it presents a utilitarian analogue to the leading theme of post-structuralism. Its intellectual background is not an idealist meditation on the instability of language, so much as a materialist response to the arrival of medical transplants and genetic engineering. In this world, the separateness of persons upheld by theorists of natural rights, but ignored in their different ways by Bentham and Buddha, is to be set aside. The ethical upshot of Parfit's radical reduction of identity is no Lyotardian hedonism or Nietzschean heroics of the present, but the need for an unflinching 'moral mathematics' of the future – since, under threat of nuclear annihilation, 'the next few centuries will be the most important in human history'.[84]

The prominence of *Reasons and Persons*, in the main due to the disturbing force and strangeness of its central arguments, also owes something to its particular combination of an extended account of the self with a sustained view of the moral life. For these two preoccupations have characterized much contemporary philosophical writing, typically in tacit reference to each other, but rarely joined so expressly and directly. On the one hand, there has been a major cluster of literature on problems of agency and identity. Here the field has divided with renewed sharpness between theorists of meaning and exponents

81. See Strawson's remarks in conversation with Bryan Magee, *Modern British Philosophy*, second edition, London 1986, pp. 157–58. Magee comments in his introduction to this collection of dialogues, originally published in 1971, that it probably represented 'the last attempt that will be possible to discuss contemporary British philosophy solely in terms of British philosophers and their work', since 'British philosophy no longer seems autonomous in the way it once was – indeed, it seems on the way to becoming the chief province in a territory whose capital is elsewhere': p. 9.

82. *Reasons and Persons*, Oxford 1984, p. x.

83. 'Persons are like nations, clubs or political parties': ibid., p. 277.

84. Ibid., pp. 453–54, 351.

of causation. The strongest attack on all naturalist accounts of the self has come from Charles Taylor, for whom the constitutive feature of human agency is self-interpretation against a background of evaluation, that is, within a cultural space defined by distinctions of worth. Identity is to be conceived as a locus not of performance but of significance: irreducible to behavioural explanation, it can only be understood hermeneutically. As such, it is unamenable to calculations of utility. The project of explaining human action scientifically not only misses its target: it must itself be interpreted as a sublimated modern sequel to ancient ideals of self-denial as the path to spiritual freedom.[85] At the opposite pole, Ted Honderich's *Theory of Determinism* offers a massive statement of the case for a causal account of action grounded on the advances of neurophysiology. Reviewing the whole philosophical tradition of debates over free will, Honderich concludes that no variant of compatibilism – doctrines that seek to reconcile determination and self-origination of our acts – is defensible. A full determinism, threatening as it may seem to unreflective hopes of life, ought to inspire neither dejection nor defiance, but rather renunciation of impossible desires, and contentment with those which are within our reach as common members of nature.[86] The stoic overtones here confirm at any rate temperamental affinities between the deeper forms of classical and modern naturalism.

A third position can be found in the work of Richard Wollheim, whose view of identity derives essentially from psychoanalysis. Traditionally, Freud's thought has often been used to mediate the claims of meaning and cause. In moderate hermeneutic versions of his doctrine, such as that of Ricoeur, the emphasis falls on analysis as interpretation rather than explanation, language more than biology. This is the reading sympathetic to Taylor. Wollheim, by contrast, has always stayed closer to Freud's own conception of his work, as an explanatory theory of psychic life whose ultimate foundation lay in the mechanisms of physical drives. At the same time, this greater materialist inclination is joined to a far more holist view of identity than that of Parfit – to whom the title of Wollheim's central work may be taken as a rejoinder. *The Thread of Life* takes as its organizing theme the 'process of living',

85. *Human Agency and Language – Philosophical Papers*, vol. I, pp. 112–13. A Canadian, Taylor can – with some latitude – be included here by reason of his long association with Oxford.

86. *A Theory of Determinism*, London 1988, pp. 495–96. Honderich is also Canadian by origin (so too his former colleague G.A. Cohen).

whose phenomenology is constituted by the experience of the continuity of our mental states, dispositions and activities. Wollheim brings to these a set of categories directly drawn from Freud and Klein, illustrating his accounts of memory or phantasy with the first case-histories of psychoanalysis.[87] Where Parfit urges the emancipating force of a view of the person as divisible, even interchangeable, for Wollheim the greatest evils that can be suffered – loss of friendship, madness and death – are those that in different ways cut the thread of living. Something of the same concern can be seen in his major study in substantive aesthetics, *Painting as an Art*, which founds the intersubjective intelligibility of painting – a process requiring the spectator to retrieve the work's original meaning for the painter – on its evolutionary success in finding the thread of a continuous public.[88]

Philosophical absorption with the problems of identity has necessarily led to closer relations with different strands of psychology. If the steeping of Wollheim's work in psychoanalytic thought is a special case, analytic philosophy generally displayed a wider interest in Freud in this period – which also, however, saw a transformation in the position of psychoanalysis within British culture at large. From being a somewhat secluded, specialist enclave it became a familiar part of lay reference, as Freud's writings belatedly achieved mass diffusion and a broad influence across a range of intellectual disciplines, with an especial attraction for feminist currents within them. Paradoxically, however, public breakthrough coincided in many ways with professional recession. In its relative isolation, up to the late sixties, psychoanalysis had enjoyed a rare fertility in England; its division between Freudian, Kleinian and Middle Groups generating a richer intellectual history, with more independent talent – Riviere, Bowlby, Fairbairn, Winnicott, Laing, Bion and others – than was produced in either the USA or France. Once it entered into common circulation, however, Winnicott or Laing become staples of paperback display and Klein impersonated on the West End stage, its previous diversity and vitality seemed to lessen. If post-Kleinian work, derived mainly from Bion, has been most visible, it has also shifted furthest away from a general theory, towards a sympathetic phenomenology of mental

87. *The Thread of Life*, London 1984, pp. 130–161.

88. *Painting as an Art*, London 1987, p. 357 – a work expressly concerned with causal explanation, whose centrepiece is a remarkable revaluation of Poussin, set in effect against Blunt's great study of him.

disorder.[89] There were larger reasons for this change.

The evolution of perhaps the sharpest mind within the British School, Charles Rycroft, records some of them. Initially a leading member of the British Psycho-Analytical Society, Rycroft took critical stock of it during the sixties and became convinced that it was too inbred and undemanding an intellectual milieu, and that psychoanalysis as a whole was unwarrantably indifferent not only to the findings of experimental psychology or ethology, but also to the insights of poetic intelligence and often the claims of common sense.[90] By the late seventies, he had left the Society and in *The Innocence of Dreams* (1979) upturned one of the central pillars of classical Freudian theory, dreams being regarded not as akin to neurotic symptoms born of repression, but as nocturnal expressions of the involuntary imagination once conceived by Jean Paul or Coleridge. Significantly, the most interesting account of dreams to come from an experimental psychologist, Liam Hudson's *Night-Life* (1985), draws directly on Rycroft's ideas. Meanwhile, the effect of such a reversal within psychoanalysis itself has been reinforced by philosophical critiques from without. Focusing on the scientific status of Freud's theories, Frank Cioffi concluded that these were procedurally untestable, Adolf Grunbaum that they were testable but incompatible with therapeutic evidence.[91] In another register, Gellner's racily executed but deeply engaged polemic *The Psychoanalytic Movement* moves beyond substantive attack on the main doctrines of psychoanalysis, to propose a sweeping cultural explanation for their social impact, in what is certainly the most powerful single attempt so far to situate Freud in the wider history of European ideas.

But if psychoanalysis is 'hardly well', in Grunbaum's temperate phrase, its principal rival has been in no better condition. For native positivist psychology has in the same period suffered more than its own share of embarrassment, with the discovery of the fraud perpetrated by the patron authority of IQ studies in England, Sir Cyril Burtt, and the

89. For friendly insight into this school, see Michael Rustin, 'Post-Kleinian Psychoanalysis and the Post-Modern', *New Left Review* 173, January–February 1989, a writer who has consistently sought to articulate psychoanalytic concerns with wider cultural and political issues.

90. See *Psychoanalysis and Beyond*, London 1985, pp. 119–127, 204–206, which contains a series of crisp vignettes of leading British analysts.

91. Frank Cioffi, 'Freud and the Idea of a Pseudo-Science', in R. Borger and F. Cioffi, eds, *Explanation in the Behavioural Sciences*, Cambridge 1970, pp. 471–499; Adolf Grunbaum, *The Foundations of Psychoanalysis*, Berkeley–Los Angeles 1984, pp. 159–172 (argument from spontaneous remission).

misadventures of his student Hans Eysenck, 'the most influential of living British psychologists'.[92] Champion of behaviour therapy and author of a popular library of works deriving social and individual patterns – inequalities of race and class, differences of intelligence and personality, propensities to criminality or to smoking – from biologically inherited endowments, Eysenck gave the ultimate piquant illustration of the affinities between scientism and superstition by flirting with astrology.[93] No philosophy of identity, however resolutely reductive its programme, could find a reliable basis from quarters like this. At a time when the gap between the overt concerns of philosophy and psychology often narrowed, the actual support the latter could provide the former – whether it conceived the self as source of meaning, or nexus of cause – ironically looked, if anything, more precarious.

Alongside the new concern with identity came a revival of interest in ethics. Where once there had been little more than formal analysis of 'the language of morals', as so many familiar locutions employed in more or less humdrum situations, there now emerged rival accounts of the substance of ethical living itself. Broadly, three contrasting positions can be distinguished. For Bernard Williams, in a series of interventions, ethics are never isolate. Moral considerations always mingle among other kinds of significant valuation on one side, and are interwoven with accidents of fortune on the other: the luck of character or occasion. The notion of the purely moral therefore betrays 'a powerful misconception of life' that converts everything into obligation – whether that obligation is interpreted in Kantian or Benthamite fashion. Conceived as such, morality is an 'institution we would be better off without'.[94] In similar vein, Wollheim has rejected the view that 'morality is ultimate or over-riding', in favour of an ethics that conjoins obligation and value. Here, however, value is identified psychoanalytically, as a projection of archaic bliss grounded on a universal human

92. 'A world figure . . . no psychologist since Freud has had such an impact on contemporary thinking as Eysenck', in the words of his admiring colleague H.B. Gibson: *Hans Eysenck – The Man and his Work*, London 1981, p. 9.

93. After *The Biological Basis of Personality* (1967), *Race, Intelligence and Education* (1971), *The Inequality of Man* (1973), *Crime and Personality* (1977), came the startling news of Eysenck's organization of a colloquium of horoscopists at the Maudsley in 1979, followed by his plea for 'cosmobiology' – the study of extra-terrestrial influences on human life – in *Astrology* (1982). Even Gibson quails at this enthusiasm: *Hans Eysenck*, pp. 204–213.

94. *Moral Luck*, Cambridge 1981, pp. 20–39; *Ethics and the Limits of Philosophy*, London 1985, pp. 180, 194–96.

nature[95] – a basis refused by Williams, for whom the only possible objective foundation for morality would be a gradual social convergence on a common way of life, from which, however, future generations could well depart.

In these critiques of rule-based ethics, a vitalist strain predominates. In the work of Alasdair MacIntyre, a much more extended and vehement attack on Kantian and utilitarian ideas of right conduct – treated as equally misguided legacies of the Enlightenment – is mounted, but from the alternative of virtue rather than value. *After Virtue* presents a history of successive moral codes, from Homeric to Modern times, that seeks not only to show how each was rooted in a specific social order, but to trace the decline of what was once a coherent ethical tradition – Aristotelian and then mediaeval – into contemporary spiritual chaos. MacIntyre's theorization of the virtues, as qualities anchored in the culture of particular communities and demonstrated across the unity of a human life, is strongly anti-atomistic in intent. Yet its hostility to liberal individualism, reproached with sanctioning any subjective ethical stance, perversely ends by reproducing relativism at a higher level – that of the localized community, as opposed to the disinherited individual. The attempt to insist on both the historical rootedness of the Nicomachean Ethics in the classical *polis*, and its perennial superior merits in late industrial civilization, inevitably issues into defensive paradox, one that can only be sustained by what – contrary to appearances – is in effect a treatment of the past as parable rather than chronicle.[96]

Formally similar in strategy, and overlapping in outlook, Charles Taylor's *Sources of the Self* also pursues an extended historical enquiry to contemporary ethical conclusions. But here the object of critical reconstruction is the formation of modern identity, from the time of Plato to that of Celan, and its treatment is on a more ambitious and richer scale. The aim of the work is not an indictment of the moral wilderness of the present, but on the contrary a demonstration of the variety of its underground springs. The sources of the modern self, whose inwardness was first adumbrated in Augustinian Christianity, include the Enlightenment ideals of the dignity of science and the Romantic valencies of nature, conceptions of universal benevolence and of personal epiphany – that is, the still active legacies of theism,

95. *The Thread of Life*, pp. 215, 221–25.

96. Of which the famous ending, awaiting the mission of a modern St Benedict for 'the new dark ages which are already upon us', provides an appropriate illustration: *After Virtue*, London 1979, p. 263.

naturalism, expressivism. Where for MacIntyre these are precisely proof of the incoherence of modernity, shattered debris of incompatible traditions strewn as if by some metaphysical disaster, for Taylor they form an indispensable complex of resources for the higher morality demanded by it. In Hegelian style, each is suspended and integrated within an ontological narrative that culminates in the quest for a transcendent order, apprehensible through the visions of modernist art and readmissible as the shapes of historical hope into radical politics.

If these explorations in a temporalized ethics have a religious background – Anglican and Catholic, respectively – moral theory assumes a quite different cast in James Griffin's *Well-Being*. It too starts from a strong statement of the embeddedness of the ethical, in contrasting ways common to all these philosophies. But here the standpoint is critically utilitarian, and its focus the immanent relationships between prudential and moral values. In Griffin's version, utility becomes the fulfilment of informed desires, its maximization a rational enhancement of well-being. Prudence instructs us to pursue those ends – for example accomplishment, autonomy, understanding, enjoyment – which will confer well-being, and morality can be conceived as a set of demands overlapping but not coinciding with it. A good life will be so at once in a prudential and moral sense. But, taking two classically contrasted values, while liberty is a principle of prudence, equality – because it involves comparison between lives – is a dictate of morality, indeed 'in a way *the* moral value'. The political consequences of this ethic are no more than silhouetted. Sufficiently, however, to condemn present patterns of material distribution as 'glaringly obsolete', and to suggest their revision by an alternative principle, normal in families: from each according to their abilities, to each according to their needs.[97]

In all these bodies of work, politics looms at the edge of the ethics in question. In political philosophy itself, meanwhile, analogous changes were occurring. Peter Laslett, introducing in 1956 what was to be a series of volumes entitled *Philosophy, Politics and Society*, declared in a famous pronouncement that for the time being 'political philosophy is dead'.[98] All the contributors to that collection, headed by Oakeshott, were British. By 1967 the editors saw some signs of revival, if one

97. *Well-Being*, Oxford 1986, pp. 239, 303.
98. *Philosophy, Politics and Society*, vol. I, London 1956, p. vii.

largely limited to a 'holding operation' against the prevalent forces of positivism, in linguistic philosophy and behavioural social science. Five years later, they decided that such verdicts were 'no longer applicable'.[99] By 1979, the fifth and final volume was recording the 'most welcome happenings' in political thought 'with enthusiasm'. The principal occasion for such satisfaction was the appearance in the early seventies of John Rawls's *Theory of Justice*, which rendered defunct Berlin's dictum earlier in the series that no commanding work of political theory had appeared in the twentieth century. Next in importance was the arrival of Robert Nozick's *Anarchy, State and Utopia*. The revival had, however, been essentially American – a change registered in the contributors to the collection itself, of whom only one was now British.

The renewal of political theory in this period, like that of philosophy at large, was indeed accompanied by a new dominance of US production. In this case, the ascendancy was for a time overwhelming – as the neo-contractarian structures of Rawls and Nozick became the obsessive centre of reference of most of the discipline. Even at the height of this influence, however, there was a discernible difference in the climate of professional opinion in the two countries. In the United States, Rawls's delphic masterpiece was generally received as the standpoint of a moderate, liberal Left, within a field whose centre of gravity lay well to the right of it. There, Nozick's truculent postures scarcely marked the outer bounds of neo-conservatism, where older and wintrier theories like those of James Buchanan and the Virginia School stood guard. In Britain, on the other hand, Rawls was more generally taken as a figure of the centre; in a culture where the utilitarian traditions he rejected were stronger, his critics were typically more radical. Here the range of philosophical outlook was several degrees to the left of the American. Dummett's forthright views were not an isolated case. Entirely opposed in their accounts of human agency, it is all the more noticeable that Taylor and Honderich have largely coincided in political conviction – Taylor a founding spirit of the New Left, Honderich a trenchant critic of the silent violences of liberal society.[100] The moral philosophies of MacIntyre and Griffin may be antithetical, but their

99. The second and third volumes (1962 and 1967) were edited by Laslett and Runciman; for the fourth (1972) they were joined by Quentin Skinner; the fifth (1979) was produced by Laslett and an American colleague, James Fishkin.

100. See his important essay on the moral comparability of acting and failing to act in politics, 'Our Omissions and their Violence', *Violence for Equality*, London 1980, pp. 58–100.

social attitudes to the inequalities of capitalism are quite close. Wollheim has gone out of his way, even in such an apparently distant context as his pictorial theory, to affirm a life-long attachment to socialism.

Within political theory itself, the pattern of discussion has thus predictably also been to the left of the American. One significant theme running through it, for obvious reasons largely absent in the USA, has been the fate and future of socialism. Alan Ryan's *Property and Political Theory* (1984), which traces two distinct conceptions of ownership – instrumental versus expressive – from Locke and Rousseau onwards, concludes with a critical balance-sheet of the respective expectations of Mill and Marx that the 'futurity of the working class' would assure a transition to socialism: hopes attractive and reasonable in their time, but since disappointed by events, as work becomes less arduous and property less important. John Dunn's *Politics of Socialism* (1984) engages more widely with the record of the labour movement and of socialist thought, in both social democratic and communist variants; combining a severe judgement on their practical and intellectual failures to date with an unusual argument as to why an impetus – at once economic and cultural – towards socialism nevertheless remains inherent in the pressures of advanced capitalism itself. Dunn's principal charge against the existent politics of socialism is the weakness, if not worse, of its understanding of democracy. This is the deficiency David Held's recent work seeks to remedy. *Models of Democracy* (1987) develops a historical typology of successive conceptions of democratic government, in a way that owes much to Macpherson; but it goes on to propose the institutional outlines of a socialism that would marry liberal reserve towards political power with Marxist suspicion of economic power, by according a right of 'democratic autonomy' – equal capacity of individuals to determine their life-conditions – to its citizens. A concern with the relationship between liberalism and socialism is, in effect, a common strand of all these works.

On the heights of political philosophy in the more traditional sense, the situation is similar. The central figure here, Brian Barry, started out in the mid sixties with a work aiming to show the advantages of bringing the technical rigour of analytic philosophy, on one side, and economic models of political life, on the other, to classic normative issues of the discipline. In keeping with the times, the authority of Austin or Downs was invoked more or less uncritically in this enterprise, which hesitated between a formal survey of different species of social justification and actual commentary on the arrangements so justified. Yet for all its conventional air, the conclusion of *Political Argument* was a penetrating, prescient attack on the founding version of the public choice theory that was later to become the dominant *Staatslehre* of the radical Right in the USA – Buchanan and Tullock's *Calculus of Consent*.[101] Barry then moved to the explanatory side of the discipline, with an original two-handed critique of the contrasting theories of democracy advanced by Downs (also Olson) and Parsons – 'economic' and 'sociological' accounts of its operation whose ideological pedigree, he argued, went back to Bentham and Coleridge. *Economists, Sociologists and Democracy* (1970) found the modern versions of both these traditions – theorizing democratic stability in terms of either utility maximization or value integration – basically wanting: the one unable to explain why anyone bothers to vote at all, the other why there should be any need for an ultimate coercive authority. While judging the deductive economic models of Downs and Olson rather less sterile than the circular culturalism of Parsons, Barry pointed to Barrington Moore's historical account of the relations between state structures and social classes as an avenue of explanation escaping the nineteenth-century dichotomy they repeated.

Such interventions, however sharp their analytical edge, remained fairly reticent in political statement. *The Liberal Theory of Justice* (1973), published as class conflicts were unseating the Heath Government, marked a dramatic change of register. Amidst the mountain of blandly decorous literature on Rawls's theory of justice, this stands out as the most telling and passionate rejoinder to it. In a polemic that succeeds in being scathingly respectful, Barry taxed Rawls with uncritical acceptance of the market as a mechanism of social distribution and the nation-state as a unit of collective decision, complacency towards domestic inequalities of wealth and power in the USA, taken for a 'nearly just' society, and blindness towards international inequalities, conjured away by draping the device of the 'veil of ignorance' across just one – advanced industrial – community. The Difference Principle, Barry charges, apparently capable of bringing succour to the least fortunate within such a state, effectively issued into little more than a placebo: 'not since Locke's theory of property have such potentially radical premises been used as the foundation for something so little disturbing to the status quo.'[102] Unaware of the central influence of working-class action in diminishing the weight of injustice in Western

101. *Political Argument*, London 1965, pp. 242–285.
102. *The Liberal Theory of Justice*, Oxford 1973, p. 50.

societies through welfare legislation, Rawls was in many of his background assumptions close to an unreconstructed liberalism of Gladstonian stamp.

At the close of the eighties, Barry's own *magnum opus* has started to appear. The first instalment of a projected three-volume *Treatise on Social Justice* encapsulates the history of reflection on justice, from Plato to the present, in two fundamental alternatives. Justice has either been conceived as the dictates of rational prudence, in circumstances where social cooperation is essential to civil existence; or as the outcome of rational agreement, in conditions where bargaining power cannot be used for advantage. Barry dubs these rival conceptions 'justice as mutual cooperation' and 'justice as impartiality'. Hume and Rawls – opposites as proto-utilitarian and neo-contractualist – nevertheless each attempted to combine both these ideas in their respective theories of justice. Hume employed the former to explain how the institutions of private property arose out of rational self-interest, and the latter to account for the sentiments of extended sympathy that then sustained them. Likewise Rawls constructs his 'original position', from which a just society is chosen, out of the self-interested calculations of those who cannot know what their particular lot would be in one; but then advocates social arrangements for his eventual position which must appeal to moral principles beyond maximin outcomes. For Barry, both amalgams are incoherent: Hume has no answer to the 'sensible knave' who ignores the claims of sympathy in a civilized society, while Rawls must resort to smuggling back ethical motives as 'higher-order' interests of the actors in his original position. Barry's treatment of Rawls is far warmer than in his earlier polemic, and in one crucial respect he reverses himself directly, to underwrite what he had previously described as the Panglossian assumption of the 'chain connexion' – roughly, that anything which improves the lot of one group will also enhance that of all others – behind the Difference Principle, which now receives his qualified approval.[103] But the power of his attack on the overall framework of Rawlsian theory is even strengthened, as he extends his critique of its stoppage before international inequalities to longer-run issues of ecological injustice, affecting many future generations.

Theories of Justice ends by proclaiming the primacy of impartiality over mutual advantage, and arguing that it is possible to attain it – that is, reach rational agreement about social ends – through unimpaired

103. *Theories of Justice*, London 1989, p. 231; presumably also p. 4.

debate. The stress here is very close to characteristic themes of Habermas – whom Barry, anachronistically monoglot in reference, ignores. Unlike Habermas, however, he not only seeks to specify the empirical conditions for – or barriers to – the 'circumstances of impartiality' in existent societies, but promises institutional recommendations for the achievement of economic equity within and between nations. It remains to be seen whether the philosophical ambition he announces, of ultimately incorporating justice as mutually beneficial cooperation as a 'special case' of justice as impartiality, will be more successful than the hybrid unions he has criticized. But the political direction of the *Treatise* as a whole is already laid out in the title of his inaugural lecture at the LSE: 'The Continuing Relevance of Socialism'.[104] In a withering attack on the market failures and individualist fallacies of the Thatcher–Reagan years, Barry proposes collective control – as opposed to equality – of life-conditions as the central principle of socialism, and the practice of social insurance as its major embodiment to date.

Tension between these two conceptions – popular sovereignty or material equality – recurs, as it happens, in another body of writing whose intellectual origins lie to the left of Barry's. The prolific output of the school of Analytical Marxism has ranged across economics, sociology, history and political philosophy. Its originating work was G.A. Cohen's reconstruction of Marx's theory of history. In its subsequent flowering, as John Roemer's theory of exploitation became central to it, capitalism has been mainly discussed (from a range of different positions) as a system of social inequality. In England, Cohen – whose election to the Oxford chair once occupied by Berlin suggests some of the changes of this period – has contributed to these debates, principally with a deadly side-blow to Nozick's theory of property.[105] But the memorable conclusion of *Karl Marx's Theory of History – A Defence* does not rest its case against capitalism on the issue of equality, whether national or international. Its indictment concentrates rather on the systematic compulsion to prefer increased output to decreased labour time that distinguishes capitalism from all other social orders: 'the economic form most able to relieve toil is the least

104. Contained in Robert Skidelsky, ed., *Thatcherism*, London 1988, pp. 143–158.
105. 'Freedom, Justice and Capitalism', *New Left Review* 125, March–April 1981, pp. 3–16.

disposed to do so.'[106] Socialism, by contrast, would for the first time empower producers to choose between goods and leisure. Here it is not social insurance but free time that is the practical touchstone of a better society. But the principle coincides with Barry's: socialism is conceived in either case as collective reassertion of control over the basic conditions of economic life. These conclusions leave two issues evidently unresolved. What would be the institutional forms of a socialized sovereignty, and what would be the relative place of equality within them? It is these questions that David Miller's *Market, State and Community* addresses, in the most developed attempt to date to establish – against objections of the radical Right and sceptical Left alike – the normative foundations of a market socialism, in which co-operative enterprises leasing socially owned capital would compete with each other, and differential returns to individual desert would flow within distributive boundaries set by a strongly constitutionalist state. The aim of this conception is to reconcile autonomy and equity with efficiency, by rendering the form of the market itself a consciously chosen economic device, the 'expression of collective will'.[107] In these related emphases, a political theory remote from that of a still recent past has been emerging. Philosophy, apparently the least likely of British disciplines to display a radical temper, in fact registered some of the most various shifts of all towards one.

6. Economics

In its classical origins economics was, as is well known, intimately connected with philosophy in Britain. Smith, professing Moral Philosophy, and Mill, expounding Political Economy, embodied the association of the two disciplines. The link between them persisted through the neo-classical revolution, Sidgwick joining ethics and economics in a single corpus. Keynes's own intellectual background lay in logic, and at the height of his career he characteristically recalled the philosophical

106. *Karl Marx's Theory of History – A Defence*, Oxford 1978, p. 306. Cohen stresses that this would stand as an indictment of American capitalism 'even if the United States were a society of substantial equality, isolated from the rest of the world' – i.e. classless and unimperialist.

107. *Market, State and Community*, Oxford 1989, pp. 220–223. For all its rigour of argument and ease of manner, Miller's book combines a level-headed moral realism with a certain contextual amnesia – as if its author, in constructing an avowedly national model, had deliberately chosen to forget the encompassing international order of capitalism, where on his own premisses cooperatives could not hope to survive.

vocation of the economist. In the post-war epoch, however, as technical specialization proceeded apace in each discipline, contact between them dwindled away all but completely. Econometrics and ordinary-language analysis had little to say to each other during the arid fifties. This distance too now altered, as certain common traits came to mark the two fields, and exchange was renewed between them.

More directly than any other area of thought, economics was altered by the upheaval in its environment in these years. During the long boom, the theoretical consensus throughout the Atlantic world was Keynesian, as counter-cyclical management of demand became normal government practice, appearing to assure steady growth of prosperity at high levels of employment. After premonitory signs of trouble in the late sixties, the sudden onset of global recession in the early seventies, bringing the novel combination of sharp falls in output with steep rises in price-level, undermined this orthodoxy. A series of radical challenges to Keynesianism rapidly occupied the front of the stage. Virtually all of these came from the United States. But if the 'counter-revolution' in economics has been essentially an American phenomenon, this has itself reflected the dominance of the USA within the discipline at large. Out of the hundred names included in the standard survey of *Great Economists since Keynes*, three-quarters were American by birth or base – compared with less than a fifth from Britain; among those living, the proportions are still more pronounced, the USA outnumbering the UK ten to one.[108] Within this American ascendancy, the tide of professional opinion swung steadily to the right: the major alternatives to Keynesian doctrines that now gained influence were without exception outspokenly conservative.

Most prominent was, of course, monetarism *stricto sensu*. Milton Friedman's Presidential Address to the American Economic Association of late 1967, which appropriately opened the period, attacked the conventional view – codified as the Phillips curve – that there was any long-run trade-off between employment and inflation. The price-level was fundamentally set by the supply of money, and fiscal expansion could only accelerate inflation, briefly lifting output and cutting real

108. Mark Blaug, *Great Economists since Keynes*, London 1985. The selection of those included may not be quite as consensual as the author makes out; but compiled by an American in England, it is likely to be balanced in this respect. One point it confirms is the high degree of mobility generally among economists – a third of those based in the USA have been immigrants, just under a third in the UK. For present purposes, greater number of working years so far spent in one or the other country can be taken as the criterion of who should be counted where – e.g. Coase or Lerner in the US group, Morishima or Sen in the UK group.

wages before labour adjusted its claims in compensation, thereby restoring 'the natural rate of unemployment' inherent in any given national economy.[109] Repeated counter-cyclical stimulation of demand only generated ever greater anticipation of price rises, without corresponding rises in output or employment – hence, inevitably, stagflation. The remedy to this evil was the tightest possible control of the money supply, preferably enforced by law rather than merely pursued by government. Monetarism in Friedman's version drove the largest breach in neo-Keynesian positions, but it was soon outdone by a more radical rejection of them. The rational expectations theory formulated by Lucas and Sargent denied that there could be any interval at all between fiscal expansion and wage inflation, by modelling labour with the same immediate capacity to foresee the effects of government policy as capital. Markets always tend towards equilibrium, and pump-priming can have not even the most short-run effect in creating jobs. The upshot is the famous axiom that there is no such thing as 'involuntary unemployment': the jobless choose to be so, preferring leisure to work.

Lucas's doctrine in effect dismisses macro-economics altogether: since markets always clear, there is no distinct role for theoretical aggregation. Friedman's, allowing for delay in the adjustment of lay expectations and ascribing superior predictive powers to the economist, retains such a dimension in simplified form. An exclusive derivation of inflation from increases in monetary aggregates, however, leaves its ultimate causes unexplained – what determines the latter? The public choice theory developed by Buchanan and Tullock filled this gap. Projecting the neo-classical analytic framework from the market onto the state, the 'new political economy' of the Virginia School treated governments as essentially self-interested maximizers like firms or households – rather than the benevolently impartial authorities Keynes had assumed. Swollen budgets and abundant emissions become the natural choices of public officials, as politicians seek clienteles for re-election and bureaucrats resources for appropriation. Keynes himself, concerned with the multiplier effects of state expenditure in general, had been notoriously indifferent to its particular destinations – digging holes or building pyramids would serve the purpose. His

109. 'The Role of Monetary Policy', *American Economic Review*, March 1968, pp. 8–17: Presidential Address to the American Economic Association, 27 December 1967. 'The first and most important lesson that history teaches us about what monetary policy can do – and it is a lesson of the most profound importance – is that monetary policy can prevent money itself from being a major source of economic disturbance': p. 12.

successors, however, had stressed the public goods of a positive character – repairing 'market failures' or private externalities – that it could provide. Here the theory of property rights associated with Coase and Demsetz stepped in, arguing that it was often essentially underdefinition of private entitlements and liabilities that led to the costly illusion of a requirement for public goods at all. Finally, completing the barrage from the right, the theory of spontaneous order perfected by Hayek in his American years pointed to the restraints on trade represented by labour unions, as an independent and endemic source of inflation from below – wrongly discounted by the schools of Friedman or Lucas – that needed to be broken as well. At the same time, far beyond this, Hayek's *œuvre* furnished an encompassing philosophical carapace – cultural and historical as well as economic and political – for every technical variety of the case for a deregulated capitalism. A great deal of more traditional work, of moderate quasi-Keynesian stamp, continued meanwhile to be done, of course. But in this altered climate, even such eminences as Arrow or Samuelson lost centrality, while rare figures to the left of them like Leontief became entirely isolated.

The British scene has differed significantly. In the first half of the century, English economics had possessed its own strong and distinctive native tradition. The version of marginalism that Marshall developed was pragmatic in cast and social in concern. A focus on the partial equilibrium of particular markets, rather than general equilibrium of all of them; a price theory embracing costs of production as well as consumer utility; a social policy favouring progressive taxation, but discountenancing union militancy; an industrial outlook already anxious at Britain's lagging productivity and loss of competitive advantage – these typified Marshall's outlook. After him, the Cambridge legacy bifurcated. Roughly speaking, Pigou developed the side that was sensitive to issues of distribution, his exploration of the possibilities for divergence between private and social costs founding what was to become welfare economics; Keynes took over the interest in production, inaugurating what later became macro-economics with what – despite its title – amounted to a pragmatically limited theory of employment, born of the Depression, that effectively set aside questions of competition or productivity. If Keynes's departures from theoretical orthodoxy occasioned sharp contention in Cambridge, his practical recommendations for the Slump still commanded widespread agreement among his critics or elders there. At the LSE an alternative circle emerged in the thirties, under the guidance of Robbins and with the presence of Hayek, that was more alive to influences from Lausanne and Vienna – the variants of marginalism stemming fromWalras and Menger, which did resist Keynesian recipes ferociously, in the name of liberal orthodoxy. But it remained relatively loose-knit and lost much of its edge during the War; Robbins himself, now a convert to Keynes's programme for employment, worked with him in his final mission to secure an American loan for peace-time recovery.[110] The post-war settlement, formally dedicated to social welfare and full employment, presided over by Labour and confirmed by the Conservative governments of the fifties, consecrated the hegemony of Cambridge traditions in the wider political culture. Within the profession itself, henceforward greatly expanded, there was no probably no country where Keynesian tenets enjoyed such general assent.

Economic decline, evident from the sixties onwards, provoked little searching response in this community – Marshall's original disquiet on this score had been all too successfully displaced by Keynes. Nor did the first signs of impending world recession, towards the end of the decade, ruffle it. In the autumn of 1971, just as a feverish commodities boom was about to collapse, giving way to the worst slump since 1929, Samuel Brittan – himself an adherent to the monetarism already waxing in the USA – submitted a questionnaire to some 120 leading economists in the UK. *Is There an Economic Consensus?* found that there was indeed one, what Brittan termed a 'liberal orthodoxy' subscribed to by three-quarters of his respondents: that is, a belief in market competition and the pursuit of individual self-interest as the mainsprings of growth, but not as necessarily conducive to an equitable distribution of income or adequate supply of public goods – which required various forms of corrective state intervention. Monetary discipline, Brittan noted with regret, was not deemed sufficient for the conduct of government by his respondents; global demand-management was firmly upheld. Worse, 'an impressionistic judgement is that their egalitarian concern is greater than among economists in most other Western countries' – perhaps a 'form of the puritan legacy'.[111] The profile of British economists at this date, in other words, testified principally to the continuity of native tradition.

Three years later, amidst oil crisis and miners' strike, John Hicks published *The Crisis in Keynesian Economics*. The most original and versatile mind of the generation younger than Keynes, Hicks had

110. For this trajectory, see Robbins's relatively candid *Autobiography of an Economist*, London 1971, pp. 121–212.
111. *Is There an Economic Consensus?*, London 1973, p. 23.

started out as a member of the LSE milieu, where he was distinguished by his early interest – working back from Pareto to Walras – in the general equilibrium tradition of Lausanne, at a time when his colleagues were more attracted to Austrian economics. By the mid thirties he had taken his distance from the untempered free-market faith of Robbins and Hayek, and formalized Keynes's theory to great and lasting effect, in the most celebrated of all reviews of it, 'Mr Keynes and the Classics'.[112] *Value and Capital* (1939) sought to reconcile the stability conditions of general equilibrium analysis with the Keynesian themes of time, expectations and money that Walras had excluded – laying the foundations for the 'neo-classical synthesis' of micro- and macro-economics developed by Samuelson after the war. Hicks himself was reserved about this extension to his work, expressing antipathy to the market-idealizing and econometric biases of the US profession in this period.[113] In *Capital and Growth* (1965) he dealt a radical blow to these by developing his fundamental distinction between 'flexprice' and 'fixprice' markets, the former – in which prices are regulated by supply and demand, assumed as universal in standard theory – now being largely restricted to primary commodities, the latter – in which producers determine prices – accounting in reality for most of modern manufacturing.

Hicks's verdict on Keynesianism in the hour of its crisis thus came from one whose record of independent native authority had few equals. It was very different from those popular on the other side of the Atlantic. Hicks singled out three central deficiencies in Keynes's *General Theory*, which called not for its rejection, but for its reconstruction. Keynes had overlooked the importance of surplus stocks in fixprice markets as a condition for the operation of his multiplier (or unusually low prices in the flexprice sector), whose absence could thwart it; he had assumed liquidity preference was typically harmful for investment, because he had neglected the question of its quality for that of its quantity; and he had failed to understand that the stickiness of wages which he noted was not essentially due to trade-union pressures, but rather to the forces of customary continuity in fixprice markets, embodied in notions of 'fairness' that were in good measure a condition of efficient employment. Keynesian fiscal expansion could

112. *Econometrica*, April 1937, pp. 147–159; now in *Money, Interest and Wages*, Oxford 1982, pp. 100–115.
113. See 'The Formation of an Economist', in *Classics and Moderns*, Oxford 1983, p. 361.

thus indeed generate inflation without job creation, as monetarist critics had argued. But the worst effect of such inflation was a far cry from their obsession with flexprice models. By unsettling the basis of all industrial relations and tax/transfer payments, it tore up custom by the roots – with direct consequences for economic efficiency, not to speak of social solidarity. Economists should henceforth be 'aware, very fully aware, that prices have a social function as well as an allocative function'.[114]

Hicks's own work in this period turned with increasing concentration to the dynamics of market exchange and capital accumulation. Dissatisfied with what he had come to regard as the unduly static mould of his earlier work, for all its effort to temporalize general equilibrium analysis, and with the steady-state models of growth current in the fifties and sixties, Hicks first laid out a very bold *Theory of Economic History* centred on the emergence of the merchant as agent of intermediation in pre-modern markets. This work remains the foremost attempt by an outstanding economic thinker since Marx to marry history and theory in a single framework. In another original move, he then published a 'neo-Austrian' account of *Capital and Time*. Viennese economics had always been distinguished from Walrasian by its insistence on the importance of time – whether as differential periods of production in capital theory, or as unpredictable discovery processes in price theory. Hicks radicalized this legacy with a flow-analysis of inputs, to fixed as well as circulating capital. The most important result of his construction was to generate the novel concept of a 'traverse' – those phases, nearly always of disequilibrium, in which one growth-path shifts, under the impulse of some key invention, towards another. Hicks subsequently came to feel that even this theorization was too static, in so far as the point of departure for a traverse was still formally – but implausibly – assumed to be a steady state of prior growth.[115] No thinker in the neo-classical tradition has made such a strong and sustained effort to integrate time as a positive principle of explanation into economics.

By the early eighties the radical Right had come to power, and the Thatcher Government was pursuing a course avowedly inspired by monetarist doctrines. At the depth of the recession, the budget of 1981

114. *The Crisis in Keynesian Economics*, Oxford 1974, p. 85.
115. *Economic Perspectives*, Oxford 1977, p. 195.

imposed the tightest fiscal squeeze since the War. Reaction among British economists showed that a decade after the end of the boom, the dominant outlook in the discipline had not substantially altered. A public letter strongly attacking the regime's policy was signed by some 360 economists, including virtually the whole faculty at Cambridge, forcing the Treasury to make a rare official reply. Co-organizer of this protest was Frank Hahn, not entirely by accident Britain's most prominent general equilibrium theorist. Historically, there has on the whole been a curious inverted symmetry between the intellectual and political traits of the respective traditions descending from Walras and Menger. Austrian economics was distinguished from the start by its realist emphasis: averse to mathematical formalization, it stressed uneven time, imperfect knowledge and cyclical imbalance – themes very close to features of the Marxist tradition. At the same time, after the generation of Böhm-Bawerk and Wieser, it became the most militantly conservative school in modern economics – consistently the far right of the field. The power of the Austrian labour movement and the strength of Austro–Marxism, compared with their political and intellectual counterparts in France or England, no doubt explain this turn after the First World War. Out of this hostile intimacy came the only really searching and informed line of critique of the Marxist programme in neo-classical literature, from Böhm-Bawerk through Mises to Hayek.

By contrast the general equilibrium tradition, resting on idealized assumptions of perfect competition and complete foresight (the *Allwissenheit* Menger had vehemently criticized), was resolutely abstract and ahistorical; and as such was often perceived by critics as little more than a metaphysical sublimation of the invisible hand into the higher mathematics. Yet paradoxically this extreme formalism was to be persistently associated with progressive political sympathies. Walras himself, an admirer of Proudhon, claimed that his system for the first time brought science to socialism. If Pareto was a ferocious opponent of the labour movement, his pupil Barone was *malgré lui* the first to demonstrate the formal coherence of imperative planning. Between the wars, Lange founded his model of market socialism – in reply to the Austrian attack on the possibility of Marxist economic calculation – on the Walrasian theory of *tâtonnement*, while Lerner used Paretian ordinal utility to show that an optimal distribution of income would be fully egalitarian. Arrow's original ambition was to develop economic planning, and his eventual consummation of GET was always combined with work bearing on social justice. Persistent Austrian suspicion of the general equilibrium outlook was thus not unfounded. The affinity between an absolute theoretical formalism and relative political radicalism may have derived, in various ways, from what might be called the subversive potential of perfectionism: on the one hand, the postulate of perfect competition could well lead to reflection on the gap between ideal and reality, with critical consequences for actual market processes; on the other, the assumption of perfect knowledge might on the same grounds prompt an interest in central planning, as a more logical embodiment of it than decentralized markets.

At all events, the public sympathies of the two leading practitioners of GET in the UK have not been unusual in this tradition. Their work has differed widely in other respects. Hahn, co-author with Arrow of a massive *General Competitive Analysis* (1971), won his reputation making good the omission of money from the Walrasian framework. He was therefore well situated to meet the claims of Friedman and Lucas head-on, as he did in *Money and Inflation* (1982) and a savage subsequent address in the US, which concluded: 'Macroeconomics today is in the state in which astronomy would be if Ptolemaic theory once again came to dominate the field. There can in fact be few instances in other disciplines of such a determined turning back of the clock. A great deal of what is written today as well as the policy recommendations which have been made would be thoroughly at home in the twenties.'[116] Upholding Keynes's grasp of the realities of involuntary unemployment, while conceding Austrian insistence on the importance of dispersed information and decision, Hahn has indicated some sympathy for Lange–Lerner conceptions of market socialism, with incentives for innovation perhaps held at Swedish levels of inequality. At the same time, while acknowledging certain limitations of general equilibrium theory – its exclusion of unequal market power, interdependent agency, public goods, missing markets – he has vigorously defended it from charges of complacency or irrelevance.[117]

By contrast Michio Morishima, himself a formidable technician whose early work was concerned to develop a dynamic version of GET, under the influence of Von Neumann's growth analysis, became in the same years a scathing critic of the sterility of highly mathematized equilibrium models – of that 'wretched state of affairs' in which 'so deep and extensive has been the mathematization of economics since 1940 that it has lost all sense of balance, becoming divorced from the

116. *Equilibrium and Macroeconomics*, Oxford 1984, p. 325.

117. 'On Market Economies', in Skidelsky, ed., *Thatcherism*, pp. 107–124; 'General Equilibrium Theory', *Equilibrium and Macroeconomics*, pp. 72–87.

knowledge of economic systems and economic history.'[118] Morishima is the most striking example to date of the paradoxical genetics of the Lausanne tradition, since he is the author of profoundly admiring, scholarly studies of both Marx and Walras, and can be regarded equally as a Marxist or Walrasian. His own most distinctive work, however, moves away from the realm of reproduction schemes or equilibrium conditions towards a comparative economics grounded in sociology and history. *The Economics of Industrial Society* (1984) aims to 'analyse the price mechanism in accordance with reality' with a tableau of different types of market, customarily conflated by GET, as they operate in different kinds of national economy, diversified by size and self-sufficiency as well as by property regime – drawing contrasts both within the capitalist and communist worlds, and between them. Morishima's explanation of his own society's spectacular post-war record, *Why Has Japan 'Succeeded'?*, sets it in a historical *longue durée* centrally affected by the peculiar forms of Confucian and Taoist ideology in Japan, and their impact on state and social relationships: providing a largely Weberian framework for an essentially Marxist account of Japanese capitalism. Whatever the friction between these, the outcome of such concrete enquiries compares favourably with the fruits of the 'capital controversy', the principal focus of most economic theory on the left inspired by Sraffa in the sixties, which in retrospect left its neo-classical target substantially unscathed.

Meanwhile – in another noticeable feature of this period – there was a revival of the distributional tradition that had marked an earlier phase of English economics. After Pigou, welfare theory underwent a relative eclipse during the Keynesian meridian. The major contributions to it came, if anything, from America – Bergson and Lerner to Arrow. But whatever the degree of radical impulse behind such work, its effect was generally stymied by the conservative dogma that ruled out all interpersonal comparisons of welfare as impermissible – leaving the subject with only the *caput mortuum* of Pareto-optimal 'efficiency'.[119] Paradigmatic of the consequences was the ironic achieve-

118. 'The Good and Bad Uses of Mathematics' , in Peter Wiles and Guy Routh, eds., *Economics in Disarray*, Oxford 1984, pp. 69–70. Morishima compares Arrow and Hahn's *General Competitive Analysis* with Spinoza's *Ethics* as an example of virtually metaphysical axiomatization divorced from empirical observation.

119. That is, any distribution in which one person's welfare cannot be improved without worsening that of another; or in Routh's words, 'a Pareto-optimum is said to obtain when nothing more can be given to the hungry, the cold, the ragged and the homeless without incommoding the glutton, the miser, the usurer and the playboy': *Economics in Disarray*, p. 313.

ment of Arrow himself, personally moved by the classic concerns of a strong social conscience, yet intellectually most celebrated for a theorem demonstrating the impossibility of aggregating individual choices into collectively agreed outcomes – in effect, any welfare politics at all.[120] Against this background James Meade's *Principles of Political Economy* represented a return, in theme as well as title, to the preoccupations of Mill and Sidgwick. Once a member of Keynes's circle, Meade specialized after the war in international trade, and his *Principles* opens by remarking that the vast disparities in wealth between nations must be for the contemporary economist the equivalent of mass unemployment before the War. But the range of its four volumes actually lies elsewhere: between a stylized taxonomy of different possible combinations of property and earning-power, a survey of problems of equilibrium or growth, and a critical discussion of key theoretical issues in planning and distribution.[121] Its upshot is a study of *The Just Economy* that proceeds from a carefully argued statement of the validity of interpersonal welfare comparisons to a systematic exploration of the contexts and criteria for social redistribution. Meade's own commitments have been to radical use of taxation in a market economy to achieve egalitarian outcomes.[122] In the early eighties he designed much of the fiscal programme for the fledgling SDP; his own thinking, however, has on occasion been to the left of the party he advised. While Meade's work has been mainly conceptual, A.B. Atkin-

---

120. 'My work in economics took its original cast from the depression, during which I grew to maturity. . . . My ideal in those days was the development of economic planning.' After the War, Arrow became involved in problems of social choice while working on applications of games theory to international relations for the RAND Corporation – his original example being a set of three actors choosing between cold war, hot war and disarmament. But his own interest in them was always very different: 'perhaps the deepest motivation for study of the theory of social choice, at least for the economist, is the hope of saying something useful about the evaluation of income distribution.' *Social Choice and Justice*, Oxford 1984, pp. vii, 3–5, 87.

121. The pursuit of these themes is not wholly consistent. The second volume, *The Growing Economy* (London 1968), sketches a gamut of institutional models characterized respectively by equal earnings and equal property ownership; absolute division between (poorly) waged work and property-owning; a mixture in which some wage-earners own property and some property-owners earn incomes; a variant where taxes and subsidies largely equalize unequal incomes; complete ownership of all property by the state; regulation of incomes by manipulation of factor prices – dubbed Propdem, Plantcap, Propcap, Welstat, Plansoc and Tradcom (i.e. property-owning democracy, plantation capitalism, property-owning capitalism, welfare state, planned socialism, trade-union community): pp. 44–48. Its sequels, *The Controlled Economy* (1971) and *The Just Economy* (1976), although their topics are planning and social equity, do not, however, exploit the typology.

122. See, in particular, *The Intelligent Radical's Guide to Economic Policy*, London 1975. Meade seems to have been a significant influence on Rawls.

son's *Economics of Inequality* is more directly empirical – emphasizing the importance, against convenient scepticism, of bringing quantification in the Kuznets tradition to the distribution of wealth and income, and the need for major social insurance transfers to eliminate poverty. Atkinson's very thorough survey concludes with the observation that it is an 'indictment of economics' today that 'far too little is known about this central subject'.[123]

The most fundamental contribution to its rethinking as a general social issue has come from Amartya Sen, whose writing more than that of any other member of his generation has renewed the classical connexion of philosophy and economics. Multifarious in its interests, extending from acute critiques of conventional accounts of consumer preference, rational choice and the profit motive, to calm defences of the possibilities of planning and the values of development theory, Sen's work has been unified by a central concern with poverty and inequality. Whether demystifying the causes of famine in Bengal, brought on not by natural calamities crippling supply but the social miseries of 'ineffective' demand, or remeasuring poverty in the United States by ranks of relative deprivation, its direction has been unfailingly radical. In broad position, Sen too has sought to recover the normative ground of interpersonal comparison, but to free it from the burden of the utilitarian framework earlier associated with it – whose bias for maximization of the sum of welfare, he argues, renders it inept for determining its distribution: indeed logically inegalitarian. Rawls's alternative, to which Sen is otherwise closer, is also faulted for its insensitivity to the diversity of individual needs. Instead of 'primary goods', however generously defined, the measure of real justice would be an equalization of primary powers – that is, a basic set of positive freedoms, as so many *capabilities* whose general diffusion would require differentiation of resources according to needs.[124] The echoes of Marx are unmistakable. In his most recent work, *The Standard of Living* and *On Ethics and Economics* (1987), Sen has developed this case: criticizing 'welfarism' for ignoring the values of agency as distinct from well-being, and reducing well-being to utilities – but also noting that theories based on rights cannot escape consequentialist judgements, even if these differ in kind from the utilitarian calculus. In the most direct convergence of economic and philosophic cultures in this period, Sen has collaborated with Bernard Williams in a collection

123. *The Economics of Inequality*, London 1983, pp. 280–81, 285.
124. *Resources, Values and Development*, Oxford 1984, p. 323.

devoted to moving *Beyond Utilitarianism*. Yet in a comparative perspective the revival of welfare economics in Britain plainly owes much to the strength of an enlightened utilitarian tradition; it is far less surprising than Sen avers that opponents of economic equality should have so frequently blamed utilitarian thinking for promoting it.

On the other hand, perhaps the most elegant and original contribution to welfare economics of all in these years was one that reversed the dominant problematic of the field in Britain. Fred Hirsch's *Social Limits to Growth* (1977) pursued the consequences of prosperity rather than poverty, in an ingenious analysis of the false promises of development: the increasing importance, yet insurmountable scarcity, of positional goods – the best land, jobs, art – whose value depends precisely on the impossibility of their general possession, and where the conditions of consumption at large become at the same time ever more social. Here the interpersonal comparisons cautiously readmitted by Meade or Sen as a normative move actually become the positive motor of a social dynamic, whose inevitable frustration breeds the paradoxical discontents of rising mass incomes. Perhaps the best tribute to this work came from Hahn, who found it, from the standpoint of general equilibrium theory, on 'too grand and ominous' a scale.[125]

In these different ways, the most distinctive strands within British economics moved apart from dominant American trends, and against the grain of domestic politics. At the levers of the state, monetarist counsels were applied for a time in the early eighties;[126] and in the ideology of the regime, Austrian doctrines formed a significant intellectual background. But Walters soon returned to America, and Hayek remained offstage. The principal, perhaps the only, theoretical sector where real gains were made by the Right was development economics. There what had once been the heterodoxy of Bauer – all-out liberalization – bid fair to become a new consensus, as disillusionment with the experience of *dirigiste* nationalism in the Third World converted many

125. 'Reflections on the Invisible Hand', in *Equilibrium and Macroeconomics*, pp. 119–120. Sen's famous text, 'The Profit Motive', contains his homage to Hirsch: *Resources, Values and Development*, pp. 90–110.

126. For an account from within, see Alan Walters, *Britain's Economic Renaissance*, New York 1986. Walters himself was a sceptic about rational expectations theory, inclining instead to Fellner's 'credibility' approach – that business confidence in the self-discipline of government is the key to lowering inflation and unemployment; pp. 10, 26–31.

a previous interventionist. On the other hand, in the final years of bureaucratic stagnation throughout most of the Second World, the liveliest discussion of the possible shapes of a post-command socialism also occurred in Britain, led by Alec Nove's pioneering *Economics of Feasible Socialism*. But the spread effect of these trends at the edge of the field remained limited. Within the discipline as a whole, the ongoing changes in the First World received little sustained or substantive analysis. The advent of global recession and the reaction of the Anglo-Saxon regimes to it cast, in effect, an unflattering light on the performance of mainstream economics at large, of centre, left or right. Few major structural explanations of the world crisis or its outcomes were forthcoming from any quarter. Freely admitted in the centre,[127] it was not to be remedied on the left by even the best tracking of the local vicissitudes of British capitalism, exemplified by Cambridge Applied Economics. Nothing comparable to French regulation theory, whatever its own shortcomings, emerged in these years. Nor, for that matter, did the prescriptive programmes for recovery of the Right fare much better. Reagan and Thatcher were triumphantly re-elected, on programmes of conservative economic rectitude. The American regime engineered euphoria with massive deficit spending, the British with rapid credit expansion. If the means were opposite – sound money and fiscal laxity in the US, tight budgets and easy money in the UK – the outcome was the same. The counter-revolution against Keynes proved in each case to be bluff.

7. History

A common feature of the intellectual changes so far noted is their turn away from an abstracted present or dissociated psyche, towards the complexities of history. But what have been the principal developments within the practice of history itself? The most articulate interpretation of the trend-lines here sees the main changes as moving in virtually the opposite direction – that is, schematically, from left to right. Lawrence Stone, in probably the most influential version of this reading, has

127. See, e.g., Hicks, *The Crisis in Keynesian Economics*, p. 3; or Arrow's candid avowal in introducing a volume on vanguard topics in the profession: 'Both at ths symposium and among economists in general, there was a tendency to shy away from the grandest themes. The fundamental questions of economic change, the theme of Schumpeter's work, are not discussed. It was suggested that economists displayed strong risk aversion in their own choice of research topics.' K. Arrow and S. Honkapohja, eds, *Frontiers of Economics*, Oxford 1985, p. 19.

argued that it was the late sixties which saw the zenith of the kind of radical history, informed by and attached to the ideals of the social sciences – structural explanation of the broadest human processes – to which he himself is committed. By contrast, the ensuing twenty years witnessed a progressive retreat and erosion of this model of historiography, the reassertion of the particular and the piecemeal, the contingent and the episodic. Such outlooks were exemplified in a growing reversion to traditional narrative that 'marks the end of an era: the end of the attempt to produce a coherent and scientific explanation of change in the past'.[128] Roughly speaking, in other words, just as sociology finally discovered the macro-historical, history itself was going increasingly micro-archival. For Stone, this change of climate was an international phenomenon, affecting France or America as much as England. Its more specifically British variant has recently been sketched, with yet greater acerbity, by David Cannadine. In this account, the Golden Age of scholarly enquiry into the British past, starting in the late 1940s, reached its climacteric in the early seventies; a period in which the professional expansion of the discipline, intellectual renovation of its methods, and political resonance of its findings – not just for England, but the world at large – all marched together. Since then, the bottom has dropped out of this combination. The teaching of history has contracted, its subject matter has dwindled into dispersal and obscurity. In these brusquely altered circumstances, of fewer practitioners and narrower horizons, 'British historians today are mainly concerned to show that less happened, less dramatically, than was once thought.' After successive revisions effacing the significance of the Tudor reforms, the importance of the Civil War, the reality of the Industrial Revolution, 'it is continuity, rather than change, which now prevails in British history, humdrum happenings rather than high drama. Indeed, the two most recent syntheses – one from Oxford, the other from Cambridge – leave almost no major landmarks or themes in our recent history at all.'[129] Across the new, featureless terrain wander assorted ideologies of a resurgent Right: Cabinetary solipsism, Thatcheromorphic individualism, Jacobite obscurantism. 'British history as thus described has all the hallmarks of a declining industry.'

How far are such verdicts an accurate depiction of the field in Britain since the late sixties? In considering them, it is necessary to bear in mind that the history produced in Britain, and the history produced of

128. *The Past and the Present*, London 1981, p. 91.

129. 'British History: Past, Present – and Future?', *Past and Present* 116, August 1987, p. 183.

Britain, are two distinct matters – the latter being only one category, albeit that enjoying far the greatest public visibility, within the former. Viewed from a comparative perspective, one of the most remarkable – if least remarked on – aspects of the historiographic scene in this period is the geographical scope of the output of so many British historians, as a collective achievement. One might say that no country in the world has contributed so much to the history of others as this one. The fact is most obvious in the case of the major European countries. Central to the historical literature on their national past have, again and again, been works by historians from the United Kingdom. The most selective list suffices to make the point. The writing of Elliott, Lynch or Carr on modern Spain; Cobb or Zeldin on France; Mack Smith or Seton-Watson on Italy; Carsten, Taylor, Blackbourn and Eley, James on Germany; Roberts on Sweden; Schama or Israel on the Netherlands; Madariaga, Seton-Watson, Carr on Russia; Boxer on Portugal – constitute unavoidable references, often indeed veritable magnets of controversy, in the historiography of the societies concerned. The density of this presence can be measured against the paucity of reciprocal explorations of the British past from the Continent over the same span of time, compared with the days of Halévy or Vinogradoff, not to speak of Ranke or Guizot; as also of the limited number of major cross-national bodies of work within the Continent itself. British historians, partly perhaps because of a residual imperial perch, possibly too because of greater institutional shelter, have been more outward-looking since the post-war settlement. Beyond the confines of Europe itself, this is a discipline which has also produced – or permitted – the monumental enterprise of Needham on China; a first collective scholarly history of Latin America; the principal reworking of the pre-literate history of the Old World, in the work of Renfrew; and – the most impressive general achievement – the richest contemporary historiography of Classical Antiquity, with a striking range of theoretical outlooks and moral tones, from Syme to Finley, Ste Croix to Brown, Hopkins to Brunt, Lane-Fox to Herrin. It would be impossible to tax this side of the discipline – what might be called its ramified 'international' dimension – with lack of large themes or bold explanations, withdrawal to the parochial or accidental, easy drift in the rivulets of time.

On the other hand, the historiography of the English past itself has followed a largely separate course, and one which – because of the traditional centrality of this kind of writing to public life in Britain – has possessed much greater salience in the general culture at large. Here rival versions of national self-understanding have always competed in close proximity to current political conflicts, essentially determining the ideological centre of gravity of the field as a whole. The quantitative concentration of scholars in the domestic sector anyway ensures the hegemony of its impact over that of the more scattered and arcane 'foreign' sectors. In this area, the Left had made its principal post-war advances. Institutionally, the most significant vehicle of its progress was *Past and Present*, founded in 1952 by the nucleus of the Communist Party Historians' Group, and broadened editorially in 1958 to include a levy of non-Marxist historians, led by Stone, which in time became the liveliest historical journal in the country.[130] The strength of this formation lay in the alliance of socialist and radical-liberal forces it represented, and the accumulating output of the generation of historians on either wing. The first half of the sixties saw the appearance of *The Age of Revolution* (1962), *The Making of the English Working Class* (1963), *The Crisis of the Aristocracy* (1965), as well as the symposium *Crisis in Europe 1560–1660* which marked the publishing 'arrival' of *Past and Present* itself. But the wider influence of this kind of history came later – probably reaching its peak in the mid seventies, between the time of *The World Turned Upside Down* (1972), *Whigs and Hunters*, *The Age of Capital* (1975), and *The Brenner Debate* (1976 onwards). By this time, something approaching a continuous (if by no means homogeneous) series of interpretations of English society and politics, stretching from the mediaeval to the industrial epochs, could be constructed from this collective work and its antecedents: a variegated critical descent moving through, among others, Hilton on the Middle Ages, Tawney and Stone on the sixteenth and early seventeenth centuries, Hill and Manning on the seventeenth century, Thompson on the eighteenth and early nineteenth centuries, Hobsbawm and Kiernan on the nineteenth and early twentieth centuries. This was never a dominant current, as the most casual glance at the standard survey of developments in the field – Elton's *Modern Historians on British History* – invariably made clear. But its presence plainly marked a break from the time when the discipline mainly divided between Namier and Butterfield. A shift in the balance of viewpoints on the British past had occurred.

It was this change which in due course came under strong counter-attack from the Right. Ever since Hume and Macaulay, national history has consistently been the most politically charged branch of higher learning in England. Hence it was always likely that a radical

130. For the emergence of the journal, see the attractive account by Christopher Hill, Rodney Hilton and Eric Hobsbawm of its 'Origins and Early Years' in *Past and Present* 100, pp. 1–14.

turn to the right in the political sphere would find some corresponding movements in the historical profession. But just as the historiographic 'Left' was itself an amalgam of Marxist socialists and – often semi-Weberian – liberals, sharing certain convictions about the methods and tasks of historical explanation, so the new revisionary 'Right' was a mixture of militant Conservatives and well-wishers of the Alliance, united more by an interrelated set of intellectual *parti pris* about the discipline than by any close-knit political bonds. Yet there was one uncanny concordance between the ideology of Thatcherism and the rhetoric of revisionism. Just as the ostensible *bête noire* of the former was not just the Left, but a Centre establishment allegedly in continuity or collusion with it, so the polemical targets of the latter regularly included not only Marxist historians – obviously the prime enemies – but also 'Whig' eminences of centrist persuasion, taxed with lending involuntary aid and comfort to them. In scope, the range of offensives launched under this aegis strikingly matched that of the emplacements acquired by the Left, period by period. Alan Macfarlane sought to demolish Rodney Hilton's account of the agrarian society of the Middle Ages, but also that of Michael Postan. Geoffrey Elton attacked not only Stone's view of the late Tudor order, but Neale's interpretation of the role of Elizabethan parliaments. For the Civil War revisionists Conrad Russell and Paul Christiansen, Christopher Hill and Lawrence Stone are joined in the dock by J.H. Hexter. Rewriting the Hanoverian epoch, Jonathan Clark casts Edward Thompson and Sir John Plumb – famously opposed watchers of Walpole – into a common obloquy. Disputing an Industrial Revolution and disposing of imperialism, the American Donald McCloskey would sweep the board of Hobsbawm and Hobson alike. The pattern of rejections and dismissals is a consistent one.

What have been the driving forces behind this historiographic backlash? Two central objects of animadversion stand out. The first is any explanation of major historical processes in terms of class; the second is any discernment in them of intelligible progress. These options are, of course, quite separable, as Butterfield, the original critic of *The Whig Interpretation of History*, realized.[131] But their amalgamation into a single 'Whig–Marxist' spectre has been one of the most insistent phobias of current revisionism. Common to them, in the eyes of this opposition, is the notion that large changes are likely to have large

131. He was quite sympathetic to Marxist approaches to history at the time he wrote *The Whig Interpretation*: see 'History and the Marxian Method', *Scrutiny*, vol. 1, no. 4, March 1933, pp. 339–355.

causes – revealing some long-term structural logic, of whatever kind. Against this prejudice, the new historical Right characteristically asserts the pre-eminent role of chance: the unpredictable and improbable consequences of small causes and slight accidents, for the course of even the most momentous events. A generic aleatorism of this kind can, however, provide at most an epistemological background to specific investigations, in which the elements of contingency at work in any given historical situation remain to be identified. Here a variety of candidates come into play, according to the temperament and outlook of the historians concerned. If social class is the causal agency uniformly abhorred, at least four different substitutes for it can be distinguished as bearers of alternative, contingent explanation.

The first of these is political faction. Conceived as more or less adventitious and unstable networks of personal ambition, so many cabals or clientages devoid of larger public meaning, or anchorage in wider social forces, factional groupings become the key to understanding the downfall of the Stuart monarchy in the mid seventeenth century – the hasard of their collision occasioning the 'traffic-accident' of the Civil War, in the vision of Russell, Fletcher or Sharpe.[132] Over two centuries later, the same explanatory schema is applied to late Victorian parliamentary democracy, and even its metamorphosis after the First World War. For Cooke and Vincent, examination of the crises following the Third Reform Bill of 1884 reveals the lesson that this was a 'system where high politics is an arcane and esoteric craft whose meaning is not even intelligible to many members of the cabinet', a closed world 'whose primary interest was inevitably its own very private institutional life'.[133] The subsequent entry of the Labour Party into this order paradoxically becomes the occasion, in Maurice Cowling's work, for the most indomitable statement of a methodological principle stretchable back to Jacobean times, with only the slightest of adjustments to modernity: 'The context in which high politics was played was the context in which politicians reacted to one another. The political system consisted of fifty or sixty politicians in conscious tension with one another whose accepted authority constituted political leadership. . . . High politics was primarily a matter of rhetoric and manoeuvre. . . . Antipathy, self-interest and mutual contempt were the strongest levers of action, the most powerful motives in conflict.'[134]

---

132. The formula was originally Laslett's, before being taken up by Russell.

133. *The Governing Passion – Cabinet Government and Party Politics 1885–1886*, Brighton 1974, pp. 22, 161.

134. *The Impact of Labour*, Cambridge 1971, pp. 3–4, 6.

Here the formal circularity of this style of explanation is expressly projected as a substantive trait of the system to be explained: 'a network of plebiscitary demagogues whose chief way of understanding their impact was by understanding the reaction of other members of it',[135] and 'whose chief purpose was to jostle each other as they picked their way' through it.

The elevation of faction as a self-sufficient motor of events necessarily focuses on political life. It is the accidentalist view from above. An alternative strategy sets out to undo standard socio-economic accounts of the past. In this variant the operative principle, whose reality dispels the fictions of class, is the household. Demographic and anthropological in background, it is no less committed to the primacy of chance, from below. In the words of Peter Laslett, reverent excavator of family life in *The World We Have Lost*, 'there is no point in denying the contingency even of epoch-making historical occurrences.'[136] On the face of it, social structures would seem less promising material than statecraft for throws of the dice. Macfarlane's *Origins of English Individualism* resolves the difficulty by not so much denying efficient causes as displacing them so far back into the mists of time as to render them inscrutable. The goal of the book is to demolish the belief that there was any 'great transformation' in the nature of English agrarian society in the early modern epoch – so much as the vestige of a transition from feudalism to capitalism. Macfarlane aims to show that there had never been any custom-bound peasantry in England at all, but rather that a mobile, profit-oriented population of nuclear households, rampantly individualist in practice and outlook, had existed from the depth of the Middle Ages. Alone in Europe, 'England was as "capitalist" in 1250 as it was in 1550 or 1750.'[137] Whence it derived this privilege, from what yet earlier stroke of fortune, is not disclosed; but Macfarlane hints that the origins of our 'beautiful system' of native property and liberty are hidden in the darkness of Teutonic woods, in the age of Tacitus.

The anthropological dissolution of cause and class terminates in familiar acquisitive households. The logical step beyond it is taken by a third current, in which history becomes programmatically anecdotal, and the statistically computed household gives way to the idiosyncratic individual proper. The two masters of this genre are both historians not of England but of France, Richard Cobb and Theodore Zeldin. Their

135. Ibid., p. 11.
136. *The World We Have Lost*, London 1983, pp. 198–99, 334.
137. *The Origins of English Individualism*, Oxford 1978, p. 195.

public renown, probably unmatched by any other practitioners in the 'foreign' sector, owes something to the special position of France within the British imagination – the one European country to figure as the intimately alien, alluring Other of the national soul. As such, exploration of 'the French' in this historiographic mode moves on particularly congenial terrain – a scholarship of emotions or of eccentrics appealing to the most traditional kinds of curiosity about our Latin neighbour. Cobb, the more flamboyant of the pair, chronicler of suicides and derelicts, footpads and *filles de joie*, not to speak of his own picaresque self, flaunts a vehement general aversion to ideas, statistics, explanations, theories of any kind – an anarchism of the mind, more than of politics. Originally – in French – a historian of the French Revolution, his subsequent reputation – in English – was won with vignettes designed to show its 'irrelevance', and that of all great collective events, by exploring 'the myriad variations of individual lives' and their correlate, 'the apartness and integrity of the individual'.[138] Zeldin, more relaxed and expansive in temperament, by contrast freely systematizes rejection of all system, in the most explicit manifesto of any of the new waves, calling for complete emancipation of the profession from the tyrannies of 'class, causation and time'.[139] He theorizes the capacious procedures of an alternative miscellany in the name of a yet more radical nominalism – not so much a monadology of isolate integrity, as something closer to a post-structuralism of friable identity. 'The traditional categorization of humans into nations, classes, groups and movements is necessarily woolly. Individuals are the basic atoms in all these categories, and a more precise view of them emerges if they are looked at under the microscope'. Such 'individuals, like atoms, are made up of masses of particles struggling inside them', with a 'multiplicity of impulses and needs' and 'random behaviour'.[140] The principal conclusion of the thousand pages of *France 1848–1945* devoted to Ambition, Love, Politics, Intellect, Anxiety and Taste as 'six different approaches to life' across the Channel is that, lacking emotional stability or self-knowledge, 'the individual has not learnt to cope

138. *Tour de France*, London 1976, p. 8.

139. 'Social History and Total History', *Journal of Social History*, Winter 1976, pp. 242–243.

140. *The French*, London 1983, p. 510: a work where Zeldin's tolerance of Communists and *soixante-huitards* is otherwise in pointed contrast with Cobb's spleen towards them: compare, for example, *French and Germans, Germans and French*, London 1983, pp. 120–22, 138–39, 176.

with himself'[141] – a pathos far from the competent rational calculators discovered in earlier English individualism.

The final significant substitution of this period occurred in the history of ideas. These have always constituted a peculiar zone of tension for conservative thought. For on the one hand, the autonomy and efficacy of ideas need to be asserted against any mere materialist reduction of them to social interests. On the other hand, their power and value must not be overestimated, in rationalist delusions ignoring the superior forces of traditional custom and perennial human nature that humble the claims of all doctrines. In the post-war English historical scene, Namier gave brutally eloquent expression to the second reflex, provoking Butterfield to reaffirm the first. The occasion of the dispute was the place – or pretence – of principle in politics in the reign of George III. It is no accident that the most articulate and self-aware polemicist among the younger revisionists of the Right, J.C.D. Clark, should have embodied the polarity in his redrawing of *English Society 1688–1832* with outstanding clarity. Declaring himself an adherent of Butterfield against Namier, Clark's central theme is the all-importance of Anglican theology to the political *modus operandi* of the Ancien Régime – a primacy that lasted from the Restoration down to its dissolution in the Reform crisis, triggered not by popular pressure for suffrage but by the breakdown of barriers to heresy, with the admission of Dissenters and Catholics to the political order. The extravagance of this substantive case is matched by the heuristic credo that accompanies it – a self-declared 'idealist methodology, pushed to its conclusion', for which social perception defines social being, to the point where class is no more than a construct of a malcontent intelligentsia, and it may be doubted whether the economy itself 'has any existence outside contemporaries' perceptions'.[142]

It would seem difficult to go further in proclaiming the supremacy of ideas. Yet Clark, in the same breath, rehearses a standard Namierite demotion of them: 'a proper study of the intricacy and uncertainty of human affairs is indeed apt to reveal values as subservient to situations, and political and ethical norms as defined retrospectively, in response to events whose outcome is often unforeseen or undesired.'[143] In this version, it is the carnal machinery of high politics that governs the course of events: spiritual peripeteia are no more than its after-effects.

---

141. *France 1848–1945*, vol. 2, Oxford 1977, pp. 1169–70.
142. 'On Hitting the Buffers: the Historiography of England's Ancien Régime', *Past and Present* 117, November 1987, p. 200.
143. *Revolution and Rebellion*, Cambridge 1986, p. 18.

The same oscillation is traceable, again and again, in the judgements of the committed Right. Elton, often regarded as Namier's true successor, pioneered the deflationary attack on 'Whig' interpretations of late Elizabethan and early Stuart Parliaments as self-assertive forums of emergent constitutional principle, the nurseries of English liberty; leaving his successors to portray them as the squabbling-grounds of small-minded squires manipulated by court rivals. Yet few historians have also entertained a less sceptical view of the lofty religious purpose and moral vision of the Henrician regime. Cowling, saturnine analyst of the oligarchic self-absorption and political cupidity behind the façade of nascent British democracy, is simultaneously the straight-faced author of studies according more importance than any other contemporary writer to Anglican religion as 'public doctrine' in modern English intellectual life – volumes that are comprehensive salutes to the 'high sense of national duty and consciousness' of the 'practitioners of English High Thought', from the dimmest crannies of college piety to the most illustrious offices of state, and their vital role in forming the national mind.[144] Such divided humours – a pendular swing between derision and devotion, the impulse to debunk and the call to revere – are a regular mark of the split mentality of this kind of conservatism.

Beyond these vagaries, however, a much more formidable reconstruction of the history of ideas has been under way. Its two central figures, Quentin Skinner and J.G.A. Pocock, are far from scholars of the Right. Nevertheless, the influence of their work can be said to have tended, up to a certain point, in a parallel direction. For it too has construed a common Whig–Marxist syndrome as a prime obstacle to historical understanding, with much the same hostility to either correlation of ideas with class, or commensuration of them with progress. This was, however, only one of its starting-points. The first was a strong reaction not so much against the sociological derivation of ideas as their philosophical disembodiment into a timeless canon of 'political theory', treated in abstraction from any surrounding history. In other words, the procedures of Leo Strauss were the initial adversary. The subsequent danger – which in time loomed larger – was the approach of C.B. Macpherson, enforcing its own selective abstractions from text and context. This double rejection, of Platonism and Marxism, did not lead to the alternative of High Politics – towards which, despite occasional gestures to Namier, this tendency has remained very

144. *Religion and Public Doctrine*, vol. II, Cambridge 1985, p. xxiv.

reserved. Its original commitment was to full historical contextualization of ideas, in the inherited conflicts and conjunctures of their epoch. In practice, however, this became increasingly the pursuit of specific intellectual *œuvres* back into the more general political languages of their time, asserting the authority of what Pocock – borrowing from Kuhn – termed the collective 'paradigm' over the thought of the individual. Taken to its conclusion, the effect of this move is not so much to urge the primacy of ideas as an antidote to the specific claims of class, as to suggest the general separability of discourses from the ruck of the social.

In Skinner's *Foundations of Modern Political Thought*, this drift is checked by the presence of the major political upheavals – struggles between Emperor and Communes in mediaeval Italy, outbreak of the Reformation in Germany, eruption of Religious Wars in France – which scan the intellectual narrative, even if its weight of detail falls overwhelmingly on the multifarious inner connexions or mutations of concepts rather than their outer circumstances. In Pocock's work, on the other hand, the Cambridge turn towards a new intellectual history has yielded its most flamboyant fruits.[145] In a series of powerful readings, of extraordinary strength and delicacy, the tradition of Italian civic humanism that produced Machiavelli is traced through successive metamorphoses – in seventeenth-century England, where the vocabulary of politics was dominated by the quite distinct idioms of common law and an immemorial constitution, ruptured by Harrington but annealed again by his successors; and then into the contrasting commercial worlds of eighteenth-century Britain, the setting of Hume, Smith and Gibbon, and the insurgent American republic of Jefferson and Madison pitted against it. The effect of this epic pedigree is twofold. On the one hand, the very scale of the discursive transmigration, pursued across these distances of time and space, suggests the independence of political ideas from social contexts determined by relations of class, against Marxist assumptions. On the other, the actual language of politics given the spotlight – the doctrines of classical republicanism, with their overwhelming stress on the active citizen – serves to displace the more juridical traditions that were to issue into modern liberalism, and its relatively passive conception of citizenry, to the margins of real development, against Whig illu-

145. It is the importance of the common Cambridge background that warrants inclusion of this New Zealander, long resident in the USA, in a British survey.

sions.[146] Locke is unceremoniously bundled into the wings, as a figure who was long of little moment. But if Whig retrospections of the past elicit Pocock's mockery, the political culture of the Whig oligarchy itself, in its own time, arouses his admiration. Regret attaches to Macaulay principally for not having lived to write the history of his appropriate subject – the Georgian stabilization.

There can be little doubt of the profound renovation of the history of early modern political thought wrought by Pocock's work. But for all its authority, there is a central equivocation at its core. What are the relations between lines of discourse and patterns of power, the languages and the practices of politics? The question stares out from the mournful fates of Machiavelli and Harrington, the two central heroes of this account, not to speak of those of the cult of the Ancient Constitution in the time of Buckingham or the ideology of civic virtue under Newcastle. At the outset, Pocock promised his readers that 'we shall be constantly inquiring, to what elements of social experience the language under study can be shown to refer?' Any charge that 'we do not relate thought to social structure should be utterly untenable'.[147] But over time the emphasis changed. Fifteen years later, he was declaring that 'language is self-reflective and talks largely about itself' and dismissing any interest in its political effects from his purview – 'we are historians of discourse, not of behaviour'. But this, Pocock insists, is no restriction, since the contemporaries of Machiavelli or Hobbes were 'without exception' themselves 'concerned not with their practical political consequences, but with the challenges they present to the normal structures of discourse'.[148] Here the social and the linguistic are radically dissociated, and ideological vocabularies become all but self

146. Although Pocock took care to append some concluding strophes on behalf of a later liberalism, hinting at the dangers of an overly active conception of politics, at the end of *The Machiavellian Moment* (Princeton 1975, pp. 551–52), they were too cursory to save him from the complaints of Hexter that he had 'slithered past the central problem' of the coexistent power of the negative conception of liberty, from the outset of his story.

147. *Politics, Language and Time*, London 1972, p. 36.

148. *Virtue, Commerce and History*, Cambridge 1985, pp. 29, 14. One wonders what Clarendon, penning his *Brief View and Survey of the Dangerous and Pernicious Errors to Church and State in Mr Hobbes's Book entitled Leviathan* (where, *inter alia*, the purpose of Hobbes's theory of succession could be no other than 'to induce Cromwell to break all the laws of his country, and to perpetuate their slavery under his progeny'), would have made of this remarkable claim. Hobbes himself would have been equally dumbfounded – the portrait of Presbyterian ministry in *Behemoth* is scarcely an illustration of the Pocock doctrine.

contained orders. Pocock's own practice never quite fulfils either programme: it contains too many local insights into the tensions between systems of ideas and structures of fact for the second, and exhibits too little general cogency about them for the first. The result is to make this immensely confident work in one central respect curiously evasive. For what it never directly confronts is the dramatic gap between the intellectual vitality of the successive discourses it plots, and their institutional inconsequence. Florentine humanism, Caroline antiquarianism, Country whiggery were all in differing ways ideological misfits, sets of values or illusions without substantial purchase on the ascendant realities of their time: Absolutism, Puritanism, Old Corruption. Even classical American republicanism, the one candidate for genuine political efficacy, had – as Pocock himself notes – a short life in front of it, before spawning an order built on much of what it most feared and detested. The upshot of the monumental chain of ideas linked across *The Machiavellian Moment* appears moderate to minimal. It is as if discourse, once emancipated from undue social reference, is also delivered of explanatory power.

Across a definite range, then, variegated forces of self-proclaimed historiographic revision – not a few relishing the label of reaction – have held the initiative in recent years. On the other hand the political Right, in the narrower sense, has overlapped rather than simply coincided with these intellectual shifts. Some of its most visible publicists, prize-fighters of the press like Norman Stone, for example, have in their professional output actually been closer in approach to the best structural historians of the Left. These, in turn, have continued to produce major work challenging or undercutting the themes of the new conservatism – it is enough to cite Keith Thomas for the seventeenth century, John Brewer for the eighteenth, E.A. Wrigley for the nineteenth. History has proved the most complex, in its intersecting divisions, of all the disciplines in contention in these years. Compared with the United States, where the breakthrough of a Left that was newer came later than in Britain and has suffered no comparable counter-attack,[149] there can be no doubt of the conservative impetus of the past decade. On the other hand, viewing the period as a whole, while the significant tactical gains have been made by an intellectual Right, strategically the scattered battlefield looks less unevenly divided.

---

149. To get a sense of this, see the remarkable special issue of the *Journal of American History* of December 1987 on the Constitution, most untouchable of national values.

8. Feminism

Finally, all the fields surveyed here were affected by the spread of feminism, in ways that any simple enumeration of eminences, still male, fails to capture. The nature and degree of the impact that the women's movement has had within particular disciplines has varied widely, of course; in many cases it is probably too early – even for those most directly concerned – to assess the extent of the changes under way. But certain general developments stand out. Historically, the first wave of feminism, which secured the suffrage, also forced ajar the universities, allowing women to enter academic life. The small number who negotiated this passage soon distinguished themselves, in two generations of creative work – those born towards 1900, and those towards 1920. Their names compare impressively with those in other Western countries of the time: in literary studies, Helen Gardiner or Q.D. Leavis; in anthropology, Audrey Richards or Mary Douglas; in history, Eileen Power, Lucy Sutherland or Joan Thirsk; in economics, Joan Robinson; in philosophy, G.E.M. Anscombe or Mary Warnock; in sociology, Ruth Glass; in art history, Anita Brookner; in international relations, Susan Strange; in psychoanalysis outside the academy, Joan Riviere or Hanna Segal. Whatever their private views of sexual inequality, without doubt quite diverse, the professional achievement of women like these was characteristically independent of them. They won their positions as individuals, and the cast of their work was general, without specifically female signature.

The second wave of feminism, from the early seventies onwards, self-consciously altered this pattern. Conceiving women's liberation as a collective goal, it typically aimed to effect transformations of intellectual fields rather than simply to make contributions to them, and its organizational style was often a deliberate refusal of earlier kinds of personal accomplishment. The main part of its work took two directions, which usually followed in sequence. First, there was reclamation of the role of the second sex within the subject areas concerned, ending the silence which had so typically surrounded it. The title of one of the pioneering writings of this kind, Sheila Rowbotham's *Hidden from History* (1973), conveys the sense of an entire movement across the disciplines. The reassertion of relevant identity, producing the new rubric of women's studies, was then followed by widening efforts to reconstruct the field of – as it were – men's studies: that is, to shift the general plan of the discipline into new parameters, rather than find a distinct space within the old.

In this dual process, moving unevenly across traditional landscapes, two disciplines have been to the fore. It is probably significant that these were the areas whose totalizing impulses had set them apart within English culture in the preceding period, laying the intellectual basis for particularly strong showings by the Left in them thereafter: literary criticism and anthropology. But there were independent reasons too, of an obvious kind, why each should have offered favourable terrain for feminist advance. In England literature had long been outstanding as a creative province of women, in the nineteenth century making up the larger number of its great novelists; and anyway, quite apart from this national tradition, its most universal concern was the imagination of relations between the sexes. Women were already central to the subject here as nowhere else. In anthropology too, because kinship was classically the core concern of the field, the place of women could not be circumvented, even where little or no attention had been paid to their experience; while the cultural variability of their roles gave obvious purchase for critical reflection on contemporary arrangements. In English studies, the combination of traditional enrolment patterns and new radical energies has given women a special prominence in the discipline: five out of eight chairs at Cambridge, long the dominant department in the country, are now held by them. Here there exists an ambiguous continuum between feminine and feminist scholarship, with critics like Barbara Everett or Marilyn Butler at one end of the spectrum, Gillian Beer towards the middle, Mary Jacobus or Cora Kaplan at the other end.[150] In anthropology, where the presence of women had always been less, and the issues posed for them were starker, there was a sharper dividing-line – the new feminist scholarship of Marilyn Strathern, Caroline Humphrey or Shirley Ardener forming a body of writing with less contiguity in the local tradition.[151] The relative density of work that has marked these fields is suggested by the number of debates and overviews to which they have given rise – currently, for example, Toril Moi's *Sexual/Textual Politics* (1985) and Henrietta Moore's *Feminism and Anthropology* (1988).

The comparable ferment in the formal disciplines of history and sociology has in one sense been more limited, no doubt because the topical breadth of these does not afford such concentrated points of

150. Compare, respectively: *Poets in Their Time*, London 1986; *Romantics, Rebels and Reactionaries*, Oxford 1981; *Arguing with the Past*, London 1989; *Reading Women*, New York 1987; *Sea Changes*, London 1986.

151. See, *inter alia*, Marilyn Strathern, *The Gender of the Gift*, London 1988; Caroline Humphrey, *Karl Marx Collective: Economy, Society and Religion in a Siberian Collective Farm*, Cambridge 1983; Shirley Ardener, ed., *Defining Females*, Oxford 1978.

attack. On the other hand, each field possessed a recent empirical tradition that allowed for a relatively natural extension to feminist research: in the one case, the social history that had been given such a powerful impetus by (above all) Edward Thompson, with its emphasis on the recovery of the experience of the neglected and oppressed; in the other, the social administration descending from Titmuss, with its interests in family and welfare. While women historians continued to make their mark in traditional fields – Olwen Hufton and Linda Colley, both eighteenth-century specialists now in the USA, are major examples – women's history as such became a central focus in the development of *History Workshop*, whose concerns have reflected the expansion (also subversion) of the social into the sexual past yielded by an alliance between socialist and feminist historians. Barbara Taylor's exploration of nineteenth-century utopianism, *Eve and the New Jerusalem* (1983), or Leonore Davidoff and Catherine Hall's study in the construction of the middle class, *Family Fortunes* (1987), are representative of this inspiration. Within sociology, empirical LSE traditions have been taken into the study of suffragism by Olive Banks, housework and maternity by Ann Oakley;[152] while the more deliberately theoretical bent which came later, altering the local complexion of the discipline, has been reflected in the two outstanding syntheses on the condition of women in contemporary Britain, Michèle Barrett's *Women's Oppression Today* (1980), where feminism is critically associated with Marxism, and Sylvia Walby's *Theorizing Patriarchy* (1990), closer to the approach of the sociology of power.

Pervasive in the literary theory of feminism throughout this period, and increasing in its history, has been the influence of psychoanalysis – itself probably the other principal area where the impact of the women's movement has been most visible. In the past Freud's ideas, with their strongly biological cast and asymmetrical force, had often been regarded as fundamentally inimical to hopes of sexual equality, and were shunned as such by feminists. It was Lacan's reworking of Freud into an essentially non-instinctual theory of subjectivity, in effect substituting a dialectics of language for the economics of the libido, that altered this. Psychic formation as a symbolic process might allow cultural transformation. In a famous reading, one of the landmarks of the period, Juliet Mitchell reclaimed Freud through Lacan for the women's movement, of which she had been the earliest theorist in the

152. *Faces of Feminism* (Oxford 1981) and *Becoming a Feminist* (Brighton 1986); *The Sociology of Housework* (London 1974) and *From Here to Maternity* (London 1981).

mid sixties, in *Psychoanalysis and Feminism* (1974). Ever since, there has been lively controversy over the relationship between the two, from many different positions: Lacan taxed with a rigid sexual determinism but Freud absolved, Freud and Lacan indicted alike, Klein presented or rejected as antidote to Freud. The variety and vigour of these debates, by now probably greater than those over the relation of feminism to Marxism, has certainly owed much to the perception that, as Terry Lovell puts it, 'while psychoanalysis is every bit as male-centred as Marxism, because it theorizes sexual difference and sexed subjectivity, then feminist intervention here *must* make a difference.'[153] In the same sense, psychoanalytic themes or frames have widely informed feminist contributions to the burgeoning area of cultural studies, where the impress of the women's movement has been considerable in the analysis of film, television, romantic fiction, political imagery, outside established academic precincts.[154]

Contrasting with the favourable terrain of literature, anthropology or psychoanalysis, and the accessible one of history or sociology, the fields of philosophy and economics have remained much more inhospitable to feminism. The reason is not hard to find. Among the social disciplines, these have traditionally been characterized by the highest degree of formal abstraction, from carnal difference or empirical reference alike, and technical closure. There were few or no prior vantage-points here. Feminist presence has thus been far thinner on the ground. Individually, however, it has not been less distinguished. One of the finest single pieces of argument to be produced by a British feminist in this period was Janet Radcliffe Richards's philosophical exploration of the moral logic of sexual injustice in *The Sceptical Feminist* (1980), a critique of current usages of reason, nature and freedom employed against, and within, the women's movement. Its intellectual background lay in a lucid liberalism. The commitment of the major feminist work of political theory, on the other hand, was socialist – Carole Pateman's vigorous attack on the whole contractualist tradition from Locke onwards, for its occlusion of the conjugal servitudes within successive conceptions of citizenship, in *The Sexual Contract* (1988). In

---

153. Terry Lovell, ed., *British Feminist Theory*, Oxford 1990, p. 25; now the best general collection in the field, this contains a selection from the psychoanalytic debates.

154. On the last of these topics, see especially Lisa Tickner, *The Spectacle of Women – Imagery of the Suffrage Campaign 1907–1914*, London 1987, which derives, but also departs, from art history – where feminist writing, finely initiated by Roszika Parker and Griselda Pollock's *Old Mistresses*, has predictably been sparser than in literary studies.

economics, where the neo-classical tradition gave least foothold of all, feminism was never likely to generate simple supplementary doctrines of *mulier economica*: here too interventions, still confined to the outskirts of the discipline, have tended to be strongly to the left. The economic geography of Doreen Massey is one example, beyond the disciplinary border. The most innovative attempt so far to overcome the theoretical deadlock of plan and market, Diane Elson's outline of what an economic order without structural inequalities of sex or class might look like,[155] is another.

Across the range of fields reviewed here, then, British feminism has left its trace – uneven in extent, but concurrent in effect. From retrieval of the particular experience of women, in imagining, allying, desiring, working, reproducing, electing, it has moved to probe or redefine the most general categories in which social existence has been understood: exchange as a principle of kinship, gender as prior to desire, class as common to sex, 'new times' as designator of capital, nature as index of value, contract as integral to citizenship, ownership as key to economic life.[156] It is always possible for revisions to overshoot the mark, and it is likely that this will befall some of the feminist bids under way, or to come. The significance of sexual inequality as a social fact varies across the range of human activities, and between the marginal analytic positions it was generally accorded in the past and the unlimited reconstructive force at times ascribed it in the present, there is room for gradation. Resolution of these issues, as of the terms in which they are to be thought – including the notion of patriarchy itself, still employed and still contested – will certainly come from international rather than national debates.

In these, British feminism has had its own profile. Compared with the United States, with which there has been most intellectual exchange, its overall presence in the academy remains noticeably weaker. There were fewer women of scholarly prominence in America than England before the second wave of feminism; since, more have acquired standing in the university in the USA than in the UK, making for a significantly greater

155. 'Market Socialism or Socialization of the Market?', *New Left Review* 172, November–December 1988.

156. Compare, for example, Strathern, *The Gender of the Gift*, pp. 311–16; Jacqueline Rose, *Sexuality in the Field of Vision*, London 1986, pp. 56–64; Nicky Hart, 'Gender and Class Politics', *New Left Review* 175, May–June 1989, pp. 45–47; Walby, *Theorizing Patriarchy*, pp. 198–200; Radcliffe Richards, *The Sceptical Feminist*, pp. 57–62; Pateman, *The Sexual Contract*, pp. 231–32; Elson, 'Market Socialism or Socialization of the Market?', pp. 27–28.

collective influence.[157] Like the women's movement at large, however, the balance of outlook in this feminism has probably been less radical than in its British counterpart. Partly because of the traditional strength of the labour movement, and perhaps partly too because of its lesser integration into the established academy – its circulation in extra-curricular milieux of civil society, cross-cutting conventional intellectual boundaries – British feminism has on the whole been more consistently averse to capitalism. This has not meant any simple reinforcement for the culture or politics of socialism. At least as much feminist work has been directed against the traditional Left as against the replenished Right, possibly more. In that sense, the culture of feminism escaped ordinary alignment. Yet it always acted as a radical pressure. Within the general intellectual movement of these years, it was something like a transverse current – moving, as it were, diagonally across the wider flow, at once quickening and altering its course.

9. Conclusions

By and large, then, the political changes that came over the British intellectual scene in these years were accompanied by theoretical shifts of a related – indeed sometimes more pronounced – character, across a wide range of social disciplines. Where major sociology had once been missing, it became overarching. Anthropology and aesthetics, traditional exceptions to a purblind empiricism and insensible positivism, tilted away yet further from them. Philosophy and economics, pulled by transatlantic developments, also departed significantly from them, regaining earlier moral energies and some mutual contact. In most of these areas, historical time – once pervasively banished – re-entered reflection; material life took on new referential weight; sexual difference won lodgement. The character and combination of these alterations varied greatly, of course, within and between fields. One of the main lessons of the period is how many diversely productive ways of allying a sense of history with a respect for material reality there are. The variety that was once capitalized played its part in this transformation, as a specific line and spur to others. But the turn itself was broader and untidier than any set of doctrinal developments. In historiography

157. One index of the difference is a more even distribution of women across the disciplines, in a pattern that would include – among others – names such as Theda Skocpol, Jane Collier, Anne Mellor, Svetlana Alpers, Martha Nussbaum, Carol Gilligan, Nancy Chodorow, Judith Sklar, Barbara Bergmann, Natalie Davis.

itself, paradoxically, the potential for vitiated renditions of it was also displayed – temporality reduced to a stream of accident, materiality to the promptings of self-consideration. Yet even here there was a complication of conservative motifs, amidst the pressure of many active alternative conceptions of the past. The peculiar *Gestalt* of the post-war culture, in so many ways vacantly asocial or slackly psychologistic, had dissolved.

By the eighties, the net effect of these changes was a marked disjuncture between high culture and politics in Britain. In most European countries, such a pattern has historically been quite frequent. In many, indeed, the normal stance of intellectuals has tended to be oppositional, swinging against the pendulum of regimes rather than with it. In England, this has not been so. Here, the larger portion of the intelligentsia has generally sung in harmony, if not unison, with the established power of the day, from the time of Coleridge's first scoring of its part after the Napoleonic wars. The present position is an anomaly in this record. The one precedent for it, the extensive radicalization of the thirties, was determined more by events abroad than at home, and had less intensive impact on the academic world – yielding, at any rate in the short run, fewer intellectual results. On the other hand, its political reach through the society was far greater, creating a generous popular culture of the Left that at its height could stretch from the Rhondda pits to the Oxford Union. Between the times of Chamberlain and Thatcher, while the varieties of radical readership multiplied and the social base of the British intelligentsia broadened, the dominant structures of written production and communication became more specialized, segmented, stratified. If the development of capitalism democratizes culture, helping to prepare the long revolution foreseen by Williams, it does so in the same way that it democratizes wealth: spreading greater average levels of income or knowledge, while developing further and superior hierarchies above them.

But if no convergence of terms or audiences like that of the thirties was in sight during the eighties, the more fundamental reason was the absence of any significant political movement as a pole of attraction for intellectual opposition. The long crisis of Labourism, the short life of the Alliance, the retirement of Communism, created a vacuum that set certain unmistakable limits to the cultural turnover of these years. The one bold attempt to break the political log jam left by the debacle of the Wilson–Callaghan years, Charter 88, was an initiative of socialist and liberal forces within the intellectual world, aiming at constitutional reform. Too radical for the Labour leadership, it was modest compared with Conservative designs. For the comprehensive programme of social engineering that gave the Thatcher regime its dynamism, the swathe of measures calculated to reshape the British social landscape and entrench the power of the Tory Party over it, elicited no alternative of similar scope. Similarly, the most powerful ideological vision of the Right, the ascendant Hayekian synthesis, remained without adequate response. Situations in which cultural production fails either to reflect or affect the political direction of a country are common enough. It was Mill who wrote that 'ideas, unless outward circumstances conspire with them, have in general no very rapid or immediate efficacy in human affairs.'[158] But circumstances may also circumscribe ideas themselves. Some of the necessary ones for an effective opposition were, in British conditions, still missing.

The stability of those conditions is now a thing of the past, the year 1988 closing an epoch. Since then the collapse of the Communist order in Eastern Europe and the approach of federation in Western Europe have struck away mental fixtures of Left and Right alike. These decades were the last period during which British political life could still remain intact within the traditional framework of the Ukanian state, while its economic foundations were increasingly integrated into the Common Market. Intellectual life may have been less internationalized than commercial or financial affairs; but it was certainly more so than parliamentary routine. The quite different context ahead will inevitably shake its dispositions into unfamiliar patterns. But whatever shape the coming European home acquires, with its probable train of homeless, one might say the world of thought is more prepared for it than that of government. Beyond the state-nation that still terms itself Great, the relationship between the two is likely to be renegotiated.

1990

158. *Collected Works*, vol. 4, Toronto 1967, p. 370.

6

The Light of Europe

The fall of Margaret Thatcher in the autumn of 1990 had much of the appearance of a return of British politics to its modern starting-point in the early sixties. After a third electoral victory, and twelve years of office, Conservative rule stumbled then too. The background to the crisis of the Macmillan regime was dawning consciousness of British economic decline, its foreground Cabinet divisions and dismissals. After purging his colleagues, Macmillan eventually lost his nerve and resigned, making way for a precarious, yet more patrician successor. It was against just such grandee paternalism and its legacy that Thatcher came to power in the Conservative Party a decade later, to restore Britain's position in the world with a programme fired by lower-middle-class radicalism. After a dozen years of government, unremitting in activism and exultant in claims, crisis struck in familiar forms once more. Sliding into a recession, the Cabinet divided; senior Ministers fell away, backbenchers stirred; and after vehement initial defiance, Thatcher gave up – courtiers' bluff playing the role of physician's advice in securing a premature departure. This time too a successor was picked from the same social mould, now with a more pronounced plebeian twist. Beyond these various domestic contingencies, there stands a greater structural symmetry. Historically, the *coup de grâce* that finished the Conservative Government of the fifties was de Gaulle's rejection in Brussels of UK entry into the Common Market in 1961, destroying Macmillan's only presentable hope of last-minute escape from Britain's economic straits. The French veto left Tory negligence naked. In 1990 Thatcher, hostile to the prospect of European monetary and political union, was trapped by Andreotti and de Michelis at an EC summit in Rome that suddenly accelerated towards it. The fury of her response brought her down, disavowed by colleagues more aware of the European dynamic. Four weeks later the longest-serving prime minister since Liverpool was out of office, effectively removed by an Italian ambush. In either case a certain English insularity, bewildered by the field of continental politics, can be seen in the miscalculations of Downing Street. But the larger reality in each crisis was the difficulty of adjusting Conservative hegemony, as the traditional vector of national identity and capitalist sovereignty in Britain, to European integration.

Circumstantial similarities of party crisis and change of leadership, after a long cycle of political dominance, are one thing. The comparative record in government is another. How far has the balance-sheet of the eighties differed from the performance of the fifties? The overriding formal goal of Thatcher's regime was to restore the competitive capacity of British capitalism, by freeing all market mechanisms. Exchange controls were to be abolished, credit deregulated, income taxes reduced, public industries privatized, municipal housing sold off, trade-union power broken, local government checked. The momentum of this programme never flagged. In its third term of office, the government forced through privatization of water and electricity, imposition of a poll tax, options out of public education, monetization in the health service, and further lowering of income tax. What was the economic outcome of this legislative drive? By the time of renewed electoral victory in 1987, on the crest of a consumption spree, there was widespread celebration of economic renaissance. Official claims boasted that since the Conservative Government came to power, Britain had witnessed the highest growth-rate of productivity in manufacturing of the seven major industrial countries, and the highest growth-rate of GNP in the European Community. The elation was short-lived. In reality, the Lawson boom was primed by a credit expansion exceeding that of Barber's dash for growth in the early seventies: broad money targets were thrown to the winds as bank lending doubled in 1985–86 to hit a record £30 billion, the bulk of it fuelling the housing market.[1] So transported was the Cabinet by the success of its electoral operation that it continued to stoke demand with tax cuts into 1988. The traditional retribution soon followed. Price levels jumped, a large trade deficit opened up, and the brakes had to be jammed on. Under the pressure of draconian interest rates, the economy fell into deep recession.

The slump of 1990–91 has exposed the modest realities of British revival, as the external deficit runs at an underlying rate of £10–15

1. The first to point out how the sluices were being opened was, appropriately, a strict monetarist: Tim Congden in *The Spectator*, 'Mr Lawson's Secret Inflation', 27 June 1987.

billion a year, while household and corporate debt are at record levels.[2] Productivity gains based on shake-out of labour and fear of job loss, themselves eroded since 1987, have not been accompanied by any significant increase in investment, and have yielded no major advance in export performance.[3] Despite sectoral improvements – in steel, coal or auto – output per person-hour in the manufacturing sector is still over 20 per cent lower than in France, and 40 per cent less than in Germany.[4] Trade-union membership has been cut by a fifth – the largest drop in the OECD – but skill shortages continue to push unit labour costs up at a rate above that of the UK's competitors. Between 1979 and 1988 real earnings rose at double the rate in Japan, Germany or France.[5] The increase in the rate of profit, singled out by exponents of the regime as the surest sign of a real capitalist recovery, rose sharply through the mid eighties, but never matched American, German or Japanese levels.[6] On the eve of the recession, corporate earnings were already falling back, and have since plummeted. The overall rate of return on capital in the business sector remained the lowest in the G–7 throughout the Thatcher years. So too did the growth in capital stock. Household savings have sunk towards US levels, and net investment is currently negative. The structural transformation promised by the new Conservatism has not arrived.

But if the economic cure has failed to take, the social body has nevertheless been notably altered. Mass unemployment became a normal part of the landscape, as in all the larger Atlantic economies. In Britain, social polarization went further than anywhere else. Between

2. The best comparative overview of the period remains Ken Coutts and Wynne Godley, 'The British Economy under Mrs Thatcher', *The Political Quarterly*, vol. 60, no. 2, April– June 1989, pp. 137–151.

3. For a careful survey, see Peter Nolan, 'The Productivity Miracle?', in Francis Green, ed., *The Restructuring of the UK Economy*, London 1989, pp. 101–120; and for the rate of industrial investment, the lowest since the War: Andrew Glyn, 'The Macro-Anatomy of the Thatcher Years', ibid, pp. 72–73.

4. Bart Van Ark, 'Manufacturing Productivity Levels in France and the United Kingdom', *National Institute Economic Review*, August 1990, p. 69: the Anglo–French gap has substantially widened since the onset of the world recession in 1973.

5. *OECD Economic Outlook*, no. 48, December 1990, pp. 77–78; although 'the RPI is expected to drop quickly in the course of 1991, core inflation is likely to prove stubborn', no. 49, July 1991, p. 76.

6. 'The change in the rate of return on capital is perhaps the hardest evidence of an economic renaissance', wrote Ferdinand Mount in 'Thatcher's Decade', *The National Interest*, Winter 1988–89 – one of the most level-headed apologies for the regime, otherwise careful to eschew hostages to fortune ('over a period of ten or twenty years, there is no particular reason to expect Britain's *comparative* social and economic vigour to improve dramatically'). For the final performance of profits in 1988–91, see Wynne Godley, 'Terminal Decay', *New Statesman and Society*, 15 March 1991.

1979 and 1988, the share of the poorest fifth of the population – some 11 million people – in post-tax income shrank from 9.5 per cent to 6.9 per cent; that of the next fifth fell too, from some 13 per cent to 11 per cent; the position of the middle two-fifths was stable; while the share of the richest fifth increased from 37 per cent to 44 per cent.[7] Such were the effects of fiscal redistribution, before the further regressive measures of the third Conservative term: the premia for the wealthy in the 1988 budget, the imposition of the poll tax and then its substitution by an increase in the sales tax. Above the worst-off groups in the population, the enterprise culture contained its own opportunity and mobility. A million council houses were sold to their occupiers. The number of shareholders trebled, and by the end of the decade exceeded the number of trade-unionists in British society.[8] Boardrooms became dominated by state-educated personnel, and high-flying graduates poured into business. Self-made millionaires multiplied, accounting for roughly half the largest fortunes in the traditional British sectors: property and retailing.[9] Money became the social measure of worth as never before.

In these years it was often debated how far the new Conservatism had established a real hegemony in the civil society it was reshaping. Was its electoral success due to the moral consensus its leader had fashioned, around the values of private initiative, fiscal prudence, public security, national self-assertion – or to the material benefits of higher average earnings and increased personal wealth brought by a prolonged consumer boom? The theorists of Thatcherism around *Marxism Today* inclined towards the first answer; the poll-takers and policy-writers around *The Political Quarterly*, stressing the advantages of a divided opposition, towards the second.[10] The two were not

7. CSO, *Economic Trends*, no. 449, March 1991, p. 118.

8. Pippa Norris, 'Thatcher's Enterprise Society and Electoral Change', *West European Politics*, vol. 13, no. 1, January 1990, pp. 67–71.

9. For these developments, see Leslie Hannah, 'Anti-Business Culture and the Changing Business Establishment', *Warwick Economic Research Papers*, no. 341, July 1989; and Philip Beresford, *The Sunday Times Book of the Rich*, London 1990.

10. The most powerful and subtle case for the view that the hallmark of Thatcher's rule was its ideological dominance has been consistently articulated by Stuart Hall: see *The Hard Road to Renewal – Thatcherism and the Crisis of the Left*, London 1988, esp. pp. 6–11, 46–50, 91–92, 154–55. The contrary opinion is perhaps most bluntly stated by Paul Hirst: *After Thatcher*, London 1989, pp. 11–13, 27–33, following Ivor Crewe, 'Has the Electorate Become Thatcherite?', in Robert Skidelsky, ed., *Thatcherism*, London 1988, pp. 25–49. For the continuing tension between the two interpretations, compare Bob Jessop, Kevin Bonnett and Simon Bromley, 'Farewell to Thatcherism? Neo-Liberalism and "New Times" ', *New Left Review* 179, January–February 1990, pp. 81–102, with Colin Leys, 'Still a Question of Hegemony', *New Left Review* 181, May–June 1990, pp. 119–128.

incompatible. Thatcher never enjoyed anything like the scale of popular adhesion won by Reagan in the United States. But the pragmatic 'fitness to govern' that was to be the principal Conservative asset in successive elections was itself an ideological construct – its requirements set by the norms of an unabashed capitalist ethos that was new to British politics. The best evidence of this political ascendancy was the transformation of the Labour Party under it, the most enduring single achievement of Thatcher's rule. Here lies, indeed, the central difference between the conjunctures of 1963 and 1991.

When Home became Prime Minister, there could be no doubt which party held the initiative. Labour was confidently, even contemptuously, on the attack. The internecine conflicts of the fifties that had pitted the Left against the dominant Right of the party, appeased by the closing chapter of Gaitskell's leadership, now appeared to be resolved. Under Wilson, Labour united behind an aggressive campaign denouncing thirteen wasted years of Tory rule, and promising a radical overhaul of its legacy. Vigorous economic intervention and social reform, mobilizing all the resources of advanced technology, would galvanize Britain out of its slumber. The Conservative regime, on the defensive under an archaic leader, had little answer. Modernity as a watchword belonged to Labour. Today, the Opposition is again – after another decade of bitter internal divisions – apparently united in its pursuit of office. But there the similarity ends. Although the immediate economic situation is much worse than when Wilson became leader, rather than gaining moral ascendancy over the heritage of Conservative rule, the party led by Kinnock is a creature of ideological adjustment to it. A comparison of the programmes of the two periods tells its own story. *Signposts for the Sixties* was an uncompromising assault on the record of Conservative incumbency, calling for a new direction to be taken by British society. *Opportunity Britain* studiously avoids undue recrimination or rupture with the tenor of Thatcher's administration, envisaging few radical modifications of the status quo. In the early nineties, Labour's stance contains scarcely any animating leitmotifs. Rhetorically, modernity has passed over to the other side, as the market has become its talisman – leaving Labour to dissent from particular gaps or excesses in it. Where the party once projected a combative refusal of the existing settlement, it now suggests mainly a defensive mollification. Most of Thatcher's institutional legacy is uncontested. The intellectual shift has prompted a new public style, widely noticed. Far from trying to rouse popular passions, much of the time Labour gives the impression of trying to creep into office on tiptoe. A strategy of unobtrusiveness is intrinsically one of weakness. That is not, of course, to say that it will fail as electoral calculation. For however muted the performance of Kinnock's party as an opposition, the government may yet be condemned by the depth of the economic downturn.

If Major were to follow the fate of Home, what would be the probable outlines of a Labour experience this time, alone or in coalition? Beyond the immediate constraints of crisis management – possibly helpful rather than harmful, as a damper on expectations – the situation of a Labour Government would be commanded by Europe. The single market of 1992, and the impetus towards federal institutions beyond it, will constitute the critical new dimension of British politics. Western Europe would thus be the practical arena in which Labourism was put to tests without equivalent in its past. The same setting, however, also provides the historical context in which Labour's trajectory since the seventies is best understood. To see what is general and what is particular in the position of British Labour, it is necessary to look at the wider pattern of European Social Democracy in the last twenty years.

1. The Parabola of Social Democracy

Historically, the classical homelands of a reformist labour movement have lain in the Northern zone of Western Europe. It is there – in Scandinavia, Britain, the Low Countries, and the German-speaking lands – that the parties of the Socialist International have created the largest mass organizations, enjoyed the lengthiest periods of governmental office, and enacted the most extensive legislation. The reasons for this Northern lead are not hard to seek. The societies where classical Social Democracy flourished were or became economically the most advanced and prosperous in the continent. England, Belgium and Germany – in that order – were the three great success-stories of nineteenth-century industrialization in Europe. Austria, Scandinavia and the Netherlands developed as their privileged periphery in the twentieth century. In these countries the working class was either industrially stronger and more numerous than anywhere else – the cases of Britain, Belgium, Germany or Austria; or it enjoyed favourable social alliances with a rural population of small independent farmers – the special pattern in the Nordic countries. In this environment, Northern Social Democracy won its electoral spurs early on. It is now over eight decades since the first plurality in a parliamentary assembly was won by a party of the Second International, in Finland in 1907. Within another few years German Social Democracy, long the leading vote-winner of the country, was the largest party in the Reichstag. At a slower pace, the pattern of growth was similar across most of Northern Europe. Only in Britain had no major working-class party emerged as a national force by the time of the First World War. The outbreak of European conflict made it clear, of course, how far the accumulation of votes or members was from representing preparation for a crisis of the state or an exercise of power. In the leading belligerent countries, the parties of the Second International, contrary to every pledge, collaborated with the ruling order in the war effort; and where it suffered military defeat, did everything to avert a social-revolutionary outcome to the ensuing upheavals. The post-war crisis gave them their first opportunity of office. In the turmoil of 1919 German and Austrian Social Democracy formed coalitions with bourgeois parties in joint efforts to contain popular unrest and stabilize a parliamentary state. If the first aim was achieved, the second was not. The SPD participated ineffectually in Weimar cabinets of the early twenties; the SPÖ was ousted from its stronger position by 1927. In Belgium the Workers' Party occupied junior posts in the first peacetime coalitions. British Labour got its chance to form a minority government in 1924, but was given an even shorter lease. The historic induction of these parties into government occurred largely as temporary shock-absorbers in the great European turbulence that followed the Armistice.

The unrest of these years, which radicalized militant sectors of the working class across the continent, also politicized previously dormant or unorganized sectors, generally swelling the trade-union and electoral bases of Social Democracy. Its second political chance came when the World Depression hit Europe at the end of the twenties. In Britain and Germany, the response was the same. Lacking any distinctive policies of their own, Snowden and Hilfdering simply complied with financial orthodoxy – reacting to the onset of mass unemployment with purgative doses of deflation. The results were National Government and Nazi advance to power. Warned by this experience, the Belgian party belatedly espoused de Man's *Plan de Travail* for public works and industrial regulation, but proved quite unable to enforce it during the Van Zeeland administration of the mid thirties. In Scandinavia, on the other hand, the Slump gave Social Democracy its breakthrough. In an environment where industrialization was later and conservative forces were historically weaker, with a divided Right and agrarian Centre, the labour movement came to power in alliance with small farmers and developed less conventional policies to meet the crisis: increased social spending, devaluation, compulsory employment, agricultural protection. Denmark initiated this path in 1929, Sweden followed in 1932, Norway in 1935.[11] By the eve of the Second World War, all three parties had reached higher levels of electoral support than any of their counterparts had secured elsewhere in Europe. Although benefits remained modest and unemployment quite high, these were the advanced experiences of the inter-war period. Their success still depended, however, on rearmament in Germany and recovery in England. The region of reformist achievement remained precarious and peripheral in the larger European scene.

It was the Second World War which transformed this position, in two ways. First, and most fundamentally, global military conflict installed Keynesian economic management at the heart of capitalism. The Third Reich had pioneered practical implementation of Keynes's doctrines in its infrastructural and weapons programmes in the run-up to the war (as Keynes himself noted in the German edition of the *General Theory*). The British Treasury, traditional bastion of neo-classical doctrine, underwent a speedy conversion once German armour was in Channel ports, and was soon outdoing Berlin in *dirigiste* mobilization of resources and deficitary budgeting to finance the war effort. The USA under Roosevelt, for all the rhetoric of the New Deal still sunk in deep depression when the war broke out, was the last to discover the remedy of military Keynesianism, but then reaped most benefit from it of all. A new economic agenda for the West had been tabled by the time the War was over. Its end in turn brought a second major change in Europe. The defeat of fascism released a powerful wave of popular radicalization, as broad in extent, if not so deep in impetus, as the aftermath of the First World War. In Northern Europe, it was the Social Democratic organizations in place which received this new influx of workers into unions and politics, amidst high hopes for a different post-war world.

Britain now led the way with the Labour Party's sweeping electoral victory of May 1945, and by 1948 Social Democracy was in power throughout the Nordic zone and Low Countries. This high tide ebbed in the fifties, as London, Brussels and The Hague reverted to Conservative rule. But with the eventual rise of the SPD in Germany and the dominance of the SPÖ in Austria, Social Democracy as a governing force actually reached its peak in Northern Europe some two decades later. In 1974–75 there were Social Democratic Premiers in Bonn, Vienna, London, Brussels, The Hague, Copenhagen, Oslo, Stockholm

11. For Danish reforms during the Depression, in many ways more impressive than the better-known experience in Sweden, although unemployment remained high, see W. Glyn Jones, *Denmark – A Modern History*, London 1986, pp. 132–148.

and Helsinki. What was the general pattern of such governments in this period? After the War, Social Democracy at large emerged with a stronger mass base than ever before, and now possessed a ready-made formula for administering capitalism to the satisfaction of broad constituencies. Counter-cyclical demand management could simultaneously boost the rate of profit for capital and raise the real living standards of labour, by expanding domestic consumption through state expenditures.[12] The efficacy of this fine-tuning rested, of course, unacknowledged on the underlying dynamic of worldwide accumulation. But there, precisely, the long inter-war downswing was giving way to an unprecedented international boom, founded initially on successive reconstructions of fixed capital and then on the generalization of Fordism. Hence, amidst twenty-five years of prosperity, Social Democratic governments could typically preside over full employment, rising incomes and improved social services in their own countries. Public ownership – once formally a prime goal of these parties – was usually relegated to deficitary industries designed to provide cheap inputs for private accumulation: a 'margin' rather than a 'mixture' in the economy, that could be all but dispensed with in the most successful of all cases of Northern Social Democracy, in Sweden.

Capitalism was at once ameliorated and strengthened by these administrations. The presence of Social Democratic governments at the helm of the state was not the primary determinant of the material improvement in the conditions of life of working people in Northern Europe: in these years greater transformations of popular living standards occurred in Japan or Spain under Conservative or Fascist regimes, than in Britain or Norway under Labour governments: what was decisive was the overall growth-rate of the national capitalism in question. Keynesian devices were an invention, not of Social Democracy but of bourgeois liberalism, and could be put to use by any capitalist state of the time – as they had been by Schacht in the thirties. The most successful post-war economies, those of West Germany and Japan, had least recourse to them, the basic springs of growth lying elsewhere. From the sixties onwards, the proportion of public expenditure in the national product grew very rapidly throughout the OECD,

12. For a trenchant account of this turning-point in the fortunes of Social Democracy, emphasizing the relative barrenness of its record before the War, see Adam Przeworski, 'Social Democracy as a Historical Phenomenon', *New Left Review* 122, July–August 1980, pp. 27–58, an essay subsequently in part integrated and revised into the first chapter of Adam Przeworski and John Sprague, *Paper Stones. A History of Electoral Socialism*, Chicago 1986, pp. 13–28.

and in all countries the share of it devoted to social provision increased.[13] But Social Democracy in Northern Europe did have one distinctive achievement to its credit in this epoch, even if it was never exclusively responsible for it – Catholic forces acting in counterpoint along the Rhine and Danube as rivals and partners. In this zone there emerged the outline of a welfare state incorporating gains – in health care, public housing, pension rights, family benefits, unemployment compensation, education – which had no close equivalents in advanced capitalist states without any Social Democratic presence. The three Scandinavian countries and the Netherlands came to embody its most developed forms. Germany and Austria, with very high levels of spending on social security, offered more restrictive variants.[14] Welfare systems of this kind were not an inevitable or invariable concomitant of full employment or fast growth. The role played by Social Democracy in bringing them into being helped in turn to preserve a sense of separate class identity within the ranks of labour. In the best of cases, these two dimensions of Social Democracy were mutually reinforcing – welfare reforms promoting class confidence and organization, class mobilization giving renewed electoral mandates for further reformism, through a dense network of trade-union and party structures.[15] This dialectic was most fully realized in Sweden and Austria, least in the UK and the Low Countries – a difference no doubt partly related to international setting. In Britain, where Labour governments were active subordinates in US global strategy, the framework of the

13. The pioneering analysis of this process is to be found in Göran Therborn, 'The Prospects of Labour and the Transformation of Advanced Capitalism', *New Left Review* 145, May–June 1984, pp. 25–29.

14. For a general approach to this distinctive achievement, see Francis Castles, *The Social Democratic Image of Society*, London 1978, pp. 57–92. Göran Therborn provides a richly detailed, occasionally piquant study of the Swedish and Dutch experiences in ' "Pillarization" and "Popular Movements" – Two Variants of Welfare Capitalism: the Netherlands and Sweden', in Francis Castles, ed., *The Comparative History of Public Policy*, Cambridge 1989, pp. 192–241.

15. Przeworski and Sprague have wrongly suggested that such mobilization was incompatible with conquest of a substantial middle-class electorate, arguing that social democratic parties were everywhere faced with a trade-off between the two – greater pursuit of middle-class votes leading to lesser commitment by the working class, and vice versa: *Paper Stones*, pp. 57–79. There is little evidence for this. The Scandinavian parties consistently combined the highest levels of proletarian support for social democracy – typically 70–80%, compared with 40–60% in Britain or Germany – with the largest share of the middle-class electorate – typically about 35%: see Klaus von Beyme, *Political Parties in Western Democracies*, New York 1985, pp. 288–89; Castles, *The Social Democratic Image of Society*, pp. 105–12. For a critique of Przeworski's fork based on the experience of the UK, see Desmond King and Mark Wickham-Jones, 'Social Democracy and Rational Workers', *British Journal of Political Science*, July 1990, pp. 387–413.

Cold War circumscribed domestic horizons. In a neutral context, the Swedish or Austrian experiences had more ideological space. But to greater or lesser effect, Social Democracy everywhere linked solidarities of class with benefits of state in a distinctive political circuit.

The post-war fortune of this kind of reformism followed that of the international boom itself. When the economic climate changed in the seventies, its dependence on a high rate of accumulation that it did not itself secure left it increasingly exposed. The onset of the world recession undermined the credit of traditional Keynesian techniques for achieving macro-economic balances: first helpless before stagflation within national economies, then outflanked by the internationalization of capital flows that followed. In the new conditions, as financial markets gained increasing structural predominance over commodity and labour markets, and national monetary sovereignty declined, there was a massive general shift of power to capital-owners in the West – and a corresponding new social agenda, radically less favourable to the majority of wage-earners.[16] Politically, the crisis caught the labour movements that had relied on a Keynesian environment quite unprepared. Social Democracy in Northern Europe had no alternative formulas of regulation of its own. The result was inevitably a spreading crisis of performance and direction. Socializations as a major goal it had long relinquished. But now, as stagflation set in and unemployment started to mount, the welfare state which it had pursued came to be identified as a prime culprit of the downswing. The first major revolt against it appeared within a few months of the oil crisis, when the Progress Party erupted in Denmark in 1973.[17] Populist discontent from below was soon harnessed to monetarist doctrine above, as neo-classical orthodoxy staged a sudden and sweeping return. Lacking any outlook independent of current capitalist consensus, the Social Democratic governments running the two major economies of the region, Britain and Germany, bent to orthodoxy as in the thirties. The result was the deflationary squeeze on public spending of the Callaghan and Schmidt regimes of the later seventies, jettisoning welfare services

---

16. The outstanding analysis of these changed parameters is Fritz Scharpf, *Crisis and Choice in European Social Democracy*, Ithaca 1991, a work of diamond-like clarity that is also a critical survey of the consequences in the four cases of Austria, Britain, Sweden and West Germany.

17. For the historical background to the crisis of that year, see the remarkable essay on Danish society since the late nineteenth century by Nils Finn Christiansen, 'Denmark: The End of the Idyll', *New Left Review* 144, March–April 1984, pp. 5–32. It was the first of a series of articles, cited further below, that make up the best survey of the West European Left in this period.

and creating unemployment in direct contradiction of the policies that had been the historical *raison d'être* for Social Democracy in the post-war period. In due course Labour and SPD alike were ejected from office as large numbers of their working-class supporters went over to more consistent champions of the dynamism of market disciplines. In the Low Countries, the Social Democratic parties were ousted from coalition Cabinets after 1982. In Scandinavia, although the pattern was more sporadic and uneven, the period saw the decline of one long-standing hegemony after another. Four decades of SAP rule came to an end in Sweden in 1976; Norwegian Labour fell from power in 1981; Danish Social Democracy has been out of office since 1982. Recovery, where it occurred – till recently in Stockholm, and more erratically in Oslo – was beset with new limits and difficulties.

Thus Northern Europe, traditionally the bulwark of international Social Democracy, became in the past decade the proving ground of regimes of the resurgent Right – vigorously conservative administrations with a strong popular base, bent on curtailing or reversing much of the legacy of the social-democratic years. Once again, as in 1945, Britain set the regional trend. The Thatcher Government was not only the first experience of its kind, it was the most far-reaching. British Conservatism was throughout the pace-setter in reducing taxes, checking social services, weakening trade unions, bridling local authorities, privatizing enterprises. On the Continent, options were picked more selectively from this menu – neither Catholic social traditions nor Radical–Agrarian reflexes allowed such unhampered reaction. There the regimes of Kohl in Germany, Martens in Belgium, Lubbers in Holland, Schlüter in Denmark were cut from much the same kind of cloth. Stabilization of public finances had greater priority than privatization of public industries; fiscal redistribution, via a freezing of social benefits and take-off of capital markets, was firmer than deregulation; major strikes were crushed (public sector workers in Belgium or Holland; general stoppages in Denmark) without the aid of new labour laws; unemployment levels rose steeply, if never quite to the peak of the UK. In Norway, the shorter-lived Willoch Government applied itself mainly to free private banking and the stock market, and to decontrol urban housing.[18] At the electoral level, only Sweden and – more strikingly – Austria resisted the sweep to the right in the eighties. But there too policies started to move in the same direction. In Sweden,

18. Lars Mjøset, Jan Fagerberg, Adne Cappelen, Rune Skarstein, 'The Decline of Social-Democratic State Capitalism in Norway', *New Left Review* 181, May–June 1990, pp. 75–83.

where the bourgeois coalition of 1976–82 actually increased social spending and the public sector, it was the SAP itself which was ultimately to cut them back and unleash the most buoyant equity market of the decade.[19] In Austria, where the SPÖ steered more successfully than any sister party through this period,[20] the biggest nationalized sector of the post-war years is now coming under the hammer. Between 1979 and 1989 Social Democracy lost ground, everywhere significantly, sometimes spectacularly, in the North.

Meanwhile, however, the political trajectory of Southern Europe was moving in just the opposite direction. Up to the late sixties, this was a region that did not possess a single social democratic movement of real moment. Yet by the early eighties, as conservative regimes ruled the roost in London, Brussels, Amsterdam, Bonn or Copenhagen, there were Social Democratic Premiers in Paris, Rome, Madrid, Lisbon and Athens. What accounted for this striking reversal of pattern? Its roots lay in the uneven and compressed development of capitalism in this zone. Historically, industrialization as a whole got under way later or more slowly in Southern than in Northern Europe, and in an environment less propitious for the labour movement. In the nineteenth and early twentieth centuries a more tentative or sluggish urban capitalism developed against a more conservative rural hinterland, of peasantry and clergy. Here too there was a core area of industrial advance, and a more backward agrarian periphery; but the character and salience of each differed profoundly. French industry, which led the region, was of course considerable in size; but it never matched German in dynamism or Belgian in relative weight, within a society largely dominated by a retrograde parcellized agriculture. In Italy or Spain, where manufacturing was patchy or isolated, much of the countryside was in the grip of semi-feudal latifundia. Portugal and Greece were on a lower socio-economic rung still. In this setting, a quite distinct balance of political

---

19. Stockholm's share index rose over 1,000 per cent, twice the increase of Tokyo's and three times that of London, in the eighties: 'Sweden's Stockmarket Stunner', *The Economist*, 2 December 1989. For the extent to which the pattern of socio-economic development in the social-democratic strongholds of Northern Europe moved in the same direction as the rest of the advanced capitalist world, see Andrew Glyn's remarkable survey, 'Stability, Egalitarianism and Dynamism: an Overview of the Advanced Capitalist Countries in the 1980s', *New Left Review*, forthcoming, 1992.

20. Running against the trend of the times, the SPÖ increased its electorate in four successive polls in the seventies, when its gains outside Vienna gave it an absolute majority of votes cast in three elections in a row – a record for any social-democratic party. In the eighties, it declined from this peak but still out-performed the ÖVP.

forces resulted. On the one hand, the working class tended to generate more revolutionary traditions than in the reformist North – initially anarchist or syndicalist, subsequently communist; sometimes with limited peasant support. On the other hand, the weight of the dominant bloc – typically with a reactionary clerical component – was proportionately greater too. Labour was subjectively more combative but objectively weaker and more isolated. At the turn of the seventies, when Northern Social Democracy was still in its post-war heyday, the Southern working classes were everywhere led by Communist parties. But these were in turn either ghettoized – the PCF in France, PCI in Italy – or repressed into the underground – the PCE in Spain, PCP in Portugal, KKE in Greece. While the Northern countries were undergoing major spells of Social Democratic government within a framework of normal party competition, the Southern countries had no similar experience of either party alternation or reforming labour administration. Spain and Portugal had been ruled by fascist dictatorships since the pre-war epoch. Greece was in the grip of a military junta. Italy had been governed by unbroken Christian Democrat coalitions since the onset of the Cold War. France, after the chequered experience of the Fourth Republic, was subject to the uninterrupted dominion of the Right for twenty years after the military rising in Algeria had brought de Gaulle to power.

But this political monopoly was accompanied, from the late fifties onwards, by accelerating economic development and rapid social change. France, Spain and Italy all registered very high rates of growth at the crest of the world boom. Peasants poured off the land; manufacturing and service industries multiplied; new middle classes expanded; religious ideology weakened. Popular living standards and expectations alike were transformed in this process. By the early seventies, it was clear that major political changes would have to occur to accommodate the new social realities created by capitalist modernization. The first sign of these was the appearance of Eurocommunism. This essentially consisted in the abandonment by Southern Communist parties of the traditions of the Third International (themselves greatly altered since the twenties, but still visible as late as the sixties), and their adoption of strategic perspectives similar to those of most Northern Social Democratic parties at the beginning of their career, when they envisaged a transition to socialism based on a gradual, peaceful and constitutional road to power. The larger Southern European capitalist societies had now reached levels of economic and social development not far from those of Northern Europe. France, indeed, was actually ahead of Britain. It was thus always likely that these countries would sooner or later enter upon a similar political cycle, embarking on their own social-democratic experience once the corsets of paternalist or authoritarian reaction were loosened. The room for social and fiscal reforms was manifestly very wide in these societies. Eurocommunism represented an objective anticipation of the coming conjuncture, and an attempt to adapt to it.

But the bid for a new moderation and respectability by Latin communism was handicapped from the start. For however close to classical social-democratic themes in its ideological discourse, its organizational forms remained those of the traditional communist movement as they had set in the Stalinist epoch, and its international links – however residual or ambiguous – still associated it with the bureaucratic dictatorships in the East. The result was that Eurocommunism by and large simply prepared the way for the rise of Eurosocialism at its own expense – that is, the sudden entry of new-found or revamped social-democratic parties proper, from very modest or marginal positions to the centre of the stage. The logic of this substitution is clear. Confronted with two parties, each of them proclaiming a social-democratic politics, there was likely to be a strong tendency for electors to choose the more coherent version – the one based on social-democratic models of organization, and international affiliations. The degree to which this logic worked itself out varied in the three main countries concerned. The substitution was most dramatic in Spain. There the local social-democratic party, the PSOE, had made only a fitful and feeble contribution to the Resistance against Franco, emerging at his death with a handful of members; whereas the Spanish Communist Party was a mass organization whose cadres had provided decades of leadership of the underground struggle against the dictatorship. Yet within a few years, as the PCE jettisoned its past for adhesion to the Bourbon monarchy, national unity and capitalist constitutionalism, the relationship of forces was completely reversed. By 1982 the PSOE had won a massive electoral victory, giving it an outright parliamentary majority – while the PCE was a demoralized remnant of itself, with under 5 per cent of the vote.[21] In France, the PCF set out on a course of alliance with a newly minted and far from robust Socialist Party in the early seventies, when it was overwhelmingly stronger – the majority party of the French working class ever since the Second World War. Again, within a few years, as the PCF sought to shed some of its

21. For this history, see Patrick Camiller, 'The Eclipse of Spanish Communism', *New Left Review* 147, September–October 1984, and 'Spanish Socialism in the Atlantic Order', NLR 156, March–April 1986, pp. 5–36.

traditional doctrinal equipage, the PS was visibly gaining the upper hand. Backing away from the alliance at the last minute in 1978 merely weakened the PCF still further. By the early eighties it was reduced to the role of a helpless pawn of a Socialist regime which soon discarded it.[22] In Italy the PCI attempted to reach an understanding with Christian Democracy itself – the linchpin of the moderate Right – rather than with the Socialist Party, in the name of a Historic Compromise between the two major forces of Italian political life. Used and dismissed once its external support for governments of 'National Solidarity' had ceased to interest the DC, the Italian Communist Party has since had to witness the steady rise to power and influence of the Socialist Party it had sought to bypass – which by the early eighties had captured both the Presidency and the Premiership in a partnership with Christian Democracy at which the PCI had failed.[23]

In Portugal and Greece, substantially poorer societies with fewer of the preconditions of capitalist modernity, developments were rather different. Here the end of the old order was precipitated by the overseas adventures of their respective dictatorships, in Southern Africa and the Eastern Mediterranean, rather than by internal upheavals. In neither country did the local Communist Party show much eagerness to follow the Eurocommunist road, each remaining more traditionalist in outlook. The opening for Eurosocialism consequently took another form. Greece and Portugal were the two Western societies which came closest to social revolutions in the post-war era – Greece in 1944–48 and Portugal in 1974–75. The Communist Parties were central forces in both of these crises, which left not only the ruling classes but also urban middle strata and regional peasant clienteles traumatized by the memory. Thus when the old order was gone, and mainstays of the Right with it, there was a vacuum at the Centre that could be filled by an emergent Social Democracy. PASOK, the Greek version, was actually a descendant of the Centre Union of the 1960s. But since the effects of the Greek Civil War were more distant, it in fact proved more radical than the Portuguese Socialist Party of Mario Soares, which owed its success in the late seventies more immediately to its role as a protective windshield against the gales of April.

---

22. The self-destruction of French Communism is considered in George Ross and Jane Jenson, 'The Tragedy of the French Left', *New Left Review* 171, September–October 1988, pp. 5–44.

23. Amidst much literature on Italian Communism that alternatively lacks criticism or realism, Toby Abse's verdict on the party – amply confirmed by subsequent events – stands out: 'Judging the PCI', *New Left Review* 153, September–October 1985, pp. 5–43.

By 1982, Eurosocialism was triumphant throughout the South – Mitterrand in power in France, Craxi in Italy, González in Spain, Soares in Portugal, Papandreou in Greece. Migration to the Sunbelt appeared to have given Social Democracy a second life, as Southern Europe seemed about to enter a cycle of reformist administrations comparable to those of Northern Europe after World War II. In fact, of course, no historical experience is ever simply or exactly a repetition of the past. The fate of the Mitterrand regime was in that respect emblematic. The French Socialist administration was always going to be the central test of Southern Social Democracy. France possessed far the largest and most advanced economy of the region – a second-rank industrial and military power on a world scale. The PS controlled both Presidency and Parliament, so enjoying virtually unlimited political powers within the Gaullist constitution. The French working class had the longest history of social insurgency in Western Europe, from the June days of 1848 to the May days of 1968. Mitterrand's programme, in these circumstances, was much the most ambitious to be advanced within the ambit of Eurosocialism: a broad range of nationalizations, minimum wage legislation, reduction in the working week, increased holidays and welfare improvements were designed to increase social control over investment and to pull France out of recession by stimulating demand and restoring full employment. *Mutatis mutandis*, the scale and significance of this project can be compared to that of the Attlee Government in England in 1945–51. Its outcome was quite distinct, however. Large areas of banking, insurance and heavy industry were taken over by the state, minimum wages raised and social benefits extended. But within a year the attempt to run a Keynesian reflation had collapsed under a balance-of-payments crisis. Wage freezes, cuts in social expenditure and attacks on the unions followed. Unemployment, instead of declining, increased.[24] Educational reform and immigrant suffrage were abandoned. Amidst joblessness at home and militarism abroad, the conditions were created for the emergence of a racist front claiming 10 per cent of the vote, and the return to office of an aggressive Right which rapidly erased much of the new public sector and reduced social security to previous levels.

The checkmate of social Keynesianism in France set the boundaries for the neighbouring experiences. No other Social Democracy tried anything quite comparable. The PSOE came to power promising to put

24. For the economics of the Mitterrand experience, see Peter Hall, *Governing the Economy*, Cambridge 1986, pp. 192–226.

an end to the widespread unemployment in Spain. Once in office, however, the González regime conformed to an orthodox liberalism, concentrating on balanced budgets, tight money and export promotion. Joblessness climbed to over 20 per cent of the labour force, the highest rate in Europe, while social expenditures were held down, dismissal procedures eased, and an informal economy quietly encouraged. In Italy the Craxi administration slashed wage indexation, liberalized the stock market and started to sell off nationalized industries. The Soares governments in Portugal endeavoured to dismantle the more radical legacies of popular mobilization from 1974 to 1975, achieving nothing very spectacular but gradually eroding the trade-union power and agrarian reform won at that time. In Greece, on the other hand, PASOK initially increased wage-levels to compensate for losses incurred in previous years of inflation – a policy to stimulate domestic demand, accompanied by higher price supports and subsidized credits to small farmers. But as in France these policies were soon brought up short against soaring imports and falling investments. Conventional retrenchment ensued, with draconian anti-strike controls to pre-empt trade-union resistance to the costs of the new financial course, as unemployment inevitably rose.[25]

In the eighties Eurosocialism thus failed to reproduce the two great hallmarks of the post-war cycle of Social Democracy in the North – full employment and extended welfare provision. In every country in which Southern Social Democracy took office, the numbers of jobless increased under its rule. In no country, on the other hand, was a range of social benefits introduced that could be compared to those pioneered in its day by Northern Social Democracy. There were two basic reasons for this difference. Northern Social Democracy built its achievements during the long wave of post-war capitalist expansion, on the back of the Fordist boom. The class compromise it institutionalized was the fruit of high rates of accumulation, combined with strong labour organization. Neither of these conditions obtained when Eurosocialism set out on its cycle of office. World capitalism was sunk in a long wave of recession, with low rates of accumulation and little margin for social concessions. Moreover, capital was now – after thirty years of trade liberalization, multinational investment and financial syndication – much more radically internationalized than during the post-war years. The national economic spaces presupposed by Keynesian

25. James Petras, 'The Contradictions of Greek Socialism', *New Left Review* 163, May–June 1987, pp. 3–25.

demand management had been steadily reduced, above all in the weaker OECD states. The South European countries, however, were economies whose position on the world market was considerably more precarious than that enjoyed by Britain, Sweden or Germany at the height of their cycle. Even the France of Mitterrand and Bérégevoy today, wealthier than the UK, is a lesser and more vulnerable economy in the global hierarchy of capital than the Britain of Cripps and Attlee.

Equally important was the quite distinct position of labour in the Southern societies. Historically, Northern Social Democracy always rested on the density and tenacity of the trade-union movements beneath it. On this substructure massive party organizations could be erected – as in Sweden, West Germany or Austria; whereas in Britain, the very strength of the unions allowed an antiquated and ramshackle party organization, with low individual membership, to persist. But in all cases, it was the primary industrial strength of the working class, mobilized in trade unions committed to independent collective goals, that assured the vitality and stability of Social Democracy in the North. Nothing like this connexion lay behind Eurosocialism. For the most part the Southern Social Democracies emerged in environments with extraordinarily weak trade-union movements, by Northern standards. Whereas the rate of unionization of the labour-force in Sweden or Austria is 60–80 per cent, and in West Germany or Britain 40–50 per cent, in France it is less than 20 per cent – about the same level as in the USA today – and in Spain nearer 15 per cent. The one Southern country with a major trade-union movement is Italy, sheltered by a patronage-based public sector; but although its effects can be gauged by above-average rates of inflation, its bargaining power is less than its formal membership suggests because of the size of the Italian black economy, operating on sweated rural or household labour. The new Eurosocialist parties, for their part, had very tenuous links with any union realities in the 1980s. They were essentially electoral apparatuses, overwhelmingly dominated at their parliamentary and administrative levels by lawyers, teachers, civil servants, economists – a layer of upwardly mobile professionals without any roots in working-class life. The PS, PSOE, PSI, PSP or PASOK in this sense all functioned as avenues of social promotion for new middle strata.[26] Their instinctive commitment to corporatist defence of labour was far less than that of

---

26. In France, the average income and education of delegates to the Socialist Party Congresses in 1981 was higher than that of their opposite numbers on the Right: David Hine, 'Leaders and Followers', in William Paterson and Alastair Thomas, *The Future of Social Democracy*, Oxford 1986, p. 274.

their Northern predecessors. In fact Southern Social Democracy often tended to display a latent – sometimes outright – hostility to unions, which frequently remained areas of Communist strength even while the parties themselves were being sidelined by Eurosocialism. Under its rule, trade-union membership typically fell rather than increased, in significant contrast with the great expansion of unionization, not merely under North European Social Democracy, but even the Rooseveltian New Deal, in their time.

If these features marked off the Southern cycle of government, they did not as such pragmatically disqualify it. In France the Chirac interlude closed with Mitterrand's re-election in 1988. In Spain the PSOE won its third victory in succession in 1990. In Italy the PSI finally achieved a longstanding goal by overtaking the PCI, rebaptized if not reborn as the PDS, in the opinion polls in 1991. In Portugal and Greece, by contrast, tough conservative regimes came to power at the end of the decade, modelled on the Northern pattern.[27] The continued success of Eurosocialism in the major states of the region had two principal grounds. The first was political. The key experiences of Northern Social Democracy after the War unfolded in a stable constitutional environment, in which representative democracy was generally the product of a lengthy prior evolution of capitalist society itself. By then Social Democracy had few political tasks to complete, within the framework of the *Rechtsstaat*: it inherited liberal institutions and then tranquilly used them for social and economic ends of a moderately welfare type. In the South, on the other hand, the state structures encountered by the new Social Democracy often still fell short of the standard liberal pattern. The heritage of past authoritarian or clerical regimes characteristically persisted in various institutional forms: regressive penal codes, discriminatory civil procedures, archaic juridical regulations, or a grossly unreconstructed bureaucratic and police–military apparatus. An objective space was thus opened for Social Democracy to realize political, legal, familial or administrative reforms for the most part achieved much earlier in the North. Democratic gains could substitute for social objectives.

The actual record of changes varied considerably. In France, Mitterrand in opposition denounced the autocratic presidentialism of the Fifth Republic as a 'permanent *coup d'état*', yet in office he adopted its

27. The victory of the PSD in Portugal, where it rose from 30% to 50% of the vote in two years, was the greatest single landslide of the Right in Europe in these years. Its background is discussed in Tom Gallagher, 'Goodbye to Revolution: the Portuguese Election of July 1987', *West European Politics*, January 1988, pp. 139–145.

powers without modification. Reforms took the shape of mild regional devolution and elective local authorities; liberalization of judicial procedures and abolition of capital punishment; modest employee rights in factories. In Italy, Craxi presided over a limited fiscal reform to diminish tax evasion by the propertied and self-employed. In Spain, after the attempted coup of 1981, the stability of the González Government counted for more than any cautious laws it passed, as a consolidation of democracy. In Portugal, the PSP won its parliamentary laurels containing threats from the Left rather than the Right. In Greece, where trade-union restrictions were relaxed, civil war veterans reintegrated into public life, and family law extensively reformed, with a range of progressive measures in favour of women, the changes were most radical. None of this, of course, altered the central structures of the state in these societies, whose traditional machineries of force and surveillance – army, police and security agencies – were left intact; while within the governing parties themselves, one-man rule of a kind virtually unknown in the North has been typical, official media have been widely abused, and electoral rules exploited for selfish partisan advantage.[28] Yet for all these limitations, Southern Social Democracy succeeded on the whole in identifying itself with a liberal secular modernity.

The other side of such modernity was growth. After the acute recession at the beginning of the decade, the world capitalist economy regained momentum as the one state still able to afford major deficit financing pulled back into a protracted boom. Reagan's military Keynesianism, underwritten by the Japanese trading surplus, created conditions for a new pattern of prosperity throughout the OECD. Levels of unemployment remained historically high nearly everywhere, and rates of profit significantly lower than in the post-war golden age, but growth resumed and average incomes for the employed increased substantially, while capital markets rocketed. The result was to fortify virtually every government in place, once the boom got under way. After 1983 there were few electoral upsets anywhere. If the Right prospered from the conjuncture in the North, the opening to the Left benefited, for much the same reasons, in the South. There the strongest economies provided the base for the most durable regimes. The weakest were the two small countries which saw clear-cut conservative victories by the end of the decade. Here Eurosocialism had least growth

28. There are well-taken accounts of these aspects of the record in Tom Gallagher and Alan Williams, eds, *Southern European Socialism*, Manchester 1989, pp. 132–187.

to show, and the Right became a united force as it conspicuously failed to do in the major states.[29]

Social Democracy, then, secured itself in Southern Europe as a harbinger of greater democracy and manager of relative prosperity. But the nature of its advance there raises no less a question about its future than does its impasse in Northern Europe. The welfare state, in its most developed forms, was a product of organized labour and represented a complex of non-commodified services, its logic at variance with the rationale of capital. Liberal institutions and market dynamics have no such sociological markers. Their substitution for social welfare as the terms of political success, if it were to become general, would denote a significant mutation of the phenomenon of Social Democracy. Within the major zones of the advanced capitalist world, Western Europe has always been distinguished by the strength of the traditions that descend from the Second International. Modern Social Democracy was born there, and its ability to spread outside its homelands proved quite limited. North American and Japanese societies, despite important episodes of labour militancy and socialist organization, never produced movements of comparable strength or stability. For over four decades now, during which not a single West European capital was to be without some experience of Social Democratic administration or coalition, Washington and Tokyo have been ruled without interruption or qualification by governments devoted to big business. In Japan, the permanently oppositional JSP has only just declared itself converted to Social Democracy, but remains as far away from power as ever. In the United States, the Democratic Party has regularly confounded the illusions of those on the Left who, seeing it as an American avenue or equivalent to Social Democracy, have projected onto it a class base and social vocation it never knew it had. But an Atlantic comparison may have its lesson all the same. For what it suggests is that European parties traditionally representing themselves as a progressive alternative would not necessarily dwindle or disappear if they could no longer credibly promise greater welfare or full employment, or invoke distinct ideals of social organization before the electorate. In other words, the

29. The structural position of the PSOE is probably the strongest of any party in Southern Europe, because of the subtraction from the Spanish Right of the two natural bastions of a modern bourgeois politics, Catalonia and the Basque country, each dominated by a regional equivalent of Christian Democracy at variance with the heirs of the national conservative tradition. The division of the French Right, a lingering weakness aggravated by Le Pen's emergence, is by comparison more circumstantial and tractable.

real approximation in store could be the reverse of what was once expected by a hopeful US Left – the gradual conversion of European Social Democratic organizations into something resembling the American Democratic Party.

Such a long-term outcome was, of course, one of the express aims of Thatcher's remodelling of British society. In France, an evolution towards it is widely held to be Mitterrand's greatest achievement. In Italy, the Communist Party has given it literal force in renaming itself a Democratic Party of the Left, without reference to socialism or labour. Objective transformations of social structure appear to work in the same sense, as heavy industry has shrunk and services have expanded, plants have been decentralized and dispersed, wage spans have widened, labour forces have been feminized, the numbers of pensioners and permanently unemployed have grown. Everywhere in Western Europe, if in differing degrees, working-class identification has declined.[30] To the crisis of welfare as an extendable objective, there has corresponded a waning of labour as a conscious constituency. The relative detachment of Eurosocialism from it, the product of a local history, could thus signal wider developments ahead. The trajectory of the recent arrivals in power in the South might presage the future of the classic parties out of office in the North, or still in it.

That regional distinction itself will in any event soon be overshadowed by another, larger one. The end of the Cold War was often envisaged as the possible opportunity for a great enlargement of the space for a moderate Left in Europe. In fact the collapse of Communism in the East, far from strengthening its historical rival, has for the moment further weakened it. For all their mutual disclaimers, the two were joined as heirs of the ideals of nineteenth-century socialism. The victory of capitalism over the revolutionary attempt to replace it was never likely to leave untouched the reformist endeavour, also compromised by the idea of some social transformation. The immediate impact was, of course, the devastating defeat of the SPD in a newly united Germany, whose Eastern regions had once been bastions of the labour movement. Soon afterwards all the strands of the Social Demo-

30. But not, of course, disappeared. After typically ceasing, in Raymond Williams's terms, to project a general interest, labour has tended to shrink as a particular interest as well, but it has not thereby lost its salience for the fate of social democracy. Paradoxically, as Stefano Bartolini notes, it is because of this continuing working-class inheritance that Social Democracy has often found it more difficult than the Right to compete as a pure 'catch-all' party of the kind Kirchheimer foresaw and feared: 'The European Left since World War I: Size, Composition and Patterns of Electoral Development', in Hans Daalder and Peter Mair, eds., *Western European Party Systems*, London 1983, p. 170.

cratic predicament came together in Sweden, as the last sustained effort to avoid greater inequality and unemployment in the eighties disintegrated amidst low domestic investment, stagflation and balance-of-payments crisis, while neutrality lost its meaning with the quietus to the Warsaw Pact. Within a month of the proscription of the CPSU in Moscow, the SAP was swept from office and a Conservative premier installed in Stockholm for the first time since the twenties.

If the two strongest pillars of the Socialist International have suffered local shocks from the earthquake in the East, its general effect has so far been to disorient and isolate Social Democracy yet further. Nowhere in Eastern Europe has a convincing candidate for its ranks arisen.[31] There the emergent party systems look as if they could revert to something nearer to the conservative–liberal division that predated the emergence of Social Democracy in Western Europe, or prevented it in North America. If that were to occur, it would be unlikely not to affect the character of politics in the EC, already subject to discernible economic pressure from the two great capitalist zones unencumbered with comparable labour movements. Historical names often change less than realities, and the International and its parties will certainly persist. The broad balance between electorates of the Right and Left reveals, in fact, an eerie overall stability since the twenties.[32] But in the span between them Western Europe might increasingly resemble the United States or Japan of today. Such an ideological *Gleichschaltung* is, of course, only one possible scenario among others. But it is a reminder that the exception and the rule can change places over time. There is no guaranteed position or assured direction for Social Democracy at the end of the century. Its contours are in flux as never before.

2. Labour in the Eighties

Where does British Labour stand in this wider setting? In the seventies and eighties, the party underwent more acute inner turbulence than any

---

31. For the dismal electoral showing of Social Democracy in post-communist Czechoslovakia and Hungary, see Ulf Lindstrom, 'East European Social Democracy: Reborn to be Rejected', Department of Comparative Politics, University of Bergen.

32. This striking historical phenomenon is subjected to careful analysis by Peter Mair and Stefano Bartolini in *Identity, Competition and Electoral Availability – The Stabilization of European Electorates 1885–1985*, Cambridge 1990, who conclude that not only has the 'bias for stability' strengthened over the span of a century, but that it would have increased yet further since the mid sixties if policy differences had not narrowed among major parties, allowing a counteracting fluctuation of underdetermined voters between them: pp. 287–88, 304.

other in the area. This was a period in which challenges to official policies from the Left were not uncommon in Northern Europe. Dutch Labour was shaken by the revolt of a New Left that achieved effective dominance in the party in the early seventies, precipitating an exodus by the Right. Swedish Social Democracy was pushed under trade-union pressure, against the will of its leadership, to adopt the Meidner Plan for wage-earners' funds in the late seventies – the most radical proposal anywhere of the time.[33] Danish Social Democracy was forced away from its traditional moderation in the party programme of 1977. In Germany much of Schmidt's legacy was repudiated by the SPD, reacting to electoral competition from the Greens, in the early eighties. But nowhere was the conflict between rival forces as deep or drawn-out as in the British party.

There were two reasons for this exceptional polarization. The first lay in the experience of Labour in office during the later seventies. In a time of a general difficulty for Social Democracy, which caught all the administrations of the time more or less off-balance, the performance of the Wilson–Callaghan governments was outstandingly listless and demoralizing, earning no loyalty or respect among any faction before it petered out amidst trade-union revolt. Failure to cope with stagflation was not in itself exceptional, but in Britain it came on the heels of Labour's failure to achieve renovation during the boom of the previous decade. Two rounds of wretchedly ineffectual administration of national economic decline left the party exposed and discredited, the welfare state that was once its boast among the meanest and seediest in Europe.[34] Mutual recrimination between rival wings over responsi-

---

33. The complicated life and death, by slow puncture, of Meidner's scheme are best traced in Jonas Pontusson, 'Radicalization and Retreat in Swedish Social Democracy', *New Left Review* 165, 1987, pp. 5–33. For the subsequent melt-down of the Swedish model, at the end of the eighties, see his 'Crisis of Swedish Social Democracy', Center for Social Theory and Comparative History, UCLA, April 1991.

34. The shrunken features of British welfare – pinched in provision and bureaucratic in administration – are effectively brought out in José Harris, 'Enterprise and Welfare States: a Comparative Perspective', *Transactions of the Royal Historical Society*, vol. 40, 1990, pp. 175–195, who stresses the continuing influence of Poor Law traditions on them; and Patrick Dunleavy's major essay, 'The United Kingdom – Paradoxes of an Ungrounded Statism', in Francis Castles, ed., *The Comparative History of Public Policy*, Cambridge 1989, pp. 249–252, 269–272, which looks at the social and economic role of the state as a whole. By the late eighties, a higher percentage of the aged were in poverty in the UK than in the USA – some 29%, as against 11% in Germany and less than 1% in Sweden. Figures like these suggest why the major comparative study of contemporary welfare institutions rates Britain as increasingly in the category of 'liberal-residual' rather than 'social democratic' states: Gösta Esping-Anderson, *The Three Worlds of Welfare Capitalism*, Cambridge 1990, p. 52.

bility for the final debacle was the inevitable aftermath. At the same time, the organization of the party constituted a uniquely distorting medium for the development of post-mortem debates – fictional trade-union votes traditionally securing the parliamentary leadership from control by its real membership, in a structure designed to give the Right a dominance out of all proportion to its actual strength in the party. Since the late sixties, cross-cutting political shifts in union officialdom had rendered this spectral system increasingly unstable and unpredictable. The acrimonies of recent failure were thus compounded by those of ancient fraud.

Fired by indignation at the record of Labour government, and determined to render the parliamentary caucus more accountable, the Left of the party mounted an attack on the policies of the previous period, and on the established mechanisms for selection of Leader and MPs. Its campaign had sufficient success to thwart the natural succession to Callaghan, to drive major notables of the Right out of the party in the first serious split since 1931, and to alter the electoral rules for the leadership. But the keystone of the old order, the union block vote, was left untouched, and the majority of the parliamentary delegation unreconciled to any radical turn. Amidst continuing divisions, challenged from the right by the breakaway SDP, saddled from the left with a platform resisted by most of its front bench, and bombarded by press attacks of unprecedented violence, Labour went down to the worst defeat of its history in 1983. A quarter of its already reduced electorate of the late seventies abandoned it. In a decade of setbacks for Social Democracy in Northern Europe, no other party suffered a disaster at the polls of these proportions. The aftermath was the election of a new leadership determined to return the party to a more traditional course. The reimposition of moderate control was gradual.[35] But, assisted by Conservative ascendancy at national level, consolidating the new bounds of acceptable politics and scotching hold-outs of municipal radicalism, it eventually became all but complete. The trade unions reverted to their role as footstools of the leadership; the national executive was realigned with the shadow Cabinet; constituency parties were disciplined; the party conference was reduced to something closer to a rally. Today, Labour is more tightly integrated under Kinnock's management than it ever was under that of Gaitskell or Wilson.

---

35. Some of the difficulties it confronted, in an increasingly disparate party, are vividly conveyed in Hilary Wainwright, *Labour: A Tale of Two Parties*, London 1988, pp. 94 ff.

Restoration of unity has been accompanied by modernization of imagery. Symbols, brochures, videos, hand-outs, rallies project an up-to-date popular party not very different from its continental opposites: closer to Northern models in composition, to Southern in floral presentation. Disembarrassed of nationalizations and nuclear disarmament, forswearing any increased ratio of public spending, its programme promises mildly progressive fiscal adjustment and better social services financed by higher growth, to be secured by greater efforts in training and education of the workforce. Civil rights, regional devolution and an unspecified elective second chamber supply a constitutional dimension, and welcome is extended to European institutions from the Social Charter to a Central Bank. There is little in this package – in which reference to French, German or Scandinavian example is a recurrent note – to distinguish Labour from its sister parties today, apart from its commitment to a larger military budget than in any other state of the Community. In appearance, British Social Democracy looks generally normalized.

In reality, Labour still remains in many ways a *sui generis* formation. Compared with its Northern counterparts, its membership is very small. At some 300,000, it is about a third of the membership of the SPD in Germany, and under a tenth of the relative size of the SPÖ in Austria, which has twice as many members in a country with a seventh of the population. Probably no more than 40,000 of those who pay dues to the Labour Party are active.[36] Official campaigns to increase the membership under Kinnock have been failures, leaving the party with the lowest proportion of members to voters of any Social Democracy in the area, and far behind the Conservatives in Britain, who enrol about a million members. Labour today lacks a mass organizational base. Nor, in conditions where municipalities are weak and provinces absent, does it possess the regional substructures that lend strength to many continental parties. Its command of inherited proletarian loyalties, always less than in Scandinavia, declined steeply during the eighties, when its share of the skilled working-class vote dropped below half. If its leadership remains more popular in social origin than elsewhere in the North, it is also more traditionally male – the salience of women in the Nordic movements is far away. In its stock of ideas and arguments, the party is little better off. The Fabian tradition has faded without replacement, leaving Labour notably short of intellec-

36. For figures up to the mid eighties, see Peter Norton, 'Britain: Still a Two-Party System?', in Stefano Bartolini and Peter Mair, *Party Politics in Contemporary Western Europe*, London 1984, p. 32.

tual drawing-power. Unable to sustain a theoretical journal or a traditional weekly, it lost the *New Statesman*, closed the *New Socialist*, and failed to absorb *Marxism Today*, the natural candidate as collective intellectual for the new party. The contrast with the pattern in Europe, where the cultural relays of Social Democracy into the media and academy have tended to become increasingly important, is striking.

Such differences suggest some of the difficulties that Labour would encounter if it were to regain office today, with the unambitious mandate it seeks, confronting the latest stage in the long British crisis. Throughout Europe, the prospects of a cogent reformist politics for the nineties remain shrouded in a fog of uncertainty. In this common situation, Labour seems unlikely to lead the way out of the general dilemmas of Social Democracy. But before these could even be fully explored, specific national predicaments lie unforgiving in its path. In Eric Hobsbawm's words, 'we are, to a greater and more dramatic extent than other developed countries, an economy in decline', joined to 'a political system of theoretically unlimited central power, which lacks any effective counter-weights or controls such as those provided elsewhere.'[37] That power has so far never checked the decline. Is this because it has never been properly applied, or because it is ill suited to the purpose? Self-evidently, neither the National Plan nor the Enterprise Culture proved to be solutions. If the British State is theoretically an 'absolutism for governments with unshakeable majorities',[38] was it the governments or the absolutism that was responsible for the failure?

3. Economy and Chronology

There is a standing answer to questions such as these within the repertory of the Left. Ever since the modernity of the British economy and British State was first seriously called in question in the early sixties, socialists have been tempted to deny that the issue has reality or relevance. A long and lively literature, from many hands, has sought to

37. Eric Hobsbawm, *Politics for a Rational Left*, London 1989, p. 207.

38. 'We are saddled with an electoral system which can transform a permanent electoral minority into a permanent parliamentary majority, and we lack any legal or constitutional safeguards against Downing Street excess . . . Democracy is more acutely threatened in Britain today than in any other parliamentary democracy': *Politics for a Rational Left*, pp. 207, 240.

show that the whole problematic of Ukania is misconceived.[39] The vigour of this tradition has come from a variety of impulses. Sentimentally, the views of English history and society proposed in *New Left Review* injured patriotic feeling, under threat from European integration. Intellectually, they disturbed canonical Marxist opinion, as transmitted from *Capital*. Politically, they nettled the Labourism of reformists and the *ouvrierisme* of revolutionaries. Ideological inclination is no bar to historical insight, and the result has been a substantial body of counter-argument, too extensive to be adequately resumed here.[40] Beyond a wealth of different local contentions, however, three tropes dominate it. In the style of Albert Hirschman's taxonomy of the rhetoric of reaction,[41] but in a discourse of progress defining capitalism in England rather than condemning revolution in France, these might be called: priority – generality – purity. In one variant, the specificity of British capitalist society lies essentially in the fact that it came first in historical order – virtually everything distinguishing it followed from this early lead alone. In another, there is nothing special about British capitalism at all: it is rather a formation which exemplifies the international laws of development of capital as a whole. In a

39. In the most recent period see, *inter alia*, Colin Barker and David Nicholls, eds, *The Development of British Capitalist Society: a Marxist Debate*, Manchester 1988; Michael Barratt Brown, 'Away with all the Great Arches', *New Left Review* 167, January–February 1988; Alex Callinicos, 'Exception or Symptom? The British Crisis and the World System', *New Left Review* 169, May–June 1988; Simon Clarke, 'Configurations of Dissent: Fractions of Capital, Class Struggle and the Decline of Britain', April 1988; Ellen Meiksins Wood, *The Pristine Culture of Capitalism*, London 1991. Each of these has its particular merits. The best direct critique of my own arguments is probably Robert Looker's 'Shifting Trajectories', in Barker and Nicholls; Callinicos and Clarke are most perceptive about the creeping international pressures of over-accumulation in the present period; Wood offers the most imaginative vision of English advance; Barratt Brown provides the fullest restatement of the classical Marxist view of Victorian capitalism.

40. Itself, of course, only a fraction of the general literature on the subject: for which see the bibliography of some two thousand entries in Sidney Pollard, *Britain's Prime and Britain's Decline*, London 1989, one of the most important recent contributions to it, whose thrust is that British deterioration should not be dated back to late Victorian or Edwardian times – although its case is subverted whenever Pollard contemplates the Ukanian state: compare pp. 270–71 with 258–59. The major alternative view, covering the principal subject omitted by Pollard, is set out in Alfred Chandler's *Scale and Scope. The Dynamics of Industrial Capitalism*, Cambridge, Mass., 1990, which shows in massive detail the failure of British firms to develop the organizational capabilities necessary for competition in capital-intensive industries in this period (and beyond), by contrast with new structures of corporate management in America or Germany.

41. Albert Hirschman, *The Rhetoric of Reaction: Perversity, Futility, Jeopardy*, Cambridge, Mass., 1991, which looks at the way progressive changes have repetitiously been condemned by conservatives under three headings: as counter-productive, ineffective or over-costly.

third, what is peculiar to the United Kingdom is the purity of its native capitalism, as opposed to mongrel versions with more pre-capitalist strains elsewhere. The three lines of argument are logically distinct, but can coexist or overlap in particular polemics; in one of the most spirited, priority and purity are directly conflated in the category of the 'pristine'[42] – unsullied because unexampled, without antecedent or admixture. What is common to the trio, of course, is minimization of all those social, political and cultural features of the British record which appear at variance with the rational dictates of capital. For these, there is a set of secondary tropes to hand, which might be termed: conformity – redundancy – latency. Here, in the spirit of Bagehot, any phenomenon which at first sight looks awkward for claims of a plenary capitalism can be explained along alternative lines, as really in complete accord with it; or as of no significant moment for it; or as a useful mystification of it.[43] Much ingenious argument has developed to bring everything from Anglican theology to Georgian horticulture, Labourist sensibility to Ukanian nationality itself, into this flexibly functional fold. Whatever the merits of particular claims of this kind, the critical test for such interpretations as a whole remains, of course, as it has always been, their capacity to provide an intelligible account of the continuing – dysfunctional – decline of British capitalism.

Here there is only one serious candidate among the trio as an explanation. The figure of generality by definition provides no purchase on the specific maladies of the UK economy. At best, it seeks to square the circle by treating them simply as the most acute manifestation of a universal capitalist crisis – Britain remaining, so to speak,

---

42. Wood's case for *The Pristine Culture of Capitalism* contains no actual reflection on the category that is its *leitmotif*. The original meaning of *pristinus* was, of course, 'former' – the sense in which the underlying polemic of Wood's essay could be described as a vigorous call to the pristine culture of socialism.

43. Conformity: 'It is not the isolation of productive capitalists, but the close functional interdependence of British financial, commercial and productive capital, underlying their financial independence, which explains the fact that productive capital has never seriously contested the hegemony of financial and commercial capital' (Clarke). Redundancy: 'Conceptual absences bear witnesses to historical presences' – in other words, 'the pressure for a nationalist ideology was weaker because the reality of nationhood was stronger'; 'possessing the reality of sovereignty, the English evidently felt no conceptual need for it', (Wood). Latency: 'Within the British power bloc hegemony has shifted from land and commerce in the eighteenth century to industry in the nineteenth and finance capital in the twentieth century. Political and ideological forms have not directly corresponded to that hegemony and have in fact fulfilled their mystifying role all the more successfully precisely because of just such a disjuncture' (Nicholls).

still at its post in the forefront of historical development.[44] The figure of purity generates a reduction to absurdity, in which the most capitalist of societies avowedly becomes least successful at capitalism, and the least capitalist mysteriously most successful.[45] The figure of priority alone affords some leverage on the problem. For it does point to a real historical singularity of modern British history, even if this is often misconstrued. The claim that England was the first capitalist nation as such does not bear examination. The Dutch economy was a unified national market, driven by capitalist farming, commerce and manufacturing, well before its English rival reached a similar stage of development: down to the late eighteenth century, agricultural productivity, urbanization and popular living standards were all higher in the Netherlands.[46] What England became, of course, was the first *industrial* capitalism – a subsequent lead inseparable from superior natural endowments, in size, location and mineral resources, which had already given it imperial hegemony over its rival. The consequences of industrial priority, as of maritime supremacy, formed a major theme in the account of Britain's descent from its station as world power developed in *New Left Review*, as widely elsewhere. But that account never, of course, reduced the dynamics of decline to the sheer datum of early industrialization alone.

Nevertheless, there is reason to ask whether the secret of the modern British crisis might not, after all, lie simply in a banal chronology. For independently of debate over the fate of the UK, the past decade has

44. 'The acuteness of the British crisis derives not from the incompleteness of the rule of capital in Britain, but from the fact that Britain shows the Janus face of capital in its most developed form': Clarke, 'Configurations of Dissent', p. 3.

45. According to Wood, 'the economic logic of capitalism has been more deeply rooted and unbridled than in any other country', although this has 'often worked to Britain's disadvantage in the more competitive setting of advanced international capitalism' – as if the economic logic of capitalism were not inseparable from the process of competition. In *The Pristine Culture of Capitalism*, the lack of any developmental narrative allows this sort of conclusion: in the pursuit of an abiding purity, history becomes more like a slide-show of illustrations of a fixed theme, picked in no particular temporal order, for the purposes of the demonstration. The effect is still a vivid display.

46. See the estimates of the growth paths of the two countries in Jan de Vries, 'The Decline and Rise of the Dutch Economy, 1675–1900', in *Technique, Spirit and Form in the Making of Modern Economies. Essays in Honour of William N. Parker*, Supplement No. 3, *Research in Economic History*, 1984, p. 168; and the comparative reflections in E.A. Wrigley, *Continuity, Chance and Change. The Character of the Industrial Revolution in England*, Cambridge 1988, pp. 102– 104, and *People, Cities and Wealth*, Oxford 1987, pp. 67– 68, 181–82. In the mid eighteenth century, in an unremarkable region of Holland, 'even small settlements from 400 inhabitants upwards almost invariably had a village shop (at a time when shops were still rare in England in places of similar size), a tailor, a shoemaker and often a weaver and baker as well.'

seen the emergence of a significant cluster of mainstream economic analysis tending to suggest that historically productivity growth has essentially been a function of temporal position – countries starting industrialization earlier slowing down sooner, those coming later moving faster, in a pattern of catch-up pointing towards ultimate general convergence in average incomes. In Baumol's version, the mechanisms of this process are to be found in the spread effects of both innovation and investment from the more advanced economies on more backward ones, once the latter are drawn into trade in common branches of production, generating accelerated learning processes in the latter.[47] Alternative accounts stress the relative growth in the service sector of all the richer countries, with its structurally lower rates of productivity growth, as the principal determinant of long-term convergence.[48] Such hypotheses have been greeted with relief by at least one thoughtful scholar on the Left, who has argued that all the main Anglophone countries in the OECD share with the UK low rates of post-war growth, simply because these were once the wealthiest societies of the pre-war world: 'the much-diagnosed "British disease" should, perhaps, be seen less as a pathological condition and more as the natural consequence of Britain's role as the innovator of modern industrial progress.'[49]

The occasion for this consoling reflection was a critique of another theory of relative economic decline, of markedly neo-liberal stamp, that had seemed to hold democratic welfare politics responsible for Britain's difficulties. In Olson's influential schema, the key determinant of economic growth is the degree of unfettered competition obtaining in any given state, which tends to be subject to progressive diminution as special interests or distributional coalitions – trade unions, cartels, lobbies, bureaucracies – build up over time, covering the dynamic of the market with 'institutional sclerosis'.[50] In this account, political change – above all, revolution or war – can sweep away accumulated

47. William Baumol, 'Productivity Growth, Convergence and Welfare: What the Long-Run Data Show', *American Economic Review*, December 1986, pp. 1072–1085.

48. Steve Dowrick and Duc-Tho Nguyen, 'OECD Comparative Economic Growth 1950–1985: Catch-Up and Convergence', *American Economic Review*, December 1989, pp. 1010–1030.

49. Francis Castles, 'Democratic Politics, War and Catch-Up', *Journal of Theoretical Politics*, vol. 3, no. 1, 1991, p. 21.

50. For Olson's treatment of the UK, see *The Rise and Decline of Nations*, New Haven 1982, pp. 77–87; Castles's essay takes the form of a critique of Olson, who has recently seen hope for England in the triumph of monetarist principle over market impediments: 'Is Britain the Wave of the Future? How Ideas Affect Societies', in Michael Mann, ed., *The Rise and Decline of Nation-States*, Oxford 1990, pp. 91–113.

impediments to economic development, permitting leaps forward after slowdown. But in conditions of long-term constitutional stability, its logic too runs in the same direction: the older an economy, the more sluggish it is likely to be. To the strength of the conclusion, however, there corresponds in neither of these versions – economic versus sociological – real specification of how the mechanisms of decline operate. Statistical correlations, notoriously pliant, substitute for detailed explanation.

In the work of the original theorist of convergence, on the other hand, economic and sociological hypotheses are integrated, in an account that is much more precise and nuanced. Abramowitz, who pioneered discussion of productivity growth in the OECD, argued that while a technological gap was favourable for catch-up by more backward economies, there had to be a social capability as well. If the principal handicap of earlier starters was the extent of 'tangible capital' sunk in interdependent production complexes that made renewal by individual firms difficult and costly, there was also the problem that 'intangible capital', in the form of specific institutions of education and entrepreneurship, could become inertial too; while the main challenge for later arrivals could be seen as the development of the intangible capital necessary to exploit their chance for newer industrial units effectively.[51] Working quite independently on the long-term downswing of the world economy since the early seventies, Robert Brenner has arrived at similar conclusions in the framework of a general Marxist theory of modern capitalist development. In any given economic space, new blocs of capital possess an inherent competitive advantage over old, since they embody later technology, but their entry into the same branches of industry typically leads, not to a reallocation of factors of production out of them, but to persistence by traditional firms in selling at reduced prices to realize their sunk investments – leading to over-competition, falling rates of profit, and eventually crisis. Originally operative at national level, this process became increasingly global as

---

51. Moses Abramowitz, 'Catching Up, Forging Ahead, and Falling Behind', *Journal of Economic History*, June 1986, pp. 385– 406; he first posed the relevant issues in 'Rapid Growth Potential and Realization: the Experience of the Capitalist Economies in the Post-War Period', in Edmond Malinvaud, ed., *Economic Growth and Resources*, London 1979, pp. 1–30. Behind the recent literature on this theme looms, of course, the great shadow of Thorstein Veblen, who advanced what is still the most striking general theory of the cultural advantages of the borrower over the initiator of techniques or institutions, as well as probably the earliest reflection on the 'systemic obsolescence' of interrelated complexes of fixed capital across English industry: *Imperial Germany and Industrial Revolution*, London 1915, pp. 22–37, 124–27.

international competition intensified from the sixties onwards. In the battle for overstocked markets, the most advanced blocs of Japanese capital emerged as decisively superior to American, not only because they embodied later technology but also because they had developed more effective institutional forms for long-term adjustment of investment, with the *keiretsu*, and for productive control of labour, with lifetime employment through company unions.[52] The advantages of lateness were thus cumulative, forcing US manufacturing firms into increasingly disadvantaged positions, amidst a general slowdown of world growth.

All of these theories may be called *ordinalist*, in the sense that they give critical explanatory weight to a country's relative position in the temporal chain of industrializations in accounting for its contemporary pattern of development. They all, too, suggest the disadvantages of an early appearance in the sequence. Where they differ is in the conclusions they draw from the ordinal series itself. In one version, its upshot looks like inexorable convergence of all advanced economies on a common standard of life and growth. In another, its logic seems to favour late-comers systematically to win and hold a lead over early-starters. In a third, neither mechanical convergence nor structural supersession is fated: new arrival is certainly a potential asset, but there is more to the hierarchy of competitive advantage than temporal order, and countries can move up and down it independently of starting-date. Historically, there can be little doubt which of these conclusions is better grounded. If we wish to see whether modern British decline necessarily ensued from the early arrival of industrialization in England, it is enough to glance at the history of the country whose industrial revolution was most nearly coeval with it. Belgium was a close second-comer, with rapid development based on the Victorian pattern of coal, textiles, iron and steel from the 1830s onwards – achieving an overall growth rate that was probably higher than in Germany or France down to the First World War.[53] Its parliamentary system predated the Reform Bill, and its economic culture was as rigidly liberal as that of England. The one institutional innovation that set it apart was the investment bank, which it pioneered. But when crisis came after the First World War, the great Belgian banks had no industrial strategy, withdrawing to the role of holding companies while

52. Robert Brenner, 'International Crisis and US Decline', *New Left Review*, forthcoming 1992.

53. Alan Milward and S.B. Saul, *The Development of the Economies of Continental Europe 1850–1914*, London 1977, pp. 180–81.

depression and retardation set in.[54] With a small domestic market and still negligible colonial wealth, Belgium fared worse than England in the thirties. It emerged after the War with a backward, stagnant economy that became the subject of a classic theoretical study of industrial decline. In a remarkable analysis Lamfalussy showed that the response of Belgian firms in the fifties to static or shrinking markets was further 'defensive investment' in them to cut costs to survive, rather than venturing into new lines of production. His conclusion was that 'capital expenditure and growing fixed assets are not incompatible with falling demand and declining profit rates, so that inadequate profits, instead of inducing disinvestment, may call forth a particular type of investment'[55] – in other words, just the logic explored by Brenner on a world scale thirty years later. If Belgium shared with Britain the lowest overall rate of capital expenditure in Western Europe, the composition of its industry was significantly less modern. Its financial balance was by now also more dependent on colonial inflows, soon to cease with an unprecedented abruptness. In this smaller, weaker and more exposed economy, everything seemed set for a steeper slide than could await the UK.

In fact, the sixties saw a reinvigoration of the Belgian economy. With a home market offering little shelter from international competition,[56] size constrained persistence in inertia – if it was the consolidation of the EEC that transformed the dynamic of Belgian capitalism, this was not a passive change. Belgian diplomacy played a key role in negotiating the Treaty of Rome, securing Brussels as the administrative capital of the new economic space, and the Belgian state henceforward actively promoted inward foreign investment, maximizing the potential of the country as a favourable base for American expansion into the Com-

54. Robin Hogg, *Structural Rigidities and Policy Inertia in Inter-War Belgium*, Brussels 1986, pp. 147–54, 181–85; for the rationale of what then became the key Belgian financial institutions, see Herman Daems, *The Holding Company. Essays on Financial Intermediation, Concentration and Capital Market Imperfections in the Belgian Economy*, Louvain 1985, pp. 59–74, who concludes that 'the holding company structure is probably the poorest way in a modern economy to organize control' of industrial enterprises.

55. Alexandre Lamfalussy, *Investment and Growth in Mature Economies: the Case of Belgium*, London 1961, p. xiv. For his general theory of defensive – as opposed to enterprise – investment, see pp. 79–94. Lamfalussy subsequently argued that it must have been applicable to the case of Britain too: *The United Kingdom and the Six*, London 1963, pp. 106–108.

56. The proportion of the Belgian economy subject to international competition is eight times as large as that of the USA: Peter Katzenstein, *Small States in World Markets. Industrial Policy in Europe*, Ithaca 1985, p. 82 – the outstanding comparative study of corporatism in the Low Countries, Scandinavia, Switzerland and Austria.

mon Market. The result was a rapid modernization of the engineering, electronics and chemical industries, shifting the centre of gravity of the economy to Flanders. If the recessions of the early seventies and eighties brought acute difficulties for a period, the underlying extent of industrial renovation is clear today. Between 1950 and 1985, the growth rate of average incomes in Belgium was nearly half as much again as in Britain.[57] In 1991, as the UK laboured under high inflation, trade deficits and declining output after a decade of Thatcher's neo-liberal medicine, Belgium under Martens's more corporatist regime combines price stability, fast growth and an export surplus.[58] The result is no idyll. The Belgian Right presides over unemployment that till recently was comparable to British levels, or in Wallonia even to Spanish; its tightly enforced incomes policies have shifted the share of profits sharply upwards at the expense of wages; regional disparities remain deep; racial tensions are mounting in the big cities. But just such latter-day resemblances between British and Belgian capitalism, evocative of a common past, are also reminders that similar beginnings can have rather different endings. National fortunes are not just fates inscribed in industrial birth-certificates. They are also formed by variable natural endowments, socio-cultural structures and political institutions. The last of these can resist, as well as follow, the entries given in the first.

4. Sovereignty and Equity

The logic of serial slowdown, in other words, is amenable to selective correction. The principal correctors of the post-war epoch have been specific types of civil bureaucracy, banking system or labour movement. The British experience has known none of these. The Treasury was a far cry from MITI or the *Commissariat au Plan*; the City had little in common with *Grossbanken* or *keiretsu*; the Labour Party was no DNA or SPÖ. Every principal form of effective regulation was

57. See the calculations in Castles, 'Democratic Politics, War and Catch-Up', p. 24.

58. 'Economic growth in Belgium continued at a very brisk pace in 1989, real GDP rising by 4% compared with 4.5% in 1988. The increase in gross fixed capital formation in the private sector was once again one of the driving forces behind the buoyancy of activity. Given capacity utilization rates not seen since 1974, high and growing profit margins enabled firms to maintain a substantial investment effort. . . . Thanks in particular to the additional employment prompted by these developments and also to increases in real wages, households saw their real incomes climb sharply. . . . In all, domestic-demand growth accelerated last year to a rate appreciably greater than that sustained by Belgium's main neighbouring countries.' *OECD Economic Surveys 1990–1991 – Belgium/Luxembourg*, Paris 1990, p. 15.

missing. These have represented contrasting solutions to market anomie, in sharply differing social and institutional contexts. They nevertheless have one fulcrum in common – the state. *Dirigiste* administration, exemplified by French planning in the Fourth and early Fifth Republics, is the most direct form of public authority. But the steerage functions performed by the financial system in Germany depend indirectly on the peculiar power of the Central Bank as the ultimate guardian of monetary stability. These variants draw on the executive branches of the State, as collective functionary or lender of last resort. The force of the concertation practised in Austria or Sweden, on the other hand, derives from the legislative branch as seat of popular sovereignty, conferring legitimacy on a negotiated corporatism. In Habermasian terms, these might be described as a coordination of the market principally through the medium of bureaucracy, money or democracy. The English State has afforded little purchase for any of them. The reasons why the civil service and financial system of the United Kingdom have been so unsuited for economic reconstruction are generally understood. The bearing of the legislature on the curve of decline remains less widely noticed. But since the last sort of regulation is in principle of most relevance to Labour, the obstacles to it require particular comment. These are located in the archaic mainframe of the Ukanian state itself.

The first is to be found in the paradox of parliamentary autocracy at the national level – a legislative power untrammelled by any constitutional restraint. The second is electoral monopoly at the local level – the winner-takes-all of simple plurality in single-member constituencies. Britain's lack of a written constitution is, of course, the most immediate sign of the pre-modern character of its polity. Venerated as an immemorial tradition, it is in fact the product of the defeat of the English Republic in the seventeenth century, which produced not only the first draft democratic constitutions in the Leveller Agreements of the People, but also the first effective written constitution of European history, in the Protectorate's Instrument of Government. It was the Hanoverian stabilization of the eighteenth century which bequeathed the customary settlement whose form remains unbroken to this day. Under its arrangements, since king-in-parliament is sovereign, not the people, the juridical issues of democratic representation – what branches of government should exercise which powers within what limits, as mandated bearers of popular sovereignty – have never arisen. The first modern constitution was born precisely out a revolt against the British doctrine of parliamentary sovereignty, when the American War of Independence gave rise to a quite different conception of political legitimacy. The principle of a formal codification of the fundamental powers and liberties of the state then acquired general momentum with the French Revolution. The successive constitutions of France – from the limited monarchy of 1791 to the radical republic of 1794 and the plebiscitary autocracy of 1799 – not only set the pattern for lands conquered by French arms, in the Low Countries, Switzerland, Italy and Germany. Within Napoleonic Europe, the original French model inspired the Spanish Constitution of 1812, proclaimed against Bonaparte's rule, which coined the name of liberalism. In Sweden, the Form of Government adopted by the Riksdag in 1809 became the most durable constitutional monarchy of the continent, while Norway produced a more liberal basic law five years later, expressly grounding all legislative power in the people.[59]

The victory of the old order at Leipzig and Waterloo could reinstate traditional dynasties, but not cancel constitutional memories altogether. The legitimism of the Restoration epoch was obliged to produce its own characteristic codes of government – the *chartes octroyées* of royal rulers formally granting revocable concessions to their subjects in France, the Netherlands and Southern Germany, often imitating what were believed to be norms in Britain, where no dangerous ideas of popular sovereignty had raised their head. Further East, in Austria, Prussia and Russia, Absolutism proper still reigned. Congress Europe was soon overtaken by the revolutionary waves of 1830–31 and 1848–49. Belgium became the classical limited monarchy, instituted by a constitutional assembly in the name of the nation. France regained universal male suffrage with the Second Republic, formally upheld by the Empire that succeeded it. Switzerland created the first federal constitution in Europe. Piedmont acquired the *Statuto* that was eventually extended to a unified Italy. In Germany, the Frankfurt Parliament laboured in vain, but at the moment of counter-revolutionary victory over it even the Prussian monarchy had to issue a legitimist charter. In England the Reform Bill widened the franchise, but the Chartists were seen off, and there was no alteration in the practice of government. When the next phase of political turbulence hit the continent, the pattern was similar: the Second Reform Bill could be run up by Disraeli without further adjustment, while the price of German Unification was the Imperial constitution and manhood suffrage, the Habsburg monarchy was forced to institutionalize the *Ausgleich* by the Hungar-

59. John Hawgood, *Modern Constitutions since 1787*, London 1939, pp. 97–101, 53–58.

ian gentry, and the Third Republic joined Parliament and Presidency. In the final decade before the Great War, Europe was once again swept by revolutionary pressures for a new political order, as national and social movements shook the Russian, Austrian and Ottoman Empires – producing a Charter in Finland, universal male suffrage in Austria, independence for Bulgaria, even a Turkish constitution. In the United Kingdom too, there was unrest: but Home Rule was fended off and the Lords remained intact. After the War, the world of Versailles brought the Weimar Constitution, Kelsen's framework for the Austrian Republic, the political settlements of the Little Entente, constitutional reforms in Scandinavia and Holland. The British State's contribution to the new era was to shed Southern Ireland, and retain control of the North: Stormont was the sum of its architectural innovation between the wars. In a Europe subsequently engulfed by fascism, such unchanging stability could stand out as an admirable monument of unbowed institutional liberalism. But what were solitary values in 1940 had become futile self-satisfactions by 1960.[60] When Western Europe was democratized after the Second World War, Germany, Italy and France each underwent a profound institutional reconstruction, which laid the basis for their convergence in the treaty founding the EEC within little more than a decade. Meanwhile Britain was congratulating itself on the Commonwealth as its alternative, whose members were bound together in the unwritten ethos of a club. Another thirty years on, the anachronism of the political culture that produced such delusions has long become evident at home too. In a world where every other advanced capitalist state is framed by a legal constitution based on popular sovereignty, Britain alone has escaped one. Its lack of any formal framework for the exercise of power is shared only by the religious regimes of Saudi Arabia and Israel.

If the cult of parliamentary sovereignty is a survival from the eighteenth century, the rules of the electoral constituency are relics from an even remoter age. They derive from a feudal epoch when the overwhelming majority of polls were uncontested – local gentry families agreeing among themselves who should be their Member of Parliament. As late as the reign of James I, at the height of contention with the king in the Commons, over 80 per cent of seats had only one candidate. Even the Long Parliament whose divisions precipitated England into civil war was essentially picked on the basis of county

60. For the wider significance of this reversal, see the great final passage of Tom Nairn's *Enchanted Glass*, London 1988, pp. 371–76, to which one sense of the title of this chapter alludes.

consensus: two-thirds of its members had faced no opposition to their election.[61] Where there was a contest, the victor needed only a simple plurality that could be registered by 'cry' or 'view' (shouts or hands). The origins of the first-past-the-post system, in other words, lie in the self-selection of the English landed elite from mediaeval times onwards. The single candidate was a natural expression of the single class in the Commons. When political divisions eventually developed within it, informal selection gave way to contested elections within the same customary rules, although down to the nineteenth century there were always substantial numbers of seats without a challenger. Such were the appropriate procedures of what its modern admirers rightly describe as England's Ancien Régime.

Logically, the critique of this system was born from the Enlightenment. Emblematically, the first theorist of modern political representation was Condorcet. Four years before the French Revolution, he demonstrated the incoherence of the principle of simple plurality wherever there were more than two candidates. Inspired by probability theory, Condorcet's reflections on voting were also informed by acute insight into the character of the English State: if the unelected power of the monarchy and the upper chamber represented 'direct despotism', the authority of the lower chamber was an 'indirect despotism' of landed and mercantile interests, in which 'the mode of election of the members of the Commons is one of the prime causes of the servitude of England'. An admirer of English *habeas corpus* and freedom of the press, he was scathing about the 'superstitious respect for the constitution' and 'servile cult of maxims that suit the rich and powerful' surrounding Parliament, 'a sort of political religion which makes almost impossible any improvement of the constitution and laws of the land'.[62] Condorcet's own proposals for popular voting – he envisaged even female suffrage – still rested on an individualist conception of politics which, typically for the period, was deeply suspicious of parties. When a collective notion of democratic choice eventually emerged for the first time, it was to be within the socialist movement

61. Derek Hirst, *The Representative of the People?*, Cambridge 1975, pp. 111, 217–222; for the consensual process itself, see Mark Kishlansky, *Parliamentary Selection. Social and Political Choice in Early Modern England*, Cambridge 1986, pp. 22–48.

62. *Œuvres* (Condorcet-O'Connor/Arago edition), Paris 1847–49, vols IX, pp. 148–49, XII, pp. 646, 636; IX, pp. 75–76, VII, pp. 214–15. Condorcet was well aware of the history of the English Revolution, and in urging the French to adopt a codified republican constitution in 1793, recalled the fateful defeat of the Leveller efforts to secure one in 1648–49: 'Sur la Nécessité d'établir en France une Constitution nouvelle', XII, pp. 531–535.

that had developed out of the legacy of the Revolution. Its pioneer was Fourier's disciple Victor Considerant, prompted by the serial forms of the phalanstery. Pointing out that representation and deliberation are two quite different processes, 'as distinct as day and night', he criticized all existing electoral procedures for confusing the two: the result was an 'oppressive, blind and incoherent' distortion of the real distribution of opinion. 'The present form of elections *parks* the voters in territorial constituencies, tying the elector to the soil as the peasant in feudal times was bound to the land on which he was born.' Rejecting this system as a barbarous product of unreflective tradition, Considerant insisted that if majority was the appropriate principle of decision, proportionality was the only defensible principle of representation, and on the eve of the revolutions of 1848 proposed a list system to achieve a truly equitable representation in elections with competing parties.[63] The origins of proportional representation as a democratic principle thus lie in the two founding moments of modern radical politics.

In England it was not until the epoch of Palmerston that the rectitude of the customary constituency plurality was questioned, in the name of a progressive liberalism. Mill, adopting a scheme for the single transferable vote, devoted a central chapter of his *Considerations on Representative Government* to the contrast between this and the old system, as nothing less than one between 'true and false democracy'. The British antidote, however, had its own characteristic bias: STV was designed by his friend Hare to secure a 'personal representation' that would be proof against party or class organization, and ensure the election of the intelligent 'elite of the country'.[64] This was not enough to persuade established wisdom that it would be innocuous. Significantly, Bagehot's immediate reaction was to associate the single transferable vote with manhood suffrage, as the two leading menaces to the very

63. See his circular to the Constituent Assembly in Geneva after the so-called Fazy Revolution in the city: *De la Sincérité du Gouvernement représentatif ou Exposition de l'Election véridique*, Geneva 1846, pp. 2–5, 10–13. Considerant envisaged two rounds of voting – one for choice of party as such, the other for choice among its candidates. As he noted, he had earlier developed the idea of proportional representation in the Fourierist press: see his article 'La Représentation nationale est un Mensonge', *La Phalange*, 17 June 1842. Considerant lived to see the first introduction of the principle in the Ticino fifty years later.

64. The formula is Mill's, in *Considerations on Representative Government*, London 1861, p. 145. Hare, who otherwise opposed major changes in the narrow mid-century franchise, advocated an extension of electoral privileges for the educated by generalization of the double vote enjoyed by graduates of Oxford and Cambridge to those of all universities in the land: *A Treatise on the Election of Representatives*, London 1859, p. 321.

possibility of parliamentary government.[65] Not surprisingly, by the close of the century it had made no headway in Britain. The advent of mass politics in continental Europe effectively bypassed it. There, theories of proportional representation for party preference first took practical shape in Switzerland and Belgium – polyglot states where the effects of simple plurality were most obviously unacceptable – and were sometimes conceded elsewhere by minority conservative groups, as insurance against elimination by the rise of popular politics. But the main force driving for the democratization of voting systems, in the mode of the ballot as well as the extent of the suffrage, was the labour movement. Proportional representation was a general demand of Social Democracy. Included in the first article of the Erfurt Programme of the SPD, achieved by the frontrunner of the labour movement in Finland, it became a normal political goal of the parties of the Second International before the Great War.[66]

Typically, the goal was achieved at the end of the War, as an inseparable part of the broad wave of democratization that brought universal suffrage and constitutional reform to most of Western Europe. The November Revolution in Germany led the way, Social Democracy in power adopting proportional representation as 'the self-evident concomitant of democracy in accordance with the party programme'.[67] Austria, Italy, Denmark, Norway followed. In France, only a partial reform was introduced, under socialist pressure, soon rolled back. Ireland got the lees of STV, appropriately, as a parting gift from British colonialism. In Britain alone, Labour – having scarcely exerted itself to broaden the suffrage before the War – did nothing to

65. Producing some of the most comic passages of political Pooterism in *The English Constitution*. On manhood suffrage: 'If it be true that a parliamentary government is possible only when the overwhelming majority of the representatives are men essentially moderate, of no marked varieties, free from class prejudices, this ultra-democratic Parliament could not maintain that government, for its members would be remarkable for two sorts of moral violence and one sort immoral.' Ditto on STV: 'The optional transferability of votes is not a salutary aid, but a ruinous innovation . . . instead of a deliberate assembly of moderate and judicious men, we should have a various compound of all sorts of violence.' London 1867, pp. 183–4, 194, 191.

66. Belgium and Sweden were the only exceptions, although the SAP was initially in favour of proportional representation, and within the POB its leader Vandervelde advocated it. Within German Social Democracy Bernstein was, characteristically, so taken with all things English that he urged the adoption of simple plurality voting too.

67. Peter Pulzer, 'Germany', in Vernon Bogdanor and David Butler, eds, *Democracy and Elections*, Cambridge 1983, p. 88. For the general connexion between the advent of proportional representation and the broadening of the suffrage, see Dieter Nohlen, *Wahlrecht und Parteiensysteme*, Opladen 1990, pp. 247 ff., the most comprehensive and authoritative recent work on the politics of electoral systems.

democratize the ballot after it, blocking every reform in order to marginalize the Liberals, until its last gasp in 1931.[68] Symptomatically, on the other hand, where the militant Right made its breakthrough in the inter-war period, proportional representation was immediately struck down: on coming to power, Mussolini abolished it in favour of a system designed to yield 'stable government' that gave any party with a plurality of national votes two-thirds of all seats, assuring a landslide victory for fascism.

The same pattern was repeated on a larger scale after the Second World War. In Germany, the British and American occupation authorities, supported by Christian Democracy, strenuously tried to prevent the readoption of proportional representation, and impose the Anglo-Saxon system. They were thwarted by Social Democracy, aided by the Liberals. The CDU did not abandon its goal of first-past-the-post elections, and tried to force it through under Kiesinger as late as 1966 – helping to precipitate the FDP into the alliance with the SPD that ruled the country through the seventies. In France, Liberation brought proportional representation along with votes for women. By 1947 it was already being diluted and rigged to reduce Communist presence in the Assembly; and when de Gaulle came to power in 1958, it was abolished altogether, in favour of a system that gave 40 per cent of the seats to the Gaullists with 20 per cent of the vote, and 2 per cent to the PCF with 19 per cent of the vote. While in opposition, the Socialists called for the reintroduction of proportional representation, along with the Communists; once in office, they eventually passed only a selfish caricature of it, engineered to marginalize the PCF, which was promptly abolished again by the Right. In Italy, where the Resistance ensured the re-establishment of a fully proportional representation, Christian Democracy tried at the height of the Cold War to deform it with Scelba's *legge truffa* of 1953 which awarded two-thirds of the seats to any coalition with a majority of votes – a crude bid for unrestrained power that ultimately failed in the face of popular indignation. Conservative forces in Austria and Ireland – the ÖVP and Fianna Fáil – unsuccessfully tried to introduce first-past-the-post elections in the sixties. In Greece, the US Ambassador publicly intervened to force the government to scrap proportional representation for a simple plurality system in 1952, so as to ensure the victory of Marshal

68. In order to cling on to office, the Labour Cabinet briefly introduced a bill for the 'alternative vote', which disappeared into the general debacle of the MacDonald Government; for this episode, see Vernon Bogdanor, *The People and the Party System*, Cambridge 1981, pp. 138–39.

Papagos. Meanwhile, in Scandinavia traditional approximations of the D'Hondt system for proportionality were everywhere yielding to more completely equitable Sainte–Laguë rules.[69] Beyond the tactical occasions of this history, the deeper correlation of political forces and options across Europe is unmistakable. Outside it, Anglo-Saxon customs remained the most imperturbable bastions of conservatism. Their most expressive product was to be the hegemony of the National Party in South Africa, where first-past-the-post elections alone permitted the imposition of apartheid, impossible if there had been proportional representation of the white electorate after the War. In the Afrikaner mirror, the logic of the English tradition found its ultimate reflection. The United Kingdom, untouched by the popular revolutions of 1789 and 1848, or the radical shock-waves of 1918 and 1945, remains the solitary state in Europe whose basic device for choosing a government predates not only the idea of democratic representation, but even that of electoral competition.

5. Party and State

What view is taken of the legacies of the British past, economic and political, by the Labour Party today? Compared with the rhetoric of the sixties, promising transformation of industry and society at white heat, its language has become more circumspect. But the tasks of renovation are not forgotten in the new programme. Without dwelling unduly on national shortcomings, as its title suggests, *Opportunity Britain* nevertheless acknowledges that much is wanting. Labour, it pledges, will address the central problems facing the UK by fostering a 'world-class economy' and 'modern constitution' in the nineties. What is the likelihood that these undertakings will prove more realistic than their predecessors?

The Thatcher regime promised to reverse British economic decline by restoration of the pure discipline of the market, eliminating public deficits, privatizing nationalized industries and breaking trade-union power. After a decade in office, and three successive election victories, it

69. For the difference between these two, see Andrew McLaren Carstairs, *A Short History of Electoral Systems in Western Europe*, London 1980, pp. 18–23, despite its unassuming title a model of lucid judgement and synthesis.

proclaimed that it had spectacularly succeeded. Now this illusion has crumbled: a year later, Britain was once again in the grip of high inflation and deep recession, running a large trade deficit. British neo-liberalism, like Labour's would-be corporatism before it, has proved no solution to external decline. On the other hand, unlike the Wilson–Callaghan governments, the Thatcher administration has genuinely transformed the internal landscape of the country. The public sector has been extensively privatized; direct taxation has been substantially reduced; social services have been starved; home-ownership has spread yet further, with the sale of council housing. What has been Labour's response to these changes?

The new programme accepts the basic parameters of the Thatcher settlement, in much the same way that the Conservative governments of the fifties accepted the parameters of the Attlee settlement. It does not seek to extend the public sector or reverse privatization to any significant degree. It does not propose to raise the overall level of taxation, but promises to adjust its incidence in a mildly more egalitarian direction. It does not substantially depart from the laws that now regulate industrial action, while rendering them a little more favourable to trade unions. It does not abandon the British nuclear deterrent. All these changes of the Thatcher years are uncontested. What the party offers the electorate beyond these fixtures is essentially a more generous level of social provision: higher pensions, better schools, newer hospitals, purer water, cleaner streets, faster trains. There is no doubt that the public wants all of these. But how are they to be financed, if taxes are not to be raised? Labour has tried to answer this question in two ways: partly by invoking the natural increase in Treasury receipts when growth resumes, and partly by stressing the functional interconnexions between social spending and economic efficiency. Its propaganda focuses above all on the need for a better trained and educated workforce, and more scientific research, as conditions of higher productivity and greater competitive capacity. Here too there is no question of the validity of the case. But the effects of greater investment in science and education can only be long-term. In the immediate future, British capitalism – marked by historically lower rates of productivity, and greater tendencies to inflation than most of its continental competitors – is not only entering a sharp recession, but confronts a severe test with the arrival of the European Single Market in 1992. In this period, the oil surplus which has done so much to finance the illusions of progress in the Thatcher epoch will also run out. The secular decline of the British economy, in other words, is likely to undergo a further twist of the spiral downwards. The Labour Party's programme contains no coherent set of measures to meet this eventuality. Welcome though its social promises are – however modest, in a comparative perspective – there is no guarantee that they will be implemented, if the party should enter office during a time when fiscal revenues are receding.

If the social dimension of the new programme is limited and precarious – it makes no promise of a return to full employment, for example – what of its political programme? The unbridled authoritarianism of the Conservative regime, exercised with full parliamentary legitimacy, and the impotence and division of the opposition to it in the 1980s, have finally awakened a certain public awareness of the archaic and pre-democratic structures of the UK State. The liveliest recent movement within civil society, Charter 88, has mounted an important campaign to end these longstanding anomalies, with proposals for a written constitution, juridical liberties and electoral reform. Under its impact, Britain's last original politician of the Left has produced something like a latter-day Agreement of the People, and the first new research centre of the Left a comprehensive and detailed Instrument of Government.[70] Amidst the wide range of measures canvassed in these, electoral reform remains, as it has always been, the key to any qualitative change. Fair matching of votes to seats extends freedom of choice, supposedly a central value for both principal parties – where in fact they have long colluded to stifle alternative tickets. It increases turnout – where electoral participation in Britain is now the third lowest in Western Europe. It also promotes the election of women to legislatures – where Britain again has one of the lowest percentages in the EC.[71] Equitable funding of parties, from public finances, is its logical complement – a democratic reform whose spread through

70. The thrust of Tony Benn's *Commonwealth of Britain Bill* (May 1991) is more radical in its abolition of the constitutional monarchy, established church and honours system, and its provision for equal representation of the sexes in two elected chambers. The Institute for Public Policy Research's *Constitution of the United Kingdom* (September 1991), on the other hand, is more advanced in its provision of an equitable voting system for the Commons (German-style proportionality), and decentralization of powers and revenues to regional assemblies. It also, of course, possesses the great merit of offering a full-scale model, rather than an indicative synopsis, of a democratized state.

71. For participation, see André Blais and R.K. Carty, 'Does Proportional Representation Foster Voter Turn-Out?', *European Journal of Political Research*, no. 18, 1990, pp. 167–181. For women: Francis Castles, 'Female Legislative Representation and the Electoral System', *Politics*, vol. 1, no. 2, November 1981, pp. 21–27. Even Switzerland, where the suffrage itself only ceased to be male in 1971, now has twice as many women in Parliament as Britain.

Northern Europe coincided with the zone of greatest Social Democratic influence.[72]

In a situation in which many of the traditional social objectives of the labour movement, embodied in the Keynesian welfare state, have been suspended or diluted, these goals represent one obvious and overdue line of advance for the Left in Britain. Labour's programme remains far behind them. If its prospectus today contains fewer promises of economic *dirigisme* than in the past, and expresses more concern for political rights, the constitutional agenda it proposes remains strictly limited and self-interested. It accepts a Bill of Rights, concedes a parliament for Scotland, promises regional assemblies and gestures towards a different second chamber, although without explaining its composition. Such changes are, of course, desirable. But they do not touch the two central arrangements at Westminster. The Labour establishment continues to refuse any serious commitment to either electoral reform or a written constitution. It visibly still hopes to utilize the pre-democratic structures of the British State, as Thatcher has done, for its own ends.[73] The standard official pretext for rejecting proportional representation – the sanctity of the personal dispensary for complaints offered by MPs to their constituents – says everything. Redress of individual grievances has, of course, nothing to do with political representation, whose function is public decision-making; the simulacrum of it in Britain, a dim memory of feudal custom, is merely evidence of the lack of any democratic protections in administrative law. The real 'accountability' of MPs is naturally – where it counts, in the lobbies – to the whips only. To their credit, increasing numbers of ordinary members of the party are starting to resist the myopic cynicism of its leadership, and to press for real constitutional change. To temporize, an 'independent' report canvassing variants of electoral reform has been released, naively designed to baulk any real upset to the status quo.[74] If even this

72. West Germany 1959; Sweden 1965; Finland 1967; Norway 1970; Austria 1975.

73. As Michael Dummett remarks, 'No body of people engaged in making decisions, and free to choose by what means they shall arrive at those decisions, has ever chosen to employ the relative majority procedure. That is reserved for elections in Britain, the United States, and some other countries, because the electors are not free to choose the method of election they are forced to employ, the choice being left to those who are elected by this method, and who may be afraid they would not be elected by any other': *Voting Procedures*, Oxford 1984, p. 171.

74. The main conclusion of the suitably named *Plant Report* ('marvellously helpful': Roy Hattersley) is that 'there is a powerful case for leaving the central elements of the representative and electoral system which we believe to be of vital importance to the legislative function in place.' Perhaps first-past-the-post elections might be given up for a

placebo has been received with suspicion by most of the PLP, the reason lies in the structure of the party as a whole. For what ultimately makes it difficult for Labour to conceive or advocate any significant democratization of the State – let alone a republican reconstruction of the kind valiantly tabled by Benn – is that it is itself, brazenly and obdurately, far less democratic even than the *un*reformed Ancien Régime at Westminster.

For behind the surface contrasts discussed above, two structural features set the Labour Party more deeply apart from its continental opposites. Internally, it still remains the creation of its trade-union progenitors: a party in which nine out of ten votes cast at its conference rest on a constitutional sham.[75] The block vote was always the working-class version of the rotten borough – Old Sarum inverted, as it were, with an inflation rather than reduction of numbers proper to principles of collective organization. Over time it raised up a Leviathan of dead souls, whose mythical millions enabled party leaderships to crush rebellions and to finance elections – enforce discipline and amass funds – without otherwise unduly exerting themselves. In recent years, the fiction of this army has become ever more hollow. In 1983 the total Labour electorate was not much larger than the official membership of the party, individual and 'block', and was smaller in size than the TUC. The same election highlighted the other major determinant of Labour's peculiar profile within European Social Democracy. Externally, the party has enjoyed the uncovenanted benefits of an electoral system that has given it a monopoly of representation on the Left, and a repression of representation in the Centre, unique of its kind.[76] Throughout the

---

second chamber, since it would be of so much less importance, but then – the authors ingenuously confess – 'there is a danger that if it were to be elected on a proportional basis, it could claim greater legitimacy in some constitutional deadlock with the Commons'! The intellectual quality of the document can be judged from its only significant comparative argument. The German electoral system – which plainly threatens Westminster most, because of its potentially attractive combination of proportional with territorial principle – is held unacceptable on the grounds that it allows a party to change a government without recourse to an election: as if the arrangements that produced MacDonald warranted solemn doubts about Genscher.

75. The Social Democratic parties of Norway and Sweden have also known collective affiliation, but at local level only, with no block vote; residual in the DNA, this has now been abolished in the SAP. The nearest counterpart to the structure of Labourism is in many ways the system of institutional representation in Austrian clericalism, which supplies the notional bulk of the members of the ÖVP.

76. The fact that Labour was never able to convert this repression into a complete elimination of Liberalism, despite every attempt and opportunity, has been one of the historical signs of 'the shallow penetration of the labour movement', as Dunleavy puts it in his shrewd discussion: 'Paradoxes of an Ungrounded Statism', pp. 261–63.

post-war epoch, with the exception of the fifties, Labour has been handed more seats than its share of votes – with an average premium larger than the parliamentary majority enjoyed by every third government. In 1983 it polled 2.2 per cent more votes than the Alliance, and received 700 per cent more seats. No other Social Democratic party has come near this record of consistently disproportional representation.

The two voting mechanisms, within the party and outside it, have had symmetrical effects on Labour. Each confers a major advantage, secured by procedural artifice rather than political mobilization. The block vote made the recruitment of a genuine mass party, with an active membership capable of sustaining it economically (as well as governing it democratically), of secondary importance. The simple-plurality system avoided the need to win a popular electorate with a free choice of ideological options before it, or to negotiate with competing forces. In the double sense of the term, these were the historical facilities of Labour. They smoothed its path and enfeebled its sinews. The regressive nature of Labourism as a political culture is rooted in the customs and privileges of this legacy. Sociologically, in the absence of a native peasantry, the English working class was long an absolute majority of the population in a way that it was in no other European country. Constitutionally, the English electoral system gave the party sole rights to representation of the Left and a possibility of governing with large absolute majorities in Parliament – something that not even the Swedish or Austrian parties ever possessed. Enjoying these assets, it was in the first years after the War the most powerful Social Democracy in Europe. By the mid eighties, it had become one of the weakest and most demoralized – an impotent spectator at the triumphal advance of the radical Right. The immediate reason for this dramatic change of fortune was, of course, its terms in office during the sixties and seventies, when national economic decline became deeply identified with party failure. But if we ask why the Labour regime of Wilson and Callaghan proved so completely incapable of halting the descent of the economy, the answer lies in the extent to which the party did indeed mirror the vices of the country. The development of English capitalism, the first and most powerful of the nineteenth century, was fettered and vitiated by its imperial past in the twentieth – still living on too many inherited assets to be forced to adjust to new competitive conditions after the Second World War, cocooned in every kind of nostalgic delusion. In much the same way, the Labour Party was corrupted and immobilized by the institutional heirlooms it received and for which it never had to struggle – a massive, ramshackle trade-union movement delivering nominal members and automatic funds, and a barnacled parliamentary order yielding plenary legislative power without any commensurate popular majority. The structure of its own organization, at the mercy of a handful of trade-union leaders, sergeants of the dead souls, was even more undemocratic and indefensible than that of the British constitution itself, in which at least formally one person counted for one vote. The agues of the national economy and parliamentary sovereignty that call for real medicine of reform in Ukania are thus lodged in Labour's own body. The combined humbugs of card-vote and constituency, trade-union bluff with parliamentary cant, Deakin crossed with Burke, have long been its life and blood. In its whole *modus operandi* Labour is tied to a past which in its rhetoric it vaguely calls upon the nation – not for the first time – to leave behind.

In the most favourable of hypotheses, then, the British Labour Party may regain office with a well-intentioned but not well-costed social programme, in the midst of an economic recession, without any political programme to mobilize the bruised and dormant energies of civil society – governing with a parliamentary majority that rests on an electoral minority. If trade unions are likely to be more docile than in the past, the balance of trade is likely to be more vulnerable. The chances of avoiding a repetition of the disastrous performance of the past do not therefore look reassuring. In all probability, a condition of relative industrial revival in Britain is now some political reorganization, as the decline of the economy appears inseparable from the arrest of the state. Sooner or later, the Westminster system will in any case be undone by federation in Europe, which no major British party yet accepts and none will be able to resist. Various sorts of reconstruction can be envisaged, before or in that process itself – some leading to further concentration and rationalization of executive power, others away from it. But so far there is only one kind in the capitalist world that has linked economic success to democratic deepening. Social-democratic concertation only works where political representation is fully equitable, and governments can negotiate and ensure common lines of economic growth because they rest on genuinely broad social forces.[77] Where these conditions are established, even modest initial goals can provide the momentum for a rolling agenda of reforms across successive administrations.

Even in the straitened circumstances of this period, there is no shortage of radical proposals with a strategic edge, capable of unblock-

77. The most forceful case for this connexion has been made by David Marquand, *The Unprincipled Society*, London 1988: esp. pp. 161–174.

ing the present logjam of the Left in advanced capitalism. Among them a range of potential avenues of attack on the mean and brutal settlement of recent years are open. One would take the statutes of company law as its central target, pressing on the increasingly institutional ownership of corporate property to break the secrecy and autocracy of management in large industrial firms, and to introduce legally binding norms of social responsibility and employee representation in private enterprise. Another would give greater priority to full employment than to industrial democracy, working on the costs and dangers of an endemically jobless underclass to establish a universal right to work as a legal entitlement, secured by wage subsidies in the private sector and project creation in the public sector. A third would proceed from current acceptance of high rates of unemployment to disconnect livelihood from waged labour by guaranteeing a basic monetary income to all as a social dividend. A fourth, on the other hand, would pick out the growing crisis of the school system in most Western countries as the Archimedean point for changing their social structures, by committing resources to public education matching those now spent on private education, on the principle of every child's right to an equal opportunity for self-realization. A fifth, by contrast, would focus on the decline of the traditional family and marriage, and tackle contemporary sexual inequality at its root by lifting the double pressure of work and child-rearing on women, with maternity entitlements of comparable level to waged labour.[78] All of these approaches start from acknowledged existing strains within the new capitalist societies of the nineties, and then test the limits of what this social order can afford as humane solutions to them. Each of them involves a set of rights, based on widespread needs. Ideologically, they share a common conception that is classically described as the idea of social citizenship.[79] There can be little doubt that this now holds out the best

78. For these emphases, see respectively: Paul Hirst, *After Thatcher*, London 1989, pp. 206–214; Michael Rustin, *For a Pluralist Socialism*, London 1985, pp. 147–172; Philippe Van Parijs, *Arguing for Basic Income*, London 1992; Paul Auerbach, 'On Socialist Optimism'; Nicky Hart, 'Procreation: the Substance of Female Oppression in Modern Society', *Contention*, nos. 1–2, Fall 1991–Winter 1992.

79. The notion itself, of course, goes back to the lectures T.H. Marshall gave in 1949 on 'Citizenship and Social Class'. It is their scheme of an advancing frontier of rights that forms the framework for Hirschman's study of the stock responses of reaction to them. The idea of social citizenship today, when it is foregrounded as the most effective ideological vision of the Left – as, for example, in Michael Mann's *Socialism Can Survive*, London 1985 – has tended to acquire a more radical sense than it possessed for Marshall himself, who was rather ambiguous about the ultimately egalitarian logic of citizenship as a category.

promise of practical advances in equality and emancipation in Western Europe at large. But it is illusory to think that these could be realized in the United Kingdom – in whatever incipient forms or partial combination – without the idea of political citizenship itself becoming for the first time a reality. It is no accident that so little has been achieved in British welfare since Marshall originally developed his theory of social citizenship, he himself having complacently assumed that the political variety already existed. To think that furtherance of the one can bypass fulfilment of the other today would be an error even on a broader stage – as if in the European Community itself, with the prospect of greater concentration of bureaucratic authority in the Commission and the coming Central Bank, it will be possible to confine demands to social provision without political democratization.

The terrain of the state-nation that miscalls itself a united kingdom is steadily being undermined, as the international integration of capital proceeds. There is a long, and not dishonourable, tradition on the Left that rejects any consideration of it as a meaningful battlefield, on principle. What have socialists to do with the vicissitudes of any particular capitalist society, when their task is to confront the system as a whole? The question is to be respected. But national differences, however relative compared with conditions outside the metropolitan zone, continue to count for those who fall under them. Lives and liberties differ substantially across the range of societies that comprise the developed world – from the great pools of misery and despair in New York or Naples to the more decent securities of Oslo or Stuttgart – and no effective opposition to capitalism can morally neglect these contrasts. The politics of a rational Left needs to be international in a new and more radical way today: global in its conclusions. But it has not yet ceased to be national in its conditions. To attend to these is not to accept the limits of the present social order, as it spreads further round the world. If its end is more unfathomable today than ever before, its strains remain. Competition is its permanent principle, and over-competition the periodic price of it. The system has stifled the symptoms of that disorder for twenty years, but has not mastered their sources. When its outbreak can no longer be deferred, the disciplines of the market will look different again. For better or for worse, new beginnings may ensue.

1991

Index